T0318200

Contemporary Employers' Organizations

This book argues that employers' organizations are resilient organizations that adapt to changing circumstances by developing new practices. Adaptation has been prompted by changing economic and social contexts, including state interventions and union activities. Contexts vary over time, across countries and world regions. The purpose of the book is to explore these variations and their impacts on employer organization.

The book covers the following themes across four book sections: theoretical perspectives on employer collective action; employers' organizations in different types of capitalism; different types of employers' organizations; and international and comparative employer interest representation. Theoretical explorations examining employer power, political preferences, meta-organizing, and ideological foundations are complemented by studies of employers' organization in China, Denmark, Australia, Germany, Turkey, Canada, and the UK. Different types such as regional and international employers' organizations are also examined. The book is one of the few edited volumes to examine employer collective action within work and employment, and is the first since 1984 to consider western and non-western contexts.

The book will be of interest to employment relations and sociology of work researchers, scholars, advanced students, and practitioners as it brings new perspectives to an understudied actor in employment relations: employers' organizations.

Leon Gooberman is a Lecturer in Employment Relations at Cardiff Business School, Cardiff University, UK.

Marco Hauptmeier is a Professor of International Human Resource Management at Cardiff Business School, Cardiff University, UK.

Routledge Research in Employment Relations
Series Editors: Rick Delbridge and Edmund Heery
Cardiff Business School, UK

Aspects of the employment relationship are central to numerous courses at both undergraduate and postgraduate level.

Drawing from insights from industrial relations, human resource management and industrial sociology, this series provides an alternative source of research-based materials and texts, reviewing key developments in employment research.

Books published in this series are works of high academic merit, drawn from a wide range of academic studies in the social sciences.

Contemporary Employers' Organizations
Adaptation and Resilience

Edited by Leon Gooberman and
Marco Hauptmeier

Routledge
Taylor & Francis Group

NEW YORK AND LONDON

First published 2022
by Routledge
605 Third Avenue, New York, NY 10158

and by Routledge
4 Park Square, Milton Park, Abingdon, Oxon, OX14 4RN

*Routledge is an imprint of the Taylor & Francis Group, an
informa business*

Library of Congress Cataloguing-in-Publication Data
Names: Gooberman, Leon, editor. | Hauptmeier, Marco, editor.
Title: Contemporary employers' organizations : adaptation and
resilience / edited by Leon Gooberman and Marco Hauptmeier.
Description: 1 Edition. | New York, NY : Routledge, 2022. |
Series: Routledge research in employment relations | Includes
bibliographical references and index.
Identifiers: LCCN 2021054382 (print) | LCCN 2021054383
(ebook) | ISBN 9780367611941 (hardback) | ISBN
9780367611972 (paperback) | ISBN 9781003104575 (ebook)
Subjects: LCSH: Employers' associations--Case studies. | Industrial
relations--Case studies.
Classification: LCC HD6943 .C66 2022 (print) | LCC HD6943
(ebook) | DDC 658.3/15--dc23/eng/20220105
LC record available at https://lccn.loc.gov/2021054382
LC ebook record available at https://lccn.loc.gov/2021054383

ISBN: 978-0-367-61194-1 (hbk)
ISBN: 978-0-367-61197-2 (pbk)
ISBN: 978-1-003-10457-5 (ebk)

DOI: 10.4324/9781003104575

Typeset in Sabon
by MPS Limited, Dehradun

Contents

Figures

Tables

About the Authors

Mona Aranea, Independent Researcher, Germany; Mona Aranea has a PhD from the University of Oviedo and worked at Cardiff University and the Hans Böckler Foundation. She researches topics within European employment relations, including European Works Councils, board-level employee representation in European Companies, European social dialogue, and most recently European Employers' Organizations.

Martin Behrens, Hans Böckler Foundation, Germany; Martin Behrens is Senior Researcher at the Institute of Social and Economic Research (WSI) of the Hans Böckler Foundation and Lecturer at the Institute for Social Sciences of the Heinrich Heine University Düsseldorf. His research focuses on German employers' associations, works councils, labour unions and comparative industrial relations.

Kevin Farnsworth, University of York, UK; Kevin Farnsworth is Reader in International Social Policy at the University of York. He has published widely on the political economy of social and public policies and the power and influence of business.

Leon Gooberman, Cardiff University, UK; Leon Gooberman is Lecturer in Employment Relations at Cardiff Business School. His research interests include the evolving nature and role of employers' organizations and employer collective action in the UK, as well as the processes and impacts of regional deindustrialization.

Marco Hauptmeier, Cardiff University, UK; Marco Hauptmeier is Professor of International Human Resource Management at Cardiff Business School. He was a researcher at the Max Planck Institute for the Study of Societies and has a PhD from Cornell University. His research in employment relations focuses on collective actors such as labour unions, European Works Councils and employers' organizations.

Markus Helfen, Freie Universität Berlin, Germany; Markus Helfen is Senior Research Fellow in the Management Department in the School of Business and Economics, Freie Universität Berlin. He researches topics within employment relations, HRM and organization theory, focusing on collective action and institutional work. These include global labour standards, and employment relations, in interorganizational settings.

Laurence Hopkins, Spark New Zealand; Laurence Hopkins is Remuneration, Systems and Data Specialist at Spark New Zealand. Previously he was Head of Research and Reward at the Universities and Colleges Employers Association in the UK, after working for The Work Foundation and The Change Institute where his specialities included employment and diversity policy.

Christian Lyhne Ibsen, University of Copenhagen, Denmark; Christian Lyhne Ibsen is Associate Professor at FAOS (Employment Relations Research Centre) in the Department of Sociology, University of Copenhagen, where he also earned his PhD in sociology. His research focuses on collective bargaining; trade unions; employers' associations; and the future of work and employment relations.

Mélanie Laroche, Université de Montréal, Canada; Mélanie Laroche is a full professor at the School of Industrial Relations of the Université de Montréal and teaches labour relations strategies and collective bargaining. Her main research interests include the logic of representation and employer action in Canada, unions, professional equality, and the evolution of labour relations.

Cangheng Liu, University of York, UK; Cangheng Liu undertook his doctoral research into business needs in China at the University of York. He is currently undertaking research on international business and trade union perspectives on social and public policies.

Cathie Jo Martin, Boston University, USA; Cathie Jo Martin is Professor of Political Science at Boston University and former chair of the Council for European Studies. Her book with Duane Swank, *The Political Construction of Business Interests* (Cambridge 2012) received the APSA Politics and History book award.

Glenn Morgan, University of Bristol, UK; Glenn Morgan is Professor of Management at the University of Bristol. He has been visiting professor at universities including Copenhagen Business School, where he was Velux Guest Professor. He was President of the Society for the Advancement of Socio-Economics in 2015 and has published widely on business and society.

Steen E. Navrbjerg, University of Copenhagen, Denmark; Steen E. Navrbjerg is Associate Professor at FAOS (Employment Relations Research Centre) in the Department of Sociology, University of Copenhagen. Among his research interests are MNC's employment practices; the relations between employers and employees at workplace level; employers' organizations; and how national IR-systems are affected by changing international value chains.

Thomas Paster, University of Roskilde, Denmark; Thomas Paster is Assistant Professor at the University of Roskilde, Department of Social Sciences and Business. He specializes in business-politics relations, corporate taxation, and welfare state politics. Recent publications include *The Role of Business in the Development of the Welfare State and Labor Markets in Germany* (Routledge, 2012).

Lisa Ahsen Sezer, University of Leicester, UK; Dr. Lisa Ahsen Sezer is Lecturer in Work and Employment at the University of Leicester. She is interested in employers' organizations' power resources, social networks, and identity-work; and how these shape the politics and outcomes of collective bargaining, HRM policies, and policy-making influence.

Peter Sheldon, University of New South Wales, Australia; Peter Sheldon is Honorary Professor, School of Management and Governance, UNSW Business School, Sydney. He publishes on comparative industrial relations and industrial relations history. His work on employer strategies and employers' associations focuses on Australia, Italy, China, South Korea, and Singapore.

Louise Thornthwaite, Macquarie University, Australia; Louise Thornthwaite is Professor, Department of Management, and Deputy Director of the Centre for Workplace Futures, Macquarie University, Sydney. She researches employers' associations, public policy analysis, social media and privacy at work, individual rights at work and the regulation of health and safety in road transport and logistic supply chains.

Geoffrey White, University of Greenwich, UK; Geoffrey White is Emeritus Professor of Human Resource Management at the University of Greenwich Business School. His research interests include reward management and human resource management, and he has advised the Local Government Pay Commission, the NHS Staff Council, the Hong Kong Government and the Universities and Colleges Employers Association.

Judith Shuqin Zhu, University of Newcastle, Australia; Judith Shuqin Zhu is Senior Lecturer in International Business at the University of Newcastle, Australia. Her research interests include employer coordination in China and Chinese multinationals' employment practices. Her work experience with the Shanghai labour authority has provided her with valuable insights about industrial relations in China. Her publications include contributions to *Human Resource Management* and *Work, Employment and Society*.

1 The Adaptation and Resilience of Employers' Organizations

Leon Gooberman and Marco Hauptmeier

Introduction

The first book on Employers' Organizations (EOs) with an international scope spanning several continents was Windmuller and Gladstone (1984).[1] The book considered the role and functions of EOs in Western countries and Japan in their historical context, focusing on the period since World War II. This context was characterized by significant economic growth and limited international competition as trade barriers constrained national markets. Meanwhile, EOs grew both in terms of their membership and functions. Collective bargaining coverage increased and EOs and unions set pay and working conditions for large parts of national workforces. EOs took part in tripartite concertation with the state and unions, where they participated in governing national training regimes, welfare state programmes and income policies although their involvement varied across countries. Overall, EOs were key actors within the political economies of Western countries during the post-war era.

The period since the 1980s saw impacts on EOs differ to those of previous decades. Many governments were influenced by the emerging neoliberal paradigm to deregulate and liberalize national economies. Liberalization combined with technological advances to enable the internationalization of trade and production that in turn prompted the development of global value chains and platform work (Newsome et al. 2015; Tilly 1995; Wood 2020). Union membership waned (Ebbinghaus and Visser 1999), collective bargaining coverage declined (Doellgast and Benassi 2020), and governments relied less on tripartite coordination (Culpepper and Regan 2014; Streeck 2003). These changes combined to increase the discretion of individual employers when managing the employment relationship (Baccaro and Howell 2017) although trends varied across liberal and coordinated market economies. Employer incentives to counter union power, and collectively coordinate activities with unions and the state reduced. Such activities were central to EOs, and as collective Employment Relations (ER) declined (Purcell 1995), a corresponding EO decline was often assumed but was rarely tested

DOI: 10.4324/9781003104575-1

through research. Barry and Wilkinson (2011), for example, examined five major ER journals published between 2000 and 2011 and identified only three studies on EOs.

Our book contributes to a more recent literature that explores 'the strange non-death of EOs' (Brandl and Lehr 2019; Barry and Wilkinson 2011; Behrens and Helfen 2019; Benson et al. 2017; Boumans 2021; Gooberman et al. 2018, 2019a; 2020b; Ibsen and Navrbjerg 2019; Martin and Swank 2012; Sánchez-Mosquera 2021; Sezer 2019; Sheldon et al. 2016, 2019; You and Barry 2016; Zhu and Nyland 2017). Our book argues that EOs are resilient organizations that adapt to changing circumstances by developing new practices to ensure organizational survival. EOs are impacted by changing economic and social contexts, including state interventions and union activities. These contexts vary significantly over time, across countries and world regions. EOs interpret changing contexts and respond to new challenges by developing new strategies, activities, and organizational forms that assist EOs and employers in adapting to evolving environments. Adaptation can be observed across democratic and authoritarian political systems as well as in countries where economies and ER institutions have transformed, demonstrating EOs' organizational resilience.

This broader argument builds on the more recent EO literature, including the chapters in this volume, within which five main trends can be identified. First, EO adaptation to changing socio-economic contexts has been studied in new country contexts including those in Asia (e.g., Benson et al. 2017) and in Eastern and Central Europe (e.g., Aguilera and Dabu 2005; Delteil and Kirov 2016). This volume contributes chapters by Zhu on China and by Sezer on Turkey.

Second, the literature identified distinct types of EOs beyond those that primarily conduct collective bargaining. Some target structures and regulation above and below national levels. This volume contains chapters by Farnsworth and Liu on international EOs, by Aranea et al. on European EOs, and by Larouche and Gooberman et al. on subnational EOs in, respectively, Canada and the United Kingdom (UK).

Third, the role of EOs in regulating ER evolved as the decline of collective bargaining in recent decades was not total, and important pockets of bargaining remained. EOs' continuing role in collective ER is a crosscutting theme in this volume and is examined, for example in Germany by Behrens and in Denmark by Ibsen and Navrbjerg. EOs also engage in new forms of unilateral, private employment regulation through codes of conduct, benchmarking, and certification. Helfen's contribution to this volume uses a meta-organizing perspective to contrast such private regulation with traditional collective regulation.

Fourth, political representation of EOs has evolved. Pluralist lobbying by EOs targeting employment and labour laws has become more important where corporatist institutions declined or disappeared. But EOs operating elsewhere have retained involvement in social pacts, whether in Asia (Benson et al. 2017; Kuruvilla and Liu 2010) or Europe (Bender and Ebbinghaus 2021). In this volume, Morgan examines the political power of EOs in the UK while Paster develops a differentiated account of German EO preferences on social programmes.

Fifth, EOs' service provision has evolved especially where collective regulation has declined most, prompting EOs to develop services to appeal to new or prospective members to maintain and grow subscription revenue, as explored in the chapter on Australia by Sheldon and Thornthwaite and the comparative chapter on higher education EOs by White and Hopkins.

The remainder of this chapter is structured as follows. The next section focuses on the historic growth and decline of EOs in Western countries, until recently the focus of ER research on EOs. The subsequent section explores the adaptation and resilience of EOs based on the evidence presented in this book and other recent EO literature. The conclusion distils key points about contemporary EOs and identifies gaps for future research.

The Growth and Decline of EOs in Western countries

The post-World War II decades were a growth period for EOs in Western countries across memberships, number of organizations, and functions. This period saw significant economic growth while product and labour markets were protected by trade barriers. Policy making was informed by the Keynesian economic paradigm that stipulated a role for EOs and unions within economic governance (Hall 1989). Tripartite governance between EOs, unions, and the state assumed three primary forms. The first was income policies and coordination between economic policy and collective bargaining that aimed to ensure aggregate demand without generating excessive inflation (Scharpf 1991). The second was that EOs and unions were granted new or expanded roles in organizing training regimes that often covered the bulk of national workforces (Gospel and Edwards 2012). The third form was prompted by the expansion of welfare states, within which EOs and unions participated in the governance of social programmes.

These forms reflected how states sought to integrate interest groups in various policy areas, as set out by theories of corporatism (Lehmbruch and Schmitter 1982; Schmitter 1974; Schmitter and Lehmbruch 1979; Schmitter and Streeck 1999). Corporatism suggested that by involving associations with specialized knowledge, states reduced their role in governing complex or conflictual societal domains like ER. Nevertheless, EO involvement varied across countries ranging from the US which saw no corporatist involvement of EOs in policy domains, to more coordinated economies that saw their full involvement.

But EOs' primary activity throughout this period remained collective bargaining (Clegg 1979; Plowman 1988; Sisson 1987) even as their other governance activities expanded. Collective bargaining coverage expanded, and union power grew. Locking unions into binding collective agreements had advantages for EOs. The first was that multi-employer bargaining moved a source of conflict, negotiations over wages, away from the workplace (Sisson 1987). The second was that bargaining prevented whipsawing where unions sought to play firms off against each other in the absence of multi-employer agreements to ratchet up wages and working conditions. Finally, bargaining reduced competition within industries as it took wages out of competition, reducing the ability of low-cost entrants to undercut wages while also preventing more profitable companies from poaching skilled staff (Swenson 1991). The benefits of bargaining were spread unevenly across EO memberships. For example, large employers in Germany benefited most as wage settlements were linked to average productivity increases by industry, making them more affordable to larger businesses with higher productivity growth while hampering the ability of EOs to reconcile the competing interests of larger and smaller members (Thelen 2000).

The literature also identified how forms of multi-employer bargaining varied across countries. A prominent typology used to explore these patterns is Varieties of Capitalism (Hall and Soskice 2001) with its identification of liberal market economies (LMEs) and coordinated market economies (CMEs), although later contributions identified further diversity in bargaining forms and EOs roles within both types. Within LMEs, Colvin and Darbishire (2013) set out three models. The first was the 'Wagner Act' model of the USA and Canada where ER revolved around private governance, with representation and collective bargaining centred on firms or enterprises although during post-war decades unions established pattern bargaining in many industries. The second was the 'voluntarist' model of the UK and, to some extent, Ireland. In the UK, bargaining outcomes were not legally enforceable. Implementation was underpinned by the relative actor power and a supportive but inobtrusive state (Howell 2005). A dual system emerged in key industries where informal and fragmented shop floor bargaining co-existed with more formal multi-employer bargaining (Flanders 1974). The final model was the 'award system' of Australia as analyzed by Sheldon and Thornthwaite in this volume, and New Zealand, where arbitration and award mechanisms were stimulated by state action, such as the 1906 Arbitration Act in Australia (Plowman 1989) that set out industry and occupational awards, followed by more recent iterations such as the Australian Fair Pay Commission, Fair Work Australia, and the Fair Work Commission.

CMEs also featured different patterns. A first was nationally centralized bargaining covering the entire economy. As examples, peak organizations in the Nordic states and Austria bargained to regulate the labour market, often encompassing welfare issues such as pensions (Swenson and Pontusson 2000; Traxler 2004). A second focused on sectoral collective bargaining with informal coordination between different sectors. One example was Germany where agreements in the metal sector provided a closely followed benchmark for other sectors (Traxler et al. 2008). A third was a multi-level combination of agreements. In Italy, Belgium, and France, national agreements determined broad issues such as hours of work, but more detailed topics were resolved through industry or enterprise agreements (Traxler 1998). Assessments of the efficiency of these patterns varied, although a prominent study (Calmfors and Driffill 1988) argued that highly centralized (such as in Austria and the Nordic countries) or decentralized bargaining systems (Switzerland and the US) performed better in terms of overall economic outcomes than intermediate systems (such as Belgium and the Netherlands).

In the post-war decades, EOs often conceded to higher union wage demands in collective bargaining (Golden et al. 1999). However, higher wages also resulted in higher aggregate income in the more sheltered national economies that underpinned aggregate demand, firm profits, and economic growth. However, this equilibrium came under pressure in the 1970s (Scharpf 1991). Two interrelated economic processes then transformed economic regimes, especially in Western countries: liberalization and internationalization. Governments and international governmental organizations had been slowly liberalizing economies and removing trade barriers since the 1950s but informed by the neoliberal economic paradigm (Blyth 2002), this process accelerated in the 1980s. Neoliberal reforms aimed to liberalize labour markets, curtail social programmes, and weaken collective ER institutions such as unions and collective bargaining. Parallel economic internationalization was supported by technological advances, prompting increased cross-border trade, cross border organization of production and services (including outsourcing, platform work, and global value chains), and growth in the number of multinational companies (Newsome et al. 2015; Tilly 1995; Wood 2020).

This changing economic context altered the rationale for employers and EOs to participate in multi-employer collective bargaining. First, employers felt less able to pay high wage bills given international competition. Research on the UK, for example, showed that employers exposed to international competition were more likely to stop bargaining collectively compared to those operating in sheltered sectors (Brown et al. 2009). Second, as union influence waned and new international exit options emerged, employer power increased, and they became less dependent on the protective elements of multi-employer collective bargaining. Employers instead preferred individualized, market-based, or firm-based wage setting and promoted intra-firm plant competition to facilitate labour concessions

(Greer and Hauptmeier 2016). Third, formal and informal collective institutions that constrained employers depended on government support (Howell 2005; Streeck 1997). But when such support weakened, employers felt less obligated to take part in collective institutions, further weakening collective ER. Fourth, early research found a positive relationship between comprehensive collective bargaining systems and macro-economic performance (Calmfors and Driffill 1988), but other research did not confirm such positive economic impacts in the context of economic internationalization (Traxler 2003; Traxler and Kittel 2000; see also Olson 1982), further weakening the rationale of employers to take part in multi-employer bargaining.

These dynamics impacted to different degrees across CMEs and LMEs. In LMEs, notably the US and the UK, multi-employer bargaining largely disappeared in the private sector. Decline was less marked in the public sector, but collective approaches often became less prescriptive as they evolved towards framework agreements while individual rights legislation gained in importance (Heery 2010). Meanwhile, EO involvement in economic coordination diminished or disappeared as governments strengthened market mechanisms for economic governance. In CMEs, however, EOs retained their role within collective bargaining despite some erosion. EOs often also retained involvement in corporatist structures governing training regimes and social programmes. In the 1990s, for example, some European countries reformed labour markets and welfare states through tripartite concertation (Ebbinghaus and Hassel 2000). Nevertheless, there was a departure from such joint coordination and policy making in the first half of the 2000s in the context of Third Way labour market policies in Europe. One case was Germany where the Social Democratic-led government abolished a social pact with EOs and unions, curtailing their role in governing labour markets and national social insurance programmes. Some observers saw this as 'the end of the century of corporatism' (Streeck 2003).

Change across both types of national systems was paralleled by decentralization as bargaining moved to lower levels such as company or plant (Katz 1993). Traxler (1995) argued that two types of decentralization existed. One was un-coordinated decentralization, typically found in less co-ordinated systems such as those of the UK and New Zealand. EOs exited multi-employer bargaining and wage setting reverted to plant or company levels, often assuming a form that excluded unions from involvement. The other was co-ordinated decentralization, generally found in more co-ordinated systems where sector level agreements remained but left space for lower-level agreements to set standards. EOs often retained influence over how bargaining results were implemented. Opening clauses enabled employers to deviate from multi-employer agreements in some economic circumstances, but EOs and unions had to agree to such deviation (Ellguth and Kohaut 2010).

Despite cross-national variation across Western countries, the neo-liberal period saw a weakening of unions, declining collective bargaining impact and coverage, and decreasing reliance by governments on tri-partite coordination. As countering unions through collective bargaining, and tripartite coordination, were widely seen as key reasons for EO existence, it was generally assumed that EOs would lose relevance and research with an explicit focus on such organizations became rare (Barry and Wilkinson 2011).

Adaptation and Resilience

Despite the trends described in the preceding section, a new literature on EOs emerged in the 2010s that highlights the adaptation and resilience of EOs across varied contexts. This literature has an explicit focus on EOs, instead of considering them in the context of other topics such as collective bargaining, social partnerships, training regimes, social pacts, or Varieties of Capitalism. The scope of this new literature has also broadened compared to previous research to include studies on countries in Asia as well as Eastern and Central Europe, new types, new activities, and new roles. This section explores EO adaptation and resilience by considering interest representation, new country contexts, and different types of EOs.

Interest Representation

The political representation of EOs has evolved as governmental approaches to coordinating and regulating ER have changed. Pluralist interest representation has become more important for EOs where governments abandoned or weakened corporatist institutions. EOs in these contexts lobby to favour employers, either through shaping employment, labour, and social laws, or preventing such laws from being enacted. This focus on lobbying can be observed in different national contexts. One example is the UK where lobbying has become the most frequent EO activity (Gooberman et al. 2018). EOs also organize and lobby above and below the national level where they target regional governments and international governmental organizations, as discussed below.

Chapters in this volume with a focus on political representation include those by Morgan and Paster. Morgan examines the power of EOs and revisits the conditions under which they can exercise political power. EOs have a strong track record of influencing governments in democratic countries due to the structural power of employers (Culpepper 2015; Lindblom 1977; Paster 2012, 2015). The state is dependent on the economic success and investments of employers as they influence economic outcomes seen as crucial for the political survival of politicians. This structural dependence made politicians susceptible to 'quiet' behind the scenes influencing of government policy by EOs. However, the rise of populism in some countries prompted the emergence of 'noisy politics' where EOs were labelled as elitist, weakening EOs traditional interest representation. For example, UK EOs proved unable to decisively influence the political process that resulted in Brexit. The theme of political preferences is further developed in Paster's chapter. He argues that employers often oppose social benefits because they weaken incentives for employees to take up employment. But in periods of overstaffing, employers tend to support social benefits as they facilitate their efforts to shed labour.

As well as lobbying, EOs continue to engage within tripartite concertation, social pacts, and corporatist institutions whose decline was not uniform across all national contexts. A first example is how some countries addressed the impacts of the 2007/2008 global financial and economic crises through social pacts (Bender and Ebbinghaus 2021) that supported labour adjustments with social programmes, helping employers to avoid dismissals while unions exercised constraint in their wage demands when bargaining collectively. A second example is that some long-standing corporatist institutions, including national training regimes in Denmark and Germany proved resilient, in part because political and economic actors saw them as contributing to economic competitiveness. Finally, new tripartite institutions were introduced in some countries. The German government, for example, introduced a federal minimum wage in 2015, delegating governance and wage setting to a new tripartite Minimum Wage Commission.

Beyond EOs' political representation, their employment regulatory role also adapted to evolving contexts. Collective bargaining declined in many countries, though exceptions to this trend exist. Martin's chapter examines the cultural origins of different ER systems, drawing on the historic literature corpus of the UK and Denmark. In Denmark, cross-class collaboration was seen as contributing to nation building but, in the UK, class-based conflict was commonly articulated. Differing moral views contributed to the creation of varied ER systems and EO roles, and the consequences can still be observed today. As Ibsen and Navrbjerg show in their chapter on Denmark, EOs and unions continue to negotiate collective agreements for large parts of the national workforce with collective bargaining coverage increasing from 80 per cent in 2007 to 83 per cent in 2015. They argue that EOs and unions have a mutual interest in keeping the state out of employment regulation, although autonomy depends on producing widely accepted negotiated outcomes that balance economic efficiency with social justice. Meanwhile, Behrens's chapter examines Germany where collective bargaining has declined although workforce coverage remains in excess of 50 per cent. Behrens argues that EOs have responded to threats posed by bargaining decline by developing a new 'bargaining free' membership category that enables employers to join EOs but avoid involvement in bargaining (Behrens 2018; Behrens and Helfen 2019).

But in liberal market economies such as the UK and the USA, the decline of EOs' role in collective bargaining has continued and is much more severe than in CMEs (Gooberman et al. 2019b). Collective bargaining has largely disappeared in private sectors although significant pockets remain within the public sector, albeit with some weakening of EO authority over members as many collective agreements have become less prescriptive.

While collective employment regulation has declined, individual and voluntary forms of EO employment regulation have become more important (Aranea et al. 2021a, 2021b; Demougin et al. 2021; Heery et al. 2022). EOs voluntarily promote labour and employment standards through codes of conduct, certification, and benchmarking of practices. Such private voluntary regulation has emerged where EOs face new state regulation or the juridification of work and ER, aiming to help members in the management of legal risk. Moreover, private voluntary regulation by EOs serves the purpose of obviating additional regulation by governments, signalling to the state that employers are capable of self-regulation. The shifting forms of labour regulation from collective to individual forms are examined in Helfen's chapter that proposes a meta-organizing perspective to analyze EOs. He interprets their standard setting as a form of collective self-discipline, in contrast to the beneficial constraints imposed on EOs by the state and unions in institutional ER.

Member services such as legal advice, education and training, and data provision have long been important to EOs (Windmuller and Gladstone 1984). However, the decline of collective bargaining, to which post-war EOs dedicated most of their resources, has prompted service provision to become central to contemporary EO activity (Demougin et al. 2019). Researchers explored such services through the analytical lens of Olson's (1965) collective action problem that could be overcome by offering services to persuade employers to join EOs. Sheldon and Thornthwaite's chapter traces Australian EOs' shift away from the provision of collective goods to selective and elective goods. The decline of collective ER required strategic and innovative adaptation by EOs with a new focus on "selective goods and elective goods that members purchase, respectively, through price-tiered membership levies or via commercial fees." In a similar vein, White and Hopkins's chapter demonstrate the importance of service provision to higher education EOs in the UK, Canada, and Australia, all of whom provided members with data on settlements and pay levels.

New Country Contexts

A limitation of the previous EO literature was that it focused narrowly on Western countries (including Australia) although Japan was studied regularly (e.g., Sako 1997). This limited scope entailed the risk that the conclusions of EO research could lack broader applicability. For example, the development of EOs in much of Asia, and Eastern and Central Europe, took place in contexts distinctive from Western countries. Many countries underwent political and economic transformations impacting on EO formation and development. These included shifts from authoritarian to democratic structures although such processes are still underway in some countries while others, such as China, remain firmly authoritarian. Meanwhile, Eastern and Central European countries and some Asian countries liberalized their economies but in other Asian economies state economic control and planning remain important.

The edited volume 'Employers' Associations in Asia' (Benson et al. 2017) was an important contribution to the literature, covering Japan, India, South Korea, China, Vietnam, Indonesia, Singapore, Malaysia, and Hongkong. The book explored how differing country-level economic development, political and institutional contexts, including democratic and authoritarian state structures, affected the nature of employer collective action while economies adopted, or were moving towards, more market-oriented economic arrangements. As examples, the density of Japanese EOs remained high but their wage setting role declined, and they focused increasingly on political representation and service provision (Benson 2017). In Korea, collective bargaining coverage and EO density were low (Lee et al. 2017). Tripartite structures existed, but EOs were often hostile towards unions and had little interest in joint regulation and developing collective bargaining. EOs in Singapore were involved in tripartite coordination and wage settings (Leggett et al. 2017), but those in Hong Kong were primarily service providers (Chan and Warner 2017). Finally, the chapter on Indonesia explored how the operational focus of a leading EO evolved from state corporatism towards member services and interest representation (Sitalaksmi 2017).

The study of EOs in authoritarian countries is emerging as a key theme. EOs in such countries are not independent but instead are either instructed directly by state authorities or act within parameters set by the state. EOs in Vietnam are tasked with promoting 'industrial harmony' while conflicts over wages and working conditions have become more frequent, prompting the government to promote tripartite coordination. China is a regular focus of study (e.g., Jiang and Zhu 2017; Zhu and Nyland 2017), given its economic rise and growing global influence. Zhu's chapter in this volume argues that Chinese EOs act as a 'transmission belt' between the party-state and employer-members. They provide a channel for the articulation of employer views to the party-state, and for communicating party-state decisions to employers. The party-state involves EOs and unions in discussions and coordination around wages and working conditions, to mediate and limit industrial conflict.

In Eastern and Central Europe, independent EOs only emerged during the 1990s transformation from socialist planned economies to capitalist market economies (Aguilera and Dabu 2005; Delteil and Kirov 2016; Trif 2004). Governments sought European integration and reconstructed their economies on western models with their norms of independent employer and employee representation. In the 1990s, state, unions and EOs in Eastern and Central European countries engaged in tripartite concertation to deal with shocks caused by privatization and exposure to international competition (Iankova 1998), although coordination was shallow as actors and representational structures were not fully developed (Ost 2000). Along with EO and union formation, independent collective bargaining was established with state support but bargaining levels and EO density have often remained low (Drahokoupil 2008). But variation exists and Poland is an example of a less co-ordinated system. Collective bargaining coverage declined from 25 per cent in 2000 to 18 per cent in 2017 (Czarzasty 2019: 466) while the association rate of employers remained stable at some 20 per cent. Polish EOs have shown little interest in supporting bargaining above company level, focusing instead on political lobbying. Slovenia, however, is a contrasting case (Feldmann 2014). EO membership was initially obligatory but legislative change in 2006 made membership voluntary, prompting the association rate to fall to less than 60 per cent in 2013 (Cazes et al. 2019). Meanwhile, although collective bargaining coverage declined from 100 per cent in 2000 to 79 per cent in 2017 (Stanojević and Poje 2019: 545), extension clauses exercised by the Slovenian government helped maintain bargaining at a relatively high level, indicating the importance of state support for employer organization and collective ER.

Sezer (2019) extended the geographic focus of study by examining EOs in Turkey, arguing that religious EOs arose to countervail the state, an argument developed in this volume through a historical exploration of the relationship between employer communities influenced by religion and a range of political actors operating in areas beyond ER regulation. A broader hypothesis derived from Sezer's study is that state threats towards autonomous collective actors in ER, civil society and the political system can push employers into coordination, which might explain EO origin in other countries within the 'Global South'.

Types

The recent EO literature identified a variety of types beyond those that conduct collective bargaining. One set are those that operate at international and regional levels. Farnsworth and Liu's chapter in this volume focuses on international EOs such as the International Organization of Employers formed from over 150 EO members to represent the interests of employers within social and employment policy at the United Nations, the G20 group of large economies, and most importantly, the International Labour Organization (ILO). The International Organization of Employers takes part in the ILO's tripartite structure via the Employers' Group, where it has long stalled progressive policies or initiatives (Baccaro and Mele 2012; Thomas and Turnbull 2020). Areana et al's chapter in this volume focuses on European EOs. European EOs strengthened their lobbying of European Union institutions within employment and social policy topics in the 1990s when the European Commission attempted to develop a social dimension to balance accelerating economic liberalization. This social dimension included sectoral and intersectoral social dialogue, EU-level institutions that aimed to facilitate cooperative relationships between unions and EEOs. However, EEOs have been a 'reluctant social partner' and have generally avoided developing binding joint regulation with unions, representing member interests instead through lobbying, service provision and voluntary standard setting.

Two chapters in this volume focus on regional EOs. Laroche examines EOs in Quebec, a Canadian province with a distinctive language, political culture, and institutions. EOs take part in sectoral or provincial consultative institutions where they aim to influence formal and informal employment norms and engage in collective bargaining and tripartite coordination. EOs contribute to diverging ER in Quebec compared to other Canadian provinces and territories. Meanwhile, Gooberman and Hauptmeier examine territorial EOs within the UK that focus on the politically devolved territories of Wales, Scotland, and Northern Ireland. They argue that these EOs have assumed a new purpose as they respond to new sub-national governing institutions. These studies on regional EOs connect to the literature on the origins of employer collective action, which observed that EOs originated at local and regional levels in the 19th century to counter unions (Commons 1964; McIvor 2002; Slate 1957).

Other types of EOs include those responding to specific social issues in a context of declining collective ER. In the UK, for example, the juridification of ER and the legislative introduction of new individual rights, including within equality and diversity, posed new challenges for employers prompting their collective organization within Employer Forums (Bowkett et al. 2017; Demougin et al. 2021). These EOs unilaterally develop and promote labour standards in their member firms, typically exceeding legally required minimums, through instruments such as assessment tools, best practice certification, benchmarking, and codes of conduct.

Going beyond the EO types discussed above, researchers have developed typologies of EOs. For example, a study in Quebec (Delorme et al. 1994) identified four types of collective bodies based on their degree of involvement within collective bargaining, while a recent UK project differentiated between negotiating, standard-setting, lobbying, and service-providing EOs (Gooberman et al. 2020a). The defining feature of these new typologies is their inclusion of EOs that have a role within ER, but do not confine their activities to traditional functions such as collective bargaining.

Conclusion

EOs have continued to adapt to changing political, social, and economic contexts, developing their practices and organizational forms to retain their relevance in a changing world. Despite some decline of collective bargaining and tripartite concertation when compared to the post-war decades, both continue to exist in many country contexts. Some EOs also unilaterally promote working and employment standards through codes of conduct, certification, and benchmarking, engaging in private voluntary regulation. Such dynamics mean that EOs remain involved in ER regulation in many contexts. Meanwhile, EOs expanded their lobbying of governments while emphasizing their provision of member services. These developments can be observed in Western countries, but also in countries that were not previously the focus of EO research such as those in Asia, and Eastern and Central Europe. To deal with new challenges and regulatory pressures, employers have also organized in different types of EOs, including international EOs, European EOs, regional EOs, and Employer Forums.

The newer EO literature to which this book contributes has increased our knowledge of employer collective action but gaps remain. First, the literature has produced new insights into EOs in Europe, Asia, and English-speaking countries like Australia, but we know less about EOs in Latin America, Africa (including Arabic countries), and Russia. Second, empirical research focuses on EOs and their representatives but the users of EOs, individual employers, receive scarce attention. This gap implies that the reasons and interests of individual employers prompting their decisions to join EOs are mostly deduced from interviews with EO representatives. Third, the governance and internal structures of EOs largely continue to be a black box (one exception is Behrens's chapter on Germany) and we lack evidence as to how EOs form policies and goals within their governance structures. Tensions and different interests between EO members and representatives might exist, requiring mediation through negotiation processes that could shape EO adaptation. There is some evidence that democratic governance in EOs has weakened, even in mature democracies, but the internal governance of EOs has yet to be examined systematically. Fourth, the literature on different types of EOs has focused on democratic countries and excluded organizations in authoritarian systems. Future research might develop and contrast EO types across both sets of political systems. Such comparisons might benefit from consulting an older corporatist literature that examined the incorporation of associations in fascist regimes in the first half of the 20th century (Schmitter 1974). Fifth, the EO literature on developing, emerging, and authoritarian countries has interrogated EO relationships with state authorities with contrasting results. In this volume, Zhu suggests that EOs in China are dependent on the state, prioritizing state interests over member interests. Sezer's study of Turkey, a country with a mixed democratic record, comes to a different conclusion by arguing that the foundation of religious EOs was a reaction to the suppression of collective actors by the government, contributing to an emergent civil society independent of the state. Future research might reveal additional relationships between the state and EOs.

ER researchers and practitioners might welcome the message of the book that EOs are adaptable and resilient organizations, as unions need a counterpart to conduct collective bargaining and the continuing existence of EOs keeps the prospect of collective ER alive despite a decline in collective bargaining. However, such an EO role in collective ER requires an ideological commitment by employers (Behrens and Helfen 2016), which is more likely to develop in contexts where employers are obliged to work with labour unions. Such nurturing constraints refer to various kinds of state inventions that includes direct instructions in authoritarian regimes, binding collective regulation in coordinated economies, unobtrusive state support of collective ER in voluntarist countries, as well as union and social movement pressures that force employers to engage. As the chapters in this book show, EOs continue to face such social and regulatory pressures in many contexts, but where they weaken and collective ER becomes a voluntary choice for employers, EOs have continued to erode collective institutions or have already moved beyond a role in collective ER towards impacting work and employment through lobbying, service provision, and unilateral voluntary regulation.

In conclusion, EOs have emerged and developed in different political and economic systems since the 19th century. It is uncertain how EOs will fare in the future but if the past is an indicator, they will adapt to evolving social, regulatory, and economic pressures and help individual employers to cope with challenges that require strength in numbers.

Note

1 We would like to thank Martin Behrens, Edmund Heery, Magnus Feldman, Krzysztof Jasiecki, and Joey Soehardjojo for insightful comments on previous drafts of this chapter.

References

Aguilera, R. V. and Dabu, A. (2005). Transformation of employment relations systems in Central and Eastern Europe. *The Journal of Industrial Relations*, 47: 16–42. 10.1111/j.1472-9296.2005.00156.x

Aranea, M., Demougin, P., Gooberman, L. and Hauptmeier, M. (2021a). *Handbook of European Employers' Organisations*. Hans Böckler Foundation Working Paper No. 225. Düsseldorf. https://www.boeckler.de/fpdf/HBS-008096/p_fofoe_WP_225_2021.pdf [accessed 8 September 2021].

Aranea, M., Gooberman, L. and Hauptmeier, M. (2021b). What Do European Employers' Organisations Do? Hans Böckler Foundation Working Paper No. 226. Düsseldorf. https://www.boeckler.de/fpdf/HBS-008113/p_fofoe_WP_226_2021.pdf [accessed 24 September 2021].

Baccaro, L. and Howell, C. (2017). *Trajectories of Neoliberal Transformation: European Industrial Relations since the 1970s.* Cambridge: Cambridge University Press.

Baccaro, L. and Mele, V. (2012). Pathology of path dependency? The ILO and the challenge of new governance. *ILR Review, 65*: 195–224. 10.1177%2F001979391206500201

Barry, M. and Wilkinson, A. (2011). Reconceptualising employer associations under evolving employment relations: Countervailing power revisited. *Work, Employment and Society, 25* (1): 149–162. 10.1177%2F0950017010389229

Behrens, M. (2018). Structure and competing logics: The art of shaping interests within German employers' associations. *Socio-Economic Review, 16* (4): 769–789. 10.1093/ser/mwx037

Behrens, M. and Helfen, M. (2016). The foundations of social partnership. *British Journal of Industrial Relations, 54*: 334–357.

Behrens, M. and Helfen, M. (2019). Small change, big impact? Organizational membership rules and the exit of employer associations from multi-employer bargaining in Germany. *Human Resource Management Journal, 29*: 51–66. 10.1111/1748-8583.12210

Bender, B. and Ebbinghaus, B. (2021). When governments include social partners in crisis corporatism: Comparing social concertation in Europe during the Great Recession. In: B. Ebbinghaus and J. T. Weishaupt (eds.) *The Role of Social Partners in Managing Europe's Great Recession.* London and New York: Routledge, pp. 24–50.

Benson, J. (2017). Employers' associations in Japan: Fragmented conservatism. In: J. Benson, Y. Zhu and H. Gospel (eds.) *Employers' Associations in Asia: Employer Collective Action.* London and New York: Routledge, pp. 38–59.

Benson, J., Zhu, Y. and Gospel, H. (2017). *Employers' Associations in Asia: Employer Collective Action.* London and New York: Routledge.

Blyth, M. (2002). *Great Transformations: Economic Ideas and Institutional Change in the Twentieth Century.* Cambridge and New York: Cambridge University Press.

Boumans, S. (2021). Neoliberalisation of industrial relations: The ideational development of Dutch employers' organisations between 1976 and 2019. *Economic and Industrial Democracy,* Published online before print. 10.1177%2F0143831X211020086

Bowkett, C., Hauptmeier, M. and Heery, E. (2017). Exploring the role of employer forums—the case of Business in the Community Wales. *Employee Relations, 39* (7): 986–1000. 10.1108/ER-11-2016-0229

Brandl, B. and Lehr, A. (2019). The strange non-death of employer and business associations: An analysis of their representativeness and activities in Western European countries. *Economic and Industrial Democracy, 37* (1): 73–94. 10.1177%2F0143831X16669842

Brown, W., Bryson, A. and Forth, J. (2009). Competition and the retreat from collective bargaining. In: W. Brown, A. Bryson, J. Forth, et al. (eds.) *The Evolution of the Modern Workplace.* Cambridge: Cambridge University Press, pp. 22–47.

Calmfors, L. and Driffill, J. (1988). Bargaining structure, corporatism and macroeconomic performance. *Economic Policy*, 3 (6): 14–64. 10.2307/1344503

Cazes, S., Garnero, A. and Martin, S. (2019). *Negotiating our Way up: Collective Bargaining in a Changing World of Work*. Paris: OECD Publishing.

Chan, A. W. and Warner, M. (2017). Employers' associations in Hong Kong. In: J. Benson, Y. Zhu and H. Gospel (eds.) *Employers' Associations in Asia: Employer Collective Action*. London and New York: Routledge, pp. 102–124.

Clegg, H. (1979). *The Changing System of Industrial Relations in Great Britain*. Oxford: Basil Blackwell.

Colvin, A. and Darbishire, O. (2013). Convergence in industrial relations institutions: The emerging Anglo-American model? *Industrial relations and Labor Relations Review*, 66 (5): 1047–1077. 10.1177%2F001979391306600502

Commons, J. R. (1964). American Shoemakers, 1648-1895: A sketch of industrial evolution. *Labor and Administration*. New York: A. M. Kelley, reprinted from *Quarterly Journal of Economics*, November 1909.

Culpepper, P. D. (2015). Structural power and political science in the post-crisis era. *Business and Politics*, 17: 391–409.

Culpepper, P. D. and Regan, A. (2014). Why don't governments need trade unions anymore? The death of social pacts in Ireland and Italy. *Socio-Economic Review*, 12: 723–745. 10.1093/ser/mwt028

Czarzasty, J. (2019). Collective bargaining in Poland: A near-death experience. In: T. Müller, K. Vandaele and J. Waddington (eds.) *Collective Bargaining in Europe: Towards an Endgame*. Brussels: European Trade Union Institute, pp. 465–481.

Delorme, F., Fortin, R. and Gosselin, L. (1994). L'organisation du monde patronal au Québec: Un portrait diversifié. *Relations Industrielles/Industrial Relations*, 49 (1): 9–40.

Delteil, V. and Kirov, V. N. (2016). *Labour and Social Transformation in Central and Eastern Europe: Europeanization and Beyond*. London and New York: Routledge.

Demougin, P., Gooberman, L., Hauptmeier, M. and Heery, E. (2019). Employers' organizations transformed. *Human Resources Management Journal*, 29 (1): 1–16. 10.1111/1748-8583.12222

Demougin, P., Gooberman, L., Hauptmeier, M., Heery, E. . (2021). Revisiting voluntarism: Private voluntary regulation by Employer Forums in the United Kingdom. *Journal of Industrial Relations*, Published online first. 63 (5): 684–705.10.1177%2F00221856211038308

Doellgast, V. and Benassi, C. (2020). Collective bargaining. *Handbook of Research on Employee Voice*. Cheltenham: Edward Elgar Publishing.

Drahokoupil, J. (2008). *Globalization and the State in Central and Eastern Europe: The Politics of Foreign Direct Investment*. Abingdon: Routledge.

Ebbinghaus, B. and Hassel, A. (2000). Striking deals: Concertation in the reform of continental European welfare states. *Journal of European Public Policy*, 7: 44–62. 10.1080/135017600343269

Ebbinghaus, B. and Visser, J. (1999). When institutions matter: Union growth and decline in Western Europe, 1950–1995. *European Sociological Review*, 15: 135–158. 10.1093/oxfordjournals.esr.a018257

Ellguth, P. and Kohaut, S. (2010). Escape from collective bargaining? Exits and the influence of opening clauses. *Industrielle Beziehungen*, 17 (4): 345–371.

Feldmann, M. (2014). Coalitions and corporatism: The Slovenian political economy and the crisis. *Government and Opposition*, 49: 70–91.

Flanders, A. D. (1974). The tradition of voluntarism. *British Journal of Industrial Relations*, 12 (3): 352–370. 10.1111/j.1467-8543.1974.tb00012.x

Golden, M. A., Wallerstein, M. and Lange, P. (1999). Post-war trade union organisation and industrial relations in twelve countries. In: H. Kitscheldt, P. Lange, G. Marks and J. Stephens (eds.) *Continuity and Change in Contemporary Capitalism*. Cambridge: Cambridge University Press, pp. 194–230.

Gooberman, L., Hauptmeier, M. and Heery, E. (2018). Contemporary employer interest representation in the United Kingdom. *Work, Employment and Society*, 32 (1): 114–132. 10.1177%2F0950017017701074

Gooberman, L., Hauptmeier, M. and Heery, E. (2019a). The evolution of employers' organisations in the United Kingdom: Extending countervailing power. *Human Resource Management Journal*, 29: 82–96. 10.1111/1748-8583.12193

Gooberman, L., Hauptmeier, M. and Heery, E. (2019b). The decline of employers' associations in the UK, 1976 to 2014. *Journal of Industrial Relations*, 61 (1): 11–32. 10.1177%2F0022185617750418

Gooberman, L., Hauptmeier, M. and Heery. E. (2020a). A typology of employers' organizations. *Economic and Industrial Democracy*, 41 (1): 229–248. 10.1177%2F0143831X17704499

Gooberman, L., Hauptmeier, M. and Heery, E. (2020b). The decay and revival of sub-UK employer organization: A response to Dr Ritson. *Labor History*, 61 (5–6): 417–422. 10.1080/0023656X.2020.1830958

Gospel, H. and Edwards, T. (2012). Strategic transformation and muddling through: Industrial relations and industrial training in the UK. *Journal of European Public Policy*, 19 (8): 1229–1248. 10.1080/13501763.2012.709023

Greer, I. and Hauptmeier, M. (2016). Management whipsawing: The staging of labor competition under globalization. *ILR Review*, 69: 29–52. 10.1177%2F0019793915602254

Hall, P. A. (1989). *The Political Power of Economic Ideas: Keynesianism Across Nations*. Princeton, NJ: Princeton University Press.

Hall, P. and Soskice, D. (2001). *Varieties of Capitalism*. Oxford: Oxford University Press.

Heery, E., Hann, D. and Nash, D. (2022). *The Real Living Wage: Civil Regulation and the Employment Relationship*. Oxford: Oxford University Press.

Heery, E. (2010). Debating employment law: Responses to juridification. In: P. Blyton, E. Heery and P. Turnbull (eds.) *Reassessing the Employment Relationship*. London: Palgrave Macmillan, pp. 71–96.

Howell, C. (2005). *Trade Unions and the State: The Construction of Industrial Relations Institutions in Britain, 1890–2000*. Princeton, NJ: Princeton University Press.

Iankova, E. A. (1998). The transformative corporatism of Eastern Europe. *East European Politics and Societies*, 12: 222–264. 10.1177%2F0888325498012002003

Ibsen, C. L. and Navrbjerg, S. E. (2019). Adapting to survive: The case of Danish employers' organizations. *Human Resource Management Journal*, 58 (5): 1–15. 10.1111/1748-8583.12182

Jiang, Q. and Zhu, Y. (2017). Employers' associations in China: Promoting interaction among the key stakeholders. In: J. Benson, Y. Zhu and H. Gospel (eds.) *Employers' Associations in Asia, Employer Collective Action.* London and New York: Routledge, pp. 125–143.

Katz, H. C. (1993). The decentralization of collective bargaining: A literature review and comparative analysis. *Industrial and Labor Relations Review,* 47 (1): 3–22. 10.1177%2F001979399304700101

Kuruvilla, S. and Liu, M. (2010). Tripartism and economic reforms in Singapore and the Republic of Korea. In: Fraile, L. (ed.) *Blunting Neoliberalism. Tripartism and Economic Reforms in the Developing World.* London: Palgrave Macmillan, pp. 85–127.

Lee, H.-J., Rowley, C. and Yu, G.-C. (2017). Employers' associations in South Korea: Increasing importance of industrial relations. In: J. Benson, Y. Zhu and H. Gospel (eds.) *Employers' Associations in Asia, Employer Collective Action.* London and New York: Routledge, pp. 60–81.

Leggett C., Kuah A. and Gan B. (2017). Employers' associations in Singapore: Tripartite engagement. In: J. Benson, Y. Zhu and H. Gospel (eds.) *Employers' Associations in Asia, Employer Collective Action.* London and New York: Routledge, pp. 82–101.

Lehmbruch, G. and Schmitter, P. C. (1982). *Patterns of Corporatist Policy-Making.* London: Sage.

Lindblom, C. (1977). *Politics and Markets.* New York: Basic Books.

Martin, C. J. and Swank, D. (2012). *The Political Construction of Business Interests: Coordination, Growth, and Equality.* Cambridge: Cambridge University Press.

McIvor, A. (2002). *Organised Capital: Employers' Associations and Industrial Relations in Northern England, 1880-1939.* Cambridge: Cambridge University Press.

Newsome, K., Taylor, P., Bair, J., Rainnie, A. (2015). *Putting Labour in its Place: Labour Process Analysis and Global Value Chains.* London: Palgrave.

Olson, M. (1982). *The Rise and Decline of Nations: Economic Growth, Stagflation, and Social Rigidities.* New Haven: Yale University Press.

Olson, M. (1965). *The Logic of Collective Action: Public Goods and the Theory of Groups.* Cambridge, MA: Harvard University Press.

Ost, D. (2000). Illusory corporatism in Eastern Europe: Neoliberal tripartism and postcommunist class identities. *Politics & Society,* 28 (4): 503–530.

Paster, T. (2012). *The Role of Business in the Development of the Welfare state and Labor Markets in Germany: Containing Social Reforms.* London and New York: Routledge.

Paster, T. (2015). Bringing power back in: A review of the literature on the role of business in welfare state politics. *MPIfG Discussion Paper,* 15: 1–38.

Plowman, D. H. (1988). Employer associations and bargaining structures: An Australian perspective. *British Journal of Industrial Relations,* 26 (3): 371–396. 10.1111/j.1467-8543.1988.tb00757.x

Plowman, D. H. (1989). Countervailing power, organizational parallelism and Australian employer associations. *Australian Journal of Management,* 14 (1): 97–113. 10.1177%2F031289628901400106

Purcell, J. (1995). Ideology and the end of institutional industrial relations: Evidence from the UK. In: C. Crouch and F. Traxler (eds.) *Organized Industrial Relations in Europe: What Future?* Aldershot, Hants, England, Brookfield, Vt., USA: Avebury, pp. 101–119.

Sako, M. (1997). Wage bargaining in Japan: Why employers and unions value industry-level co-ordination. *CEP Discussion Papers dp0334*. Centre for Economic Performance, LSE.

Sánchez-Mosquera, M. (2021). Somewhat more than path dependence: The Spanish employers' peak organisation and social dialogue in light of the crisis of the industrial relations system. *Economic and Industrial Democracy.* Published online before print. 10.1177%2F0143831X211024717

Scharpf, F. W. (1991). *Crisis and Choice in European Social Democracy.* Ithaca, NY: Cornell University Press.

Schmitter, P. C. (1974). Still the century of corporatism? *The Review of Politics,* 36: 85–131.

Schmitter, P. C. and Lehmbruch G. (1979). *Trends Toward Corporatist Intermediation.* Beverly Hills and London: Sage Publications.

Schmitter, P. C. and Streeck, W. (1999). The organization of business interests: Studying the associative action of business in advanced industrial societies. *MPIfG Discussion Paper,* 99: 1–96.

Sezer, L. (2019). Employers' organizations as social movements: Political power and identity-work in Turkey. *Human Resource Management Journal,* 29 (1): 67–81.10.1111/1748-8583.12209

Sheldon, P., Della Torre, E. and Nacamulli, R. (2019). When territory matters: Employer associations and changing collective goods strategies. *Human Resource Management Journal,* 29 (1): 17–35.10.1111/1748-8583.12201

Sheldon, P., Nacamulli, R., Paoletti, F. and Morgan, D. E. (2016). Employer association responses to the effects of bargaining decentralization in Australia and Italy: Seeking explanations from organizational theory. *British Journal of Industrial Relations* 54: 160–191. 10.1111/bjir.12061

Sisson, K. (1987). *The Management of Collective Bargaining: An International Comparison.* Oxford: Basil Blackwell.

Sitalaksmi, S. (2017). Employers' Associations in Indonesia: The transformation from state corporatist to professional organization. In: J. Benson, Y. Zhu and H. Gospel (eds.) *Employers' Associations in Asia, Employer Collective Action.* London and New York: Routledge, pp. 183–204.

Slate, D. M. (1957). Trade union behaviour and the local employers' association. *Industrial and Labor Relations Review,* 2: 55. 10.1177%2F001979395701100104

Stanojević, M. and Poje, A. (2019). Slovenia: Organised decentralisation in the private sector and centralisation in the public sector. In: T. Müller, K. Vandaele and J. Waddington (eds.) *Collective Bargaining in Europe: Towards an Endgame.* Brussels: European Trade Union Institute, pp. 545–562.

Streeck, W. (1997). Beneficial constraints: On the economic limits of rational voluntarism. In: J. R. Hollingsworth and R. Boyer (eds.) *Contemporary Capitalism: The Embeddedness of Institutions.* Cambridge: Cambridge University Press, pp. 197–219.

Streeck, W. (2003). No Longer the Century of Corporatism: Das Ende des "Bündnisses für Arbeit".

Swenson, P. (1991). Bringing capital back in, or social democracy reconsidered: Employer power, cross-class alliances, and centralization of industrial relations in Denmark and Sweden. *World Politics*, 43 (4): 513–544. 10.2307/2010535

Swenson, P. and Pontusson, J. (2000). The Swedish employer offensive against centralized wage bargaining. In: T. Iversen, J. Pontusson and D. Soskice (eds.) *Unions, Employers, and Central Banks: Macroeconomic Coordination and Institutional Change in Social Market Economies*. Cambridge: Cambridge University Press, pp. 77–106.

Thelen, K. (2000). Why German Employers cannot bring themselves to dismantle the German Model. In: T. Iversen, J. Pontusson and D. Soskice (eds.) *Unions, Employers, and Central Banks: Macroeconomic Coordination and Institutional Change in Social Market Economies*. Cambridge: New York: Cambridge University Press, pp. 138–172.

Thomas, H. and Turnbull, P. (2020). From a 'moral commentator' to a 'determined actor'? How the International Labour Organization (ILO) orchestrates the field of international industrial relations. *British Journal of Industrial Relations*, 59 (3): 874–898. 10.1111/bjir.12578

Tilly, C. (1995). Globalization threatens labor's rights. *International Labor and Working-class History*, 47: 1–23. 10.1017/S0147547900012825

Traxler, F. (1995). Farewell to labour market associations? Organized versus disorganized decentralization as a map for industrial relations. In: C. Crouch and F. Traxler (eds.) *Organized Industrial Relations in Europe: What Future*. Aldershot, UK: Avebury, pp. 3–19.

Traxler, F. (1998). Collective bargaining in the OECD: Developments, preconditions and effects. *European Journal of Industrial Relations*, 4 (2): 207–226. 10.1177%2F095968019842004

Traxler, F. (2003). Bargaining (de) centralization, macroeconomic performance and control over the employment relationship. *British Journal of Industrial Relations*, 41: 1–27.

Traxler, F. (2004). Employer associations, institutions and economic change: A crossnational comparison. *Industrielle Beziehungen/The German Journal of Industrial Relations*, 11 (1/2): 42–60.

Traxler, F., Brandl, B. and Glassner, V. (2008) Pattern bargaining: An investigation into its agency, context and evidence. *British Journal of Industrial Relations*, 46: 33–58.

Traxler, F. and Kittel, B. (2000). The bargaining system and performance: A comparison of 18 OECD countries. *Comparative Political Studies*, 33: 1154–1190.

Trif, A. (2004). Overview of industrial relations in Romania. *SEER-South-East Europe Review for Labour and Social Affairs*, 2: 43–64.

Windmuller, J. P. and Gladstone, A. (1984). *Employers' Associations and Industrial Relations: A Comparative Study*. Oxford: Oxford University Press

Wood, A. J. (2020). *Despotism on Demand*. Cornell University Press.

You. K. and Barry, M. (2016). Intra-industry competition among employer associations: A case study of the retail sector. *Labour and Industry*, 26 (2): 120–137. 10.1080/10301763.2016.1162937

Zhu, J. S. and Nyland, C. (2017). Chinese employer associations, institutional complementarity and countervailing power. *Work, Employment and Society*, 31: 284–301. 10.1177%2F0950017016643480

Part I

Theoretical Perspectives on Employer Collective Action

2 Employers' Organizations: Sources of Power and Limits to Power

Glenn Morgan

Introduction

The purpose of this chapter is to consider the conditions under which Employers' Organizations (EOs) are able to exercise power in the political arena. How are they able to influence state policy against the opposition of other organized groups in society? Conventional accounts broadly define power as the ability of actor A to get actor B to do something significant that would not have been done without the intervention of actor A and is, in some way, against the interests of B (Lukes 1974). The core of the problem for EOs is that prior to the advent of liberal democratic forms of the state, state power was exercised by traditional landed elites and the rising manufacturing employers class, combining physical coercion, economic necessity, and long-standing religious and moral legitimations of hierarchy and status. Conflicts between these elites often offered the entry point for widening the franchise, leading politicians to support an extended electorate in the hope that they could build on existing systems of deference and status to create 'working class conservatives' (Ziblatt 2017).

However, once liberal democratic forms of representation became embedded from the late 19th century in Europe, then in theory the state was controlled by 'the people' through the mechanism of elections where political parties, including socialist and social democratic ones, presented contrasting platforms for government. The tensions such changes brought about were revealed starkly in the rise of fascism and authoritarianism in many European countries in the 1930s as some landed and industrial elites sought to defend their power and destroy rising social democratic and communist movements by destroying democracy (Kershaw 2015). The post war restoration in Western Europe of liberal democracies ushered in a period where elites moved to shape politics not through violence and coercion but by other mechanisms, utilizing democracy in order to ensure that business friendly parties dominated the state.

In this chapter, therefore, the primary focus is on approaches which examine how EOs exercised power within post-war liberal democratic societies to ensure the maintenance of a business-friendly environment.

DOI: 10.4324/9781003104575-3

Two main sets of mechanisms are described – the instrumentalist approach and the structural approach. Whilst these approaches lay a framework for understanding business power, they are insufficient in themselves as they are unable to account for the instances where EOs fail to achieve their key objectives. In the second part of the chapter, recent approaches which provide answers to this problem are discussed in the context of firstly the increasing fragmentation of business in the 2000s (Mizruchi 2013) and secondly the politics of the late 2010s and 2020s driven by the rise of populism (Moffitt 2016; Mudde and Kaltwasser 2017; Muller 2017) in which the voice of business was increasingly delegitimized. Both these features led to significant disruptions in the power of EOs to influence the state, e.g. as in the Brexit process in the UK or in aspects of Trump's policies of protectionism. The chapter concludes by calling for more detailed studies of the power of EOs in the light of the increasing fragmentation of business, the instabilities of contemporary liberal democracies and the challenges set by the rise of populism.

Theories of Power

Instrumental Approaches to Power

Instrumental approaches to power are based on the idea that the state is an instrument that can be controlled and used by particular groups to forward their interests. Therefore, whoever holds the state, holds the key instruments of power which can be exercised over other groups and has the capability to influence the key outcomes of policy decisions. In the liberal democracies which began to develop in the late 19th century and became dominant in Western industrialized economies in the 1950s and 1960s, there was the possibility that a majority of the electorate could be mobilized against the wealth and power of big business and could itself control the state in ways which went against the perceived interests of business. Business associations and EOs sought to avoid electoral contests which might lead either to radical versions of socialism, with expropriation of the ownership class, or more social democratic versions (based on gradual and incremental changes and redistribution of wealth, income and life chances through taxation of the rich and the creation of the institutions of the welfare state and more equality of opportunity). Through the 20th and 21st centuries, business associations and EOs have sought strategies to limit the radical potential of democratic politics by finding ways to ensure that when the 'people' got the vote, the impact of this was limited because sufficient of them would vote in a conservative, business friendly way to stave off fears of socialism. Persuading elements of the electorate to vote for conservative friendly policies could also be achieved by not opposing all efforts at ameliorating the effects of markets and market inequality. On occasions business friendly parties might themselves initiate limited welfare state reforms in order to forestall more radical demands from emerging (Korpi 2006; see also Iversen and Soskice 2019). Both these strategies required establishing business friendly parties that appealed to not just the core business constituency (ranging from large firms through to self-employed crafts people and shop owners) but also to a wider section of the population (including the growing white collar and technical group of employees).

Crucial to this has been the support which EOs have given to establishing and maintaining business friendly political parties. Businesses and wealthy individual businesspeople have provided funds to support the development of national party structures for policy-making and fighting elections. Most liberal democracies now have some sort of constraints over the levels of funding which can be provided by individuals and corporations directly or indirectly to support election campaigns. However, more recently these restrictions have been undermined by a combination of legal judgments (in the US, the *Citizens United v. Federal Election Commission* in 2010) and the rise of social media enabling new and less visible ways to contact and influence electors. For most of the century, business friendly parties (receiving support from EOs, corporations and wealthy individuals) have been able to significantly outspend socialist and social democratic parties (which have generally been dependent on trade union contributions and individual membership fees, with a limited number of business donors at particular points). Such funding has been effective in buying advertising space in print and broadcasting media and, in recent years, in targeted messaging on social media. It has also been important in the ability of conservative, business-friendly parties to develop and sustain strong organizational structures and social infrastructure (such as clubs and societies) in and around national legislatures but also across regions and cities crucial for achieving electoral majorities.

The influence of business in developing business-friendly parties is reflected in the degree of interconnectedness between the parliamentary membership of such parties, EOs, and businesses (Scott 1997). Shared social and cultural capital developed in educational settings, professional networks and interlocking membership of corporate boards and the boards of important cultural institutions make it relatively simple for such individuals to move backwards and forwards between politics and the business sector, including through EOs and to use this as a basis for establishing lobbying operations with close contacts with decision makers. The British Conservative MP, Angela Knight, for example had a post-university career as an engineer and manager of a business, won her parliamentary seat in 1992 and lost it in 1997. She subsequently served as Chief Executive of the British Bankers Association and, having left the BBA in 2012, then became Chief Executive of Energy UK, the trade association for the sector. Finally, she became Chair of the Office for Tax

Simplification set up within the Treasury in 2015, leaving in 2019 having accrued a number of non-executive directorships in other UK-based companies.

Compared to labour or to social movement organizations, EOs have access to much more funding especially when the need is perceived to mobilize against specific measures that could damage business. Lobbying can take place directly through the contact between EOs and the government or via intermediary professional lobbying operations. Individual companies depending on their scale and sense of threat may pursue their lobbying efforts and/or participate in collective efforts. Lobbying may start before the electoral process with businesses finding candidates which they can rely on to follow their interests even before they arrive at the legislature. Lobbyists provide candidates with ready-made policies and expertise, often in areas where the individual has little personal knowledge. Business associations and EOs are able to access the state as an instrument and use this power to support their own interest.

The power of business associations and EOs is also related to the increasingly complex nature of decision-making and the need for expertise to frame and develop the cognitive and normative structures for rules and regulations. For example, Hertel-Fernandez (2019) in his study of the development of labour legislation in the US over the last decade described how right-wing lobby groups funded by billionaires such as the Koch brothers provided draft legislation to weaken labour rights to state legislators who were generally ignorant of labour law though committed to undermining trade union power. This in turn relates to the broader issue of how neoliberal ideas on the nature of the labour market and labour market regulation became dominant from the 1980s undermining previous institutional settlements in which labour and its representatives had a major role. Baccaro and Howell (2017) trace these processes over five European countries since the 1970s, focusing on how in different countries and over different timelines, EOs and firms encouraged changes in the law in order to increase their discretionary power over labour in the workplace. This in turn led employers to experiment with new strategies that involved new contractual forms for labour. Under these redefined legal obligations, shifts occurred, particularly in the US and the UK, from a discourse of collective rights enforced by collective bargaining to a discourse of individual rights enforced through legal tribunals (Dundon et al. 2020; Piore and Stafford 2006). The specific role of EOs in these liberalization processes and the degree to which they initiated such reforms by providing legal templates, temporary placements of their own employees into government or simply influencing specific ministries and their consultation processes varied according to the particular institutional structure of different capitalisms (Baccaro and Howell 2017; Thelen 2014; on the specific role of ideas, see Morgan and Hauptmeier 2021).

This reflects what Lukes describes as the third face of power (Lukes 1974) where broad hegemonic discourses about the nature of markets and capitalism become part of the taken for granted way in which policy is constructed. As neoliberalism established itself, labour markets were increasingly deregulated through forms of legislation strengthening employers and weakening labour as a collective actor and changing managerial and HR practices towards individual employees. Central to these processes has been a change in the nature of the state (Howell 2021). As governments, encouraged by employers, have privatized agencies, utilities and a broad range of services, they have facilitated a weakening of trade union representation, undermining pay and conditions that had been built up through collective representation over decades. As they slimmed down the public sector, they became reliant on external agencies such as EOs and consultants to provide them with advice on policy and implementation.

The scale of this role of business in setting the agenda for state services is seen in the UK in the development of Academy Schools run by private businesses, National Health Service (NHS) services operated by the private sector and using outside management consultants to resolve organizational problems (Sturdy et al. 2021), the outsourcing of employment and training to private sector contractors (Greer et al. 2017), and the analysis of policy problems and the development of possible solutions being outsourced to prestigious and expensive management consultants. Busemeyer and Thelen (2020) describe this as a form of institutional power in the sense that once state services are privatized, the state itself becomes increasingly reliant on the expertise, knowledge and strategy formulation processes in the private sector amongst firms and EOs. Business associations and EOs became powerful shapers of public policy either directly through their role inside the machinery of government or because as intermediary associations, they take over the role of government in regulating particular areas. In doing so, they shape the ideas and frameworks within which social actors interpret their world. The battle of ideas over how to respond to issues of inequality, unemployment, gig work, sustainability and global climate change is one in which business friendly organizations, including mass media outlets, can easily outspend social movements and left-wing media. The result is not ideological closure but an asymmetrical access to the public sphere of ideas that facilitates in many cases the hegemony of business-friendly messages, carried into the inner reaches of government by EOs and business associations.

Structural Approaches to Power

The concept of the structural power of business describes the way in which business interests are taken into account by state actors as an automatic part of its functioning and decision-making. States are, in this argument, dependent on the economy in order to provide the taxes and revenues that enable the state to provide essential services. If the economy collapses, state services start to collapse with electoral consequences for those politicians in charge of the state. In a capitalist economy, therefore the first concern of the state is to maintain the conditions for capitalist reproduction (Culpepper 2015; Przeworski and Wallerstein 1988). By contrast with instrumental power, structural power is exercised not through political action but through economic action on the part of business. Business is centrally concerned with its profitability. If that is threatened because the public policy context is no longer favourable to processes of capital accumulation, then business will adapt. Young et al. (2018) describe one form of this adaption in terms of a 'capital strike', where businesses as a whole reduce investments in a particular context with the effect of reducing employment, tax revenues etc. Foreign businesses cease to direct investment into such contexts, whilst home-based companies either invest overseas or bury their capital into financial assets that are spread in global wealth chains that are often difficult to identify and more particularly tax (Seabrooke and Wigan 2014). Business considers these decisions as purely 'economic', driven by the necessities of sustaining their profitability.

This power is often particularly helpful for employers where the collective power of trade unions or social democratic parties appears strong. Financial markets have been the crucial intermediary, quickly showing when governments are losing the confidence of business. As financial traders sell off currencies or downgrade debt instruments (raising their effective interest rates and therefore the level of state repayments), they weaken the ability of government to maintain its policies and push it towards retrenchment and austerity, which in turn leads to political tensions (Blyth 2013). These political tensions may lead to elections in order to establish consensus for a new way forward. Thus, decisions in the economic realm reverberate back into the political sphere as in the UK during the 1970s 'profit squeeze' (Glyn and Sutcliffe 1972) and the rise of trade union power, leading to the idea that Britain was becoming 'ungovernable' resulting in two closely contested elections in 1974 that left a Labour minority government struggling to stay in control. In the end, Labour stayed in control until 1979 by going to the International Monetary Fund (IMF) to borrow sufficient funds for managing everyday operations of the state. Structural power was being exerted in the sense that in order for the British state to continue in anything like its current form, government had to act in a way which began the gradual restoration of employer power that gathered pace in the Thatcher era. It was the Labour Government that recognized the structural bind that its particular pattern of economic development had placed it in, and it was the leaders of that government, Prime Minister Callaghan and Chancellor of the Exchequer Denis Healey who articulated the sea change necessary, announcing in December 1976 a package of swingeing public spending cuts as a condition of receiving funds from the IMF. Callaghan stated to the Labour Party conference that year 'We used to think you could spend your way out of a recession and increase employment by cutting taxes and boosting spending. I tell you in all candour that option no longer exists'. Later, the economist Diane Coyle in the Financial Times stated that 'the conditions imposed by the IMF hammered nails into the Keynesian coffin' (9 January 2017) even though the loan itself was barely called on as the self-imposed cuts were so stringent.

It was the structural power that capital exerted over the UK state that enabled EOs to at last begin to fight back against trade unions and under the extended years of Thatcher to again exert visible instrumental power in resetting relations between labour and capital in the workplace and in the wider social and economic context.

The lesson learnt by many was that the confidence of the markets and those trading in the markets had to be retained by governments (see Fairfield 2015 for an analysis of how structural power undermined Lula's radical agenda in Brazil). Otherwise, businesses following their own economic interests would take decisions which could damage the wider economy. The structural power of business operates through market signals to governments when they are moving beyond policies that business supports. Business does not have to say anything political or engage directly with policymakers. It simply continues to do what its structural position demands, i.e. that it takes strategic decisions about how, where and when to make profits. Such decisions have collective consequences for governments as they are dependent on business for taxation, revenue and employment and this is why governments are subject to the structural power of business. Governments have to take account of the effects of their actions on the business decisions of the private sector or reckon with the consequences of failing to do so in terms of markets, employment and tax revenues. This gives business associations and EOs power over crucial issues. However, as discussed, this does not mean that opposition to business power disappears in democratic contexts as the next section of the chapter discusses.

Unpacking the Limits to Business Power

The previous section laid out the broad arguments about why business has power in democratic capitalist societies. In this section, the chapter probes into more detail about the circumstances under which this power is limited. Two aspects in particular are discussed: firstly, the distinction between 'noisy politics' and 'quiet politics' and secondly the issue of the increased fragmentation of business. Both issues have become particularly salient over the recent period of rising populist politics as politicians have taken decisions and implemented policies which have had major adverse impacts on sections of business, e.g. Brexit in the UK.

'Quiet' Versus 'Noisy' Politics

The first modification to the power of EOs derives from the debate about quiet versus noisy politics, originally developed in Culpepper (2011). From the point of view of business, power works best when it is exercised in a 'quiet' way, in other words when business can act quietly behind the scenes to influence government policy through the means discussed earlier such as providing expert insider advice on how to regulate markets. In these contexts, social networks and the social and cultural capital on which they are based can work to connect individuals, firms and other organizations and lubricate and facilitate decision-making, taking for granted the business perspective on problems and solutions. As a result, much of the political work gets done behind the scenes and is shaped as a technocratic approach to making things work better. Electorates barely get to see this activity or evaluate it other than in elections. Often, they may not perceive many of these activities as salient and important for their lives. Whilst in its early stages during the Reagan and Thatcher era, the establishment of neoliberalism required a noisy politics of undermining Keynesianism and propounding revived views of market deregulation etc., once this hegemony became established, a quiet politics of influencing how regulations were constructed and implemented behind the scenes became the norm for EOs.

However, as commentators such as Crouch (2006) and Mair (2013) pointed out, the result was two-fold in the 1990s and 2000s. On the one hand, political parties in power tended to move towards the centre as they cohered around policies that supported business for the reasons discussed. On the other hand, voters became increasingly disillusioned about the narrowness of the choices they had between the main parties, turnout declined and extreme parties began to gain a foothold. These populist parties were far from quiet; on the contrary, they had to make themselves heard above the previously dominant parties (De Vries and Hobolt 2020) and central to this was criticizing the failure of the traditional centrist parties on the grounds that they represented an establishment elite which had lost touch with 'the people'. Certain issues that could be made noisy such as immigration, elite corruption, and bureaucratic interference, were drawn on as were techniques of using social media to create new storms of controversy leading to the rise of what Hopkin (2020) describes as 'anti-system politics' that rejects the current establishment and its policies. Electors may start to come out on the streets to protest and to vote for non-traditional parties with anti-system views where populist leaders 'perform' their authenticity as angry representatives of an 'angry people' through breaking with the usual norms of political behaviour (Lonergan and Blyth 2020; Moffitt 2016). Quiet politics becomes interpreted as the site of self-interest and corruption and its practitioners are condemned as self-interested elites.

In this context, business finds itself identified by populist politics as the enemy of the people. Populism and its influence on government policy becomes more limited especially where previously business friendly parties have become overtaken by populist minorities, e.g. in the UK Conservative Party. For example, in the Brexit debate, whilst the bulk of British business supported remaining in the European Union (EU), many of them kept silent for fear of antagonizing their customers or becoming the target of Twitter storms (Feldmann and Morgan 2021). Brexit went against the arguments articulated by most business associations and EOs and over the next few years, the influence of business over the conduct of negotiations and the terms of departure was limited (Anderson 2019). Issues of labour and labour migration, for example, were one area where these conflicts surfaced. Labour migration into the UK under the free movement pillar of the single market was strongly favoured by most UK employers and EOs. This labour enabled the expansion of many emerging market areas because of its willingness to work flexible hours, in inconvenient locations, for relatively low wages. The importance of EU labour in hospitality industries, in the emerging gig economy of delivery drivers, in the personal social services involved in nursing home and hospital care, in the agricultural sector as well as in a range of building and construction jobs was crucial to the expansion of the UK economy in the 2000s and its recovery in the 2010s. In the emerging populist politics of the era, however, this led to deep conflict as parties like the UK Independence Party (UKIP) and later the Brexit Party, as well as many elements of the Conservative Party blamed this opening up, particularly the enlargement process bringing in Eastern European economies, as keeping wages low and acting as a drain on access to housing, health and education and as undermining national identity and cultural homogeneity in towns, cities and countryside. On this issue EOs such as the Confederation of British Industry (CBI) found themselves charged by the populists with 'destroying the country'. Whilst British attitudes to immigration in the post war period had generally been negative amongst much of the population, it was only as the salience of this issue was increased by linking it to wider grievances in the aftermath of austerity that large areas of the country had been 'left behind' that it became particularly powerful. In the Brexit referendum, those in favour of Remain generally made their argument in terms of what became known as Project Fear – if we leave things will get so much worse. But this was unconvincing to many electors who felt that things had got worse for them under EU membership and therefore any change could only be for the better, a positive, upbeat message which the Leave campaign symbolized by its claim that leaving the EU would mean the UK could spend an extra £350 million a week on the NHS.

In the years following the Brexit vote, EOs continued to argue for ways to ameliorate the impacts of Brexit on supply chains, on labour markets, on exports and non-tariff barriers. However, their pleas have often fallen on deaf ears as the Brexit deal was increasingly interpreted in ways which maximized the negative impact on business, e.g. by leaving the customs union and the single market (Anderson 2019). The Withdrawal Agreement and the Treaty negotiated by Prime Minister Johnson achieved only the most minimal trade agreement; whilst tariffs were set at zero for traded goods, non-tariff barriers emerged as adding significantly to export and import costs. Services more generally were left out of the Treaty, creating many new barriers for businesses in finance, professional services, entertainment and creative/digital industries (Grey 2021). The issue of labour supply which was now under UK control became increasingly complex with EU migrants leaving the UK to return home due to the uncertainties created by Brexit, whilst new arrangements were slow in emerging and subject to continuing controversy. Thus, in this context of noisy politics, business found itself relatively powerless to reshape Brexit in a business-friendly way. This reflects the potential threat to business power by noisy politics in general and by the rise of populist politics in particular in the current context.

Business and the Fragmentation Thesis

This situation has been exacerbated by the increasing fragmentation of the business interest particularly in the liberal market economies. Some differentiation of business interests is inevitable given the nature of different sectors, markets, rules and regulation. The question is the nature and degree of this fragmentation, the forces which make it stronger or weaker and the degree to which it impacts on business influence in politics. Much of the time such differentiation remains dormant, and the influence of business may seem strong and united; however, when faced with particularly acute political choices such as free trade or protectionism, low currency valuation versus high currency valuation, easy lending versus tight credit conditions, labour market coordination versus flexible labour markets, such differences may start to show.

At such moments, institutional structures which have been built to facilitate business unity show their strength and capacity or their weakness. In liberal market economies, the strength of business associations in the post war period was slowly undermined from the 1970s onwards. As Mizruchi (2013) has argued, the rise of shareholder value, institutional investors and dynamic financial markets undermined the unity necessary to sustain a sense of collective identity for business (Davis 2009). Business leaders were increasingly pressurized to increase their earnings and push up the value of their shares. Distributing back to their shareholders through dividends, through rises in the price of shares and through the buying back of shares led to less direct investment in the company and more financial manipulations via replacing shares with bonds, engaging in leveraged merger and acquisitions activities, linking executive pay to share price performance. As part of this, the managerial elite became more international and diverse in scope; social and cultural connections between managers were lost and new more financially literate and internationally experienced managers emerged to cross national boundaries in search of the most profitable opportunities (e.g., Davies 2018, on changes in the UK).

The fracturing of collective identities and action under the pressure of shareholder value driven ideology did not lead to the disappearance of business from politics but rather, as discussed earlier, each large company now employed its own lobbyists to place its own people in the quiet corridors of power where the technical and expert decision-making goes on. However, this change undermined firstly the interests and capacities of many businesses to participate in supporting EOs and in particular their ability to speak in a unified way about major social and political issues. As the Brexit vote showed, the consequence of this fragmentation in the context of noisy populist politics was that business can suffer a heavy defeat over key objectives. Mizruchi argues that similar processes in the US left a political void where previously big business would have engaged collectively with major social issues as it did during the 1960s (Mizruchi 2013). The result was the deep penetration into US politics of anti-system populism which has threatened to destroy long established norms of US government. Groups within traditional parties, such as the Tea Party and later the Trump Republicans in the US, Brexit supporters in the UK Conservative Party and the volatile growth of UKIP and then the Brexit Party in the UK occupy the gaps left by business's abdication from collective responsibility for society's big problems. The result has been to make politics highly volatile and noisy where policies emerge that are highly problematic for business as a whole in liberal market economies.

Coordinated market economies have missed some of this fragmentation and its consequences (Martin and Swank 2012). Nevertheless, there has been some weakening in the coverage of business associations and EOs in terms of membership and of the areas over which they engage in collective action (see chapter by Behrens on Germany in this volume). The solidarity of business in some of these contexts has been undermined over recent years as large multinational companies (often based overseas) have opted out of the associations and national agreements, seeking to make their own deals with trade unions enabling more plant level bargaining and labour market flexibility. This reflects also the fracturing processes discussed earlier in terms of the degree of penetration into coordinated market economies of shareholder driven ideology and an increasing focus on the firm's specific requirements rather than a willingness to compromise in order to sustain a collective cross-business alliance. However, because of their deep institutional embeddedness, EOs continue to play a significant role in training, technical standards and labour markets as well as maintaining a role collectively in stabilizing the political environment and recognizing the potential threat of populist politics. For example, Kinderman (2020) has shown that business associations have been active in trying to prevent the rise of right-wing populism in the German context in a way which has not occurred in the UK and the US where companies have been much more focused on their own interests rather than the 'collective good'. German business associations have recognized the threat to their interests arising from anti-system politics and have sought to stave off its rise.

The issue of business fragmentation is also particularly affected by the strength of labour and its degree of challenge to the existing system. Where labour organizations and political parties are effective at organizing the bulk of the workforce, then business potentially faces a threat that requires a united front. In coordinated market economies, corporatist type institutions have worked to neutralize this threat and turn a potentially confrontational situation into one of 'beneficial constraints' (Streeck 1997). In liberal market economies, firms and businesses that might have avoided membership of associations or informal collective action with other businesses may feel compelled to become more cooperative. For example, in the 1975 referendum in the UK over continued membership of the European Economic Community (EEC, as the EU was then known), almost the whole of the UK business community actively supported the campaign to say yes to membership (Feldmann and Morgan 2021; Saunders 2018). They were united in the sense of threat and in the belief that staying in the EEC was crucial to their ability to defeat this threat. Over the few years following the referendum victory, British business started to regroup and actively work with the new Conservative Party led by Margaret Thatcher which decisively broke with the corporatist tendencies of the Heath Government and espoused free market liberalism. By contrast in the 2016 Brexit referendum, the level of support from business to remain in the EU in the noisy politics of the time was much less (Feldmann and Morgan 2021). Trade unions had been considerably weakened in the intervening period and Labour's policies, particularly under Prime Ministers Blair and Brown had shifted towards the centre, supportive of business and finance. The threat level from the left was minimal and therefore from this political point of view, businesses had little incentive to overcome their fragmented state and become actively involved as a collective body.

In general, when labour is weak, business can rely on governments which are supportive and so the incentive to join EOs and engage in high levels of activity to combat labour militancy are low. Businesses find it easy enough to access governments when they need to, even if that involves the help of intermediary lobbying firms. The business interest as a whole is so dominant amongst policy-makers that there appears little need for business as a whole to organize for its representation. Therefore, the fragmentation deriving from the structural features of shareholder capitalism is reinforced by the lack of threat from labour. However, unexpectedly another form of threat to business emerged with the rise of populist politics which has propounded policies that disrupt global value chains, internationalization of investment and international trade agreements. Populists have argued for more state interventionist policies towards infrastructure investment, more protectionist trade policies, more nativist and nationalistic immigration policies, all within a framework of disruptive politics conducted through noisy social media and dramatic performances of 'people power' (as in the storming of the Capitol building in January 2021). Through coordinated action, these groups have captured control of traditional business-friendly parties such as the Republicans in the US and the Conservatives in the UK and threatened the bonds that have in the past connected businesses to the party. The fractured nature of business in these liberal market economies has weakened their ability to influence such governments even though labour as a social force is weak. EOs desperately try to find a way through this confusion but are often ineffective and dependent on the electorate to defeat populism and restore some form of normalcy (and quiet politics), as happened with Trump but not with Johnson in the UK.

In conclusion, the ability of business to act in a unified way is affected by a range of factors that can be understood by reference to background institutions, the power of labour and its threat to business, the structure of the economy in terms of the range of sectors and its degree of internationalization and finally the nature of firms, their managements and their shareholders. In recent years, the rise of populism with a number of policies which undermine business interests has undermined quiet politics and led to some notable defeats for sections of an increasingly fragmented business sector.

Conclusions

The main point of this chapter is that in democratic capitalist societies, business does exert a powerful influence on policy making even though it continually faces the challenge that electors may choose to pursue policies that are antagonistic to business interests. Issues such as egalitarian tax policies, state regulation of markets for social purposes, nationalization of key sectors, improved workers' rights in the labour market and in the workplace and welfare systems that act to provide a safety net rather than a mechanism to force workers back to work as soon as possible constitute policies to which employers are mostly resistant. Defeating such proposals or keeping them off the agenda formally and informally constitute the three dimensions of power identified by Lukes (1974).

By contrast, business and EOs may struggle, in the age of fragmentation, populism and noisy politics, to maintain the popularity of business-friendly policies where these are identified with highly visible levels of inequality, insecurity, poor work conditions, and a disciplinary welfare state. Business has been peculiarly successful for much of the industrial period in maintaining its position in spite of economic and political crises but now it faces a challenge. In order to understand how business has achieved this and how it is losing its power, it is important to identify the specific mechanisms through which this has occurred.

Building on previous work, the chapter distinguishes between instrumental and structural power. Instrumental power is based on the idea of controlling the state like an instrument that can be used for whatever purpose its controllers wish. This has led business associations and EOs to support parties and politicians that espouse business friendly policies by providing funding and personnel giving them a financial advantage in most elections in western democracies. Businesses have 'quietly' cultivated connections inside government, facilitated in many contests by shared social and cultural capital. As governance has become more complex in modern societies, business associations and EOs have increasingly provided the expertize to government to deal with technically difficult areas of regulation and policy making. In recent decades, private businesses have penetrated deep into government, providing advice directly to ministers and running whole swatches of contracted out public services. Governments have made themselves dependent on business.

This is reinforced by the structural power of business, that means government is dependent on continued investment by business to keep up employment, tax revenues and financial markets. Failure to sustain this confidence rapidly translates into crises on the financial markets. Therefore, governments always have to keep an eye on how their policies are being perceived by business. Business itself may not even recognize that it is exercising power; it is just pursuing its own strategies for profitability, but the consequences are crucial for governments.

However, the chapter emphasizes that business does not always succeed in achieving its goals. Business will have high levels of influence under quiet politics but once politics becomes noisy and politicians have to listen more directly to their electorates then the interests of business may be sacrificed. Business does not have the power to keep everything quiet and when issues become noisy, it either participates (with the risk that it can be publicly defeated and often humiliated with long lasting effects as in the Brexit referendum) or it can stand back, in which case again it may find itself defeated. In some circumstances it can engage in noisy politics and win but this is high risk.

Such calculations may relate to the degree of unity which business will show. The chapter discussed the range of variation in business unity which has occurred over time and across different institutional settings.

Liberal market economies have increasingly weakened and fragmented business associations in terms of their ability to influence major issues of policy (as revealed by Brexit and the Trump years); coordinated market economies have been able to retain more unity and have been able to ward off the most volatile populist elements so far, even if cracks in this unity are appearing. Labour also plays a role in this. Where labour is powerful and antagonistic to business, then business is likely to become more unified but if labour is weak, incentives for business to act together as opposed to lobby on behalf of their own interests will decline.

Finally, there are limits to business's power that have emerged with the rise of populist politics. As electorates have begun to support anti-system politics and populist parties, business has found itself treated with a certain contempt, as part of the establishment which failed 'the people' during the 2010s and is now reaping the whirlwind. Populist leaders do not owe their positions to the support of business and if they are going to retain their position, they have to keep renewing the faith of their supporters by continuing to attack the old establishment. To varying degrees across Europe and the US, business power is facing a new environment where its previous mechanisms of power are weakening. Central to the development of the capitalist democracies over the next decade is whether business can re-establish its power, by aiding the return to power and influence of those parties or groups within parties which they previously supported and the mode of governance which they supported (i.e. quiet politics). Or alternatively will business find ways to adapt to the new era of noisy politics driven by populist leaders and volatile economic and political policies and reassert aspects of its power and interests in a new environment?

References

Anderson, I. (2019). *F**K Business: The Business of Brexit*. London: Biteback Publishing.

Baccaro, L. and Howell, C. (2017). *Trajectories of Neoliberal Transformation*. Cambridge: Cambridge University Press.

Blyth, M. (2013). *Austerity: The History of a Dangerous Idea*. Oxford: Oxford University Press.

Busemeyer, M. and Thelen, K. (2020). Institutional sources of business power. *World Politics*, 72 (3): 448–480. 10.1017/S004388712000009X

Crouch, C. (2006). *Post Democracy*. Cambridge: Polity Press.

Culpepper, P. D. (2011). *Quiet Politics and Business Power*. Cambridge: Cambridge University Press.

Culpepper, P. D. (2015). Structural power and political science in the post-crisis era. *Business and Politics*, 17 (3): 391–409. 10.1515/bap-2015-0031

Davies, A. (2018). *Reckless Opportunists: Elites at the End of the Establishment*. Manchester: Manchester University Press.

Davis, G. F. (2009). *Managed by the Market*. Oxford: Oxford University Press.

De Vries, C. and Hobolt, S. (2020). *Political Entrepreneurs: The Rise of Challenger Parties in Europe*. Princeton NJ: Princeton University Press.

Dundon, T., Martinez Lucio, M., Hughes, E., Howcroft, D., Keizer, A. and Walden, R. (2020). *Power, Politics and Influence at Work*. Manchester: Manchester University Press.

Fairfield, T. (2015). Structural power in comparative political economy: Perspectives from policy formulation in Latin America. *Business and Politics*, 17 (3): 411–441. 10.1515/bap-2014-0047

Feldmann, M. and Morgan, G. (2021). Brexit and British business elites: Business power and noisy politics. *Politics and Society*, 49 (1): 107–130. 10.1177% 2F0032329220985692

Glyn, A. and Sutcliffe, B. (1972). *British Capitalism, Workers and the Profit Squeeze*. London: Penguin.

Greer, I., Breidahl, K., Knuth, M. and Larsen, F. (2017). *The Marketization of Employment Services*. Oxford: Oxford University Press.

Grey, C. (2021). *Brexit Unfolded*. London: Biteback Publishing.

Hall, P. and Soskice, D. (2001). *Varieties of Capitalism*. Oxford: Oxford University Press.

Hertel-Fernandez, A. (2019). *State Capture: How Conservative Activists, Big Business and Wealthy Donors reshaped the American States and the Nation*. New York: Oxford University Press.

Hopkin, J. (2020). *Anti-System Politics: The Crisis of Market Liberalism in Rich Democracies*. Oxford: Oxford University Press.

Howell, C. (2021). Rethinking the role of the state in employment relations for a neoliberal era. *Industrial and Labor Relations Review*, 74 (3): 739–772. 10.11 77%2F0019793920904663

Iversen, T. and Soskice, D. (2019). *Democracy and Prosperity: Reinventing Capitalism through a Turbulent Century*. Princeton, NJ: Princeton University Press.

Kershaw, I. (2015). *To Hell and Back: Europe 1914–1949*. London: Penguin.

Kinderman, D. (2020). German business mobilization against right-wing populism. *Politics & Society*, 49 (4): 489–516. 10.1177/0032329220957153

Korpi, W. (2006). Power resources and employer-centred approaches in explanations of welfare states and varieties of capitalism. *World Politics*, 58 (2): 167–206. 10.1353/wp.2006.0026

Leonard, C. (2019). *Kochland: The Secret History of Koch Industries and Corporate Power in America*. New York: Simon and Schuster.

Lonergan, E. and Blyth, M. (2020). *Angrynomics*. London: Agenda Publishing.

Lukes, S. (1974). *Power: A Radical View*. London: Macmillan.

Mair, P. (2013). *Ruling the Void*. London: Verso.

Martin, C. J. and Swank, D. (2012). *The Political Construction of Business Interests: Coordination, Growth and Equality*. Cambridge: Cambridge University Press.

Mizruchi, M. (2013). *The Fracturing of the American Corporate Elite*. Cambridge: Harvard University Press.

Moffitt, B. (2016). *The Global Rise of Populism*. Stanford: Stanford University Press.

Morgan, G. and Hauptmeier, M. (2021). The social organisation of ideas in employment relations. *Industrial and Labor Relations Review*, 74 (3): 773–797. 10.1177%2F0019793920987518

Mudde, C. and Kaltwasser, C. R. (2017). *Populism: A Very Short Introduction.* Oxford: Oxford University Press.

Muller, J.-W. (2017). *What is Populism?* London: Penguin.

Piore, M. J. and Stafford, S. (2006). Changing regimes of workplace governance, shifting axes of social mobilization and the challenge to industrial relations theory. *Industrial Relations*, 45 (3): 299–325. 10.1111/j.1468-232X.2006.00439.x

Przeworski, A. and Wallerstein, M. (1988). Structural dependence of the state on capital. *American Political Science Review*, 82 (1): 11–29. 10.2307/1958056

Saunders, R. (2018). *Yes to Europe!: The 1975 Referendum and 1970s Britain.* Cambridge: Cambridge University Press.

Scott, J. (1997). *Corporate Business and Capitalist Classes.* Oxford: Oxford University Press.

Seabrooke, L. and Wigan, D. (2014). Global wealth chains in the international political economy. *Review of International Political Economy*, 21 (1): 257–263. 10.1080/09692290.2013.872691

Streeck, W. (1997). Beneficial Constraints: On the Economics Limits of Rational Voluntarism. In: R. Boyer and J. R. Hollingsworth (eds.) *Contemporary Capitalism: The Embeddedness of Institutions.* Cambridge: Cambridge University Press, pp. 197–219.

Sturdy, A. J., Kirkpatrick, I., Alvarado, N. R., Blanco-Oliver, A. and Veronesi, G. (2021). The management consultancy effect: Demand inflation and its consequences in the sourcing of external advice, *Public Administration*, Published online before print. 10.1111/padm.12712

Thelen, K. (2014). *Varieties of Liberalization and the New Politics of Social Solidarity.* Cambridge: Cambridge University Press.

Young, K. A., Banerjee, T. and Schwartz, M. (2018). Capital strikes as a corporate political strategy: The structural power of business in the Obama era, *Politics & Society*, 46 (1): 3–28. 10.1177%2F0032329218755751

Ziblatt, D. (2017). *Conservative Parties and the Birth of Democracy.* Cambridge: Cambridge University Press.

3 Meta-organizing Employers: From Beneficial Constraints to Collective Self-discipline?

Markus Helfen

Introduction

From an organization theory perspective, Employers' Organizations (EOs) can be understood broadly as a variant of interorganizational coordination in the "negotiated environment" (Pfeffer and Salancik 2003: 144). Although such a view does not preclude the formation of other specialized organizations for facilitating collaboration among business firms in various political arenas or strategic action fields (Fligstein and McAdam 2011), EOs have been regarded as the archetypical form. Consequently, within analyzes of the political economies of Western democracies of the post-World War II era, EOs have been predominantly viewed through the lens of the association, i.e. collective actors created for interest representation to foster private business' interests within the sphere of formal state politics (e.g. Korpi 2006; Schmitter and Streeck 1999; Traxler 1993). With the gradual devolution of the political process into fragmented political sub-arenas with diverging interest constellations, the emergence of influential multinational firms, un- or underrepresented sectors and firms, this dominant view of the association has lost much of its grip in understanding how EOs work in their variety and for what ends. Already using the term "organization" resonates with irritations on how to handle the new organizational look of employer interest politics (Gooberman et al. 2018).

For theory development, these irritations represent a welcome opportunity for rethinking the common wisdom on what EOs are in organizational terms and for opening the debate towards new views. Here, the use of a meta-organizing lens is suggested for such a widening of the analytical horizon to account for EOs in their variety. Usually, meta-organizations are defined as organizations whose members are organizations themselves with the profound repercussion that these meta-organizations do not possess strong authority over their members (Ahrne and Brunsson 2005). Here, a different perspective is chosen that emphasizes the meta-organization as a relational entity, i.e. one that entertains various relationships with "inside" actors, such as member organizations, and partnering other

DOI: 10.4324/9781003104575-4

meta-organizations ("federations"), but also with state agencies, other parties (and even individuals) as well the media and public. From this relationality, meta-organizing is understood as a process in which EOs deploy interorganizational management practices (Sydow and Windeler 1998). Whether such a meta-organizing view leads to a dramatic re-evaluation of the EO, or a reconfirmation of its special role, is hard to tell in a world in flux, politically, economically, and environmentally. Nevertheless, a reconsideration of the organizational foundations might bring new insights into the differentiation and multi-faceted nature of today's organized business interest politics. In an era of civil regulation (Williams et al. 2011a, 2011b), setting the focus on a meta-organizing view is helpful for understanding the current shift away from democratically devised "beneficial constraints" (e.g. Wright 2000) towards a precarious and fragmented collective self-discipline of employers in their dealings with various stakeholders.

In what follows, a recombination of various views is presented that takes the organizing dimension of employers' collective agency out of the black box. Building on a brief discussion of the commonalities and differences of closely related concepts from organization and management studies (Ahrne and Brunsson 2005; Berkowitz and Dumez 2016; Perks et al. 2017; Provan and Kenis 2008; Gawer 2014), a meta-organizing view is developed that allows an understanding of EOs by focusing on their meta-organizing practices. From this discussion, a practice-based view of meta-organizing is derived explaining how meta-organizing of employers occupies a larger territory and shows a greater variety of organizational forms than the traditional associations' interest articulation and collective bargaining in formalized political processes. Such a practice-based view connects structures, i.e. levels, domains, and history as well as actors and resources, with meta-organizing practices like selecting members, allocating resources, regulating action, and evaluating outcomes as well as negotiating rules. The chapter concludes by mapping further directions for inquiry with respect to understanding and typifying employers' meta-organizing especially with an eye on current dynamics in negotiated varieties of conflict resolution.

Understanding the Meta-organization: Concepts and Directions

The traditional views of organized collective action see associations as an outcome of the political processes in economic interest articulation and collective bargaining, in which organizations such as employer' associations and trade unions participate as representatives of their class (Müller-Jentsch 2004). In such a *political view*, the divergent class interests are key which are to be transformed by collective actors into the social fabric of interest aggregation and decision-making in relation to the state. There have been two dominant perspectives: (1) The economic theory of collective action explaining the rational choice of businesses to engage collectively in political action, for example, firms' decision to join a member association, despite "free-rider" problems (e.g. Olson 1965; Van Waarden 1992) and (2) in critical symbiosis with the former, the neo-corporatism debate explaining how class structures, organizability of interest groups, and the mechanisms of interest aggregation affect the dealings between organized capital, organized labour, and the state in the political process (e.g. Offe and Wiesenthal 1980; Schmitter and Streeck 1999; Traxler 1993).

Employers' Organizations in Political Macro-exchange

In situations of state-led governance arrangements, for example tripartite coordination between the state, organized business, and organized labour (Croucher and Wood 2015; Streeck 2009), one important question for the political view is how and under what circumstances the tripartite interaction structure produces collaborative outcomes, and how any structural shifts in such macro-arrangements also explain changes in country-specific economic policies or business strategies (most prominently Hall and Soskice 2001). Assuming a tripartite structure consisting of organized labour, organized capital, and the state (both administration, and government) as a given, one aspect is whether dominant coalitions can be identified as shaping the meta-rules of collective bargaining and social welfare politics.

For their part, associations represent organized capital and act in their capacity to mediate between member firms interests ("internal stakeholders") and external stakeholders such as state authorities or unions (e.g. Child et al. 1973). The associations' ability for reconciling contradictory demands of external stakeholders with their members' interests by compromising on the one hand ("influence logic"), and by representing member firms according to their goals and ambitions on the other ("membership logic"), has been identified as the essential organizational dilemma of the association (e.g. Child et al. 1973; Schmitter and Streeck 1999). In collective bargaining, for example, associations alter the interaction between member firms and trade unions, by transforming the conflicts between workers and firms into negotiated agreements with unions (e.g. Turner 1998; Walton et al. 2000), notwithstanding structural class conflict (Schmidt and Kochan 1972; Wright 2000).

In studies concerned with welfare politics, policy change has been linked to associations. Paster (2012), using Germany's social history as an example, concludes that employers' associations, if not trying to directly stop developments towards social reform, largely tried to slow them down most of the time in the 19th and 20th centuries, even against temporary coalitions between organized labour and social democratic parties in government. However, as Paster argues in this volume, this does not necessarily mean that employers are always and universally opposed to any social reform; rather, their opposition or even support for social reform depends on the dominating assessment of labour market situations in the employers' camp. During over-employment employers may even support social reforms which facilitate firms' restructuring. Martin and Swank (2012), building from a comparison of Anglo-Saxon, Scandinavian, and continental European countries, connect the peculiar role of associations as an engine for coordinated social reform policies to the structure of party politics. In between the two, Korpi delineates the expansion of welfare states within what has become known as coordinated market economies (Hall and Soskice 2001) to party politics by further differentiating between protagonists, consenters, and antagonists in the employers' camp (Korpi 2006, see also Afonso 2011). The analytical focus is then to identify the conditions for coordinated welfare politics such as varying configurations and structural shifts in actor constellations over time depending on the "political type" of employers.

Here, there is neither the space for elaborating on the various advantages and insights of this political view, nor for delineating its shortcomings and unsettled debates. Rather, the point is made that the *organizational practices* needed to manage (create, maintain, change) coordination, cooperation, and collaboration between employers is a relevant complement to these analyzes, but too often remains only implicit in studies following a political view. With an eye on the erosion of traditional associations as well as the increased variety of EOs, this is a relevant shortcoming for capturing the current fragmented landscape of employers' collective action as well as the more diverse universe of civil regulation (Williams et al. 2011a).

A few observations in support of this claim may be in order: (1) With the erosion of countervailing forces, especially the decline of unions, and with the neoliberal reforms in Western welfare states, traditional EOs have lost some of their relevance in the political process (e.g. Streeck 2009); (2) The expanded size of multinational firms (e.g. Laroche 2010) and profound limits of the nation state in regulating cross-border business operations (e.g. Scherer et al. 2016) reduce the integrative capacities of EOs traditionally confined to territorially bounded interest politics; (3) the shifts in the structural composition of the population of firms with regards to new business segments, new varieties, and network forms of organizing businesses (e.g. Grimshaw and Rubery 2005) and production (e.g. Sorge and Streeck 2018) provide obstacles for an interest formation built from a traditional membership logic (e.g. Ibsen and Navrberg 2019, already Traxler 2004); even more so where new types of businesses raise the question anew what an employer is at all (Davidov 2014); (4) these fundamental shifts have given rise to more fragmented forms of political articulation, exemplified by advocacy groups, NGOs, or the social media (e.g. Fransen and Burgoon 2015); and (5) and partly as a response, alternative, and to a certain extent more flexible organizational forms such as direct lobbying, special purpose NGOs, consultancies, and think tanks have gained in importance in employers' policy making (e.g. Fransen and LeBaron 2019).

In their combination these trends neither do away with the association as such, nor do they mark the end of political influence seeking and mobilizing by employers (e.g. Clemens 2015; Walker and Rea 2014), but they clearly indicate that the association as a peculiar organizational form occupies only a fraction of the territory of business collective action. Taking the field of employment relations as an example, even within this one field other forms of EO include mediating agencies between labour supply and demand, standard-setting agencies, and social purpose vehicles of all sorts and varieties (e.g. Berkowitz et al. 2017; Hawley and Combes Taylor 2006; Marques 2017; Waddock 1989, 2008). Furthermore, agencies like lawyers, law consultancy firms, and think tanks act on behalf of (groups of) firms as these are subjects of regulatory acts or arbitration and due diligence procedures (e.g. Edelman and Suchman 1997).

The Meta-organization

Usually, meta-organizations are defined as organizations whose members are organizations themselves with the profound repercussion that these meta-organizations do not possess strong authority over their members (Ahrne and Brunsson 2005). This a very general definition that includes international organizations in which states are members, as well as civil society organizations, third-sector associations, or cooperatives. Where business firms are members of a meta-organization, these members usually command more resources, show higher status, entertain pronounced identities, and are led by top managers more influential than the association's management itself (Ahrne and Brunsson 2005). At the same time, the competition among resourceful members with strong identities as well as the need to meet demands from external interest groups can prompt conflict over meta-organizations' jurisdiction (for elaborations in the German context see Helfen and Nicklich 2017).

Like the political view, a meta-organizing view locates EOs also in the field of law and politics, acting on behalf of (groups of) firms as these are subjects of regulatory acts, arenas of rule enforcement, and actors influencing legal regulation (e.g. Edelman and Suchman 1997). A meta-organizing view diverges from a political view, however, in three ways: (1) in considering collective action also in relation to organizing business itself, (2) in considering employers' societal influence with regards to relationships with other actors than the state, and (3) in focusing on the organizational practices of associative action. In other words, being constrained by the political environment and members' interests, employers' meta-organizations are engaged in a broader spectrum of activities for different purposes, also including the economic coordination of business firms and "softer" variants of societal influencing (Berkowitz and Dumez 2016).

Management and Governance of Interorganizational Relations

The first two distinctions of the meta-organizing view are especially resonant with concerns about the management and governance of interorganizational relations. In various areas of the more recent management literature from innovation and strategy to public management, one observes the emergence of terms trying to capture how collaborative structures among firms and other organizations such as associations or state agencies are organized and managed. Among others, terms include "network governance" (Provan and Kenis 2008); "network orchestration" (Bartelings et al., 2017; Paquin and Howard-Grenville 2013; Perks et al. 2017), "architecture of collaboration" (Fjeldstad et al. 2012) or "platform" (Gawer 2014). As these views on network governance and management share many aspects, occasionally even the term (e.g. Berkowitz and Bor 2018; Gawer 2014), with the meta-organizing view developed here, it is also important to note some important differences.

Management accounts prioritize how single lead firms can organize collaborative structures with other firms for creating and reaping relational and collaborative advantages for themselves, i.e. by cultivating positive network externalities, making use of additional resources created by participating firms, joint knowledge creation, as well as cost savings, and risk sharing (e.g. Dyer and Singh 1998). Here, instead, the collectivity of firms that pool their resources for joint production (Ostrom 2017) is taken more seriously. Many relational benefits are not available for the single firm, they take on the character of a local public good that emerges from a permanent, recurrent, and continuous collaboration among those organizations involved as group or collective (Barnett and King 2008). Also, for capturing the political aspect of the meta-organization, the relevant resources need to be defined more broadly as containing capabilities that differentiate all sorts of organizations' performances including intangible assets such as the societal support for a network's activities (Maurer et al. 2011) or cultural-political assets (Gillespie 2010). In other words, if markets are cultural-political constructions (e.g. Fligstein 1996) they are also subject to meta-organizing by firms and others. In combination with the idea that goals and rules are also formed by stakeholders' collective action, also interorganizational coordination and collaboration can be conceived of as a "political economy" in which a complex rule system is shaped on different levels: (1) the single organization, (2) across organizational boundaries between participants, and (3) the whole set of interorganizational relations of a network (Provan et al. 2007).

Relationality and Partiality of Meta-organizations

Building on these considerations, Figure 3.1 illustrates a relational view of the meta-organization. Meta-organizations' *relationality* stems from the various relationships the meta-organization entertains with inside actors, such as member organizations, and partnering with other meta-organizations (federations), but also with external organizations such as state agencies, third parties (and even individuals) as well the media and the public. Seeing the meta-organization as a genuinely relational entity, i.e. mediating between various groups of societal sectors allows to avoid a focus on formal politics only, and reinstating the broader notion of resource-dependence in the negotiated environment triggering a demand for regulating competition, but also for coordination and collaboration (Pfeffer and Salancik 2003).

Furthermore, this approach enables meta-organizing to be placed as being meant for meta-purposes, i.e. collective action that goes beyond single members' rationality and formed within contexts from within or outside a group (Ostrom 2017). These contexts might be of a societal-cultural (normative ideas, social problems), political (state), and economic kind and the respective meta-organizing can be directed towards

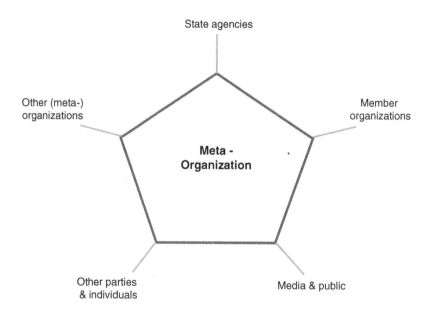

Figure 3.1 The meta-organization.

various fields: economic (resources-related), political (state-related), and societal (civil society oriented social purposes) as well as combinations thereof. Inasmuch as employers' meta-organizations are concerned, these imply, at least in degrees, that competitors are organized, prompting the dilemma between simultaneously collaborating and competing.

This organizational dilemma is mitigated by the meta-organization through operating as a partial form of organization. As a generalized idea, *partiality* captures the observation that organizing does not necessarily combine all elements used to classify the "complete order" (Ahrne and Brunsson 2011) of the traditional hierarchical bureaucracy: a clearly de-lineated membership, internal procedures and decision rules, monitoring, evaluation, resource allocation as well as incentives and sanctions. With this idea of partiality, Ahrne and Brunsson (2011) expand the range of meta-organizations to include other forms of partial organizing; for ex-ample, standards and standardization fall under partial organizing (Brunsson 2000). For EOs, this incompleteness affects various aspects of regulating work and employment. In particular, the notion of partiality makes it easier to understand the organized character of arrangements such as inter-firm networks, electronic labour market platforms, em-ployers' mimicry of social movement organizing, and standard-setting agencies. At the same time, partiality assists in understanding the un-organized appearance of much what is going on inside meta-organizations of a more fluid and temporary kind like social media campaigns.

A Practice-View on Meta-organizing

A unifying feature of meta-organizations and their managerial neigh-bours is their restricted authority over the contributions and resources of participating organizations. Hence, much depends on the *organizing* of meta-organizations as a practice. Furthermore, meta-organizing is better understood as a process rather than a structure; a process in which po-litical influence does not necessarily take the form of a member-based, formal organizational structure. Rather, meta-organizing occurs through and translates into inter-organizational management practices (Sydow and Windeler 1998) which can be recombined and reshuffled into var-ious types and forms. Hence, a meta-organizing view allows to under-stand a broader class of employers' organizing through examining interorganizational management practices (Sydow and Windeler 1998). At the same time, meta-organizing institutionalizes structure, i.e. a set of rules, actors, and practices, which can only be understood through the relational practices that meta-organizations and those meta-organized use in the process of meta-organizing (Ringel et al. 2018; Vaara and Whittington 2012).

Building on these considerations, EOs are understood through the "structuration" (Giddens 1984) of meta-organizing. Although intertwined in structuration, in what follows the structural contingencies and practices of meta-organizing are discussed separately for the purpose of exposition. As for the structural dimension the domains, levels, and history of meta-organizing are discussed alongside actors and resources. These structural contingencies are juxtaposed to the practices of meta-organizing. Like broader considerations of inter-organizational collaboration, these relational practices include (1) selecting, i.e. how the members are chosen from the broader group of relevant firms, (2) allocating of competences, resources, and benefits within the meta-organization, (3) regulating collaboration and responsibility among the members, and (4) evaluating contributions to and outcomes of the meta-organization. The peculiar relational character of meta-organizing is captured through (5) negotiating as a practice in dealing with inside and outside stakeholders.

Structures of Meta-organizing

Domains, levels, and history

Meta-organizing may occur on various levels and domains of social organization ranging from meta-organizing at the macro-level, such as negotiating labour standards and other forms of regulating work and employment in the political sphere and international organization (e.g. Garaudel 2020), and meso-level meta-organizing in sectors and fields, e.g. employers' associations and the organization of professions, to the micro-level in which firms (and individuals) are mediated into particular jobs through electronic platforms and other agencies, for example. As for private business' meta-organizations, the field either defined them in terms of the organizations involved providing for structuration of meta-organizing practices, i.e. the collectivity of firms distinguished by criteria like engaging in similar business activities (DiMaggio and Powell 1983) or in broader terms of the strategic action field resting on the dynamics of collective action (Fligstein and McAdam 2011). Similarly, territories (global, regional, national, local) (Crouch et al. 2009) or issues (economic, social, cultural, technological, etc.) might provide for institutional environments of meta-organizing (e.g. Hoffman 1999; Lawrence and Suddaby 2006). Regardless of the source, the respective domains and levels of meta-organizing carry a structuration in the form of an institutional legacy, at least as defined in Greve and Rove (2014: 28) as those "structures created at one time in one domain [that] have spill over effects by triggering later organization building in the same community but in a different domain" or "[structures that] can drive diverse organization building over time due to a self-reinforcing cycle of organization creation in each community". Whether defined as legacies or as imprints (Marquis 2003), what counts is that the historical context conveys rules and resources that enter into the structuring conditions of how actors perform meta-organizing within their respective domain and level (e.g. Martin and Swank 2008; Reveley and Ville 2010), depending of course, on how these are enacted in the recursive interplay between structure and agency (e.g. Hauptmeier 2012; Pierson 2004).

Actors and resources

In Figure 3.1, one archetypical configuration of the actor constellation in meta-organizing employers for political purposes at the macro-level has been given. An even more differentiated view, more apt for the meso-level of meta-organizing, can be derived from Provan and Kenis' (2008) distinction of organizational structures of network governance. In direct analogy, meta-organizing could be (1) shared between the organizations in a mutual and participative self-organization; in this case, close collaboration between all organizations involved as well as frequent interactions and multiplex relationships among these are to be expected; (2) arranged by a lead organization, i.e. one participant or a small group of participants assumes the role of the meta-organizer; and (3) an administrator separated from the group of organizations as a specialized unit for meta-organizing; of course, it is possible that this meta-organizing unit is a formal association or federation; for example. Actor-wise, then, the meta-organizing depends, beyond the levels, domains, and time, on the quality of the relationships between the organizations as well as contingencies such as the number and type of the participating organizations, their heterogeneity in resources, size and views, their different positioning in the network, or the degree to which participants of the network depend mutually on each other in reaching their objectives. In this, as well as in other actor constellations of meta-organizing one relevant question becomes who controls the stream of resources when and where (i.e. in which context and situation). Among the relevant resources in meta-organizing, we can consider capital, information, and knowledge, but also legal structures, societal legitimacy, political influence, and cultural capital.

Practices of Meta-organizing

Depending on the levels, domains, and time as well as the actors and resources as structural conditions, like other forms of arranging inter-organizational collaboration, meta-organizing consists of a bundle of different inter-organizational practices (Sydow and Windeler 1998).

Selecting

Meta-organizing implies a set or bundle of activities around selecting those organizations being members of the meta-organization within a certain domain and level. Respective practices are the definition of criteria for selecting members, but also the procedures and rules for ending membership. Through these practices the meta-organization is situated in relation to its inter-organizational environment and demarcates its organizational boundaries. At the same time, selection practices decide over whether an organization's membership is rather homogeneous or heterogeneous with regards to the domains selected, e.g. industry, sector, size classes, regional, and locality. When the meta-organization is already in existence, excluding and including new organizations, expelling existing ones opens up new connections or closes old ones to different sets of resources, thereby contributing to the change and adaptation of the meta-organization over time. Selecting has a performative dimension in that it shapes the other practices.

Allocating

Meta-organizations bundle (or "pool") resources from within their membership and acquire additional resources from the outside and influence how these resources are allocated among the meta-organization's members as well as between the meta-organization and its members. In combination with the allocation of responsibilities, the resourcing of certain activities has an impact on a meta-organization's performance as well as its ongoing capacity for producing local commons and potentiality for collective action. Insofar as a meta-organization's own resources are concerned, they might gain in organizing autonomy if they are institutionalized. For example, where there is a continuous exchange relationship with outside actors like the state or another organization, these relational arrangements can be regarded as a meta-organizing resource. With an eye on EOs, however, the meta-organization might remain in an auxiliary role for the dominant resource holders among the membership.

Regulating

Meta-organizing also includes the definition of the rules for collaboration of the respective group of firms. These include boundary rules for selecting members, choice rules for allocating resources among members, pay-off rules for evaluating a meta-organization's performance, and position rules for regulating itself (Ostrom 2017). The definition of these procedural and substantive rules are part and parcel of meta-organizing and include the meta-rules for meta-organizing, i.e. who is allowed to participate in setting the rules of a given meta-organization. With regards to EOs, regulating implies a rather complex interplay between internal and external rule-setting. Internally, standardizing certain members' activities and organizational practices also serves an external purpose, externally, rights granted from the interplay with outside actors' spill-over into a sanctioning tool, for example, in situations where legal entitlements are granted to a meta-organizing body.

Evaluating

Looking at evaluating closely reveals a broad array of possible yardsticks applied to meta-organizing by input, process, and outcome, from within as well as from the outside. Obviously, evaluating also depends on the members selected as well as the relational structure that characterizes the domain of the meta-organization. As for EOs, evaluating outcomes from the outside means identifying their effects on quantitative and qualitative labour market outcomes, for example. Evaluating processes from within includes the meta-organization's contribution transforming the interests of a heterogenous membership into viable political demands and standards. Also, meta-organizations evaluate their members and partners as well as the quality of relationships of the parties they connect by developing "valuation frames" (Bessy and Chauvin 2013) such as ratings and standards.

Negotiating

In contrast to the managerial accounts of inter-organizational coordination and collaboration, a meta-organizing view emphasizes EOs' associative character (Ahrne and Brunsson 2005). In other words, meta-organizing also means negotiating, since meta-organizations act in and through brokerage, i.e. "the process of connecting actors in systems of social, economic, or political relations in order to facilitate access to valued resources" (Stovel and Shaw 2012: 141). A wide variety of practices such as collective bargaining, dialogue, mediation, and arbitration procedures in conflict resolution involves negotiating of the meta-organization with internal and external stakeholders, mostly other organizations such as firms, unions, state authorities, NGOs, or meta-organizations and consultancies; a distinction adequately captured with the notion of an "intermediary organization" (Müller-Jentsch 2004) including a special role in the political organization of societies. From this view, meta-organizing enables participants to coordinate also in a non-hierarchical way by facilitating negotiated solutions (Ahrne and Brunsson 2005). This is achieved through standards or meta-rules of interaction, for example when procedural rules for members' interaction among each other are settled in statutes. This holds also for the meta-organization's dealings with third parties. For example, meta-organizations might select under which circumstances they act collaboratively or competitively, using diverging styles of representing and negotiation modes such as distributive bargaining or joint problem solving (Walton et al. 2000). Another aspect of negotiating is the sub-practice of ideational brokerage. Following on from Campbell (2004), "ideational brokerage" means the transporting of ideas across the boundaries between societal groups. Inasmuch as meta-organizations reconcile their members' ambitions with the demands of external groups by negotiating, they also enact a process of ideational brokerage, i.e. making ideas flow between distinct societal spheres and groups. Thereby, the meta-organization also influences the quality of relations among the parties they connect (Obstfeld et al. 2014). For EOs, one example is the conveying of social partnership across the divide between employers and unions (e.g. Turner 1998).

Conclusions

As for the world of EOs, the recent proliferation of new forms and practices of meta-organizing provides challenges for more traditional forms such as the association. Of course, this also parallels profound structural changes in the socio-political arena around regulating work and employment. One of the more radical forms is the implicit transformation of associations' function by the private agency types of meta-organizing not easily accounted for by more traditional views concentrating on the association-type. This peculiar form of organizational re-intermediation in the sphere of labour politics and regulation does not imply that there are no traditional EOs any longer, on the contrary, the institutional work carried out in establishing temporary work agencies for example shows an orchestration of various strands of meta-organizing (e.g. Helfen 2015). Similar processes are under way in the current era of platform work where the contractual disconnection between employers and the electronically mediated jobholders requires agencies to electronically connect these across space and time (Palier 2019; Vallas and Schor 2020); those EOs engaged in traditional interest politics, however, struggle to get a standing in this arena, exactly because the platforms' partial meta-organizing circumvents the extant regulations of work and employment in their business domain.

While the traditional interest aggregation and intermediation in and through collective bargaining by associations is weak to non-existent in the new arenas of platform work (with some notable exceptions in Scandinavia, e.g. Ilsøe 2020), at the same time, also the arenas of traditional employment show a rather well documented bifurcation (Palier and Thelen 2010), even fragmentation (e.g. Grimshaw and Rubery 2005), of regulating working and employment conditions. This development also entails an erosion of traditional EOs from within (for Germany see Behrens and Helfen 2019; Silvia and Schroeder 2007; Streeck 2009; Streeck and Hassel 2003). Whether more traditional varieties of meta-organizing get rejuvenated through the manifold crises of and political challenges to private business more generally (Barnett 2012), remains an open question requiring further investigation. Nevertheless, with respect to the weaknesses of the association type, one might conclude that associations' regulatory capacity has weakened in the last decades. With respect to the institutions of industrial relations, hence, it may be expected that the relaxation of the beneficial constraints of earlier settlements (Wright 2004) also erodes the future capacities for formally meta-organizing employers in the future.

At the same time, new forms of meta-organizing have emerged that may bring about some sort of employers' collective self-discipline in an era of civil regulation through involving societal actors of various sorts. For example, and by contrast with the decline of associations, in other fields of labour politics, alternative forms of meta-organizing are mushrooming. A prominent example is Corporate Social Responsibility (CSR), an arena where there is a widespread proliferation of various social purpose vehicles and standard-setting agencies arranging for self-regulatory initiatives of employers (e.g. Barnett and King 2008; Vogel 2010). With such meta-organizational vehicles, employers engage in societally relevant activities around certain public goods in voluntary, but purpose-driven collaboration with third parties from civil society (e.g. Selsky and Parker 2010; Williams et al. 2011b). Also, in the arena of global labour standards similar meta-organizations articulate and negotiate certain standards within multi-stakeholder dialogue; and the collaboration among these various meta-organizations has already been identified even as some form of "meta-governance" (Albareda and Waddock 2018; Waddock 2008). Nevertheless, it remains largely an open question whether these new forms of employers' meta-organizing create new and innovative regulation. In the field of work and employment, it remains highly doubtful whether these new varieties could replace formal negotiation processes structured around the association-type, because their regulating concentrates on managing the societal expectations in an informal way and neither hard law nor binding agreements with other organizations are usually sought.

To find answers to these and similar questions requires more research capable of deepening our understanding of meta-organizing, also by engaging in a multi-disciplinary dialogue beyond organization theory. On empirical grounds, more research is also needed that seeks for examining more closely the variation in meta-organizing practices and their accompanying organizational embodiments (for promising beginnings in that direction see Gooberman et al. 2018). For example, identifying typologies of the various forms of meta-organizing based on the structural contingencies (domains, levels, history, actors, and resources) and practices (selecting members, allocating resources, regulating action, evaluating outcomes, and negotiating the exchange with third parties) discussed above, would assist in gaining more fine-grained insights into the emerging reality of employer organizing. Such a typology could contain meta-organizing forms such as the voluntary association, the standard-setting agency, the market-driven intermediary, and the social-purpose vehicle. Of course, such a typology has its limitations as there might be additional types and subtypes depending on the various combinations of the respective practices. Another important area for future research would be to examine the impact of meta-organizing's variety for the conflict resolution capacity within the diverging industrial relations systems of various country settings (for example, building on, but also extending the more traditional comparative literature such as Deeg and Jackson 2007; Katz and Wailes 2014). Also, a further inquiry into the natural persons carrying the collaboration, organizing, and institutional work of meta-organizing's legal persons is a worthwhile endeavour. Such research could include the study of the individuals enacting the meta-organizing, their socio-demographic characteristics as well their varying attitudes (for an early example of a study in this direction see Friedman and Podolny 1992).

In concluding, one important, but unsettled question for research and practice is highlighted with respect to the voids not covered by the traditional associations: To what extent, in what domains, and at what levels do these alternative forms of meta-organizing produce an effective capacity for self-regulation? Certainly, it may be too harsh a criticism to accuse these new varieties of business meta-organizing of exerting undue political and societal influence under the masquerade of public benevolence. However, in the eyes of the wider public such meta-organizing falls short of what is usually expected from civil society organizations (for the fundamentals in disentangling these complexities around the distrust in corporations controlling politics see Clemens 2015). In this broader societal meaning of meta-organizing, it is not settled at all whether we are entering a new period of "civil regulation" (Williams et al. 2011a; b) of regulating business activities by softer variants of "collective constraints" (Sorge and Streeck 2018: 591), or whether the complex deficits in the political process culminate in a "refeudalization" (Neckel 2020) bearing the inherent risk that democratic constraints are relaxed, i.e. the rules and procedures formalizing interest politics in a representative democracy, and replaced by a voluntarism in which employers deal with those stakeholders they prefer the most.

References

Afonso, A. (2011). Employer strategies, cross-class coalitions and the free movement of labour in the enlarged European Union. *Socio-Economic Review*, 10: 705–730. 10.1093/ser/mws008

Albareda, L. and Waddock, S. (2018). Networked CSR governance: A whole network approach to meta-governance. *Business & Society*, 57 (4): 636–675. 10.1177%2F0007650315624205

Ahrne, G. and Brunsson, N. (2005). Organizations and meta-organizations. *Scandinavian Journal of Management*, 21: 429–449. 10.1016/j.scaman.2005. 09.005

Ahrne, G. and Brunsson, N. (2011). Organization outside organizations: The significance of partial organization. *Organization*, 18 (1): 83–104. 10.1177% 2F1350508410376256

Barnett, M. L. (2012). One voice, but whose voice? Exploring what drives trade association activity. *Business & Society*, 52 (2): 213–244. 10.1177%2F000765 0309350211

Barnett, M. L. and King, A. A. (2008). Good fences make good neighbors: A longitudinal analysis of an industry self-regulatory institution. *Academy of Management Journal*, 51 (6): 1150–1170. 10.5465/amj.2008.35732609

Bartelings, J. A., Goedee, J., Raab, J. and Bijl, R. (2017). The nature of orchestrational work. *Public Management Review*, 19 (3): 342–360. 10.1080/14 719037.2016.1209233

Behrens, M. and Helfen, M. (2019). Small change, big impact? Organisational membership rules and the exit of employers' association from multiemployer bargaining in Germany. *Human Resource Management Journal*, 29 (1): 51–66. 10.1111/1748-8583.12210

Berkowitz, H. and Bor, S. (2018). Why meta-organizations matter: A response to Lawton and Spillman. *Journal of Management Inquiry*, 27 (2): 204–211. 10.1177%2F1056492617712895

Berkowitz, H., Bucheli, M. and Dumez, H. (2017). Collectively designing CSR through meta-organizations: A case study of the Oil and Gas industry. *Journal of Business Ethics*, 143: 753–769. 10.1007/s10551-016-3073-2

Berkowitz, H. and Dumez, H. (2016). The concept of meta-organization: Issues for Management Studies. *European Management Review*, 13: 149–156. 10.1111/emre.12076

Bessy, C. and Chauvin, P. (2013). The Power of market Intermediaries: From information to valuation processes. *Valuation Studies*, 1 (1): 83–117.

Brunsson, N. (2000). Organizations, markets, and standardization. In: N. Brunsson and B. Jacobsson (eds.) *A World of Standards*. Oxford: Oxford University Press, pp. 21–39.

Campbell, J. L. (2004). *Institutional Change and Globalization*. Princeton: Princeton University Press.

Child, J., Loveridge, R. and Warner, M. (1973). Towards an organizational study of trade unions. *Sociology*, 7: 71–91. 10.1177%2F003803857300700105

Clemens, E. S. (2015). The democratic dilemma: Aligning fields of elite influence and political equality. *Research in the Sociology of Organizations*, 43: 223–241. 10.1108/S0733-558X20150000043020

Crouch, C., Schröder, M. and Voelzkow, H. (2009). Regional and sectoral varieties of capitalism. *Economy and Society*, 38 (4): 654–678. 10.1080/03 085140903190383

Croucher, R. and Wood, G. (2015). Tripartism in comparative and historical perspective. *Business History*, 57 (3): 347–357. 10.1080/00076791.2014.983479

Davidov, G. (2014). Setting labour law's coverage: Between universalism and selectivity. *Oxford Journal of Legal Studies*, 34 (3): 543–566. 10.1093/ojls/ gqu003

Deeg, R. and Jackson, G. (2007). Towards a more dynamic theory of capitalist variety. *Socio-Economic Review*, 5: 149–179. 10.1093/ser/mwl021

DiMaggio, P. J. and Powell, W. W. (1983). The iron cage revisited: Institutional isomorphism and collective rationality in organizational fields. *American Sociological Review*, 48: 147–160. 10.2307/2095101

Dyer, J. H. and Singh, H. (1998). The relational view: Cooperative strategy and sources of interorganizational competitive advantage. *Academy of Management Review*, 23 (4): 660–679. 10.5465/amr.1998.1255632

Edelman, L. B. and Suchman, M. S. (1997). The legal environments of organizations. *Annual Review of Sociology*, 23: 479–515. 10.1146/annurev.soc.23.1.479

Fjeldstad, Ø. D., Snow, C. C., Miles, R. E. and Lettl, C. (2012). The architecture of collaboration. *Strategic Management Journal*, 33: 734–750. 10.1002/smj.1968

Fligstein, N. (1996). Markets as politics: A political-cultural approach to market institutions. *American Sociological Review*, 61: 656–673. 10.2307/2096398

Fligstein, N. and McAdam, D. (2011). Toward a general theory of strategic action fields. *Sociological Theory*, 29: 1–26. 10.1111%2Fj.1467-9558.201 0.01385.x

Fransen, L. and Burgoon, B. (2015). Global labour-standards advocacy by European civil society organizations: Trends and developments. *British Journal of Industrial Relations*, 53 (2): 204–230. 10.1111/bjir.12017

Fransen, L. and LeBaron, G. (2019). Big audit firms as regulatory intermediaries in transnational labor governance. *Regulation & Governance*, 13: 260–279. 10.1111/rego.12224

Friedman, R. A. and Podolny, J. (1992). Differentiation of boundary spanning roles: Labor negotiations and implications for role conflict. *Administrative Science Quarterly*, 37: 28–47. 10.2307/2393532

Garaudel, P. (2020). Exploring meta-organizations' diversity and agency: A meta-organizational perspective on global union federations. *Scandinavian Journal of Management*, 36 (1). Online only at 10.1016/j.scaman.2020.101094.

Gawer, A. (2014). Bridging differing perspectives on technological platforms: Toward an integrative framework. *Research Policy*, 43: 1239–1249. 10.1016/j.respol.2014.03.006

Giddens, A. (1984). *The Constitution of Society*. Cambridge: Polity.

Gillespie, T. (2010). The politics of 'platforms'. *New Media & Society*, 12 (3): 347–364. 10.1177%2F1461444809342738

Gooberman, L., Hauptmeier, M. and Heery, E. (2018). Contemporary employer interest representation in the United Kingdom. *Work, Employment & Society*, 32 (1): 114–132. 10.1177%2F0950017017701074

Greve, H. R. and Rao, H. (2014). History and the present. Institutional legacies in communities of organizations. *Research in Organizational Behavior*, 34: 27–41. 10.1016/j.riob.2014.09.002

Grimshaw, D. and Rubery, J. (2005). Inter-capital relations and the network organisation: redefining the work and employment nexus. *Cambridge Journal of Economics*, 29 (6): 1027–1051. 10.1093/cje/bei088

Hall, P. A. and Soskice, D. (2001). An introduction to varieties of capitalism. In: P. Hall and D. Soskice (eds.) *Varieties of Capitalism. The Institutional Foundations of Comparative Advantage*. Oxford: Oxford University Press, pp. 1–68.

Hauptmeier, M. (2012). Institutions are what actors make of them—The changing construction of firm-level employment relations in Spain. *British Journal of Industrial relations*, 50 (4): 737–759. 10.1111/j.1467-8543.2012.00891.x

Hawley, J. D. and Combes Taylor, J. (2006). How business associations use interorganizational networks to achieve workforce development goals: Implications for human resource development. *Human Resource Development International*, 9 (4): 485–508. 10.1080/13678860601032601

Helfen, M. (2015). Institutionalizing precariousness? The politics of boundary work in legalizing agency work in Germany, 1949–2004. *Organization Studies*, 36 (10): 1387–1422. 10.1177%2F0170840615585338

Helfen, M. and Nicklich, M. (2017). Mitgliedermanagement von Metaorganisationen: Arbeitgeberverbände und ihre Mitglieder. In: Schroeder, W. and Weßels, B. (Hrsg.) *Handbuch Arbeitgeber- und Wirtschaftsverbände in Deutschland*. Wiesbaden: Springer, pp. 227–247. 10.1007/978-3-658-08176-8_9

Hoffman, A. J. (1999). Institutional evolution and change: Environmentalism and the U.S. chemical industry. *Academy of Management Journal*, 42 (4): 351–371. 10.5465/257008

Ibsen, C. L. and Navrberg, S. E. (2019). Adapting to survive. The case of Danish employers' organizations. *Human Resource Management Journal*, 29: 36–50. 10.1111/1748-8583.12182

Ilsøe, A. (2020). *The Hilfr agreement. Negotiating the platform economy in Denmark*. FAOS Research Paper 176. Copenhagen: University of Copenhagen.

Katz, H. and Wailes, N. (2014). Convergence and divergence in employment relations. In: A. Wilkinson, G. Wood and R. Deeg (eds.), *Oxford Handbook of Employment Relations*. Oxford: Oxford University Press, pp. 42–61.

Korpi, W. (2006). Power resources and employer-centered approaches in explanations of welfare states and varieties of capitalism. *World Politics*, 58: 167–206. 10.1353/wp.2006.0026

Laroche, M. (2010). Mondialisation et action collective patronale: deux réalités conciliables? *Relations Industrielles_Industrial Relations*, 65 (1): 134–154. 10.7202/039531ar

Lawrence, T. B. and Suddaby, R. (2006). Institutions and institutional work. In: S. R. Clegg, C. Hardy, T. B. Lawrence and W. R. Nord (eds.) *The Sage Handbook of Organization Studies*. London: Sage Publications, pp. 215–254.

Marques, J. C. (2017). Industry business associations: Self-interested or socially conscious? *Journal of Business Ethics*, 143: 733–751. 10.1007/s10551-016-3 077-y

Marquis, C. (2003). The pressure of the past: Network imprinting in intercorporate communities. *Administrative Science Quarterly*, 48: 655–689. 10. 2307%2F3556640

Martin, C. J. and Swank, D. (2008). The political origins of coordinated capitalism: Business organization, party systems, and state structure in the age of innocence. *American Political Science Review*, 102 (2): 181–198. 10.1017/ S0003055408080155

Martin, C. J. and Swank, D. (2012). *The Political Construction of Business Interests. Coordination, Growth, and Equality*. Cambridge: Cambridge University Press.

Maurer, C. C., Bansal, P. and Crossan, M. M. (2011). Creating economic value through social values. Introducing a culturally informed resource-based view. *Organization Science*, 22 (2): 432–448. 10.1287/orsc.1100.0546

Müller-Jentsch, W. (2004). Theoretical approaches to Industrial Relations. In: B. E. Kaufman (ed) *Theoretical perspectives on work and the employment relationship*. Champaign, IL: ILRA, pp. 1–40.

Neckel, S. (2020). The refeudalization of modern capitalism. *Journal of Sociology*, 56 (3): 472–486. 10.1177%2F1440783319857904

Obstfeld, D., Borgatti, S. P. and Davis, J. (2014). Brokerage as a process: Decoupling third party action from social network structure. *Research in the Sociology of Organizations*, 40: 135–159. 10.1108/S0733-558X(2014)0000040007

Offe, C. and Wiesenthal, H. (1980). Two logics of collective action: Theoretical notes on social class and organizational form. *Political Power and Social Theory*, 1: 67–115.

Olson M. (1965). *The Logic of Collective Action, Public Goods and the Theory of Groups*. Cambridge: Harvard University Press.

Ostrom, E. (2017). *Governing the Commons. The Evolution of Institutions for Collective Action*. Cambridge: Cambridge University Press [1990].

Palier, B. (2019). Work, social protection and the middle classes: What future in the digital age? *International Social Security Review*, 72 (3): 113–133. 10.1111/issr.12218

Palier, B. and Thelen, K. (2010). Institutionalizing dualism: Complementarities and change in France and Germany. *Politics & Society*, 38 (1): 119–148. 10.1177%2F0032329209357888

Paquin, R. L. and Howard-Grenville, J. (2013). Blind dates and arranged marriages: Longitudinal processes of network orchestration. *Organization Studies*, 34 (11): 1623–1653. 10.1177%2F0170840612470230

Paster, T. (2012). *The Role of Business in the Development of the Welfare State and Labor Markets in Germany: Containing Social Reforms*. London: Routledge.

Perks, H., Kowalkowski, C., Witell, L. and Gustafsson, A. (2017). Network orchestration for value platform development. *Industrial Marketing Management*, 67: 106–121. 10.1016/j.indmarman.2017.08.002

Pfeffer, J. and Salancik, G. R. (2003). *The External Control of Organizations. A Resource Dependence Perspective*. Stanford [1978].

Pierson, P. (2004). *Politics in Time, History, Institutions and Social Analysis*. Springer: Princeton/Oxford.

Provan, K. G. Fish, A. Sydow, J. (2007). Interorganizational networks at the network level: A review of the empirical literture on whole networks. *Journal of Management*, 33 (3): 479–516.

Provan, K. G. and Kenis, P. (2008). Modes of network governance: Structure, management, and effectiveness. *Journal of Public Administration Research and Theory*, 18: 229–252. 10.1093/jopart/mum015

Reveley, J. and Ville, S. (2010). Enhancing industry association theory: A comparative business history contribution. *Journal of Management Studies*, 47 (5): 837–858. 10.1111/j.1467-6486.2010.00926.x

Ringel, L., Hiller, P. and Zietsma, C. (2018). Toward permeable boundaries of organizations? *Research in the Sociology of Organizations*, 57: 3–28. 10.1108/S0733-558X20180000057001

Scherer, A. G., Rasche, A., Palazzo, G. and Spicer, A. (2016). Managing for political social responsibility: New challenges and directions for PCSR 2.0. *Journal of Management Studies*, 53 (3): 273–298. 10.1111/joms.12203

Schmidt, S. M. and Kochan, T. S. (1972). Conflict: Towards conceptual clarity. *Administrative Science Quarterly*, 17 (3): 359–370. 10.2307/2392149

Schmitter, P. C. and Streeck, W. (1999). *The Organization of Business Interests: Studying the Associative Action of Business in Advanced Industrial Societies.* MPIfG Discussion Paper 99/1, Cologne [1981].

Selsky, J. W. and Parker, B. (2010). Platforms for cross-sector social partnerships: Prospective sensemaking devices for social benefit. *Journal of Business Ethics*, 94: 21–37. 10.1007/s10551-011-0776-2

Silvia, S., and Schroeder, W. (2007). Why are German employer associations declining? Arguments and Evidence. *Comparative Political Studies*, 40: 1433–1459. 10.1177%2F0010414006293444

Sorge, A. and Streeck, W. (2018). Diversified quality production revisited: Its contribution to German socio-economic performance over time. *Socio-Economic Review*, 16 (3): 587–612. 10.1093/ser/mwy022

Stovel, K., and Shaw, L. (2012). Brokerage. *Annual Review of Sociology*, 38: 139–158. 10.1146/annurev-soc-081309-150054

Streeck, W. (2009). *Re-Forming Capitalism. Institutional Change in the German Political Economy.* Oxford: Oxford University Press.

Streeck, W., and Hassel, A. (2003). The crumbling pillars of social partnership. *West European Politics*, 26 (4): 101–124. 10.1080/01402380312331280708

Sydow, J. and Windeler, A. (1998). Organizing and evaluating interfirm networks: A structurationist perspective on network processes and effectiveness. *Organization Science*, 9 (3): 265–284. 10.1287/orsc.9.3.265

Traxler, F. (1993). Business associations and labour unions in comparison. Theoretical perspectives and empirical findings on social class, collective action and associational organizability. *British Journal of Sociology*, 44: 673–691. 10.2307/591416

Traxler, G. F. (2004). Employer associations, institutions and economic change: A crossnational comparison. *Industrielle Beziehungen*, 11 (1&2): 42–60.

Turner, L. (1998). *Fighting for Partnership. Labor and Politics in Unified Germany.* Ithaca/London: Cornell University Press.

Vaara, E. and Whittington, R. (2012). Strategy-as-practice: Taking social practices seriously. *Academy of Management Annals*, 6 (1): 285–336. 10.5465/1 9416520.2012.672039

Vallas, S. and Schor, J. B. (2020). What do platforms do? Understanding the gig economy. *Annual Review of Sociology*, 46: 273–294. 10.1146/annurev-soc-121919-054857

Van Waarden, F. (1992). Emergence and development of business interest associations. An example from the Netherlands. *Organization Studies*, 13 (4): 521–564. 10.1177%2F017084069201300402

Vogel, D. (2010). The private regulation of global corporate conduct. Achievements and limitations. *Business & Society*, 49 (1): 68–87. 10.1177%2 F0007650309343407

Waddock, S. (1989). Understanding social partnerships. An evolutionary model of partnership organizations. *Administration & Society*, 21 (1): 78–100. 10.11 77%2F009539978902100105

Waddock, S. (2008). Building a new institutional infrastructure for corporate responsibility. *Academy of Management Perspectives*, 22 (3): 87–108. 10.54 65/amp.2008.34587997

Walker, E. T. and Rea, C. M. (2014). The political mobilization of firms and industries. *Annual Review of Sociology*, 40: 281–304. 10.1146/annurev-soc-071913-043215

Walton, R. E., Cutcher-Gershenfeld, J. E. and McKersie, R. B. (2000). *Strategic Negotiations. A Theory of Change in Labor-Management Relations*. Ithaca: ILR Press.

Williams, S., Abbott, B. and Heery, E. (2011a). Civil regulation and HRM: The impact of civil society organisations on the policies and practices of employers. *Human Resource Management Journal*, 21 (1): 45–59. 10.1111/j.1748-8583. 2010.00134.x

Williams, S., Heery, E. and Abbott, B. (2011b). The emerging regime of civil regulation in work and employment relations. *Human Relations*, 64 (7): 951–970. 10.1177%2F0018726710391687

Wright, E. O. (2000). Working-class power, capitalist-class interests, and class compromise. *American Journal of Sociology*, 105: 957–1002. 10.1086/210397

Wright, O. E. (2004). Beneficial constraints: Beneficial for whom? *Socio-Economic Review*, 2: 407–414. 10.1093/soceco/2.3.407

4 Facilitating Labour Shedding or Enhancing Labour Supply?: An Analysis of German Employers' Organizations' Views on Work Incentive Effects of Social Programmes

Thomas Paster

Introduction

Employers' Organizations (EOs) bargain with labour unions over wages and working conditions, and also influence governments' social and labour market policies through lobbying and negotiations with government policymakers and labour unions. Governments frequently consult with EOs on major social policy and labour market reforms, either formally or informally, not least because such reforms can affect employers' hiring decisions and thus, at the macro-level, investment and employment. Government policymakers thus find it relevant to know how firms will react to the adoption of new or changes in existing policies.

A growing field of research investigates the character and the determinants of the social policy preferences of employers. Yet, no consensus on how to describe and explain those preferences has so far emerged. A variety of analytical perspectives exist in this field, sometimes at odds with each other and with no consensus on which determinants are the most important, or on how EOs' impact on social policymaking is best characterized. However, we do see some consensus on the view that employers' views on social policies vary in that they are not universally and uniformly opposed to all and any forms of social protection to workers (for detailed reviews of this research field see Paster 2015, and Oude Nijhuis 2019). Variation across time, countries, and types of employers matters. How can we describe and explain that variation?

In this chapter, I argue and show that how EOs perceive the impact of social benefits on work incentives is crucial for how they position themselves on social policy issues. Social programmes can either strengthen or weaken individuals' willingness to work and can thus affect the supply of labour. They strengthen work incentives if benefit entitlements depend on work requirements and activation rules. They weaken work incentives if they allow individuals to make a living

DOI: 10.4324/9781003104575-5

without working or seeking work, an effect of social programmes called de-commodification. In other words, social benefits can either maintain or weaken individuals' dependence on the labour market, they can either *re*-commodify or *de*-commodify labour (cf. Greer 2016).

The chapter shows that work incentives are a key concern for employers, yet the intensity and character of this concern varies. As a result of this varying assessment of work incentives, employers sometimes oppose, sometimes support de-commodification. Two variables matter in explaining this variation: Labour market conditions and firms' own staffing policies. Labour market conditions can be characterized by an under-supply (labour shortages) or an over-supply. An over-supply, in turn, can take two forms: A high level of unemployment or over-staffing by firms. Over-staffing means that firms keep more employees on their payroll than they need for production. It can occur when labour market regulations, strong unions, or co-determination rights by employees make labour shedding costly to employers. This conceptualization thus results in a total of three scenarios: Under-supply of labour (aka labour shortages), high unemployment, and over-staffing. Figure 4.1 depicts these three scenarios. They serve the purpose of capturing the context in which employers assess the relevance of work incentives.

I argue in this chapter that how employers assess the desirability of de-commodification will differ depending on which of these three scenarios they experience, because the maintenance (or, alternatively, weakening) of work incentives matters to them in different ways depending on the scenario. In the first two scenarios they will oppose de-commodifying social policies, albeit for different reasons. When faced with an under-supply of labour they will oppose de-commodifying social policies because of the work disincentives they generate. When unemployment is high, they will also oppose de-commodifying social policies, not because of a need to protect work incentives, but in order to avoid higher labour costs. In the third scenario, over-staffing, however, employers will welcome de-commodifying social policies, since they do, in this scenario, have an interest in policies that facilitate labour shedding. When barriers to labour shedding exist, de-commodification can serve as such a facilitator, because it can make lay-offs more acceptable to unions and employees.

Empirically, the chapter demonstrates the plausibility of this argument for Germany based on an analysis of three reform episodes from different periods. Through this cross-temporal comparison, changes in EOs' perceptions of the desirability of work incentives and related changes in labour market conditions and staffing policies are documented. The reform episodes chosen are (a) the introduction of public social insurance under Bismarck in the 1880s, (b) the adoption of unemployment insurance in the 1920s and (c) the adoption of policies to facilitate early retirement in the 1980s. The focus is on these three reforms because of their potential negative impact on work incentives.

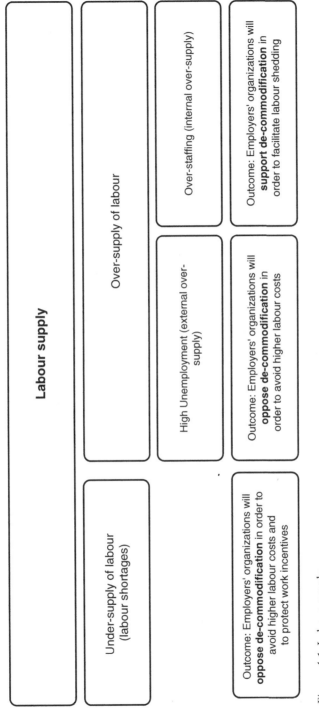

Figure 4.1 Labour supply.

The empirical analysis focuses on the positions taken by the peak federations of German EOs, rather than on sector-level organizations, since in Germany social policy issues are handled primarily by the peak federations. Statements by local or sectoral organizations are occasionally used to further document a position. Different peak federations existed in different periods. During the social reforms under Bismarck, the Central Federation of German Industry (Centralverband deutscher Industrieller, CDI), formed in 1876 by the organizations of heavy industry and textiles, was the main peak federation. During the adoption of unemployment insurance, the Federation of German Employers' Associations (Vereinigung deutscher Arbeitgeberverbände, VDA), founded in 1913, was the main peak federation. During the post-war period, the Confederation of German Employers' Associations (Bundesvereinigung deutscher Arbeitgeberverbände, BDA), founded in 1949 as the successor to the VDA, was the main federation.

The results show that while, in general, employers worried that social policies would generate work disincentives, they welcomed work disincentives during the period of over-staffing in the 1970s and 1980s, when employers intended to shed labour. Due to the limited number of cases, and focus on one country, the results primarily illustrate the plausibility of the argument, rather than providing a definite test, and the empirical scope would need to be expanded to other countries to conclusively assess the importance of work incentives for EOs cross-nationally.

We need to take note also of the fact that the reform episodes studied are taken from historical periods that differ greatly not just in terms of labour market conditions and staffing policies, but also in many other ways, economically, socio-culturally, institutionally, as well as politically. The decision to use a research design that compares policy reforms across a long stretch of time offers the advantage of demonstrating the role of labour market conditions and staffing policies more clearly than what an analysis of a shorter period, during which labour markets and staffing policies may not have changed drastically, would allow. The price paid for this is the difficulty of controlling for other societal and political changes that have occurred during the same period, which, in the case of 20th century Germany, were clearly enormous. For the purpose of this chapter, though, the very focused and narrowly specified character of the research question justify this research design, bearing in mind that, rather than aiming at a comprehensive explanation of welfare state development, the chapter zooms in on one specific aspect: employers' assessment of work incentives. The empirical sections will also briefly discuss broader changes in political and socio-economic environment and their possible relevance for employers' attitudes towards social programmes. Before turning to the empirical analysis, however, the next section will introduce theoretical debates on the social policy preferences of EOs and relate the theoretical argument to existing work.

Employer Preferences on Social Policy

We can divide theoretical perspectives on the social policy preferences of employers into two broad groups: efficiency-theoretical perspectives and conflict-theoretical perspectives. Both agree that the positions of EOs on various aspects of public social policy, such as benefit generosity or principles of coverage, vary, but they differ in how they explain those differences. Efficiency-theoretical perspectives identify economic benefits of social programmes to firms as sources of support; conflict-theoretical perspectives identify political-strategic considerations as sources of employer support for social programmes (for in-depth reviews of these debates see Martin 2006; Oude Nijhuis 2019; Paster 2015). This section will discuss both perspectives before turning to the role of work incentives for employers.

Efficiency-theoretical perspectives locate the reasons for employer support for public social policy in their expectations of economic benefits. Greater labour productivity and employee motivation are examples of such benefits. Yet, these goods do not provide a rationale for firms to back public social programmes, since company welfare will give them greater discretion at rewarding productivity and employee loyalty. Public social programmes may even crowd out company welfare programmes and weaken employee loyalty to the firm.

Efficiency-theoretical perspectives have focused however not on employee loyalty and productivity, but on the generation of incentives for employees to invest in what is called specific skills. Skills are specific if they cannot be transferred to other firms or other sectors. Theory predicts that employees will prefer to invest in transferable skills rather than in specific skills (see Paster 2019a: for a more detailed discussion of efficiency-theoretical perspectives). According to one view, public social programmes, and unemployment insurance in particular, can make investments in specific skills more attractive to employees by protecting the value of the skill investment in case of job loss (Estévez-Abe et al. 2001: 180–181). From this perspective, a developed welfare state may represent a competitive advantage to firms dependent on specific skills. According to Torben Iversen, the welfare state constitutes 'simultaneously an arena for redistributive struggles and a source of comparative advantage' (Iversen 2005: 13). Following the same logic, Estevez-Abe et al. predict that 'in economies where companies engage in product market strategies that require … firm- and industry-specific skills, …, a strong alliance between skilled workers and their employers in favour of social protection … is likely to emerge' (Estévez-Abe et al. 2001: 147).

Another strand of research highlights redistribution of costs of social policy across sectors as a source of EOs' policy preferences. To use an example, a nationwide public programme of work injury insurance may redistribute the costs of compensating injured workers from sectors with a high risk of injury to those with lower risks, if employers are otherwise liable to compensate workers. Applying this logic, Isabela Mares found for inter-war Germany and France that workers as well as employers in sectors with high risk of unemployment favoured the introduction of public unemployment insurance with broad coverage, while workers and employers in low-risk sectors both opposed such a programme (Mares 2004; Mares 2003a: 106–165; Mares 2003b: 245).

Conflict-theoretic perspectives identify the sources of employer support for particular social policy reforms in political-strategic considerations. Accepting social reforms can sometimes be a 'lesser evil' for employers. For instance, EOs may offer backing for the adoption of a particular social programme in exchange for concessions in other policy fields, such as for instance trade policy or taxation. Here, acceptance of social programmes serves as a bargaining chip or is part of a larger packaged deal and is thus not motivated by any analytic assessment of the effects of a social programme for productive efficiency.

Following this perspective, several studies have documented that business support for the social policy reforms of the New Deal period in the US was influenced greatly by such strategic considerations (Amenta and Parikh 1991; Hacker and Pierson 2002; Skocpol and Amenta 1985). These studies responded to others that argued that those reforms were the product mainly of business interests (Jenkins and Brents 1991; Quadagno 1984). Later, the work by Peter Swenson re-asserted the argument that business support for welfare reforms was genuine, rather than a strategic accommodation to the political context: 'employers were not merely resigned to hegemonic Social Democrats ...They knew what they wanted. Sometimes they liked best what they got and got what they liked best' (Swenson 2002: 11). In my own earlier research, I documented how the goal of pacifying discontent parts of the labour movement motivated German EOs to back social reforms, such as the Stinnes-Legien agreement signed in November 1918 (Paster 2013: 427–31; Paster 2012: 75–83).

Conflict-theoretic perspectives differ from efficiency-theoretic perspectives in their assumed preferences that underlie EOs' policy stances. Efficiency-theoretic perspectives imply that employer support for public social policies is genuine, conflict-theoretic perspectives that it is strategic; an adaptation to political constraints. The preference modelling of the conflict-theoretic perspective rests on the considerations that, if enhancing productive efficiency is their motivation for backing social benefits, employers will be better off with voluntary company welfare programmes than with compulsory public programmes. Company welfare programmes allow greater discretion to the individual firm and enable management to cultivate a sense of loyalty among employees.

Equally important, though, is the protection of work incentives. Company welfare benefits maintain work incentives, since they are tied to employment in the firm. In contrast, public social programmes can be designed in such a way that they allow benefit recipients to make a living without work, even though, whether this is in fact the case, will depend on details of the benefit entitlement rules. Yet, the fear of an erosion of work incentives and, as a consequence, a shrinking of the labour supply, may be expected to prompt employers to view public social programmes sceptically. This view was expressed, for instance, by Esping-Andersen who uses the concept of de-commodification to capture the ability of individuals to make a living without employment: '[d]ecommodification strengthens the worker and weakens the absolute authority of the employer. It is for exactly this reason that employers have always opposed decommodification' (Esping-Andersen 1990: 22).

Social policies do however differ in their degree to which they decommodify labour. The extent to which benefit recipients can make a living without gainful employment depends on benefit generosity and on benefit entitlement rules. Today, benefit entitlements are often linked to requirements of participation in activation measures and a willingness to accept job offers, often including offers for jobs that are below one's certified level of skills training. Moreover, and equally important, social programmes differ in terms of the type of risks they protect against, with different vulnerabilities towards benefit abuse. Work injury insurance, as well as sickness and disability insurance benefit only those with specified health conditions, which often require verification by a medical officer, and do thus not reduce the supply of able-bodied workers, except for undetected or tolerated benefit abuse by malingerers.

In contrast, benefits to the unemployed are more likely to reduce labour supply, since the willingness of an unemployed person to accept work is more difficult to monitor and benefits may drive up workers' reservation wage, possibly generating labour shortages in low-wage sectors. In short, if employers' social policy preferences are driven by the goal of protecting work incentives, we will expect that they will oppose benefits to the unemployed more strongly than those to the sick, the injured and the disabled. This hypothesis differs clearly from the skills investment thesis, discussed earlier, since the later predicts employer support, in particular for unemployment insurance.

The remainder of this chapter will investigate how the assessment of work incentives influences employers' social policy preferences through a case study of German welfare state history. The analysis will show how German employers initially, up to the inter-war period, feared an erosion of work incentives as a result of the adoption of new social programmes, in particular unemployment insurance. During the post-war period, German EOs came to see social protection as compatible with work incentives as long as it followed the Bismarckian model of earnings-based benefits. During the 1970s and 1980s, a period of over-staffing, German employers came to see value in negative work incentives and endorsed in particular early retirement schemes as a tool for reducing labour supply. Since the 1990s, with the emergence of new labour shortages, EOs abandoned support for early retirement programmes and came to push for stricter work requirement rules in social programmes and activation.

Bismarck's Social Insurance Project (1880s)

Germany was the first country to adopt public social insurance programmes during this period, under the rule of Chancellor Otto von Bismarck. The overall goal of government was to strengthen working class loyalty to the political regime, the nation state founded in 1873 as a semi-authoritarian regime with elections and political parties, but with government accountable to the emperor, not parliament. The social policy legislation co-existed with anti-socialist legislation, which constrained the political activities of the Social Democrats, though without banning the Social Democratic Party. Unemployment during this period was below 5 per cent and the expanding heavy industry experienced labour shortages, many of its workers came from Eastern Europe and Silesia (cf. Galenson and Zellner 1957, Table 1). The labour market was thus characterized by shortages, although mitigated by open borders and migrant workers.

The social programmes adopted were health insurance (1883), work injury insurance (1884) and old-age and disability pensions (1889). All programmes relied on compulsory coverage for large parts of the economy, even though white-collar employees were included only from 1911 on and civil servants were already insured with separate programmes. Contributions by employers and employees funded the programmes, and business interest organizations and unions played a role in programme administration. Pension benefits were in general too low for subsistence, meaning that workers either had to continue to work or rely on family support. Work injury insurance replaced the pre-existing employers' liability legislation, which mandated employers to compensate injured workers, if the worker could prove negligence by the employer (for a detailed account of the reforms in English see, for instance, Hennock 2007).

The main federations of industry supported the reforms, primarily because they accepted the need to pacify the working class, but also because they hoped to influence policy details (Breger 1982, Oechelhaeuser 1889: 109). Support came in particular from heavy industry and from the national peak federation of industry, the Central Federation of German Industrialists (CDI), which was dominated by heavy industry and textiles (Bueck 1903). The CDI was originally founded in 1876 as a pressure group for trade protectionism during the economic crisis of the 1870s, had cultivated close ties to the ministerial bureaucracy, and when the government announced its plans for social reform, shifted its focus from trade to social policy (Kaelble 1967: 109–11). Its executive director, Henry Axel Bueck, praised Bismarck's social insurance reforms as 'a work of civilization of the highest order' (Bueck 1905a: 791–792).

Support for the reforms was weaker in manufacturing and chemical engineering, but those sectors were still small at that time and their political influence weak due to lack of a peak federation (Ullmann 1979: 592–4, Paster 2012: 62–63). Manufacturing formed its own peak federation, the League of Industrialists (Bund der Industriellen, BdI), in 1895 (Ullmann 1976). These two sectors, heavy industry and manufacturing, differed in their approach to labour unions, with heavy industry refusing to accept unions, and manufacturing being less hostile to unions. Ullmann estimates that during the 1880s, the CDI represented about 2 per cent of all German firms, employing about one-third of all workers (Ullmann 1979: 594). In short, the CDI at that time was far from representative for German business at large, yet it represented big industry, in particular in heavy industry, and was the politically most influential of all business interest organizations.

Did industrialists fear social insurance to erode work incentives? To answer this question, I consulted the edited collection of primary sources by Wolfgang Ayass, Florian Tennstedt and colleagues (Ayass et al. 2003a Ayass 2003, 2003b), as well as the three-volume historiography of the CDI written by its long-term executive director (1887–1916), Henry Axel Bueck (Bueck 1905a, 1905b). In the case of health insurance and work injury insurance these sources do not contain any statements by business representatives pointing to a fear of negative work incentives. In the case of disability pensions, business representatives did voice concerns that benefit abuse might undermine work incentives. Business representatives called on the government to delay the adoption of pensions because of the expected cost increases, but also cautioned about benefit abuse. The following statement by Henry Axel Bueck, made at the general assembly of the Association of Iron and Steel Industry in Rhineland and Westphalia in November 1881, articulates these concerns:

> If the state would promise every worker from the outset a pension for disability and old age as a legal entitlement, this would diminish the sense of individual responsibility, and this would be the greatest damage that we could do to our society … I have said … "to be poor must never stop being a misfortune", This may sound very harsh, very heartless, but simply remove the perspective that presents misery, deprivation and poverty as a consequence of carelessness, indolence, idleness and dissoluteness, and at the same moment a large share of the poor will stop to make an effort, which today, with all their energy and most of them with success, endeavour to avert this sad fate[1] (document no. 23 in Ayass et al. 2003a: 97).

To sum up, fears of an erosion of work incentives did not play a dominant role in employers' assessment of Bismarck's social reform plans, and where they existed, they took the form of suspicion of benefit abuse. Fears of an erosion of work incentives, even where they existed, were not strong enough to prevent industrialists from supporting Bismarck's reform plans. This is most likely the result of the fact that the programmes on the agenda targeted those either unable to work, that is, the injured and sick, or those too old to work. Remarkably, though, unemployment was not among the risks covered by Bismarck's social insurance reforms. As we will see in the next section, unemployment insurance was introduced only in 1927 and met profound resistance from industry.

The Adoption of Public Unemployment Insurance (1927)

Public unemployment insurance was the branch of social insurance that German employers opposed most. During the Wilhelmine Empire, up to 1914, political support for a public programme to support the unemployed was weak among all political actors. Support for the unemployed was provided by the municipalities, in the form of means-tested social assistance, and by the unions, through what we today call the Ghent system, voluntary insurance based on contributions by members. The labour unions wanted to protect these schemes since they offered a tool for mobilization. Thus, they did not prioritize a public programme.

After World War I, the democratization of the political system that ended with the passing of the Weimar constitution in 1919 and high levels of unemployment in the aftermath of the war resulted in a different political and economic context. The unions had come to support a public programme because their own schemes were in financial difficulties. At the same time, a means-tested programme to support the unemployed, called unemployment assistance (Erwerbslosenfürsorge), had been introduced in 1914 in response to the rise in unemployment with the start of the war. This programme was intended as temporary, to be abolished after the war. After the war, however, the new Social Democratic-led provisional government continued this programme, to serve as a stop-gap solution until a permanent programme of unemployment insurance could be adopted (Faust 1987; Lewek 1992: 25; Wermel and Urban 1949).

Parliament adopted a public programme of unemployment insurance on 16 July 1927, after about nine years of debate. The government had presented its first bill to parliament in November 1919, but only the fourth bill found a majority in parliament; 344 deputies voted in favour of the final bill, 47 against. The ministerial bureaucracy and the Minister of Labour, Heinrich Brauns of the Centre Party, which represented political Catholicism, were the driving forces. The final bill had the support of all the major centre-right and centre-left parties. The Communists, the

German National People's Party and the NSDAP voted against (Führer 1990: 189).

The debate about the adoption of unemployment insurance took place during a period when the number of unemployed workers was rising. During the Wilhelmine Empire and during World War I, unemployment had been low and labour shortages had intensified during the war. The rate of unemployment reached a low of 1.0 per cent in 1917. After the war, unemployment went up and fluctuated between 6.8 and 18 per cent during the 1920s (Galenson and Zellner 1957, Table 1). Yet, the rate was still lower than during the Great Depression, when it reached an all-time high of 24 per cent in 1932. Nevertheless, the over-supply of labour did not result in EOs backing demands for unemployment insurance.

The EOs were among those actors most fervently opposed to un-employment insurance and had campaigned against its adoption up to 1924 (Lewek 1992: 156–157; Paster 2011: Table 3). The main organizations involved were the Federation of German Employers' Associations (Vereinigung deutscher Arbeitgeberverbände, VDA) and the Federation of German Industry (Reichsverband deutscher Industrie, RDI). The first was the peak federation of EOs, later the peak federation of industry associations, resulting from a 1918 merger of CDI and League of Industry. In addition, the German Diet of Industry and Commerce, the peak federation of the Chambers of Commerce, was active on this topic. All three had initially, until at least 1918 and partly also thereafter, opposed public support for the unemployed (for instance CDI 1913; DIHT 1920: 56; RDI 1925: 17–18; VDA 1924: 3–4).

Between 1918 and 1927, they gradually shifted to a stance of prag-matic cooperation, realizing that a majority in parliament supported unemployment insurance, and that cooperation would thus be more effective than opposition in influencing the legislation, as a meeting of the social policy committee of the VDA on 27 January 1925, had con-cluded (VDA 1925). Similarly, the social policy committee of the RDI decided in a meeting on 16 December 1920, that unemployment in-surance would be preferable to unemployment assistance, calling the first 'the lesser of two evils' because 'if unemployment assistance continues, the employer has no influence over the use of the funds' as the munici-palities administered unemployment assistance. With 16 votes in fa-vour, and 5 votes against, the RDI's social policy committee decided in the end to endorse the adoption of unemployment insurance (RDI 1921).

The publications by the VDA, as well as other business interest as-sociations frequently mention two arguments against unemployment insurance: cost increases to industry and suspected 'rewards for laziness' (VDA 1922: 27; VDA 1923: 35–36). The following quotes illustrate these arguments. In 1914, the executive director of the local EO of Nuremberg-Fürth, Franz-Xaver Zahnbrecher, wrote in a memorandum to government that unemployment insurance would have the effect that 'the need to seek work will be ... eliminated and the motivation of our people [to work] will cease' (Zahnbrecher 1914: 34). An employer periodical argued in October 1920 that 'a public insurance against unemployment would lead to carelessness among the lower classes, and generate opportunities for indolence' (DAGZ 1920: 1–2).

Notably, the EOs argued for strict work requirements for benefit recipients and argued that benefit recipients' vocational training and previous occupation should not be taken into consideration when deciding which types of jobs an unemployed person would be allowed to refuse without losing benefits. Different from what the government bill had proposed, the VDA insisted in 1926 that the unemployed be required to 'accept jobs that are not in line with existing vocational training or previous occupation' (VDA 1926: 36 and 36R). Similarly, the DIHT argued in 1920, in response to the first government bill, that 'acceptable employment is any employment that the insured person is physically capable of, even if it is outside of his place of residence or occupation' (DIHT 1920: 56). The evidence presented here thus contradicts the thesis that German employers backed the adoption of unemployment insurance in order to protect skill investments (Mares 2003a: 148).

In short, employers were much more concerned about negative work incentives in the case of unemployment insurance, compared to the other branches of social insurance. This appears because unemployment insurance benefits able-bodied workers and benefit abuse is more difficult to monitor. Rising unemployment did not turn EOs into supporters of unemployment insurance, since the over-supply of labour did not take the form of over-staffing, and thus did not generate any need for employers for decommodifying policies.

Over-staffing and Early Retirement Schemes (1970s and 1980s)

During the post-war period, social benefits were increased in many programmes, most notably in public pensions, where a major reform adopted in January 1957 raised benefit levels by about 65 per cent and introduced wage indexation of benefits. In contrast to the Weimar period, the social policy reforms of the post-war period were largely based on a broad cross-party consensus and shaped by electoral competition for pro-welfare voters (Alber 1989: Table 43).

During the post-war period, employer attitudes towards the welfare state also underwent a transformation. In contrast to its predecessor in the Weimar period (the VDA), the national peak federation, the BDA, accepted the political need for a welfare state. The BDA largely refrained during this period from attacking social programmes in principle, and instead focused its efforts on shaping the details of social policy legislation.

Unemployment declined throughout the 1950s and reached a low point in the 1960s at about 1 per cent, before starting to increase again with the oil price crisis in the 1970s, reaching a preliminary peak of 9.3 per cent in 1985, and rising further after unification, peaking at 13 per cent nationwide in 2005, before beginning to fall in the period since, to 5.5 per cent in 2019 (Bundesanstalt für Arbeit [Federal Agency for Labour], 2021).

Unlike during the Weimar Republic, the over-supply of labour since the 1970s was reflected not only in rising unemployment, but also in over-staffing. Industrial change in the 1970s and 1980s resulted in many companies wanting to shed labour, in particular older workers, yet facing resistance from unions and works councils. In this context, EOs became less concerned with protecting work incentives and, to the contrary, came to support social policies that reduced work incentives, in particular policies that facilitated an early exit of older workers from the labour market (Ebbinghaus 2006: 43–45; Jacobs et al. 1991: 200–205). These policies allowed firms to shed workers without risking industrial conflicts or political discontent. Changes in the labour market and industrial restructuring plans had thus changed the way employers viewed the importance of work incentives.

These changes are also reflected in the stances of the national peak federation. The BDA supported in the 1980s the extension of the duration of unemployment insurance benefits from 12 to 24 months for older workers, a measure intended to allow unemployed older workers to transition into retirement after that period (BDA 1985: 49). The BDA also backed the Early Retirement Law (Vorruhestandsgesetz, VRG) adopted in April 1984, which introduced a new benefit for employees that retire early (Vorruhestandsgeld). The BDA argued that:

> Early retirement offers an opportunity to mitigate the imbalances in the labour market that are caused temporarily by demographic developments and to enhance the occupational chances of those cohorts with high birthrates that are entering the labour market
>
> (BDA 1984: 56)

At the same time, however, the BDA also emphasized that early retirement policy should be seen as temporary. The BDA's executive director, Hans-Gerhard Erdmann, argued in 1984 that

> [i]f employers are open towards the idea of early retirement, then only under the aspect that during a temporary, exceptional situation special, additional support is needed. The current tensions in the labour market, caused by demographic changes, need to be mitigated
>
> (Ebert 1984: 12)

From the late 1980s on, the BDA took a more sceptical stance towards early retirement. In 1989, the BDA argued that the Early Retirement Law of 1984 had:

> [b]y and large not lived up to expectations. It certainly made a small contribution to solving the problem of unemployment, so that the law cannot be considered a failure. The approach used was however expensive
>
> (BDA 1989: 69)

At that time, the BDA criticized early retirement merely because of its effects on social expenditure, but not because of any reduction in labour supply. From about the mid-1990s onwards, however, the BDA began again to emphasize the need to strengthen work incentives. BDA president Dieter Hundt argued in 2008 that:

> We can no longer afford to push out of their job employees in good health. In the face of a shortage of skilled workers and the declining number of school leavers, companies need both, the young and the old ... I call on the government to continue the ... path of extending working life
>
> (BDA 2008: 1)

Demands by the BDA for supply-side reforms of the labour market, such as activation measures and stricter work requirement rules, further confirm this shift in the BDA's assessment of the desirability of strengthening work incentives. The BDA supported in particular the Agenda 2010 and Hartz IV reforms, which aimed to bring unemployed people back into jobs through a combination primarily of less generous social benefits, activation requirements, and stricter rules on what kind of jobs an unemployed person could refuse to accept without losing benefit rights (Hassel and Schiller 2010: 110–116). The BDA supported the gist of these reforms, and found that they did not go far enough in terms of deregulating the labour market. Moreover, the BDA criticized the adoption of national minimum wage in 2014 as making it more difficult for the long-term unemployed to re-enter the labour market (BDA 2014a: 4).

To sum up, the BDA thus changed its position from one of cautious support for early retirement to opposition. This position is evident, for instance, in the BDA's opposition to the introduction in 2014 of a rule that allows workers with at least 45 years of contribution payments to retire at the age of 63, instead of 65, without actuarial benefit cuts (BDA 2014b: 9–12). At the same time, however, the BDA explicitly endorsed benefit improvements in disability pensions, that is, benefits for employees who due to health reasons have a reduced earnings capacity and thus can receive benefits already before the statutory retirement age of

65 (BDA 2014b: 1,12) These differences in the BDA's positions towards benefits for people capable and not capable to work indicates that its opposition is not motivated only by expected cost increases, but primarily the fear of reduced work incentives. To conclude, the evidence shows that the BDA welcomed work disincentives during times of over-staffing but opposed them during periods of labour shortages.

Table 4.1 summarizes the above discussed views of German EOs on the effects of social policy reforms on work incentives within the selected reform episodes.

Conclusions

Drawing on three reform episodes from the history of the German welfare state, this chapter has shown how employers' perceptions of de-commodifying social policies have changed in response to changing labour markets and firms' staffing policies. When faced with labour shortages, German employers pushed for regulations that strengthened work incentives, such as activation and stricter entitlement rules. In contrast, when during the 1970s and 1980s firms were over-staffed and wanted to shed labour, they welcomed social policy-generated disincentives to work. The expansion of these social programmes did however increase labour costs and resulted in German EOs taking a more critical stance towards social policy-induced labour shedding from the 1990s on. Subsequently, the emergence of new labour shortages in some occupations from the mid-2000s on resulted in employers gaining a renewed interest in the strengthening of work incentives, and, together with their interest in containing labour costs, resulted in German EOs calling for more restrictive access to social benefits.

The chapter advances debates between conflict-theoretical and efficiency-theoretical explanations of employer preferences by showing how the relative importance of political conflict and economic efficiency as drivers of employers' social policy support vary depending on labour market conditions and firms' staffing policies. During the core period of the construction of welfare state programmes, from Bismarck up to the Weimar years, political conflict drove employers' engagement with reform initiatives, when they intended to pacify workers and avert the adoption of more radical proposals. Later, during the 1970s and 1980s large employers came to temporarily see efficiency benefits in social programmes, as tools for facilitating labour shedding. Faced with new labour shortages and with higher non-wage labour costs, German EOs turned against those policies from the 1990s on and became supporters of activation and a tightened access to benefits. These changes in EOs' social policy preferences are related to changing staffing policies, which turned social policies from a tool to facilitate labour shedding into a cost burden and obstacle to work incentives.

Table 4.1 German EO's views on the effects of social policy reforms on work incentives

Reform plan	Year	Labour market scenario	Did German EOs expect the programme to weaken work incentives?	How did German EOs view the expected work disincentives (positively or negatively)?
Work injury insurance	1881	Under-supply	No	NA
Health insurance	1883	Under-supply	No	NA
Disability and old-age pensions	1889	Under-supply	Partly (benefit abuse)	Negative
Unemployment insurance	1927	Over-supply/High Unemployment	Yes	Negative
Early retirement scheme	1970s–1980s (several reforms)	Over-supply/Over-staffing	Yes	Positive

In addition, the chapter documented how the intensity of EO concerns about work incentives varied depending on the type of social programme. The comparison of EO positions on the adoption of new social programmes during the core period of welfare state construction shows that unemployment insurance was the programme they opposed most strongly. Statements in EO publications show that negative work incentives were indeed the main reason for German EOs to oppose unemployment insurance, a fear that mattered less to them with respect to the other types of social insurances.

The historical record does not support the thesis developed in particular by Mares (2001: 197) that an interest in skill investment induced the EOs representing large firms to support social protection for workers. During the Wilhelmine Empire and the Weimar Republic, fears of negative work incentives, together with expected increases in labour costs, were the main motives for employers to oppose social reforms, even though the intensity of the concerns about negative work incentives varied across programmes. While German employers during the post-war period became more supportive of social protection, they did not do so because they expected an enhanced supply of specific skills, but because they expected easier labour shedding during periods of industrial restructuring.

Since 2005, unemployment has gone down in Germany, from 13 per cent to 5.5 per cent (2009), and the focus of German EOs shifted from over-staffing to fears of labour shortages in some occupations, which, for demographic reasons, are expected to intensify in the 2020s. These changes require staffing policies different from those in the 1970s and 1980s, intended to attract qualified employees. In this changed labour market environment, German EOs became advocates of activation and tighter benefit rules in social programmes.

Note

1 All quotes in the text have been translated from German by the author.

References

Alber, J. (1989). *Der Sozialstaat in der Bundesrepublik 1950–1983*. Frankfurt am Main, New York: Campus.

Amenta, E. and Parikh, S. (1991). Capitalists did not want the social security act: A critique of the "Capitalist Dominance" Thesis. *American Sociological Review*, 56: 124–129. 10.2307/2095678

Ayass, W., Tennstedt, F. and Winter, H. (eds.) (2003a). *Von der Kaiserlichen Sozialbotschaft bis zu den Februarerlassen Wilhelm II. (1881–1890) Band 1. Grundfragen der Sozialpolitik: die Diskussion der Arbeiterfrage auf Regierungsseite und in der Öffentlichkeit*. Darmstadt: Wissenschaftiche Buchgesellschaft.

Ayass, W., Tennstedt, F. and Winter, H. (eds.) (2003b). *Von der Kaiserlichen Sozialbotschaft bis zu den Februarerlassen Wilhelm II. (1881–1890) Vol 1 Grundfragen der Sozialpolitik: die Diskussion der Arbeiterfrage auf Regierungsseite und in der Öffentlichkeit*. Darmstadt: WBG.

BDA (1984). Jahresbericht der Bundesvereinigung der Deutschen Arbeitgeberverbände. In: *Bundesvereinigung der Deutschen Arbeitgeberverbände* (ed.). Cologne: BDA.

BDA (1985). Jahresbericht der Bundesvereinigung der Deutschen Arbeitgeberverbände. In: *Bundesvereinigung der Deutschen Arbeitgeberverbände* (ed.). Cologne: BDA.

BDA (1989). Jahresbericht der Bundesvereinigung der Deutschen Arbeitgeberverbände. In: *Bundesvereinigung der Deutschen Arbeitgeberverbände* (ed.). Cologne: BDA.

BDA (2008). *Arbeitgeberpräsident Dr. Dieter Hundt: Eine Rückkehr zur Frühverrentung darf es nicht geben, Presse-Information Nr. 050/2008*. Berlin: Bundesvereinigung der Deutschen Arbeitgeberverbände.

BDA (2014a). *Gesetzentwurf für Mindestlohn schwächt Tarifautonomie und schafft Einstiegsbarrieren am Arbeitsmarkt: Stellungnahme zum Gesetzentwurf zur "Stärkung der Tarifautonomie"*. Berlin: Bundesvereinigung deutscher Arbeitgeberverbände.

BDA (2014b). *Rentenpaket: Annahme verweigern: Stellungnahme zum Entwurf eines "Gesetzes über Leistungsverbesserungen in der gesetzlichen Rentenversicherung" (RV-Leistungsverbesserungsgesetz)*. Berlin: BDA.

Breger, M. (1982). *Die Haltung der industriellen Unternehmer zur staatlichen Sozialpolitik in den Jahren 1878–1891*. Frankfurt am Main: Haag + Herchen.

Bueck, H. A. (1903). *Soziale Reform*. Berlin: J. Guttentag.

Bueck, H. A. (1905a). *Der Centralverband Deutscher Industrieller, 1876–1901*. Berlin: J. Guttentag.

Bueck, H. A. (1905b). *Der Zentralverband Deutscher Industrieller, 1876–1901. Band II*, Berlin.

Bundesanstalt für Arbeit [Federal Agency for Labour] (2021). *Arbeitslosigkeit im Zeitverlauf 03/2021* [Excel File]. In: Bildung, B. f. P. (ed.). Bonn: BPB.

CDI (1913). *Zur Arbeitslosenversicherung*. Berlin: Centralverband Deutscher Industrieller.

DAGZ (1920). Die moralischen Gefahren der reichsgesetzlichen Regelung der Arbeitslosen-Versicherung. *Die Deutsche Arbeitgeber-Zeitung. Zentralblatt deutscher Arbeitgeberverbände*, 31 October (no. 44), 1.

DIHT (1920). Arbeitslosenversicherung. *Handel und Gewerbe. Zeitschrift für die zur Vertretung von Handel und Gewerbe gesetzlich berufenen Körperschaften. Im Auftrag des Deutschen Industrie- und Handelstags*. Deutscher Industrie-und Handelstag.

Ebbinghaus, B. (2006). *Reforming Early Retirement in Europe, Japan and the USA*. Oxford: Oxford University Press.

Ebert, R. (1984). Probleme eines vorgezogenen Ruhestands. *Der Arbeitgeber*, 36: 11–12.

Esping-Andersen, G. (1990). *The Three Worlds of Welfare Capitalism*. Princeton: Princeton Univ. Press.

Estévez-Abe, M., Iversen, T. and Soskice, D. (2001). Social Protection and the Formation of Skills: A Reinterpretation of the Welfare State. In: P.A. Hall and D. Soskice (eds.) *Varieties of Capitalism. The Institutional Foundations of Comparative Advantage.* Oxford: Oxford University Press, pp. 145–183.

Faust, A. (1987). Von der Fürsorge zur Arbeitsmarktpolitik: Die Errichtung der Arbeitslosenversicherung. In: Abelshauser, W. (ed.) *Die Weimarer Republik als Wohlfahrtsstaat.* Stuttgart: Steiner.

Führer, K. C. (1990). *Arbeitslosigkeit und die Entstehung der Arbeitslosenversicherung in Deutschland 1902–1927.* Berlin: Colloquium.

Galenson, W. & Zellner, A. (1957). International Comparison of Unemployment Rates. In: Universities-National Bureau (ed.) *The Measurement and Behavior of Unemployment.* NBER.

Greer, I. (2016). Welfare reform, precarity and the re-commodification of labour. *Work, Employment & Society*, 30: 162–173. 10.1177%2F0950017015572578

Hacker, J. S. and Pierson, P. (2002). Business power and social policy: Employers and the formation of the American welfare state. *Politics & Society*, 30: 277–325. 10.1177%2F0032329202030002004

Hassel, A. and Schiller, C. (2010). *Der Fall Hartz IV: wie es zur Agenda 2010 kam und wie es weitergeht.* Frankfurt: Campus.

Hennock, E. P. (2007). *The Origin of the Welfare state in England and Germany, 1850-1914: social policies compared.* New York: Cambridge University Press.

Iversen, T. (2005). *Capitalism, Democracy, and Welfare.* Cambridge: Cambridge University Press.

Jacobs, K., Kohli, M. and Rein, M. (1991). Testing the industry-mix hypothesis of early exit. In: M. Kohli, M. Rein, A.-M. Guillemard and H. Van Gunsteren (eds.) *Time for Retirement. Comparative study of Early Exit from the Labor Market.* Cambridge: Cambridge University Press, pp. 67–96.

Jenkins, J. C. and Brents, B. G. (1991). Capitalists and social security: What did they really want? *American Sociological Review*, 56: 129–132. 10.2307/2095679

Kaelble, H. 1967. *Industrielle Interessenpolitik in der Wilhelminischen Gesellschaft: Centralverband Deutscher Industrieller 1895–1914.* Berlin: de Gruyter.

Lewek, P. (1992). *Arbeitslosigkeit und Arbeitslosenversicherung in der Weimarer Republik 1918–1927.* Stuttgart: Franz Steiner.

Mares, I. (2001). Firms and the Welfare State: When, Why, and How Does Social Policy Matter to Employers? In: P. A. Hall and D. Soskice (eds.) *Varieties of Capitalism. The Institutional Foundations of Comparative Advantage.* Oxford: Oxford University Press, 184–212.

Mares, I. (2003a). *The Politics of Social Risks. Business and Welfare State Development.* Cambridge: Cambridge University Press.

Mares, I. (2003b). The sources of business interest in social insurance: Sectoral versus national differences. *World Politics*, 55: 229–258. 10.1353/wp.2003.0012

Mares, I. (2004). Economic insecurity and social policy expansion: Evidence from interwar Europe. *International Organization*, 58: 745–774. 10.1017/S0020818304040238

Martin, C. J. (2006). Consider the Source! Determinants of Corporate Preferences for Public Policy. In: D. Coen and W. Grant (eds.) *Business and Government: Methods and Practice.* Opladen & Farmington Hills: Barbara Budrich Publishers, pp. 51–78.

Oechelhaeuser, W. (1889). *Soziale Tagesfragen*, Berlin: J. Springer.

Oude Nijhuis, D. (2019). Analyzing the role of business in welfare state development. In: Oude Nijhuis, D. (ed.) *Business Interests and the Development of the Modern Welfare State*. Abingdon: Routledge.

Paster, T. (2011). German employers and the origins of unemployment insurance: Skills interest or strategic accommodation? *MPIfG Discussion Paper*, 2011: 32.

Paster, T. (2012). *The Role of Business in the Development of the Welfare State and Labor Markets in Germany: Containing Social Reforms*. London: Routledge.

Paster, T. (2013). Business and welfare state development: Why did employers accept social reforms? *World Politics*, 65: 416–451. 10.1017/S0043887113000117

Paster, T. (2015). Bringing power back in: A review of the literature on the role of business in welfare state politics. *MPIfG Discussion Papers*, 15.

Paster, T. (2019a). Varieties of Capitalism und Sozialpolitik: Thesen und empirische Befunde. In: H. Obinger and M. G. Schmidt (eds.) *Handbuch Sozialpolitik*. Wiesbaden: Springer, pp. 255–273.

Quadagno, J. S. (1984). Welfare capitalism and the social security act of 1935. *American Sociological Review*, 49: 632–647. 10.2307/2095421

RDI (1921). *Geschäftliche Mitteilungen für die Mitglieder des RDI Vol.3 Issue 1*. Berlin: Reichsverband deutscher Industrie.

RDI (1925). *Deutsche Wirtschafts- und Finanzpolitik*. Berlin: Selbstverlag des Reichsverbandes der Deutschen Industrie.

Skocpol, T. & Amenta, E. (1985). Did capitalists shape social security? *American Sociological Review*, 50: 572–575. 10.2307/2095440

Swenson, P. A. (2002). *Capitalists against markets: the making of labor markets and welfare states in the United States and Sweden*. New York: Oxford University Press.

Ullmann, H.-P. (1976). *Der Bund der Industriellen: Organisation, Einfluß und Politik klein- und mittelbetrieblicher Industrieller im Deutschen Kaiserreich 1895–1914*. Göttingen: Vandenhoeck & Ruprecht.

Ullmann, H.-P. (1979). Industrielle interessen und die entstehung der deutschen sozialversicherung 1880–1889. *Historische Zeitschrift*, 229: 574–610.

VDA (1922). Geschäftsbericht über das Jahr 1921 erstattet von der Geschäftsführung. *Berichte*. Berlin: Vereinigung der Deutschen Arbeitgeberverbände.

VDA (1923). Geschäftsbericht über das Jahr 1922 erstattet von der Geschäftsführung. In: VDA (ed.) *Berichte*. Berlin: Vereinigung der Deutschen Arbeitgeberverbände.

VDA (1924). Stellungnahme der Vereinigung der Deutschen Arbeitgeberverbände zu Erwerbslosenfürsorge und Arbeitslosenversicherung. *Mitteilungen der VDA*, Appendix to "Mitteilungen" Nr. 23: 1–4.

VDA (1925). Stichworte der Geschäftsführung zur Sitzung des Sozialpolitischen Ausschusses, 27.1.1925. *State Archive Hamburg Files Blohm/Voss 1326 Vol.2*. Hamburg: State Archive.

VDA (1926). *Stellungnahme zu den Grundfragen der Arbeitslosenversicherung*. Berlin: Vereinigung der Deutschen Arbeitgeberverbände.

Wermel, M. and Urban, R. (1949). Arbeitslosenfürsorge und Arbeitslosenversicherung in Deutschland. *Neue Soziale Praxis*, 6: 111.

Zahnbrecher, F. X. (1914). *Arbeitslosenversicherung und Arbeitgeber*. Nuremberg: K. Hofbuchhandlung Schrag.

5 Culture and Coordinated Industrial Relations

Cathie Jo Martin

Introduction[1]

The road to coordinated and liberal employer organization is a hotly debated issue in industrial relations studies. Power resources theorists argue that countries with militant labor movements, well-represented by their strong unions and social democratic parties, successfully forced employers to organize in order to engage in collective bargaining arrangements. Countries with strong class divisions produced well-organized labor movements capable of wresting concessions from the capitalist class (Korpi 1980; Lipset and Rokkan 1967; Paster 2012; Sisson; 1987; Stephens 1979). Others point to the crucial role of employer organization in the logic of industrial coordination and suggest that strong employers' organizations arise from favorable preindustrial economic arrangements (i.e. guilds) and political institutions (proportional parties). In this case, cooperation emerged in countries with more muted class antagonisms (Crouch 1993; Hall and Soskice 2001; Iversen and Soskice 2019; Martin and Swank 2012; Thelen 2004).

This chapter suggests another factor contributing to the evolution of corporatist and pluralist employers' organizations, namely that diverse varieties of capitalism have different moral economies of the employment relationship. Specifically, I suggest that countries developing corporatist and pluralist employers' organizations have entirely different cultural views of labor, skills, cooperation and the state, and that these views provide a backdrop for the collective organization of employers in the 19th century. Cultural depictions of labor relations have meaning for employers' preference for social investments in skills, labor market competition versus coordination and a substantial role for the state in industrial relations.

To substantiate my claims about the different moral economies of liberal and coordinated countries, I investigate depictions of labor embedded in 18th-, 19th- and early 20th-century national literatures. I apply computational text analyses to large literary corpora from Britain, Denmark, France and Sweden from 1770 to 1920 to assess the frequency with which authors in liberal and coordinated countries make reference

DOI: 10.4324/9781003104575-6

to skills, cooperation, states and markets in passages about labor. I illustrate the quantitative findings with brief presentations of British and Danish fictional works referencing industrial relations.

I find that authors in the coordinated countries of Denmark and Sweden present the labor relationship differently from those in the liberal countries of Britain and France, and that these differences date back to the 18th century. Danish and Swedish writers have significantly more references than British and French authors to skills, coordination and states in snippets of text around labor during most periods. British and French authors have significantly more references to markets in their passages about labor. Qualitative assessments of British and Danish authors' works reinforce the quantitative findings about strong cross-national differences in narratives about labor. British social reform authors have great pity for the working class; however, they make limited references to the positive benefits of social investments in workers and assume that class relations are inherently conflictual. Danish authors view the productive contributions of workers and peasants as necessary to national ambitions, view social investments in workforce skills as an essential part of this national project, and urge cooperation among social classes for the benefit of society. British authors doubt state capacities to remedy social injustices; Danish authors view the state much more positively and urge that all citizens contribute to a strong society and robust state.

Cultural analysis has theoretical implications for the evolution of industrial relations systems and sheds light on competing scholarly accounts of liberal versus coordinated labor relations. Cultural depictions of labor, skills, cooperation and the state diverge in liberal and coordinated countries long before the emergence of employers' organizations, unions and even political parties. I surmise that these cultural depictions contribute to the framing by both employers and workers' conceptions of their preferences, and that cultural products help to reinforce cross-national differences in the construction of class cleavages (Spillman 2012). Cultural work sheds light on the moral economies underlying diverse varieties of capitalism and addresses questions about the dynamics of political economies that materialist explorations overlook.

The chapter also adds to the trend in industrial relations to explore the role of ideas in industrial relations (Hauptmeier and Heery 2014; Morgan and Hauptmeier 2021; Schulze-Cleven and Weishaupt 2015). Much of this excellent literature explores the institutional framework that influences the interpretation of new policy ideas about labor relations. Yet I diverge in developing a separate literary cultural channel for the transmission of ideas about labor that is somewhat separate from the institutional framework for processing policy ideas.

Finally, the paper addresses why familiar practices in labor relations continue despite wild shifts in economic conditions over time; in this way, it contributes to work on processes reinforcing continuities at moments of institutional change. Cultural touchstones, in this case the symbols and narratives of literature, are passed down by authors from one generation to another. Fiction writers inherit symbols and narratives from past generations of authors, and they collectively rework these cultural touchstones to address contemporary issues. Because the symbols and narratives are recursive and repeating, they have bearing on the national continuities in the packaging and adoption of new paradigms by successive generations of policymakers. Unlike path dependencies laid down at a specific moment of policy creation, enduring cultural touchstones provide a continuity in the imagining of labor across time. These cultural touchstones are dynamic and subject to alteration over time; moreover, these are not deterministic in specific episodes of labor relations. Yet they provide insight into why familiar features of labor relations within national settings tend to reappear through time and under very different economic circumstances. The cultural touchstones lend a sense of familiarity in our patterns of social class engagement.

Varieties of Employer Organization

Scholars sort industrial relations systems and employers' organizations into two or more categories. Hall and Soskice (2001) differentiate between liberal and coordinated market economies (see also Estevez-Abe et al. 2001; Streeck 1992). Employers' organizations are labeled pluralist and macrocorporatist (or neocorporatist) and some add a third level of sectoral coordination (Crouch 1993; Martin and Swank 2012; Schmitter 1981). The systems of industrial relations and employer organization vary in the characteristics of industrial groups, their incorporation into public policymaking processes, and their types of skill formation. These stylized versions neglect cross-national variations in modes of production, forms of cooperation, skills producing institutions (Amable 2003; Deeg and Jackson 2007; Lane and Wood 2009; Morgan 2005). Yet these typologies are useful for observing correspondence between culture and labor relations.

First, coordinated/corporatist societies have encompassing, centralized and consensus-oriented national employers' and workers' organizations, while pluralist systems have weak and decentralized organizations. Collective bargaining tends to be more centralized and cooperative in corporatist than in pluralist countries (Schmitter 1981; Stephens 1979).

Second, corporatist/coordinated systems integrate "social partners" into state-sponsored tripartite commissions to form policy; whereas pluralist systems lack these extra-legislative forms of policymaking. Thus, employers in coordinated/corporatist countries presuppose more consensual, cooperative relations among the social partners and recognize a more positive view of state involvement than do employers in liberal/pluralist countries (Hall and Soskice 2001; Martin and Swank 2012; Oude Nijhuis 2013).

Third, employers in coordinated/corporatist countries, often with open economies, compete on the basis of quality in high-value-added market niches and need a highly-skilled workforce; therefore, they support human capital investments in and social protections for labor. Employers in liberal countries historically develop Fordist manufacturing processes using semi-skilled labor, are likely to use price competition, and are more likely to produce for domestic markets (Cusack et al. 2007; Hall and Soskice 2001); therefore, they seek workers with lower skills and cooperate less with organized labor and with one another than their peers in coordinated countries (Hall and Soskice 2001; Schmitter 1981; Streeck 1992; Swenson 2002; Wilson 1990). Industrial relations systems were fully formed after the Second World War, yet industrial unions and employers' organizations emerged during the 19th century and peak organizations and courts for labor disputes developed around the turn of the 20th century (Crouch 1993; Martin and Swank 2012).

The concept of "preference" is underdeveloped in Hall and Soskice's original formulation, as the authors largely attribute the divergence in employers' strategic choices to the different production strategies of firms in coordinated and liberal market economies. Preferences arise from material interest shaped by institutional structures, and there is little room for the interpretation of preference. Hall (1993) elsewhere writes extensively about the role of ideas in policy change; however, ideas are not central to musings on varieties of capitalism.

Scholarly work investigating the origins of pluralist and corporatist employers' organizations also largely focus on interests and organization, to the neglect of ideas. First, power resources theory suggests that co-ordinated labor relations were forged through the fires of labor radicalism. Strongly-organized unions and parties representing workers wrested concessions from employers and motivated business to form employers' organizations in response (Galenson 1952; Korpi 1980; Lipset and Rokkan 1967; Paster 2012; Sisson 1987; Stephens 1979; Tolliday and Zeitlin 1991; Windmuller and Gladstone 1984). In these stories, countries that ultimately achieved the most industrial coordination were those in which labor was sufficiently radicalized, rather than reformist (Lipset 1983).

Second, another theory suggests that contemporary coordinated countries, compared to liberal countries, had stronger preindustrial co-operative institutions (guilds) and norms; these enabled early consensual engagement across the class divide. Guilds created assumptions about patterns of cross-class cooperation, as employers develop shared interests with labor in a production strategy relying on a skilled workforce (Crouch 1993; Cusack et al. 2007; Hall and Soskice 2001; Stråth 2017; Sundberg 2004; Thelen 2004). In contrast, liberal countries developed craft unions that drove wedges among segments of the working class and worked against coordination (Clegg 1979; Unwin 1966).

Third, a related explanation suggests that political institutions influenced the development of different types of employers' organizations. Martin and Swank (2008, 2012) suggest that right party politicians in countries with proportional representation had incentives to delegate power to employers' organizations because business thought that it could win more fighting labor in private channels than fighting labor and farmers in legislatures. Industrial organization occurs when the state has a particularly activist agenda, as policymakers mobilize business from the top-down to achieve their political objectives (Grant and Marsh 1977; Martin 1991). Crouch (1993) maintains that social partners were able to wrest policymaking away from bureaucrats in countries where business and labor were strongly organized (Crouch 1993). Forms of coordination influence the manner in which employers express collective preferences for productivity-enhancing social pacts (Streeck 1992; Visser and Hemerijck 1997; Martin and Swank 2012; Nijhuis 2013).

While these theories do not directly address the role of ideas, they suggest somewhat contradictory views about radicalism and reformism in countries destined to become coordinated and liberal market economies. Writing from a power resources perspective, Lipset (1983) suggests that workers were *more radical* in countries that ultimately developed high levels of industrial coordination, because preindustrial status groups created a shared corporate identity within the working class and were able to gain power from capital. But the literature emphasizing preindustrial coordination suggests the obverse: guilds etc. made workers *less radical* and more oriented toward consensual negotiation in countries that later developed highly organized labor market institutions (Cusack et al. 2007; Thelen 2004; Unwin 1966).

Ideas, Culture and Employer Organization

Scholars have recently accorded greater attention to ideas in the cross-national divergence of industrial relations systems; they recognize that ideas as well as institutional complementarities bolster practices of cooperation and conflict in labor relations. The interpretation of ideas becomes a tool for mobilizing action in labor relations (Hauptmeier and Heery 2014). Industrial relations (as well as governmental) institutions have normative legacies that sustain patterns of cooperation or conflict at moments of historical institutional change (Schulze-Cleven and Weishaupt 2015). The "social organization of ideas," or the processes of knowledge production and transmission, shape choices of industrial relations and are particularly important during episodes of paradigmatic change. Ideas as a causal or contextual variable may help to explain continuities at moments of political institutional change. Policy entrepreneurs are guided by ideas when they translate or adopt new hegemonic ideas into country-specific policies (Ban 2016; Blyth 2002; Edling et al. 2014).

I am deeply sympathetic to these arguments; however, they cannot address the role of ideas in the initial construction of labor relations institutions, before the modern evolution of institutions for knowledge production. We learn from E.P. Thompson (1991) that the English crowd had a moral economy that guided labor resistance to the ills of industrial capitalism. But one wonders whether employers and workers had a different type of moral economy in the countries destined to become coordinated market economies.

Exploring how literature in coordinated and liberal countries diverges in depictions of labor also gives us an independent way to think about cultural influences. Ideas are often evaluated by considering their apparent manifestation in institutions, and indeed, symbolic elements together with social practices and material resources constitute a core component of institutions (Scott 2001: 48–51). Yet it is possible to study ideas apart from the institutions in which they are manifest through the symbols and narratives embedded in cultural artifacts.

I suggest that that fiction writers collectively depict labor in culturally-specific ways and that cross-national variations in these depictions may be observed in national corpora of literature. Countries have a "cultural toolkit" (norms, symbols and narratives) that actors use to ascribe meaning and develop solutions to problems (Swidler 1986: 273–276). The toolkit includes "repertoires of evaluation," or scripts that define positives and negatives, and draw boundaries between groups (Lamont and Thévenot 2000: 5–6). The heterogeneous cultural toolkit cannot predict specific choices; however, symbols, narratives and repertoires of evaluation are unevenly distributed across countries and citizens in one country are more likely to access specific cultural tools than citizens in others (Lamont and Thévenot 2000: 5–6). Authors draw from a cultural toolkit in processes of bricolage that contribute to shifting manifestation of political philosophies and institutional change (Carstensen and Vivien 2016).

Fiction writers constitute a mechanism by which the cultural toolkit is transmitted from one generation to the next. Authors act collectively as purveyors of cultural symbols and narratives, and draw upon cultural artifacts inherited from the past to depict new challenges and solutions (Martin 2018). The collective voices and silences of the corpora transcend the agency of individual writers (Guy 1996: 71; Poovey 1995; Williams 1963). Familiar touchstones inform the "political unconscious," (or gap between authors' intended goals and their subtext messages) that is unacknowledged by the text (Jameson 1981). The symbols and narratives, or cultural touchstones, that authors use to depict labor are repeating and to some extent enduring across time. Country-specific depictions of policy problems endure across epochs, even as paradigm shifts effect subtle changes in the causes, agents and effects of problems; the iterative manifestation of cultural depictions transcend individual reform episodes. Kipling recognizes the power of the national corpus when he writes: "The magic of Literature lies in the words, and not in any man ... a bare half-hundred words breathed upon by some man in his agony ... ten generations ago, can still lead whole nations into and out of captivity" (Kipling 1928: 6).

Cultural artifacts have bearing on the construction of collective social identities and class cleavages. Cultural scripts or "imaginaries" help to define class relations, organize economic action and create markets (Beckert and Bronk 2018: 4). Cultural production influences norms of economic exchange and the preferences of economic actors (Dobbin 1994; Spillman 2012: 159). Novels' depictions may politicize or demobilize marginal groups and stories of resistance become crucial weapons in movement mobilization (Ewick and Silbey 2003; Lamont and Thévenot 2000; Swidler 1986). Narratives and symbols convey expectations about the psychological articulation of "self," the relationship between individual and society, conformity to the social order and collective identities (DiMaggio and Markus 2010: 351; Griswold and Wright 2004; Korsgaard 2012; Polletta et al. 2011).

Certainly, there is also a reciprocal impact of power relations on cultural development, as dominant interests give preference to certain cultural voices. Although the barriers to publishing were lower in the 18th and 19th centuries, publishers gave a platform to chosen authors (Altick 1986). Yet characteristics of cleavage formation – the strength of antagonisms, individual attachment to the collective, and distance between core and peripheral groups – may well endure through shifting power relations driving institutional change.

Thus, I suggest that cultural views toward industrial relations and institutions for employer organization co-evolve. Cultural depictions are influenced by preindustrial institutions for cooperation such as guilds and cameralism (Archer 1979: 3); these cultural views, in turn, reinforce industrial relations choices of cooperation versus conflict. If these ideas and cultural depictions are important to the emergence and continuation of industrial relations systems, one should be able to observe differences in the cultural touchstones of liberal/pluralist and coordinated/corporatist countries. Specifically, coordinated market economies should include more references to skills, government and cooperation in passages about labor; liberal market economies should include more references to markets in reflections on labor.

Quantitative Methods

This chapter relies on computational test analyses (using Python) to systematically test observable differences in corpora of British (562),

Danish (521), French (500) and Swedish (411) novels, poems and plays between 1700 and 1920 (after which copyright laws limit access). Denmark and Sweden represent coordinated market economies and Britain and France represent liberal market economies. The national corpora are drawn from online lists of important literary works (poems, plays and novels) and country collections of national literature (e.g. the Archive of Danish Literature). The corpora include virtually all full-text files available from Denmark, France and Sweden and a large, representative sample of British texts compiled from online lists. Full text files are provided by HathiTrust. Because available full-text files are often not first editions, I manually alter the dates of works to reflect their initial publication. The timing of publication is crucial for establishing the sequential relationship between cultural artifacts and reform moments.

I hypothesize that if distinctive literary depictions are associated with choices in industrial system development, one should find cross-national variation in the cultural scripts of large corpora of national literature that correspond to our predicted differences in evolution of industrial systems. Snippets of fifty-word text are built around words that reference the concept of labor; I then stem the corpora and take out stop words. The words (in English) include worker, guild, craftsman, journeyman, apprentice, farmer, peasant, serf, mechanic and labor; and I translate these words into Danish (presented in an online Appendix).

To compare theoretically-derived concepts in snippets of text surrounding labor in national corpora, words are chosen that represent core concepts including skills, coordination, state and market. I use a supervised learning model to compare word frequencies across countries. A dictionary-based approach allows one to identify words in each core concept, by searching core terms in an online dictionary and thesaurus. Although excellent psychosocial dictionaries (e.g. the Moral Foundations Dictionary and the Linguistic Inquiry and Word Count) enable measures of norms and values, the categories specific to modes of collective political engagement require a custom-made specification (Bonikowski and Gidron 2016). I have widely read fiction from Britain and Denmark and have authors on other articles from France and Sweden who have also ensured that we use historically-appropriate words.

A supervised learning model is appropriate for calculating temporal and cross-national variations in word frequencies because our categories are specified by theory: the object is not to assess how an individual document fits into a corpus, but to assess cross-national and temporal differences among works that are presorted by country, language and time (Laver et al. 2003; Hopkins and King 2010).

Findings

The quantitative data largely confirm the predicted differences between the coordinated countries of Denmark and Sweden, and the liberal countries of Britain and France. In Figure 5.1, we see that all countries talk about work and the working class. Britain, where the industrial revolution has most progressed, makes the highest level of references to labor.

Yet writers in coordinated Denmark and liberal Britain discuss the working class in quite different ways. Danish authors celebrate farmers and workers as the backbone of Danish society, at least from the late 18th century when serfdom ended. Positive views of peasants and workers in Denmark date back to at least the 18th century with Ludvig Holberg's 1741 international best seller, *Niels Klim's Journey Underground*, which advocates for a free and educated peasantry. In the novel's subterranean utopia, respect is paid to those who contributed most to society and prior laws favoring the elevation of certain classes are revoked as contrary to "the general interest" (Holberg 1845, loc 446). Holberg gives his fortune to the Sorø Academy, which then hires Holberg's students, such as Jens Schelderup Sneedorff, who writes passionately about peasants (Larsen et al. 2013: 54–69). Adam Oehlenschlager's famous play, *Hakon Jarl*, expresses similar views about class. The evil Hakon deeply offends Scandinavian sensibilities in preferring to rely on slaves rather than on his own people (Oehlenschläger 1840: 105). When Hakon tries to seize the throne, peasants stage an uprising and meet at the Thing to choose an alternative king (113, 170). In Bernhard Severin Ingemann's heroic stories

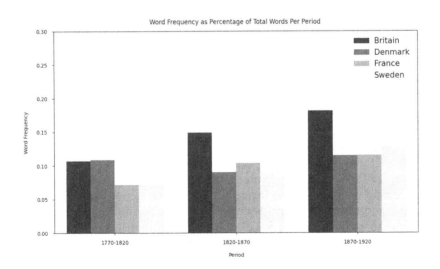

Figure 5.1 Labour references in entire corpora.

Labor words include: work, worker, guild, craftsman, journeyman, apprentice, farmer, peasant, serf, mechanic, labour.

about the Danish middle ages, the people constitute the power in those "days of departed glory ... If it [the power] flashes not from many thousand eyes united, and pours not forth from every heart in Denmark, the greatest king in the universe cannot ... restore to the people the lofty spirit of our ancestors" (Ingemann 1913, loc 7602). Nikolaj Frederik Severin Grundtvig (poet, priest and scholar of Nordic mythology) believes that the folk constitute a historical body unified by spiritual unity and a common language, and he builds on conceptions appearing in the ancient Nordic myths. Social solidarity is central to this conception of the organic society, but Grundtvig also views some equality as necessary to the unity of the people, as expressed in the stanza:

"Far more of those metals so white and so red
Find others by digging and selling
We Danes though can point to everyday's bread
In even the lowliest dwelling –
Can boast that in riches our progress is such
That few have too little, still fewer too much"
(Lindhardt, p. 27.)

British Victorian novelists are famously sympathetic to the tribulations of the working class; however, they stop short of envisioning workers as contributing to the well-being of society. Thomas Malthus sets the stage for this interpretation with his *An Essay on the Principle of Population* (1797) that provides a logic for viewing the poor in negative terms and for blaming the victims. Population will increase with a rise in the means of subsistence, unless population growth is limited by checks such as moral restraint (late marriage), vice (prostitution) and misery (starvation) (Malthus 1809: 27-8).

Although critics denounce Malthusian pessimism, the right and left converge on concerns about overpopulation and excessive reproduction among the lower classes (Steinlight 2018). Writers such as Dickens, Bronte and Gaskell help to foster a view of the working class as suffering from a culture of poverty, even while they are highly critical of social injustice. Their works highlight the suffering of women and children – often at the hands of drunken, destitute men – and these invoke sentiments of charity rather thoughts about working class contributions to society (Guy 1996; Poovey 1995: 57). Charles Dickens, writes *A Christmas Carol* to attack the Second Children's Employment Commission report and tells the leading author of the report, Southwood Smith, that his book will have "twenty thousands time the force" of a pamphlet on the issue (Henderson 2000: 140–143). Elizabeth Gaskell (22) with *Mary Barton* similarly expresses sympathy for "the weaver, who thinks he and his fellows are the real makers of this wealth, is struggling on for bread for his children, through the vicissitudes of lowered wages, short hours." Gaskell believed that it is the job of reform-oriented bureaucrat James Kay-Shuttleworth's and essayist Thomas Carlyle's to research objective conditions; her role is to teach people sympathy rather than political economy (Pollard 1965: 34–41). In *The Netherworld,* George Gissing stresses the cruelty of the urban poor: "Clem's brutality [and] ... lust of hers for sanguinary domination was the natural enough issue of the brutalizing serfdom of her predecessors in the family line" (Gissing 1889; Loc 95). Socialist HG Wells fears cultural degradation associated with mass culture and describes the "extravagant swarm of new births" as the "essential disaster of the 19th century" (Wells 1934; Carey 1992: 1).

Skills

Figure 5.2 demonstrates that in passages referring to working class people, labor snippets in coordinated Denmark and Sweden include significantly more references to skills than do British and French snippets. These findings appear in bas relief when comparing Danish and British writing about labor. Danish authors consider industrialization to be an important collective project and seek expanded mass education of workers to meet the collective goals of building society, national strength and economic prosperity. They depict advances in agricultural and industrial productivity as a national project, and workers' skills becomes an issue of national security. Grundtvig believes that peasants should be both literate and educated about Danish history in order to participate fully in Danish society: they are the

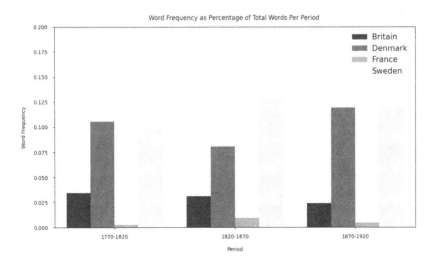

Figure 5.2 References to skills in labour snippets.

Skills words include: skill, ability, competency, proficiency, qualification.

"workmen of the sun" (Grundtvig 1968). In *Montanus den Yngre*, Thomasine Gyllembourg (1837; 2019) links social solidarity, education, economic productivity and a positive industrialization project to cope with the 1818 to 1828 depression. Conrad is brash, inconsiderate and disruptive to social harmony, but he has great ideas; for example, he recognizes that unemployment can develop with mechanization but he argued that expanded production will increase employment (loc 696). Conrad insults a bureaucrat, but the civil servant still offers Conrad a state subsidy for the factory because "I honor my land's well-being, and such a factory I hope will become a great gift for the land" (loc 2028). The book describes Conrad's personal growth and offers a blueprint for how Denmark as a society may integrate new technology, preserve social harmony, avoid harm to redundant workers and espouse a national project for economic growth.

In contrast, British novelists make few references to workers' skills. Education and skill-building is an individualistic affair to further self-development rather than an investment for building a strong society. Matthew Arnold explains, "The best man is he who most tries to perfect himself, and the happiest man is he who most feels that he is perfecting himself" (Arnold 1867–1868: 46). Coleridge warns that "a man ... unblest with a liberal education, should act without attention to the habits, and feelings, of his fellow citizens"; education would "stimulate the heart to love" (Coleridge 1796, #IV.) John Stuart Mill (1829) posits education as *the* mechanism for the cognitive and moral development of the (primarily upper and middle class) individual.

Cooperation/Coordination

Figure 5.3 reports frequencies of cooperation/corporatism words in snippets of text surrounding labor. As predicted, Denmark and Sweden have significantly higher levels of references than Britain and France to cooperation/coordination words with one important exception. Cooperation words drop in Sweden during 1820 to 1870, a period of significant class conflict. This finding gives credence to labor power theories about the rise of the working class in Sweden (Korpi 1980; Stephens 1979) and suggests that the labor mobilization in Denmark and Sweden took quite different routes (Anthonsen and Lindvall 2009; Knudsen and Rothstein 1994).

Danish and British literature offers clear differences on coordination and cooperation; indeed, Danish works are replete with narratives stressing cooperation. Hermann Drachmann's "There once was," the most performed play in Danish history, ends with a song, "We love our land," that is still sung every year on the summer solstice to reinforce community and collective identity (Frederiksen 2020: 6). The third stanza emphasizes Denmark's love of peace and commitment to defending the country against external enemies and internal discontent:

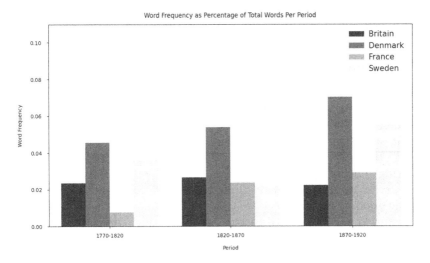

Figure 5.3 References to coordination in labour snippets.

Coordination words include: agreement, arbitration, bargaining, coalition, collaboration, collective, compromise, cooperation, coordination, negotiation, pact, settlement, unanimous, unity, confederation, federation and union.

Each town has its witch and each parish its troll,
We keep them from life with joy that we hold,
We will have peace here in this land, Saint Hans, Saint Hans,
Peace can we win if hearts never be cold
            (Drachmann 1902: 121; translated by C.J. Martin.)

Danish authors express sympathy with unions, farmers' organizations and other cooperative institutions. For example, in *Lucky Per*, Henrik Pontoppidan (winner of the Nobel prize) decries the collateral damage imposed by industrialization on workers, and views favorably unions, education and social protection as the best way to compensate for expanding industrial risk. Protagonist Per admires workers and their collective spirit: "It struck him what a fresh and active sympathy the workmen manifested from the beginning, although most came out of Copenhagen's lower classes ... They did not quarrel with anyone and were held together by mutual respect" (Pontoppidan 2019: 480). Per's fiancé, Jacobe, notes a growing interest in "different labor movements that had such close ties with modern technical development ... She had felt insecure in the face of these grumbling millions of workers whose demands often seemed to endanger all that she most treasured in life. But ... she had now arrived at some clarity about these dark, reluctant feelings of alliance with the sooty, subjugated army of workers craving light, air, and humane treatment: the 20th century men" (Pontoppidan 2019: 199–200).

British authors believe that labor relations are inherently conflictual. Even those sympathetic to the plight of labor hold no great hope for easy resolution to class conflict and often portray the mob as frightening. In Charlotte Bronte's *Shirley*, the eponymous heroine has sympathy for the poor but would battle their rampage: "Let me listen to Mercy as long as she is near me. Her voice once drowned by the shout of ruffian defiance, and I shall be full of impulses to resist and quell" (Bronte 1907: 224). The author has sympathy for the novel's starving, unemployed Luddites; yet, they are *not* portrayed as foot soldiers in an agricultural revolution who will contribute to the economic good of the country.

Victorian novelists also mistrust unions, which they view as unreasonable and geared toward self-interest. In *North and South*, Gaskell draws unions as fatally-flawed institutions that contribute to workers' misery: John Boucher notes about organized labor that "Yo' may be kind hearts, each separate; but once banded together, yo've no more pity for a man than a wild hunger-maddened wolf" (Gaskell 180). Upon Boucher's death, the novel's heroine laments, "Don't you see how you've made Boucher what he is, by driving him into the Union against his will" (Gaskell 336). British novelists doubt that workers will ever support technological innovation. In Bronte's *Shirley*, the Luddite "sufferers hated the machines which they believed took their bread from them; they hated the buildings which contained those machines; they hated the manufacturers who owned those buildings" (Bronte 1907: 26–27).

State

Figure 5.4 reports findings for the frequency of government words. As predicted, Denmark and Sweden have significantly higher frequencies of words associated with government than do Britain and France, except for Sweden in the middle of the 19th century. The frequencies of government words decline in late 19th-century Denmark, as industrial self-regulation becomes a central aspect of the Danish model; however, the Danish level remains higher than that of Britain and France.

These findings resonate in fictional narratives. British authors doubt government's capacity to ameliorate social ills. Dickens ridicules self-interest in the legal system: *David Copperfield's* Mr. Spenlow remarks, "the best sort of professional business ... [is] a good case of a disputed will ... [with] very pretty pickings" (366). William Morris – a pillar of the

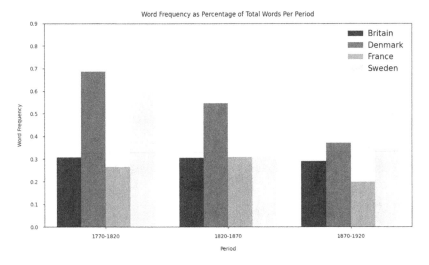

Figure 5.4 References to state in labour snippets.

Government words include: nation government, ministry, authority, law, legal, illegal, judgment, judge, council, commission, committee, public municipality, parish king, kingdom, crown, throne.

Democratic Socialist Federation and later the Socialist League – is deeply sympathetic to workers, yet in his utopian novel, *News from Nowhere*, all institutions (states *and* markets) disappear. A guest from the past is told that the "whole people is our Parliament" (Morris 1890: 72).

Danish authors offer a positive view of government that is grounded in the will of the people. Ingemann reflects on state authority: "The mere external domination, which has not its roots in the deepest heart of the people, is worthless and despicable" (Ingemann 1913: 8264). Writers recognize that government serves a positive role in promoting industrial projects, as when the protagonist in Lucky Per develops an ingenuous plan for a waterway to capture power from waves and wind that is greeted with great interest by local authorities and investors. (Per's own flawed personality and attention deficit disorder make him abandon the project, but the idea itself is sound) (Pontoppidan 2019). Government interventions help to offset corruption. For example, Jacob Knudsen in *The Old Priest* describes the corruption entailed in a private effort to build a new folk high school; the corrupt cabal designing the project is "almost unregulated, in any case erratic – also in a moral sense" and external regulation and oversight is necessary to stop private abuse of power (Knudsen 1901: 29).

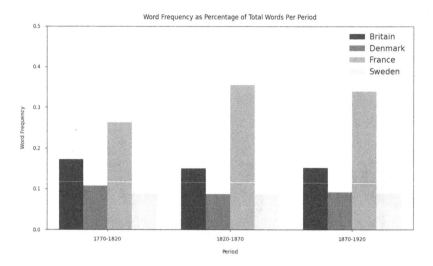

Figure 5.5 References to markets in labour snippets.

Market words include: market, sell, buy, exchange, supply, demand, price, cost, trade, commerce.

Market

Figure 5.5 reports findings for the frequency of words associated with markets. As predicted, the liberal countries have higher frequencies of market words in labor snippets than do the coordinated countries. The French words may be somewhat elevated due to the inclusion of the word "demande," which connotes the opposite of supply in labor markets and a question word. British novelists such as Dickens and Eliot view the market as damaging but necessary, and they seek private charity to offset market devastation. In contrast, charitable appeals to rescue the poor are largely missing from Danish works; rather the poor seek their own cultural development. In H.C. Andersen's *Only a Fiddler*, Christian's kind landlady read books from the local lending library to follow "the advance of literature as well as she could in a provincial town" and wonders "why should not poverty enjoy the advantage?" (Andersen 1908: 117-8).

Conclusion

This chapter demonstrates that British and Danish authors depict the working class in entirely different ways in the 18th, 19th and early 20th century. Cultural expectations about labor relations have deep historical roots, and cultural narratives provide a context for the emergence of industrial relations systems. Danish authors view labor as essential to the nationalizing and industrializing projects and, with their stories, they draw connections between workforce skills development and the socio-economic well-being of the country. British authors write tales that pluck at our heartstrings about destitute members of the working class that suffer greatly from social ills; however, these stories do not posit workers as critical players in national economic and social development. It is stunning how much authors on both the right and left converge in their view of farmers and workers as valued contributors to the strength of the Danish nation and to its economic and political ambitions. This perspective differs dramatically from the British view that the working classes – with their propensity toward over-breeding and cultural corruption – constitute a threat to British well-being.

An analysis of cultural work is not meant to diminish other factors driving the evolution of industrial relations systems. Certainly, working class power and the willingness of employers to agree to negotiated settlements matter to the emergence of employers' organizations and institutions for industrial relations (Huber and Stephens 2001; Paster 2012; Swenson 2002). Moreover, the political rules of the game and party structures have an impact on political choices made in the evolution of labor and social policies (Cusack et al. 2007; Huber et al. 1993; Kitschelt 1992; Martin and Swank 2008, 2012).

Yet workers and employers do not calculate their interests in a cultural vacuum. Stories about the essential role played by labor in national projects undoubtedly ease the willingness to make social investments in the working class. Authors reinforce the view that a strong and educated peasantry and working class is essential to cultivating useful citizens for nation-building and industrializing projects. Moreover, while it is beyond the scope of this paper, in other work I record the extensive interactions between authors and other class actors in political movements to develop skills-training systems (Martin, in preparation).[2] To the extent that cultural symbols and narratives provide context for the expression of business and labor preferences, this work has bearing on our understanding of the construction of social class and the institutional evolution of employment relations.

Understanding how industrial relations systems develop can help us to anticipate how these may fare in the future, as cooperative arrangements struggle with the exorbitant vagaries of the 21st century. Some believe that the era of coordination and managed capitalism has passed (Baccaro and Howell 2017; Streeck 2016). Other argue that coordinated countries will continue to maintain their cooperative practices of the past, even if these practices take different forms in the new capitalist era (Emmenegger et al. 2012; Iversen and Soskice 2019; Martin and Swank 2012; Thelen 2004; Traxler 2004). The endurance of models depends on whether preferences for coordination continue under conditions of rapidly changing modes of economic production (Schulze-Cleven and Weishaupt 2015). If cultural expectations sustain investments in the working class, then coordinated countries should be more likely than liberal ones to maintain social solidarity against the ravages of the post-industrial age.

Notes

1 The author thanks for their generous funding the National Endowment for the Humanities (Grant #20200128124651855), Boston University Hariri Institute (Research Award #2016-03-008), and Boston University Center for the Humanities. She is also grateful to Ben Getschell and Andrei Lapets for their programming assistance and to HathiTrust and Arkiv af Dansk Litteratur for files. She also thanks for their thoughtful comments Leon Gooberman, Marco Hauptmeier, Edmund Heery, Martin Bæk Christensen, Vivien Schmidt, Christian Lyhne Ibsen, Michele Lamont, Lyn Spillman, Patrick Emmenegger and Klaus Petersen.
2 For example, Julius Schiøtt, the secretary of the Industrial Federation (Industriforeningen) was a former student leader and close associate with the modernist authors in the faction entitled the Literary Left. Schiøtt organized meetings in the federation to study the contribution of skills development and school reform to economic competitiveness (Nørr 1979: 204–205).

References

Altick, R. (1986). Nineteenth-century English best-sellers. *Studies in Bibliography*, 39: 235–241.

Amable, B. (2003). *The Diversity of Modern Capitalism*. Oxford, UK: Oxford University Press.

Andersen, H. C. (1908). *Only a Fiddler*. Boston, MA: Houghton Mifflin.

Anthonsen, M. and Lindvall, J. (2009). Party competition and the resilience of corporatism. *Government and Opposition*, 44 (2): 167–187. 10.1111/j.1477-7053.2009.01281.x

Archer, M. S. (1979). *Social Origins of Educational Systems*. London: Sage Publications.

Arnold, M. (1867–1868). Culture and Anarchy. http://public-library.uk/ebooks/25/79.pdf

Baccaro, L. and Howell, C. (2017). *Trajectories of Neoliberal Transformation: European Industrial Relations since the 1970s*. Cambridge: Cambridge University Press.

Ban, C. (2016). *Ruling Ideas*. Oxford: Oxford University Press.

Beckert, J. and Bronk, R. (2018). Introduction. In: J. Beckert and R. Bronk (eds). *Uncertain Futures: Imaginaries, Narratives and Calculation in the Economy*. New York: Oxford University Press, pp. 1–38.

Blyth, M. (2002). *Great Transformations: Economic Ideas and Institutional Change in the Twentieth Century*. Cambridge: Cambridge University Press.

Bonikowski, B. and Gidron, N. (2016). The populist style in American politics. *Social Forces*, 94 (4 June): 1593–1621. 10.1093/sf/sov120

Bronte, C. (1907). *Shirley*. T. Nelson & Sons. Kindle version.

Carey, J. (1992). *The Intellectuals and the Masses: Pride and Prejudice amongst the Literary Intelligentsia, 1880-1939*. London: Faber & Faber.

Carstensen, M. B. and Vivien S. (2016). Power through, over and in ideas: Conceptualizing ideational power in discursive institutionalism. *Journal of European Public Policy*, 23(3): 318–337.10.1080/13501763.2015.1115534

Clegg, H. A. (1979). *The Changing System of Industrial Relations in Great Britain*. Oxford: Basil Blackwell.

Coleridge, S. T. (1796). *That All May Know the Truth; and that the Truth May Make Us Free*. The Watchman IV.

Crouch, C. (1993). *Industrial Relations and European State Traditions*. Oxford: Oxford University Press.

Cusack, T., Iversen, T. and Soskice, D. (2007). Economic interests and the origins of electoral systems. *The American Political Science Review*, 101 (3): 373–391. 10.1017/S0003055407070384

Deeg, R. and G. Jackson. (2007). Towards a more dynamic theory of capitalist diversity. *Socio-Economic Review*, 5(1): 149–180. 10.1093/ser/mwl021

Dickens, C. (1850). *David Copperfield*. E-book of classic edition.

DiMaggio, P. and Markus, H. (2010). Culture and social psychology: converging perspectives. *Social Psychology Quarterly*, 73 (4): 347–352. 10.1177%2F01 90272510389010

Dobbin, F. (1994). *Forging Industrial Policy*. New York, NY: Cambridge University Press.

Drachmann H. (1902). *Der Var Engang* [There Once Was]. Copenhagen: Gyldendalske Boghandels Forlag.

Edling, N., Petersen, J. H. and Petersen, K. (2014). Social policy language in Denmark and Sweden. In: D. Béland and K. Petersen (eds.) *Analyzing Social Policy Language*. Bristol: Policy Press, pp. 13–34.

Emmenegger, P., Hausermann, S., Palier, B. and Seeleib-Kaiserm M. (2012). *The Age of Dualization*. Oxford: Oxford University Press.

Estevez-Abe, M., Iversen, T. and Soskice, D. (2001). Social protection and the formation of skills: A reinterpretation of the welfare state. In: P. A. Hall and D. Soskice (ed.) *Varieties of Capitalism: The Institutional Foundations of Comparative Advantage*. Oxford: Oxford University Press, pp. 145–183.

Ewick, P. and Silbey, S. (2003). Narrating social structure: stories of resistance to legal authority. *American Journal of Sociology*, 108 (6): 1328–1372. 10.1086/378035

Frederiksen, Kurt L. (2020). *Holger Drachmann: Vi vil fred her til lands. En biografi*. Copenhagen: Gyldendal.

Galenson, W. (1952). *The Danish System of Labor Relations: A Study in Industrial Peace*. Cambridge: Cambridge University Press.

Gaskell (2012). *Mary Barton*. Ware, UK: Wordsworth Classic.

Gissing, G. (1889). *The Essential George Gissing*. Halcyon Classics Series. Kindle.

Grant, W. and Marsh, D. (1977). *The Confederation of British Industry*. London: Hodder and Stoughton.

Griswold, W. and Wright, N. (2004). Cowbirds, locals, and the dynamic endurance of regionalism. *American Journal of Sociology*, 109 (6): 1411–1451. 10.1086/381773

Grundtvig, N. F. S. (1968). Skolen for Livet og akademiet i Soer. In: K. E. Bugge (ed.) *Grundtvigs skoleverden i tekster og udkast*. Gads Forlag: Kobenhavn.

Guy, J. (1996). *The Victorian Social-Problem Novel*. London: MacMillan Press.

Gyllembourg, T. (2019). *Montanus den Yngre*. Lindhardt og Ringhof Forlag.

Hall, P. A. (1993). Policy paradigms, social learning, and the state: the case of economic policymaking in Britain. *Comparative Politics*, 25 (3): 275–296. 10.2307/422246

Hall, P. A. and Soskice, D. (2001). *Varieties of Capitalism: The Institutional Advantages of Comparative Advantage*. Oxford: Oxford University Press.

Hauptmeier, M. and Heery, E. (2014). Ideas at work. *International Journal of Human Resource Management*, 25 (18): 2473–2488. 10.1080/09585192. 2014.936235

Henderson, J. P. (2000). "Political economy is a mere skeleton unless … " what can social economists learn from Charles Dickens? *Review of Social Economy*, 58 (2): 141–151. 10.1080/003467600402512

Holberg, L. (1845). *Niels Klim's Journey Under the Ground*, trans. John Gierlow. Boston, Mass.: Saxton, Peirce & Co.

Hopkins, D. J. and King, G. (2010). A method of automated nonparametric content analysis for social science. *American Journal of Political Science*, 54 (1): 229–247. 10.1111/j.1540-5907.2009.00428.x

Huber, E., Ragin, C. and Stephens, J. D. (1993). Social democracy, Christian democracy, constitutional structure and the welfare state. *American Journal of Sociology*, 99(3): 711–749. 10.1086/230321

Huber, E. and Stephens, J. (2001). *Development and Crisis of the Welfare State*. Chicago: University of Chicago Press.

Ingemann, B. S. (1913). The Childhood of King Erik Menved. In *3 Historical Novels of Denmark*. Kindle version.

Iversen, T. and Soskice, D. (2019). *Democracy and Prosperity*. Princeton: Princeton University Press.

Jameson, F. (1981). *The Political Unconscious*. Ithaca: Cornell University Press.

Kipling, R. (1928). *A Book of Words*. New York: Charles Scribner's Sons.

Kitschelt, H. (1992). The formation of party systems in east-Central Europe. *Politics and Society*, 20 (1): 7–50. 10.1177%2F0032329292020001003

Knudsen, J. (1901). *Den Gamle Præst*. Copenhagen: The Nordic Publishing House.

Knudsen, T. and Rothstein, B. (1994). State building in Scandinavia. *Comparative Politics*, 26 (2 Jan): 203–220. 10.2307/422268

Korpi, W. (1980). Social policy and distributional conflict in the capitalist democracies. A preliminary comparative framework. *West European Politics*, 3 (3): 296–316. 10.1080/01402388008424288

Korsgaard, O. (2012). *Kampen om Folket*. Copenhagen: Gyldendal.

Lamont, M. and Thévenot. L. (2000). Introduction. In: M. Lamont and L. Thévenot (ed.) *Rethinking Comparative Cultural Sociology*. Cambridge: Cambridge University Press.

Lane, C. and Wood, G. (2009). Capitalist diversity and diversity within capitalism. *Economy and Society*, 38 (4): 531–551. 10.1080/03085140903190300

Larsen, C., Nørrog, E. and Sonne, P. (2013). *Dansk Skolehistorie: Da Skolen tog form 1780–1820*. Aarhus: Aarhus University Press.

Laver, M., Benoit, K. and Garry, J. (2003). Extracting policy positions from political texts using words as data. *American Political Science Review*, 97 (2): 311–331. 10.1017/S0003055403000698

Lindhardt, P. G. (1951). *Grundtvig*. London: SPCK.

Lipset, S. M. (1983). Radicalism or reformism. *American Political Science Association*, 77 (1 March): 1–18. 10.2307/1956008

Lipset, S. M. and Rokkan. S. (1967). Introduction. In: S. M. Lipset and S. Rokkan (eds.) *Party Systems and Voter Alignments*. New York: Free Press.

Malthus, T. (1809). *An Essay on the Principle of Population*. Washington City: Roger Chew Wrightman.

Martin, C. (2018). Imagine all the people: literature, society, and cross-national variation in education systems. *World Politics*, 70(3): 398–442. 10.1017/S0043887118000023

Martin, C. J. (1991). *Shifting the Burden*. Chicago: University of Chicago Press.

Martin, C. J. and Swank, D. (2008). The political origins of coordinated capitalism. *American Political Science Review*, 102 (2): 181–198. 10.1017/S0003 055408080155

Martin, C. J. and Swank, D. (2012). *The Political Construction of Business Interests*. Cambridge: Cambridge University Press.

Mill, J. S. (1829). Analysis of the phenomena of the human mind. https://www.gutenberg.org/files/56441/56441-h/56441-h.htm

Morgan, G. (2005). Introduction. In: G. Morgan, R. Whitley and E. Moen (eds.) *Changing Capitalisms?* Oxford: Oxford University Press, pp. 1–18.

Morgan, G. and Hauptmeier, M. (2021). The social organization of ideas in employment relations. *ILR Review*, 74(3): 773–797. 10.1177%2F001979392 0987518

Morris, W. (1890). *News from Nowhere*. Feedbooks. www.feedbooks.com. Kindle.

Nijhuis, D. O. (2013). *Labor Divided in the Postwar European Welfare State*. Cambridge: Cambridge University Press.

Nørr, E. (1979). *Det Højere skolevæsen og kirken*. Aarhus: Akademisk Forlag.

Oehlenschläger, A. (1840). *Hakon Jarl*. London: T Hookham.

Oude Nijhuis, D. (2013). *Labor Divided in the Postwar European Welfare State*. Cambridge: Cambridge University Press.

Paster, T. (2012). *The Role of Business in the Development of the Welfare State and Labor Markets in Germany: Containing Social Reforms*. London: Routledge.

Pollard, A. (1965). *Mrs. Gaskell: Novelist and Biographer*. Manchester University Press.

Polletta, F., Chen, P. C. B., Garnder, B. G. and Motes, A. (2011). The sociology of storytelling. *Annual Review of Sociology*, 37: 109–130. 10.1146/annurev-soc-081309-150106

Pontoppidan, H. (2019). *Lucky Per*. Naiomi Lebowitz (trans). New York: Random House.

Poovey, M. (1995). *Making a Social Body*. Chicago: University of Chicago Press.

Schmitter, P. (1981). Interest intermediation and regime governability in contemporary Western European and North America. In: S. Berger (ed.) *Organizing Interests in Western Europe*. New York: Cambridge University Press.

Schulze-Cleven, T. and Weishaupt, J. T. (2015). Playing normative legacies: Partisanship and employment policies in crisis-ridden Europe. *Politics & Society*, 43(2): 269–299. 10.1177%2F0032329215571291

Scott, W. (2001). *Institutions and Organizations*, 2nd ed. Thousand Oaks: Sage.

Sisson, K. (1987). *The Management of Collective Bargaining*. New York: Blackwell.

Spillman, L. (2012). Culture and economic life. In: J. Alexander, P. Smith and R. Jacobs (eds.) *Oxford Handbook of Cultural Sociology*. Oxford University Press: Oxford, pp. 157–198.

Steinlight, E. (2018). *Populating the Novel*. Ithaca: Cornell University Press.

Stråth, B. (2017). The cultural construction of equality in Norden. In: S. K. N. Bendixsen, M. Bente Bringslid, and H. Vike (eds.) *Egalitarianism in Scandinavia*. Palgrave Macmillan.

Stephens, J. (1979). *The Transition from Capitalism to Socialism*. London: Palgrave Macmillan.

Streeck, W. (1992). *Social Institutions and Economic Performance*. Beverly Hills, CA: Sage.

Streeck, W. (2016). *How will Capitalism End?* London, UK: Verso Books.

Sundberg, K. (2004). Introduction. In: K. Sundberg, T. Germundsson, and K. Hansen (eds.) *Modernisation and Tradition*. Lund: Nordic Academic Press, pp. 13–24.

Swenson, P. (2002). *Capitalists Against Markets*. New York: Oxford University Press.

Swidler, A. (1986). Culture in action. *American Sociological Review*, 51 (2): 273–286. 10.2307/2095521

Thelen, K. (2004). *How Institutions Evolve*. Cambridge: Cambridge University Press.

Thompson, E. P. (1991). *The Making of the English Working Class*. London: Penguin.

Tolliday, S. and Zeitlin, J. (1991). *The Power to Manage? Employer and Industrial Relations in a Comparative-Historical Perspective*. London: Routledge.

Traxler, F. (2004). The metamorphoses of corporatism: from classical to lean patterns. *European Journal of Political Research*, 43: 571–598. 10.1111/j.14 75-6765.2004.00166.x

Unwin, G. (1966). *The Guilds and Companies of London*. London: Frank Cass.

Visser, J. and Hemerijck, A. C. (1997). *A Dutch Miracle: Job Growth, Welfare Reform and Corporatism in the Netherlands*. Amsterdam: Amsterdam University Press

Wells, H. G. (1934). *Experiment in Autobiography*, vol. 1. New York: Macmillan.

Williams, R. (1963). *Culture and Society*. New York: Columbia University Press.

Wilson, G. (1990). *Business and Politics*. Chatham, NJ: Chatham House.

Windmuller, J. and Gladstone. A. (1984). *Employers' Associations and Industrial Relations*. Oxford: Oxford University Press.

Part II

Employers' Organizations in Different Types of Capitalism

6 Employers' Organizations in China: Transmission Belt between Members and State

Judith Shuqin Zhu

Introduction

Employers' Organizations/Associations (hereafter referred to as Employers' Organizations or EOs) are organizations established to pursue employers' collective interests in issues concerning the employment relationship (Windmuller 1984). They are generally voluntarily formed and independently represent employers' interests. Employers mobilize to countervail threats from interventionist states, trade unions and other stakeholders which may encroach on their interests. However, industrial relations (IR) literature on EOs is dominated by studies on employer coordination in developed democracies where citizens are normally given the power to shape government policy decisions, and EOs are valuable means of participation for employers to collectively exercise their power in governance. Little is known about EOs and employer coordination activities in non-democratic contexts, where states reject these modes of democratic participation and where plural interests are not well recognized. This chapter aims to narrow this knowledge gap by analysing EOs in a non-democratic country, China.

Until recently, the study of EOs in China has received very little scholarly attention. As a result, knowledge about EOs in China and employer associative behaviours is incomplete. To extend our understanding of employer coordination in China, the analysis presented in this chapter draws on insights from available literature and empirical data collected from an overarching research programme on employer coordination in China, which involved three field study trips to China between 2009 and 2019. Empirical data include interview data and documents collected from the China Enterprise Confederation (CEC) and All-China Federation of Industry and Commerce (ACFIC) at national and local levels, member firms of these associations and labour authority. In total, 29 interviews were undertaken with officials from 2 EOs and relevant officials from government departments responsible for labour relations issues, and 56 enterprise managers were interviewed. The triangulation of data was undertaken to enhance the validity of findings reported here.

DOI: 10.4324/9781003104575-8

Armed with rich data, this study argues that EOs in China differ from voluntary and independent EOs in democratic societies. EOs in China play a dual role of a party-state assistant and a representative of employers' interests with the relationship with, and interests of, the state being prioritized. EOs function primarily as a transmission belt between state and members. In their top-down transmission, they communicate state laws, regulations, directives, policy guidance etc. to members. In their bottom-up transmission, they convey members' views, interests, positions and problems to the state. EOs' transmission belt function is realized through EOs' close connection with the state as well as a range of activities undertaken by these EOs.

This chapter begins with a discussion of the literature on EOs' formation, functions and activities in democratic societies. It then discusses the relationship between business associations and the state in non-democratic societies. This is followed by an analysis of EOs' origins, roles, and activities in China.

EOs in Democratic Societies: Formation, Functions, and Activities

The IR literature on employer coordination concentrates on developed democracies. Traditionally, EOs are understood to be independent organizations formed by employers. There are two types of EOs: "pure" associations that specialize exclusively in helping employers manage human resource management (HRM) – IR activities, and "mixed" bodies that assist with both labour market and other business interests (Traxler 2008). EOs are normally formed by employers to contain union power, to respond to and shape state regulations and policies, to take wages out of competition, and to offer services that are either impossible or too costly for single firms to generate themselves (Jackson and Sisson 1976; Plowman 1989; Schmitter and Streeck 1999; Windmuller 1984). In the last three decades, the decentralization of employment relations and declining trade union power in most OECD countries have reduced employers' need for their collective bodies to countervail trade unions and involve in collective bargaining. This has triggered scholars to re-examine why and how EOs mobilize to pursue their collective interests in employment relationship issues. Some scholars argue that in such de-centralized IR regimes, employers will be motivated to mobilize in ways that enable them to countervail employee power by taking direct action and/or by inducing the state to weaken labour's capacity to bargain (Barry and Wilkinson 2011). Recently, scholars have added one more reason for employers to mobilize: to countervail the pressures from non-government/civil society organizations campaigning for improving working conditions and social outcomes for workers (Gooberman et al. 2019). In doing so, these authors have extended the concept of EOs, including employer collective bodies which do not bargain with trade unions but still actively represent employers' interests in front of other institutional actors and address employers' needs in work and employment related issues.

HRM-IR scholars have generated significant insights that help clarify why firms might join and form EOs. In so doing, scholars have identified EOs' functions and activities as including:

1 political lobbying of government;
2 public and media relations;
3 provision of forums for discussion, debate and networking;
4 collective negotiation with trade unions;
5 advocacy before tribunals and courts;
6 provision of assistance to individual members engaged in disputes;
7 limiting competition between employers for labour;
8 HRM – IR training;
9 provision of specialized services as well as legal and bargaining advice.

(Plowman 1978; Sheldon and Thornthwaite 2005;
Traxler 2008; Windmuller 1984)

In general, EOs' activities can be categorized as either interest representation or service provision (Traxler 2008). With declining trade union power and collective bargaining arrangements in recent decades, states in many developed democracies began to more comprehensively regulate employment and develop a greater focus on individual employment rights legislation. Key interventions include the introduction of minimum wage laws, minimum working standards, health and safety regulation, work related social benefits, equal employment opportunity laws and workers' participation rights (Gooberman et al. 2019). Consequently, employers' need to defend managerial prerogative and countervail state encroachment increased. EOs in many OECD countries have also accorded greater attention to political lobbying and the provision of specialist services than before (Silvia and Schroeder 2007; Traxler 2008). In some cases, EOs have shifted their focus from collective bargaining to lobbying, services, legal support, and training (Gooberman et al. 2019).

State and Business Relations in Non-democratic Societies

It is easy to understand why employers mobilize, given EOs' functions in a democratic society where citizens are given the power to shape government decisions about what interests should be prioritized. When actors favour policies and practices that employers deem unacceptable, employers may mobilize to form a common front to countervail threats from those actors and exert pressure on the state. One example is US business associations' successful lobbying campaign against the perceived threat to business interests from various social actors (Waterhouse 2009). However, in non-democratic societies where states are prone to reject democratic participation in governance, and where a plurality of views and interests are not well recognized, what is the role of EOs and what are their functions and activities? Our current understanding of these questions is limited.

Nevertheless, insights from the broad literature on business associations in societies with authoritarian political regimes casts some light on the character of these EOs, whereby they are a subgroup of business associations which focus on employers' labour market interests and their needs in work and employment issues. Some literature suggests that state actors' political strategies may lead to the formation of EOs. For example, when researching business associations in Russia, Markus (2007) notes that political actors encouraged business to organize to overcome state bureaucrats or to broaden the sources of expertise that can be tapped into by the state. Similarly, Foster (2001) argues that in the context of an authoritarian state, the design of an incorporated business association system or consultative structure may be underpinned by a mix of political goals (e.g. exerting control over society and hedging against political threats) and functional goals concerning economic and social development. Meanwhile, the relative importance of state goals affects the functioning of the associations and membership benefits as where, for example, the state focuses on economic development, incorporated business associations "play a role in the exchange of information, the coordination of policy, and the implementation of policy measures (such as the granting of subsidies to firms) designed to foster business success" (Foster 2001: 91). More recently, Nguyen (2014) studied voluntarily formed business associations in Vietnam. She argues that such associations play a crucial intermediatory role between the state and private business, and that they coalesce with bureaucratic interests in exchange for the state's accommodation. Together, these findings reveal the dominance of the state in state-civil society relationships within authoritarian states, and the possibility for civil society groups to advance their constituents' interests through deliberative engagement with the state which needs the assistance of these civil society groups to govern effectively.

In the Chinese context, scholars commonly accept that the Chinese Communist Party (CCP) is committed to a 'Market-Leninist' system and state corporatist arrangement, allowing sectoral interest organizations to mobilize under state dominance (Gilley 2011; Unger and Chan 2015; Zhang 2008). The state recognizes only one selected association as the sole interest representative of a sector. Borrowing from the Russian Leninist model which assumes a harmony of interests in a socialist state and all actors uniting to work towards the prosperity of socialism, the

CCP led government has framed these chosen sector agencies as transmission belts between their constituencies and the government, endowing them with dual roles: a government assistant and an interest representative for their constituencies. In the field of IR, the All-China Federation of Trade Union (ACFTU) was assigned to represent workers while, until 2011, the CEC was the only legitimate representative for employers (see Zhu and Nyland 2017 for an analysis of the reasons for two formal EOs). Both trade unions and EOs also act as a government assistant by helping the party-state to achieve its economic and political goals. This institutional arrangement artificially removes conflict of interests between trade unions and EOs. This, in conjunction with the political ideology of workers as the leading class and state domination in the polity (Gilley 2011), has effectively eliminated the need for EOs to countervail trade unions while accentuating the importance of their transmission belt function.

EOs in China: Formation, Roles and Activities

EOs' Formation

Both the CEC and the ACFIC were formed by the party-state. The CEC was established by the party-state in 1978 because of its decision to join the International Labour Organization (ILO) and embrace market-oriented reform. The former initiative gave rise to the need for a Chinese employer representative at the ILO while the latter led to the need to fill the institutional gap between the state and business owners/managers created by the deregulation of economic activities. Upon its establishment, the CEC was charged with assisting state-owned firms to improve the quality of their management, providing representation for China's employers at ILO conferences, and acting as a communication bridge between government and enterprise managers (CEC 2008). This agenda was expanded subsequently with the CEC being instructed to represent employers in domestic tripartite institutions when China introduced a form of ILO's tripartism in IR in the early 2000s.

In the case of the ACFIC, it was established in 1953, a few years after the CCP party-state took power and established new China. The party-state established the ACFIC to incorporate all trade and industry associations inherited from the pre-1949 period. When China initiated economic reform in 1978, the ACFIC became the sole legitimate representative of private business. In 2011, the ACFIC successfully requested to the government that it should act as a representative of private employers within IR. Now, the ACFIC is a second legitimate employer representative in China, with private business employers being its major constituents and a fourth player in China's IR tripartite system. The ACFIC has taken up the role of employer representative for non-public economic sectors and the

CEC is expected to primarily represent state-owned enterprises. As can be seen from EOs' origin in China, they are not autonomous associations formed voluntarily by employers.

EOs' Roles

Both the ACFIC and the CEC freely acknowledge that they play dual roles, as government assistant and employers' representative, acting as a transmission belt between the government and their members. In its charter, the ACFIC defines its role as "an assistant to the government in managing and serving the non-public economy" (ACFIC 2020). Similarly, the CEC states that it is an appendix of the party-state, acting as a bridge and link between the government and enterprises (CEC 2020; Zhu and Nyland 2017). Although interviewees from both EOs avowed that they strove to serve members' interests, they admitted that if employer needs conflicted with the wishes of the state, they invariably supported the latter. This is because the existence and survival of EOs will be jeopardized if they challenge the state. Further, as explained by an EO official in our interview: "We are not that kind of organization whose survival depends upon its ability to speak for its members".

These role prescriptions and priorities of EOs in China can be explained by the tight control the party-state exercised over the CEC and the ACFIC. Structurally, both the CEC and the ACFIC are integrated into the government administration system, with the ACFIC being under the United Front Work Department of the CCP Central Committee while the CEC is under the supervision of the state-owned Assets Supervision and Administration Commission which is directly under the state council. As an organization, both the ACFIC and the CEC have branches/affiliates at province, municipal, city and county levels, paralleling with government administration at different levels. Government influenced not only the building up of these two EOs' branches at different administrative levels but also their recruitment activities when they were created. The government was instrumental in establishing the ACFIC's branches at different levels of the administration system and instructed voluntary trade and industry associations to be members of the ACFIC in the early 1950s. As for the CEC, when it was created China's Economic and Trade Commission instructed all state-owned enterprises to join and local governments to establish regional enterprise associations as affiliated members to the CEC. Subsequently, the government ordered major industrial and trade associations and societal actors such as the China Young Entrepreneur Association to join. The state's recruitment effort ensured that initially the CEC membership was dominated by state-owned firms. It is worth noting that currently the CEC and the ACFIC's recruitment activities emphasize inducements offered to members through their functions and activities, as discussed below.

Both EOs have limited autonomy. The ACFIC is fully controlled, staffed and financed by the party-state whereas the CEC is, at most, a semi-autonomous association. The party-state monopolizes the appointment of executive managers to these associations. Executive staff of these associations are appointed by the CCP's Organization Department at relevant administrative levels. At national level, ACFIC's chairman and deputy chairman and the CEC's president and vice presidents are decided upon by the Organization Department of the CCP Central Committee. The current ACFIC chairman is also the deputy chairman of the National Committee of the Chinese People's Political Consultative Conference, a position taken previously by the current CEC president. Financially, the party-state fully funds the ACFIC. The ACFIC's staff are categorized as public servants and are fully paid by the government. As for the CEC, the government substantially reduced the funding it provided to the CEC and withdrew active support for membership recruitment in the late 1990s. The CEC was instructed to register as a civil society body and self-fund. These steps were taken to meet ILO requirements that an EO must be an independent association of employers. To enhance the representation capacity of the CEC as an EO and to increase financial income, the CEC opened membership to firms of all types and began aggressively marketing itself to employers in the booming private business sector and expanding its service provisions. This led to fundamental changes in the CEC's membership composition. Private firms increasingly became the major cohort of CEC members. For example, by 2009 CEC member firms in Shanghai consisted of state-owned firms (17%), domestically owned private firms (70%) and joint ventures and foreign owned firms and others (13%). Therefore, the CEC is currently more financially and organizationally independent than the ACFIC.

In brief, both the CEC and the ACFIC play dual roles, assistant to the state and representative of employers. Their role as the assistant to the state is prioritized due to tight control exercised by the party-state over these associations. However, it would be a mistake to view these associations as being alienated from employers, functioning merely as a tool for state domination of employers. As can be seen below, these associations do provide employers with benefits and opportunities generated from their close link with the party-state, which is authoritative in determining economic and IR policies, and their activities undertaken to fulfil their mandates as a transmission belt between the state and members.

EOs' Activities: A Transmission Belt between the State and Members

Both the CEC and the ACFIC act as a two-way transmission belt: top-down and bottom-up. In their top-down transmission, these EOs communicate government directives, policies, guidelines, and regulations to their members, assisting the government to mobilize employers to contribute to government's economic and social development goals. In their bottom-up transmission, the CEC and the ACFIC articulate members' interests, views, and problems to the party-state. Although EOs transmit in both directions, their top-down transmission operates more effectively than the other way around.

The CEC and the ACFIC undertake a range of activities to realize its function as a two-way transmission belt between the state and members. Some of them are ostensibly similar to those identified in the literature on EOs in developed democracies as discussed above. In reality, these activities are carried out in a fashion that is acceptable and valued within China's state corporatist system, enabling the EOs to perform either top-down or bottom-up transmission.

Top-down Transmission Activities

The ultimate objective of the top-down transmission by state corporatist associations such as the CEC and the ACFIC is goal-oriented harmony or organized consensus and cooperation from their constituencies, geared towards serving national economic and social development goals. To do so, the CEC and the ACFIC primarily rely on three mechanisms/activities: issuing policy-related directives and guidance, providing policy training and consultation, and organizing study tours and competitions. As mentioned above, both the CEC and the ACFIC are structurally and operationally linked with the state. Such embeddedness in the government administration system and EO leaders' previous career experience as government officials have led to both associations often acting like government agencies and they are perceived as government agencies (or in our interviewees' words *er zheng fu*). They are used to educate, instruct, and advise their members through issuing directives, policy guidelines and notices. An ACFIC interviewee responsible for employer work complained that he had to draft corresponding official documents such as instructions/guideline and notices whenever new IR policies were issued or new initiatives were launched, and such work claimed a large share of his time. The extent to which EOs rely on these top-down administrative measures to communicate with their members have drawn criticism from observers (Guo 2014).

Both EOs also transmit government policy guidelines to members or clarify nuances of government policies through training and consultation services. Compared to the CEC, the ACFIC is relatively weak in this regard. For example, in addition to join government labour authorities to provide free IR policy consultations, CEC organizes training programmes covering IR, HRM, and ideological and political education relating to sensitive issues arising from the economic system and enterprise reform. These programmes are normally delivered by a team consisting of full-time trainers, government officials and academics. Generally, training programmes that focus on government IR policies and practices are free. These programmes help employers interpret and better comply with government policies and regulations. They are deemed to be necessary and valuable not only because labour laws and rules are commonly written in an ambiguous manner but also because labour management is a politically sensitive issue and often needs to be discussed sotto voce.

In addition, the ACFIC and the CEC organize conferences, study tours and competitions to mobilize and incentivize employers to better contribute to national development goals. Both the CEC and ACFIC are charged with the responsibility to facilitate and diffuse innovations across firms, and with guiding enterprises to operate business with integrity and in compliance with laws and regulations. One important way for them to fulfil this mandate is to organize conferences, celebrating events such as 'Entrepreneur Day' and competitions for 'Enterprise of Excellence', or 'Entrepreneur of Excellence', 'Top 500 Enterprise in China', 'Exemplary Enterprise in Systematic Transformation', 'Enterprise Ranked for Competitiveness', and 'Non-public Economy Star Enterprises'.

Ironically, two member interest representation activities in developed democracies, collective bargaining with trade unions and representation of employers in labour tribunals, have been transformed into a type of EOs' top-down transmission activities. In these activities, EOs work in a top-down manner and act more as a government assistant in regulating IR issues than employers' interest representative countervailing trade unions. For example, in the early 1990s, China introduced an enterprise collective contract system through a bureaucratic process directed by government bodies, with the ACFIC as the major driving force. The CEC was charged with the responsibility to promote collective consultation (the Chinese equivalent of collective bargaining) and convince employers to sign collective contracts. These collective contracts are generally reproductions of officially provided model collective contracts that are prepared considering guidelines on wages, minimum labour standards and government directives (Clarke et al. 2004). They are generally signed without significant negotiation between enterprise managers and enterprise trade unions, and without EOs' participation.

It should be noted here that China's collective consultation/bargaining system has started to develop beyond the enterprise level, as regional and sectoral collective bargaining emerged (Lee et al. 2016). However, the CEC and the ACFIC are neither the driving force for this, nor the employer representatives in such bargaining. In 2003, the first multi-employer sectoral bargaining since the 1950s occurred in Xinhe town of Wenling city, and the first sectoral union, Xinhe Woollen Sweater Sectoral Union was formed. After collective bargaining between employer representatives, the autonomously formed Xinhe Woollen Sweater Trade Association and workers' representative, a collective wage agreement covering the whole sector was concluded (Wen and Lin 2015). The success achieved by this sectoral wage barging contributed to the shift of ACFTU's bargaining strategy from enterprise collective bargaining towards regional sectoral bargaining. The sectoral wage bargaining tends to happen at localities where small and medium-sized private firms are clustered geographically, with a few incidences of municipal level sectoral wage agreement as notable exceptions (Lee et al. 2016). In such regional and sectoral wage bargaining, employer representatives were either employers or sectoral industry or trade associations that were established by employers for the purpose of self-regulating intra-firm competition and industry wide wage standards.

In the case of China's labour dispute resolution system, EOs act as a neutral judge at a labour dispute tribunal, or as a government assistant in resolving collective labour disputes in a local tripartite labour dispute mediation committee (see discussion below) when such disputes cause government concerns. China's labour dispute resolution system consists of enterprise labour disputes mediation committees, local labour dispute arbitration committees and courts. At enterprise level, committees include employer representatives (normally enterprise managers), worker representatives and enterprise trade unions. The local labour dispute arbitration committee, which is administered by the local labour authority, includes representatives from the ACFTU, the CEC and the ACFIC and local labour authority. The representatives from the CEC or the ACFIC may be required to act as arbitrators when a labour dispute cannot be settled within the enterprise and thus is taken to the local labour dispute arbitration committee when it involves multiple workers. However, in such scenarios, the CEC and the ACFIC officials are not assigned the role of employer interest representative but are expected to be neutral judges. Therefore, EOs' presence in labour dispute arbitration committees is largely a formality, which only serves the function of signifying the existence of tripartite arrangements in China's labour dispute resolution process.

Bottom-up Transmission Activities

Bottom-up transmission activities are carried out to represent and serve employers' interests. Although both EOs prioritize the state's interests and goals, they also realize that the bottom-up wishes of their assigned constituencies and their ability to serve members' interests are positively associated with their own organizational interests and status within China's corporatist framework. The need for EOs to serve their members' interests was made even more evident by the CEC's loss of monopoly in employer representation due to the ACFIC's challenge on the ground that the CEC failed to effectively represent employers, especially private employers. Both EOs undertake a range of bottom-up activities. These include representing members' interests in front of the state and the public, providing specialized services, organizing forums and events for members to discuss, debate and network, and participating in tripartite consultation. As with EOs in developed democracies, their bottom-up activities can be broadly categorized into two groups: employer interest representation and service provision.

Employer Interest Representation

The CEC and the ACFIC's employer interest representation activities include representing employer interests to the party-state and to the public. In representing employers' interests to the state, both EOs have the great advantage that the government has charged the associations with acting as a communication bridge between government and enterprises. This responsibility gives them the authority required to convey to the government what employers believe constitutes 'best' IR practice. The CEC and ACFIC also assist their members by informing the state as to how firms perceive existing and proposed labour laws and regulations as well as the problems and consequences in the implementation of policies and regulations. One mechanism used to fulfil this function of lobbying and representation to the government on behalf of their members is to influence the government through its voluntary or commissioned research and policy submissions. In the case of the ACFIC, its role as a member of the China People's Political Consultative Conference under the CCP Central Committee enables it to represent the interests of non-public economy sector/private enterprises through participating in political consultation of national policies and strategies in politics, economic and social affairs.

Another mechanism that can be used by EOs to represent employers, to respond to and shape state regulations and policies is through its participation in IR tripartite consultation conferences. Parties involved in the IR tripartite system include the Ministry of Human Resources and Social Security which represents the government, the ACFTU representing workers, and the CEC and the ACFIC representing employers. At national level, the tripartite conferences focus more on framework, procedures, rulemaking, law, regulations, and policies related to labour relations. They function primarily as the venues for the three parties to analyze the impact of economic policies and social development plan on labour relations; provide advice on the formulation and implementation of laws, regulations, decrees and policies on labour relations; for the three parties to consult on problems they encountered in coordinating labour relations and to attempt to form consensus on major issues that may affect the development of labour relations. At local level, provincial, municipal, and county tripartite consultation conferences focus more on practical issues and labour relations at workplaces within the jurisdiction rather than policy formation. Provincial and municipal tripartite bodies also have the responsibility to discuss and set the minimum labour standards appropriate to local conditions.

These tripartite conferences offer a channel for the EOs to articulate their members' interests, concerns, positions and views on IR policies and regulations and thus the possibility to influence policymaking and implementation in favour of its members. It should be noted that when constructing tripartite institutions, the Chinese government embraced ILO's principle of tripartism because it encourages dependence on a top-down approach to IR (Lee et al. 2011) and a cooperative approach which entails collective debate between the state, organized workers/ ACFTU and employers/EOs (Shao et al. 2011). With the reference to ILO's tripartite consultation convention, one would expect China's tripartism in IR would improve industry democracy by giving voice, legitimacy, and autonomy to organized labour and employers. However, in reality, tripartite institutions in China are turned into authoritarian state corporatist mechanisms. The dynamics of tripartite consultation conferences reflect the power status of workers and employers in the Chinese political system, in which employers as a group or class do not have high political and social status and employers as a class have little political voice (Zhu and Nyland 2017). At tripartite conferences, it is often the case that the ACFTU actively proposes agenda items for tripartite consultation conferences to discuss. For the ACFTU, it wants to use tripartite bodies to promote collective consultation and strengthen unionization in enterprises (Shao et al. 2011). Both goals do not impose much challenge for EOs or their members due to the formalistic nature of collective consultation at enterprises, and weak enterprise unions. Government representatives dominate the decisions of the tripartite consultation conferences and act as mediator and/or, to be more exact, arbitrator for trade unions and EOs if their views diverge. In other words, the government representatives exercise most influence at the tripartite consultation conferences and the party-state has the final say about IR issues and policies. For example, although the CEC as monopoly employer association was invited to participate in tripartite debates on the new *Labour Contract Law (2008)*, few of their suggestions found a place in the final version of the law. Likewise, although the Shanghai tripartite committee initially objected to the issue of regulation on collective contracts, the Municipal People's Congress Committee insisted on formulating the regulation and the tripartite committee was simply instructed to draft the *Shanghai Municipal Labour Collective Contract Regulation,* which the state then proceeded to amend and issue (Zhu and Nyland 2017).

Service Provision

Services provided by the CEC and the ACFIC include those traditionally offered by EOs in developed democracies: information research and advice, support for individual members in disputes, and training; with network building (or what is called by Chinese EO interviewees 'platform function' *ping tai gong neng*) service as an important extension. As mentioned above, both EOs provide members with advice on labour laws, government policies and IR matters. While free information research and advice as well as training programmes form a type of top-down transmission, fee-based activities are provided on demand and tailored for each customer and thus are more oriented towards satisfying members' interests. The ACFIC's selective goods for its members focus on trade matters and target member firms' modernization, innovation, and growth (Lee et al. 2011). In comparison, the CEC are more specialized in HRM-IR related services. In general, such information research, advice and training services are not as relevant to bottom-up transmission as other services such as support for individual members in disputes and network building/platform service.

EOs transmit upward their individual members' grievances or assist them to connect upwards with government officials who can address their grievances either through their institutional connection with the government's administration system, or through personal networks. Both the CEC and the ACFIC assist employers in disputes either by providing advice or by advocating for them. These advocating or advice services are normally free of charge. The ACFIC has been very active in defending private employers, as part of the collective goods that it offers members. The CEC was also reported to have used its government channels to solve some employers' problems with labour authorities or government departments, in some cases through CEC official's personal network within the government system (e.g. Zhu and Nyland 2017). One CEC national official interviewee even shared the story of his effort in getting an unfairly convicted employer at a local level out of prison. Nevertheless, such advocating services appear to be on an ad hoc, individual basis. Comparatively, the CEC draws on its rich experience and expertise in labour relations matters to offer more extensive and specialized services to firms in labour dispute. Of all enterprises, medium, small, and privately owned firms are most likely to involve the CEC in their IR disputes. Nearly all CEC interviewees attributed this development to the fact that big firms can hire prestigious lawyers or ask government officials to solve disputes for them, while state-owned enterprises can gain help directly from government departments.

Both the ACFIC and the CEC attach great importance to the network building service. This service is the Chinese equivalent to providing a forum that enables employers to meet and debate issues related to employment issues. The network building service provided by both EOs is regarded by members as one of most valuable membership benefits. It entails the provision of venues where managers can build connections that may prove lucrative. Both EOs actively serve as a medium through which employers could meet, establish relationship with and influence government officials who can be more effective in solving their employment related issues than the EOs. These associations facilitate communication and rapport between members through organizing seminars on IR and business management issues, study tours, friendship-building parties and meetings and leisure activities such as sightseeing, tea-tasting, jade appreciation, dinner gatherings and hiking/walking. At these networking events, relationship building, business opportunity seeking and sharing of business information and experiences are major focuses for members, while debate over IR polices or employers' collective action rarely happen (Zhu and Nyland 2017). This is largely because labour relations in China have been traditionally regulated and dominated by the government so there is not much need for members to discuss such issues at meetings organized by state corporatist EOs. Moreover, for firms, especially large firms, it can be more effective to resolve IR concerns or labour disputes by leveraging their influence over government or top government officials (Zhu and Nyland 2017).

Last but not the least, the CEC and the ACFIC provide opportunities for members to promote themselves. The increased visibility of members through those promotion activities potentially endows members with more power in influencing government officials. Both EOs use their own channels such as official websites, online platforms, or publications to promote member firms' brands, products and technologies. In addition, both the CEC and ACFIC use public media to extensively promote their big employer conferences, award ceremonies, competition events and issue the outcomes of competitions. Such publicity has an effect of free advertising for participating member firms. Therefore, firms sought to participate and win prizes to enhance their influence with government officials, potential customers, and other stakeholders.

Conclusion

This chapter contributes to filling the knowledge gap about employer coordination in China by discussing the origins, roles, and activities of EOs. By so doing, it argues that within China's state corporatist system, EOs function as a transmission belt between the state and members. The chapter has shown that Chinese EOs were formed by the party-state to fulfil its needs. These EOs have dual roles in the IR arena: government assistant and employer representative, with the former being dominant. They prioritize the party-state interests over employers' interests. With the party-state dominating IR policy decisions but involving association leaders in the policy-making process through tripartite consultation mechanisms, representing, more specifically voicing, employers' interests to state is possible and bears significant value for employers. Nevertheless, the analysis of EOs' activities has revealed that their top-down transmission, communicating government policy lines to employers, outweighs bottom-up transmission, conveying employers' interests to the state. Ostensibly, Chinese EOs carry out many activities that are similar to those undertaken by their counterparts in developed democracies. However, these activities are performed in a way that is acceptable within China's state corporatist system and valuable for members. For example, their activities in the tripartite consultation and collective contract systems that are significant collective interest representation activities for EOs in developed democracies, have been transformed into a sort of top-down transmission activity. Meanwhile, EOs' network building service provided to members has the shade of bottom-up transmission, or utility value for members to push their interests upward. In sum, Chinese EOs perform their role of government assistant through a range of top-down transmitting activities. They play their role as employer interest representative by taking advantage of their corporatist association status and their close connection with the government, as well as through their various bottom-up transmission activities.

To conclude, this chapter demonstrates that Chinese EOs are not the type of EOs as depicted in classic works concentrating on democratic societies. Within China's state corporatism system, Chinese EOs serve as a transmission belt between the party-state and their members. As a two-way transmission belt, EOs' top-down transmission, communicating state positions, laws, and policies to members, takes primacy over their bottom-up transmission. It can be expected that Chinese EOs will continue to be beholden to the party-state in the near future as long as the party-state keeps its tight control over society. This is not to deny the possibility that at some future point these EOs may gradually shift in form as China's political and economic landscapes evolve. This study suggests that both EOs might become more effective in representing employers' interests. Nevertheless, even if this expectation is realized, EOs will not be allowed to have substantial autonomy and represent employer interests independently.

References

ACFIC (2020). *Introduction to the ACFIC*. All-China Federation of Industry and Commerce. http://www.acfic.org.cn/bhjj/ [accessed 5 October 2020]

Barry, M. and Wilkinson, A. (2011). Reconceptualising employer associations under evolving employment relations: Countervailing power revisited. *Work, Employment and Society*, 25 (1): 149–162. 10.1177%2F0950017010389229

CEC (2008). *The Thirty Years in the History of the China Enterprise Confederation.* Beijing: China Enterprise Confederation.

CEC (2020). *About Employer Work.* China Enterprise Confederation, viewed 5 October 2020. http://www.cec1979.org.cn/gz/about.php

Clarke, S., Lee, C. H. and Li, Q. (2004). Collective consultation and industrial relations in China. *British Journal of Industrial Relations*, 42 (2): 235–254. 10.1111/j.1467-8543.2004.00313.x

Foster, K. W. (2001). Associations in the embrace of an authoritarian state: State domination of society? *Studies in Comparative International Development*, 35 (4): 84–109. 10.1007/BF02732709

Gilley, B. (2011). Paradigms of Chinese politics: Kicking society back out, *Journal of Contemporary China*, 20 (70): 517–533. 10.1080/10670564.2011.565181

Gooberman, L., Hauptmeier, M. and Heery, E. (2019). The evolution of employers' organisations in the United Kingdom: Extending countervailing power. *Human Resource Management Journal*, 29 (1): 82–96. 10.1111/1748-8583.12193

Guo, J. (2014). *A Research on Issues Related to Strengthen and Improve the Work of the Federation of Industry and Commerce under the New Situation.* http://sttzb. shantou.gov.cn/sttzb/llwz/201402/89de0794659d4f3e8f9344958b0202b4. shtml [accessed on 10 November 2020]

Jackson, P. and Sisson, K. (1976). Employers' confederations in Sweden and the UK and the significance of industrial infrastructure. *British Journal of Industrial Relations*, 14 (3): 306–323.

Lee, C. H., Brown, W. and Wen, X. Y. (2016). What sort of collective bargaining is emerging in China? *British Journal of Industrial Relations*, 54 (1): 214–236. 10.1111/bjir.12109

Lee, C. H., Sheldon, P. and Li, Y. Q. (2011). Employer coordination and employer associations. In: P. Sheldon, S. Kim, Y. Q. Li and M. Warner (eds.) *China's Changing Workplace: Dynamism, Diversity and Disparity.* New York: Routledge, pp. 301–320.

Markus, S. (2007). Capitalists of all Russia, unite! Business mobilization under debilitated dirigisme. *Polity*, 39 (3): 277–304. 10.1057/palgrave.polity.2300083

Nguyen, T. P. (2014). Rethinking state-society relations in Vietnam: The case of business associations in Ho Chi Minh City. *Asian Studies Review*, 38 (1): 87–106. 10.1080/10357823.2013.872598

Plowman, D. (1978). Employer associations: Challenges and responses, *Journal of Industrial Relations*, 20 (3): 237–262.

Plowman, D. (1989). Countervailing power, organisational parallelism and Australian employer associations, *Australian Journal of Management*, 14 (1): 97–113. 10.1177%2F031289628901400106

Schmitter, P. and Streeck, W. (1999). *The Organization of Business Interests: Studying Associative Actions of Business in Advanced Industrial Societies.* Discussion paper 99/1. Cologne: Max Planck Institute für Gesellschaftsforschung.

Shao, S., Nyland, C. and Zhu, C. (2011). Tripartite consultation: An emergent element of employment governance in China. *Industrial Relations Journal*, 42 (4): 358–374. 10.1111/j.1468-2338.2011.00635.x

Sheldon, P. and Thornthwaite, L. (2005). Member or clients? Employer associations, the decentralisation of bargaining, and the reorientation of service provision: Evidence from Europe and Australia. In: W. J. Hausman (ed.), *Annual*

Meeting Program: Reinvention and Renewal, Annual Meeting Program: Reinvention and Renewal 2005, Minneapolis, Minnesota, USA, pp. 1–21.

Silvia, S. J. and Schroeder, W. (2007). Why are German employers associations declining? Arguments and evidence. *Comparative Political Studies,* 40 (12): 1433–1459. 10.1177%2F0010414006293444

Traxler, F. (2008). Employer organizations. In: P. Blyton, E. Heery, N. A. Bacon and J. Fiorito (eds.) *The SAGE Handbook of Industrial Relations.* London: SAGE, pp. 225–240.

Unger, J. and Chan, A. (2015). State corporatism and business associations in China. *International Journal of Emerging Markets,* 10 (2): 178–193. 10.1108/IJOEM-09-2014-0130

Waterhouse, B. C. (2009). *A Lobby for Capital: Organized Business and the Pursuit of Pro-market Politics, 1967–1986.* Cambridge, MA: Harvard University Press.

Wen, X. and Lin, K. (2015). Restructuring China's state corporatist industrial relations system: The Wenling experience, *Journal of Contemporary China,* 24 (94): 665–683. 10.1080/10670564.2014.975959

Windmuller, J. P. (1984). Employer associations in comparative perspective: Organisation, structure, administration. In: J. P. Windmuller and A. Gladstone (eds.) *Employer Associations and Industrial Relations: A Comparative Study.* Oxford: Clarendon Press, pp. 1–23.

Zhang, J. J. (2008). *Marketization and Democracy in China.* New York: Routledge.

Zhu, J. S. and Nyland, C. (2017). Chinese employer associations, institutional complementarity and countervailing power. *Work, Employment and Society,* 31 (2): 284–301. 10.1177%2F0950017016643480

7 Keeping the State out through Legitimacy: Employers' Organizations in Denmark

Christian Lyhne Ibsen and
Steen E. Navrbjerg

Introduction

In this chapter, we explain why Danish employers' organizations are still committed to collectivism and coordination in the regulation of terms and conditions of employment. We argue that Danish employers' organizations (in cooperation with unions) deliver a stable and effective system for regulating the labour market. Therefore, the Danish state accepts these organizations as a legitimate partner in maintaining and developing the welfare state. To remain legitimate, employers' organizations must be sufficiently encompassing when regulating the labour market and deliver answers to problems of the labour market and the modern welfare state. This is only possible if employers' organizations can keep trade unions close in productive bargaining relationships and if employers and trade unions represent the majority of companies and their workers (Gooberman et al. 2018; Sisson 1987).

The historical origin of employers' commitment to this model is the so-called September Compromise of 1899 that defined the main pillars of the Danish model based on principles of freedom of labour market associations and free collective bargaining. Moreover, it provided employers with extensive managerial prerogatives and a peace clause. By showing the state that the social partners were able to autonomously regulate the labour market through collective agreements, the fundamental legitimacy vis-á-vis the state was established.

This legitimacy encouraged the state at a very early stage to establish an institutional framework for collective bargaining including a highly effective conflict resolution system. The state accepted its withdrawn role in the regulation of collective bargaining, provided that the social partners delivered legitimate solutions to the most pressing labour market problems of the time: keeping industrial peace and sound wage developments.

The legitimacy of the social partners and hence their independence from the state was threatened during various 20th century crises, especially during the 1970s. However, social partners repeatedly maintained their autonomy by solving the pressing labour problems of the time, e.g.

DOI: 10.4324/9781003104575-9

wage restraint during the 1960s and 1980s, and flexibility during the 1990s and 2000s.

Legitimacy has increased with tripartite cooperation on pressing political issues ranging from occupational pensions in the 1990s over continuous education to paternity leave in the 2000s. Most recently, the social partners have been deeply involved in negotiating relief packages for industries harmed economically during the Covid-19 crisis. By taking societal responsibility, shifting governments have realized that the social partners are reliable in not only labour market regulation but also in solving major economic and welfare issues. In that way, employers' organizations and unions keep the state out of regulating wages and working conditions by staying close together.

The purpose of this chapter is to show how autonomy and cooperation foster legitimacy and thus stability in the Danish employment relations model. We do so by answering the following two questions:

1   Why does the Danish state accept such a high level of social partner autonomy in regulating the labour market?
2   Why are Danish employers' organizations still committed to collectivism and cooperation?

The chapter proceeds as follows: First, we discuss the concept of legitimacy in the context of industrial relations with a focus on the relations between employers' organizations and the state. Next, we analyze the Danish model of employment relations, as well as the employers' and unions' common vested interest in keeping the state out of essential issues in labour market regulation such as wage regulation. We do this by tracking the ability of social partners to solve major labour and welfare state problems and create legitimacy in the eyes of the state. We also show how legitimacy has decreased when social partners seemed incapable of solving major labour and welfare state problems, especially in the 1970s, and thus how autonomy and legitimacy have been tightly linked to the problem-solving capacity of social partners. Finally, we discuss the overarching perspectives of the analysis.

Legitimacy in the Context of Employment Relations

Legitimacy, in the Weberian understanding, is conformity with either formal rules or social norms (Meyer and Rowan 1977). However, this is a rather descriptive approach and the concept has been developed over the last 50 years, but quite different understandings can still be observed. Suchman (1995) identifies at least two distinct approaches: a strategic tradition in which organizations manipulate symbols to obtain societal support; and an institutional tradition in which structural dynamics generate pressure that no organization can avoid or control.

These two approaches have a likeness with a long-lasting contradictory understanding in social sciences, namely the power of the individual (or organization) vs. the power of structure (institutions). Suchman employs a general understanding of legitimacy:

Legitimacy is a generalized perception or assumption that the actions of an entity are desirable, proper, or appropriate within some socially constructed system of norms, values, beliefs, and definitions.

(Suchman 1995: 594)

However, as pointed out, there are quite different understandings on how this is obtained. In this analysis, we adhere to a strain that to some degree transcends the actor-structure controversy, namely Scharpf's (1999) understanding of legitimacy based in actor-based institutional rational choice. In Scharpf's understanding, legitimacy has three dimensions:

• Input legitimacy: The participatory process leading to rules and laws, a process ensured by institutions of representation.
• Throughput legitimacy: The processes taking place between input and output, i.e. the on-going formal and not least informal negotiations between actors.
• Output legitimacy: The ability to solve problems by means of rules and laws, with institutional mechanisms to support and implement them.

Applying these concepts to the Danish model, our argument about autonomy and legitimacy can be summarized as follows: Employers have a first-best preference for managerial prerogative in setting terms and conditions (Korpi 2006), and employers want to keep the state and unions out of its business, even when politicians have reasons to intervene. However, in political contexts where strong political parties and/or trade unions might intervene in employment relations with statutory regulation, this is hardly possible. To avoid political interference, employers will prefer corporatist policy-making and collective bargaining with strong trade unions (Martin and Swank 2012), thereby ensuring that the state views the preferences of employers (the input), collective bargaining (throughput) and the resulting collective agreements (the outcome) as conforming to general political objectives and priorities of the state (Ibsen 2015).

The ability to keep the state out of employment relations, however, depends on corporatist policy-making and collective bargaining being viewed as a legitimate alternative to legislative action by politicians. It is an ongoing process to legitimizing the employers' role in the view of the state, i.e. to show that the input and throughput lead to the output asked for by the state. If employers can realize these objectives, they would be shielded from external pressures by the state or the 'shadow of hierarchy' (Sisson 1987). If the social partners do not deliver solutions on labour market challenges, they will lose legitimacy and legislators will take over. The focus of our analysis is on legitimacy in this ongoing formal and informal bargaining between employers, trade unions and the state – the throughput. However, we are not able to understand the legitimacy of throughput without a constant eye for the interests of the employers' organizations (the input) and bargaining outcomes (the output) and how these have changed over time.

The Danish Model of Employment Relations

The regulation of salaries and working conditions in Denmark takes place through recurring national bargaining rounds, typically every two or three years. The key area is the substantial part of the private labour market that is comprised of the organizations under the two largest central organizations, Danish Trade Unions Confederation (FH: Fagbevægelsens Hovedorganisation) and the Danish Employers' Confederation (DA: Dansk Arbejdsgiverforening).

The unions and employers' organizations of these two large organizations make sectoral agreements and prescribe national standards. They furthermore prescribe procedural and economic guidelines for local negotiations on pay and working conditions. Indeed, wage setting, and regulation of working conditions are primarily left to social partners, although legislation also dominates in areas such as vacation time, health, and safety. As such, relations between the parties are based on the premise of mutual respect for their diverging interests and consensus on how to resolve conflicts (Madsen and Due 2008). The parties only have the right to engage in disputes at the time when a negotiation concerning the conclusion and renewal of agreements takes place (the conflict right). During the settlement period, there is no resort to industrial action (the peace clause). This applies, even if company-based bargaining typically takes place after the peace obligation has come into force (Due et al. 1994). These fundamental principles are still the same as stipulated in the September Compromise from 1899 (see below).

A precondition for the strength of an IR-model as the Danish example is an extensive coverage of collective agreements, high union density, high organization rate among employers and dense network of workplace representation (the right to organize in unions – also a part of the September Compromise). Overall, 83% of the Danish labour market was covered by collective agreements in 2015 – compared to 80% in 2007 and 84% in 1997 (Larsen et al. 2010; Navrbjerg and Ibsen 2017). However, coverage varies between sectors, and while the collective agreement coverage is 100% in the public sector, it is 74% in the private sector. Some sectors, such as cleaning, have significantly lower coverage.

Table 7.1 Organized employers in Denmark – in percent

	2004	2009	2015
Public Sector	100	100	100
Private Sector	53	58	53
Combined	84	80	83

Source: Based on DA Arbejdsmarkedsrapport 2004, 2009 plus table from DA 2017. Including DA, FA and (in 2004 og 2009) SALA. These numbers include employers' organizations like Kristelig Arbejdsgiverforening and Dansk Håndværk.

Trade union density has slightly declined since the mid 1990s but has remained comparatively high with 68.4% of Danish employees being union members in 2019. However, an important trend behind these figures is the fact that 'traditional unions' have lost ground to 'yellow' or 'alternative' unions. With few exceptions, these unions do not negotiate collective agreements, but merely refer their members to rights in the collective agreements negotiated by traditional 'red' unions. They are by and large ignored as social partners by the political system as they do not employ collective agreements as an important tool to solve welfare issues. The same goes for the alternative employers' organizations, i.e. The Association of Christian Employers (Kristelig Arbejdsgiverforening).

Table 7.1 shows that 53% of private sector employers (measured by share of employees) are members of employers' organizations (2015). However, it should be kept in mind that most Danish companies are relatively small; the average Danish enterprise has four employees and for many companies it makes little sense to be a member of an employers' organization.

Denmark has a comparatively organized system of employment relations with employers' organizations and trade unions as main actors in the regulation of work conditions and wages. However, this is only a result of a constant fine-tuning of throughput mechanisms of legitimacy to deliver the output that legitimize the autonomy of labour market regulations in the eyes of the state. As the history will show, this has not always been a smooth process.

Social Partner Autonomy via Legitimacy

In this section, we use legitimacy to explain the high degree of commitment to collectivism and coordination by Danish employers. The ability of the Danish model to deal with these often-conflicting objectives through the 20th and 21st century has continuously challenged legitimacy and thus the ability of employers to keep the state out. Table 7.2 shows four periods, their major labour problems, and the level of legitimacy.

Table 7.2 Major labour market problems and level of legitimacy 1890s through 2020s

	1890s–1960s	*1970s–1987*	*1987–1990s*	*2000s–2020s*
Major Labour Problems	Managerial Prerogative Labour Peace Wage Moderation	Labour Peace Wage Moderation Flexibility	Flexibility Wage Moderation	Flexibility Welfare Benefits Low Wage Work
Level of Legitimacy	Increasing	Declining	Restoring	Cementing

The Rise of Legitimacy: 1899 to 1960s

The first trial for employers and trade unions to earn legitimacy pertained to their ability to produce *labour peace* despite their strong conflicts of interest around the later 19th century. During the 1880s and 1890s, recurrent labour conflicts between local trade unions and employers became an increasing problem that crippled the economy. Employers were basically not organized, while employees were organized, but locally. The trade unions exploited this fact by applying a decentralized strategy, challenging the employers one by one, thereby improving wages. Using the leverage from one success, unions went on to the next employer using the same strategy. Employers were fragmented and could not defend themselves against this leapfrogging (Due et al. 1994: 71–72).

National trade unions were formed in 1895 and it became increasingly clear to employers that existing organizations for employers, mainly concerned with trade and competition policy and as such effectively business organizations, were no match to the unions. In 1896, The Employer' Confederation of 1896 (today Dansk Arbejdsgiverforning, DA) was established, and in 1898 The National Organizations in Denmark (originally De Sammenvirkende Fagforbund i Danmark, DsF, later LO, Landsorganisationen i Danmark) was founded.

In 1899, a decisive battle between the parties took place. After 19 weeks of conflict, the employers' organization DA and the confederation of unions LO laid down the fundament for future negotiations and conflict resolution in The September Compromise. Four ground principles were stipulated:

1　The managerial prerogative, i.e. management's right to organize, direct and divide work.
2　The peace clause, i.e. the obligation for employees and union to secure no strikes while the collective agreement is running.
3　The right to conflict, i.e. the right to strike or lock-out when a new collective agreement is negotiated.

4   The right to organize, i.e. the workers right to organize collectively in unions and the unions' right to negotiate on behalf of the workers.

The September Compromise, however, still lacked clear rules of conflict resolution. Lack of rules generally prevented settlements without costly stoppages as unions employed leapfrogging strategies while employers announced general lockouts to centralise and discipline members of unions. The parties had not solved the fundamental labour problem of the day, leading the state to intervene by setting up the August Committee of 1908 which in 1910 submitted its proposal for a formalization of conflict resolution. Subsequently, the Permanent Court of Arbitration (now Labour Court) and Industrial Tribunal (Faglig Voldgift) were established for the treatment of legal conflicts (retskonflikter) – each organization dealing with breaches and interpretation of treaties, respectively. In addition, an institution for mediation (Forligsinstitutionen) was established to deal with conflicts of interest in connection with the renewal of agreements.

The establishment of the Mediation Institution was, however, controversial. Employers wanted to give the institution a retracted intermediary role, while unions preferred a more interventionist role. The Act of 1910 reflected a pragmatic solution. Mediation was made mandatory, but proposals were not binding. The parties still had the final say over terms and conditions of employment, reflecting the August Committee's pragmatic belief in the autonomy of labour and capital (Madsen and Due 2008).

However, the right to make mediation proposals was not enough to stem the many conflicts of the early 20th century and a solution to the problem of fragmented votes on mediation proposal in federations and employers' use of general lockouts was needed. The legislative amendment of 1934 gave the Mediation Institution the opportunity to link the settlements and mediation proposal into one entity and thus a comprehensive proposal for adoption. Here we come to the core of the Danish collective bargaining model: Via *the linkage rule* employers obtained a coordinated process in which virtually all agreements expired at the same time and had to be negotiated simultaneously. Also, it guarantees an all-or-nothing decision about mediation proposal, which means that a ballot among all union members may conceal significant disagreements (Ibsen 2016).

The conflict resolution system and linkage were instrumental for solving the second labour problem in the post-war era: *wage moderation*. As seen in Figure 7.1, inflation was a challenge in the post-war era of the Danish economy, often fuelled by wage-inflation spirals. Companies exposed to international competition, e.g. manufacturing, became increasingly wary of employers in sheltered sectors, e.g. construction, giving in to union wage demands (Due et al. 1994; Ibsen and Stamhus 1993). Since employers in sheltered sectors could pass on labour costs increases to consumers – something that the exposed sectors could not – a key issue for Danish employers was how to reconcile these internal

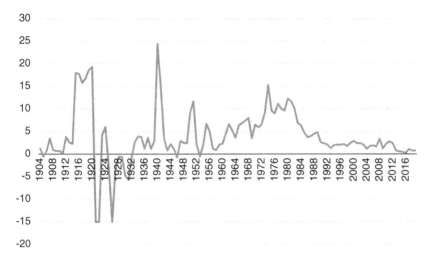

Figure 7.1 Consumer price index (1900 = 100). 1904–2019.
Source: Based on Danmarks Statistik (2020): PRIS9: Forbrugerprisindeks, gennemsnitlig årlig inflation (1900 = 100) efter type. Copenhagen: Danmarks Statistik.

differences. DA attempted to enforce discipline upon member associations and would use the linkage by the Mediation Institution to force areas that could not agree on wage moderation to be swept up in the general settlement. This strategy forced unions to coordinate – typically around a key pattern setting agreement in manufacturing and ensured control over wage developments despite high economic growth. Employers, however, needed discipline on the part of unions and this required strong unions capable of coordinating wage demands across industries and across bargaining levels (Traxler et al. 2001).

Increasingly, however, unions in sheltered industries felt deprived of the possibility of industrial action to a different result than manufacturing. Likewise, unskilled workers were worried that they would only get the minimum wage increases, whereas skilled workers would be able to top off general wage increases with local wage bargaining. These internal union tensions gradually began to undermine the employers' efforts to produce wage moderation and labour peace.

The Decline of Legitimacy: 1970s to 1980s

By the 1970s, Denmark, along with other Western European countries, had prospered for a decade but was facing inflationary pressures due to low unemployment, increasingly militant unions, and declining wage discipline among employers. Workers saw big wins on the horizon such as reducing working hours and provisions on equal pay. Thus, while times were good for employers, they were increasingly worried that their strategy of centralized bargaining would no longer produce legitimate outcomes, i.e. wage moderation and labour peace. Moreover, the equalization of wages and other terms and conditions of employment across industries and companies squeezed out many employers who could not afford the labour costs set out in collective agreements. Calls for more flexibility became commonplace among employers, but there were huge risks involved in inserting flexibility in the bargaining system, as strong unions might use it to their advantage. The diverging demands on the collective bargaining process finally led to the first major industrial conflict in 1973 and resulted in almost 4 million lost working days (Due et al. 1994). Paralyzing the economy for two weeks, the Social Democratic government intervened by passing a law that settled terms and conditions until the next bargaining round. The intervention reduced working hours to 40 per week (from 41.75) and introduced equal pay provisions. At the same time, wage increases reached double-digits in per cent, hampering both international competitiveness but also internal demand.

When the oil crisis erupted in 1973, unemployment skyrocketed and the state was under severe pressure to restore public finances. A well-functioning labour market was key in this regard, but employers and trade unions were far apart in their demands. The 1975, 1977 and 1979 bargaining rounds all ended in government interventions (Bøje and Madsen 1994; Due et al. 1994). These interventions severely undermined the legitimacy of the Danish model and the social partners. Terms and conditions of employment were *de jure* settled by politicians, albeit using bargaining agreement blueprints that had been negotiated by unions and employers but rejected by their members. In the end, the bargaining model relied on its ability to produce agreements that employers could count on during the agreement duration. During the 1970s, one could argue that the social partners were managing laws instead of bargaining collective agreements, which undermined the legitimacy of the Danish model of labour market regulation.

As shown in multiple studies (cf. Katz 1993), the oil crisis and the subsequent company restructurings pushed employers to demand bargaining decentralization and more flexibility. Faced with international competition and the need to end wage-price spirals, Danish employers were no exception and pressured their associations to demand radical change to the centralized bargaining rounds. Trade unions, on their part, were caught between radical factions who saw the end of capitalism near and pragmatic factions who fought for jobs and real wage increases (Ibsen and Jørgensen 1979). The latter faction was led by the skilled metalworkers' unions in the exporting manufacturing companies (Iversen 1996). They were increasingly sympathetic to employer demands for more

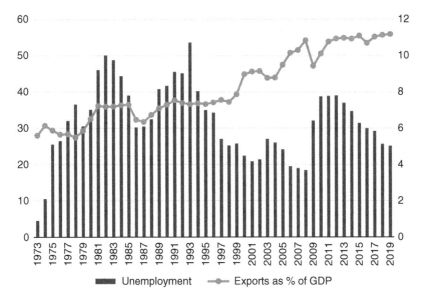

Figure 7.2 Exports as % of GDP (left axis) and unemployment (right axis) – Denmark 1973–2019.

Source: Based on World Bank (2020): Unemployment, total (% of total labour force) (national estimate); Exports as percentage of GDP. Washington D.C. World Bank Data.

flexibility and bargaining decentralization as this would move distribution of wage increases closer to management and might produce skills premia otherwise suppressed by centralized bargaining (Due et al 1994; Ibsen and Stamhus 1993). Figure 7.2 shows how exports became increasingly important in the Danish economy after the 1980s and how this change was instrumental to lowering unemployment. Restoring wage moderation and introducing more flexibility were important elements for this change to the Danish economy.

The Restoration of Legitimacy: 1980s to 1990s

The path to restore the legitimacy of employers' organizations was paved by threats of government intervention. In 1983, the Centre-right government controversially suspended indexation of wages which ensured extra wage increases in case of price inflation over a certain level. This governmental move emboldened employers to insist on wage restraint, and unions started to change strategy to focus on real wage increases rather than trying to outpace price inflation. In 1987, the tripartite "Common Declaration" between the government, employers' organizations and unions, contained a pledge to focus on employment and real wage improvements, rather than nominal pay increases. Moreover, increased private savings would pave the way for better retirement schemes whilst improving the current account deficit.

Instrumental to all these changes was the employers' organizational restructuring of the 1980s and 1990s, concentrating power among employers in the exporting industries. After a series of mergers of smaller manufacturing associations, Confederation of Danish Industry (Dansk Industri, DI) was created in 1991/1992. The new confederation of business was the result of two mergers – first between Jernets Arbejdsgivere and Industrifagene (process manufacturing industries) to form Industriens Arbejdgivere, which then merged with Industrirådet (a policy and lobby organization for manufacturing). In the meantime, there was a reorganization of DA which cut down its affiliates from 150 to 50 employers' organizations, mostly through mergers (Ibsen 2016). These organizational moves forced unions to do the same, and unions formed The Central Organization of Industrial Employees in Denmark (CO-industri) as the counterpart to DI, and gradually decreased the number of trade unions through mergers of smaller unions.

The organizational changes paved the way for the transition from a three-tiered bargaining structure at the confederate level, the industry level, and workplace level, to a two-tier system at industry and workplace level. With one level less, the vertical control of employers over wages was improved. However, horizontal control of employers between different industries was still a challenge without the confederate level. Horizontal control over wage increases was institutionalized through pattern-bargaining (Ibsen 2016) in which manufacturing set the wage increase pattern for the rest of the private and public sector. By the 1990s, this system had been fully institutionalized, producing moderate wage increases across the private sector (see Figure 7.3).

Wage moderation, however, was not the only objective during the 1990s. Employers, especially in manufacturing, were wary of wage standardization and their inability to reward performance and skills. Thus, in the early 1990s flexible wage systems were introduced for large shares of the private sector. This was followed by working time decentralization, making the length and placement of working time variable and based on local bargaining between management and shop stewards. Trade unions would keep track of local bargaining but would eventually relinquish veto rights over local bargaining. By the end of the 1990s, what has been called *centralized decentralization* was a reality (Due et al. 1994). Employers' organizations succeeded in transforming collective agreements from standardized regulation to flexible framework agreements, whilst keeping control over wage increases, a feat that had not been possible with statutory regulation or interventions. Legitimacy of the bargaining model had been restored.

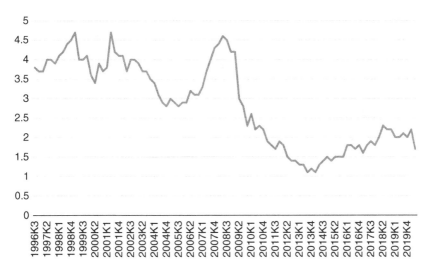

Figure 7.3 Yearly increases in hourly wages in private sector. Denmark 1996–2020.

Source: Based on Danmarks Statistik (2020): ILON2X; ILON15: Indices of average earnings in the private sector by industry. Copenhagen: Danmarks Statistik.

Cementing Legitimacy: 2000s to 2020

At the turn of the millennium, employers' organizations in Denmark delivered on most if not all the regulatory parameters needed for a successful export-oriented economy. Wages were under control but produced enough flexibility and increases to satisfy both companies and workers. Working time and other conditions were gradually decentralized to the workplace level. Work stoppages due to strikes had almost disappeared in the private sector, with the notable exception of the major industrial conflict in 1998 (more on this below). However, fiscal constraints on the welfare state, the transition to the knowledge economy, and the European Union (EU) enlargement all posed new challenges to the legitimacy of the bargaining model. Shifting governments would use these challenges as a reminder to employers that their autonomy in regulating the labour market was not guaranteed.

As we show below, collective agreements deliver key welfare benefits on occupational pensions, continuous education and training, and parental leave, further cementing the legitimacy of the bargaining model and protecting it from government intervention. In return for the decentralization of wages and working hours, the Danish trade unions in the private sector began to focus on social benefits in industry level agreements that overlapped with traditional welfare state policies (Ibsen and Thelen 2017; Madsen and Due 2008).

Public pension retrenchment and drift in public pension systems by which contributions do not follow price inflation required that compensatory schemes and occupational pensions be collective enough to be acceptable to citizens, i.e. to cover a vast majority of the population through collective agreement. For governments, it was beneficial to let collective bargaining shore up pension levels due to fiscal constraints on the welfare state. The first agreements on occupational pensions covering widely in the private sector came in 1991. Starting moderately, the occupational pensions increased during the 2000s and 2010s to 12% contributions in the private sector making it an indispensable part of the Danish pension system. Moreover, it served to increase private savings rate to a remarkably high level and kept wage inflation low. In 2011, Danish household pension savings stood at 300% of yearly disposable income (Isaksen et al. 2014). From 1988 to 2005 the share of workers (age group 30–55) covered by an occupational pension scheme increased from 37% to 69%, and the Danish pension system relies on collectively bargaining pension entitlements to be sustainable.

Turning to education, as argued by many scholars, the transition to the knowledge economy comes with new social risks and demands for protection against these risks (Morel et al. 2011). First and foremost, the attrition rate of skills has increased and large groups of workers need reskilling to remain employable. Denmark, with its long tradition for public investment in skills, already had extensive rights to continuous education and training (CET), especially for unskilled blue-collar workers. However, opportunities and incentives for employers to train their workers continuously during employment were weak. This was problematic from an employability perspective, as re-integration into employment is much easier if skills are updated continuously. In the first part of the 2000s, the government therefore began pushing employers' organizations and trade unions to figure out bilateral solutions that would incentivize both employers and workers to expand CET.

Collectively bargained agreements on CET, known from the manufacturing agreements, offered government a blueprint for funding CET by supplementing existing public funding of such education. If employers paid collectively into a CET fund, this money could then be used to pay time-off for when workers did the courses, which were paid by government. Paid CET and cost-sharing would make continuous CET attractive for both companies and workers. Thus, in 2006–2007, a sweeping tripartite agreement was reached: the government promised extra funding for continuous education and CET if the social partners could come to an encompassing solution. Negotiations settled on an extension of the skill-development fund that had been negotiated previously for manufacturing, and the agreement now gave each worker the right to two weeks of paid CET and education, plus the right to personally choose the CET to be received. These rights have subsequently been improved.

Likewise, the shadow of hierarchy was very present on parental leave. The Liberal-Conservative government threatened employers with legislation in 2003, if the bargaining parties could not find a way to ensure paid parental leave through collective funds (akin to the ones used on pensions). A breakthrough came in 2004, which developed parental leave foundations on an industry-basis. Industries which did not agree on such a foundation would be covered by the LO/DA general foundation. Moreover, the social partners agreed to a compensation mechanism ensuring that companies with large shares of female workers would not incur excessive costs (i.e. due to the costs of paying for maternity leave).

On all three issues, it was a Liberal-Conservative government that pushed (in 2004 on parental leave) or pulled (in 1987/1991 on pension and 2007 on education and CET) social partners into agreement. On all three occasions a key requirement for agreement has been the encompassing nature and solidaristic funding of schemes. The high coordinative capacity and high coverage of the bargaining system opened an avenue for collective bargaining on welfare related issues, and thus cemented the legitimacy of the model when faced with new challenges in the knowledge economy. If the government had to solve these challenges, public budgets would be stretched and taxpayers would have to pay.

Conclusion

Danish employers' organizations are still committed to collectivism and coordination due to their vested interest in strong unions to keep the Danish state out of labour market regulation. The Danish model of collectivism and coordination relies on unions and employers' organizations being sufficiently encompassing to obtain legitimacy in regulating the labour market and solve problems of the modern welfare state. This is only possible if unions represent most of the workers, if collective bargaining coverage is high, and if the employers' organization can keep unions close in productive bargaining relationships.

We explain commitment through legitimacy, understood as the conformity of bargaining processes (input and throughput legitimacy) and results (output legitimacy). In our use, this legitimacy is inherently political as we are concerned with how employers want to keep the state out of its business, even when politicians have reasons to intervene. Employers can achieve this if the state views the actions of employers and outcomes of collective bargaining as conforming to general political objectives. If employers realize these objectives on their own, they can be shielded from external pressures by the state or the 'shadow of hierarchy'.

During the 20th century and into the 21st century, these objectives tied to what actors viewed as the major labour problems of the time. We identified multiple: Managerial prerogative, labour peace, wage moderation, flexibility, welfare benefits, and low wage work. While the corporatist model of employment relations came under pressure during the 20th century, the employers again and again maintained their autonomy by solving these pressing labour problems. Indeed, legitimacy has even increased in recent decades with tripartite cooperation on pressing political issues ranging from occupational pensions in the 1990s over continuous education to paternity leave in the 2000s. More recently, the social partners have been deeply involved in negotiating relief packages concerning threatened branches during the Covid-19 crisis. Shifting governments have realized that the social partners are reliable in not only the regulation of the labour market but also in solving major economic and welfare issues. In that way, employers' organizations and unions are keeping the state out of the business of regulating wages and working conditions by staying close together.

On the flipside, the constant danger of delegating regulation and welfare benefits to employers is that bargaining coverage could fall due to the voluntarist nature of Danish collective bargaining. While a collective agreement coverage between 70% and 75% in the private sector might seem high, it is a major problem that a large group stands outside the 'normal' package of collectively provided employment conditions and benefits. Recently, this large group has come in focus due to a European Commission proposal for an EU minimum wage directive. Thus, many critical questions ensue for employers' organizations eager to retain legitimacy. How can the uncovered group be protected from low wages, if there is no statutory regulation of wages? Similarly, how will this group fare when it retires from the labour market but has not been able to obtain a decent pension through the collectively provided occupational pensions? If coverage decreases to politically unacceptable levels, politicians will feel obliged to intervene.

Moreover, there is a risk of 'double-regulation' in the sense that statutory reforms will have spill over effects on how agreed entitlements work and vice-versa. For example, should wage-earners with large occupational pension savings still receive the public pension? And what are the limits to employers' willingness to provide welfare benefits? In a changing economy in which old industries are being disrupted and new tech-based companies are making their way into the Danish employer landscape, the old way of providing employee benefits through collective bargaining might not be the preferred option anymore.

All these questions hinge upon the fundamental ability of employers' organizations to organize Danish companies in the future and deliver encompassing self-regulation. So far, this ability has been resilient even when other countries' employers' associations began to introduce non-collective bargaining membership (see chapter 9 on Germany) or pure business association membership. Today, these membership types are also possible in Danish employers' organizations, but they still constitute a minority. Should this ratio change, this might have a snowball effect putting serious pressure on bargaining coverage and the legitimacy of the Danish model of employment relations.

References

Bøje, T. P. and Madsen, P. K. (1994). Wage formation and incomes policy in Denmark in the 1980s. In: R. Dore, R. Boyer and Z. Mars (eds.) *The Return to Incomes Policy*. London: Pinter.

Due, J., Madsen, J. S., Jensen, C. S. and Petersen, L. K. (1994). *The Survival of the Danish Model. A Historical Sociological Analysis of the Danish System of Collective Bargaining*. Copenhagen: DJØF Publishing.

Gooberman, L., Hauptmeier, M. and Heery, E. (2018). Contemporary employer interest representation in the United Kingdom. *Work, Employment and Society*, 32 (1): 114–132. doi: 10.1177/0950017017701074

Ibsen, C. L. (2015). Three approaches to coordinated bargaining: A case for power-based explanations. *European Journal of Industrial Relations*, 21 (1): 39–56. doi: 10.1177/0959680114527032

Ibsen, C. L. (2016). The role of mediation institutions in Sweden and Denmark after centralized bargaining. *British Journal of Industrial Relations*, 54 (2): 285–310. doi: 10.1111/bjir.12142

Ibsen, F. and Jørgensen, H. (1979). *Fagbevægelse og stat – Bind 2: Den faglige kamp, statsindgreb og indkomstpolitik 1930–1978*. København: Gyldendal.

Ibsen, F. and Stamhus, J. (1993). *Fra Central til Decentral Lønfastsættelse*. Copenhagen: Jurist- og Økonomforbundets Forlag.

Ibsen, C. L. and Thelen, K. (2017). Diverging solidarity: Labor strategies in the new knowledge economy. *World Politics*, 69 (3): 409–447. doi: 10.1017/S0043887117000077

Isaksen, J., Kramp, P. L. and Sørensen, L. P. (2014). Household balance sheets and debt: An international country study. In: B. Winkler, A. Riet and P. Bull (eds.) *A Flow-of-Funds Perspective on the Financial Crisis*. London: Palgrave Macmillan, pp. 257–270.

Iversen, T. (1996). Power, flexibility, and the breakdown of centralized wage bargaining: Denmark and Sweden in comparative perspective. *Comparative Politics*, 28 (4): 399–436.

Katz, H. C. (1993). The decentralization of collective bargaining: A literature review and comparative analysis. *Ind Labor Relat Rev*, 47(1): 3–22. doi: 10.1177/001979399304700101

Korpi, W. (2006). Power resources and employer-centered approaches in explanations of welfare states and varieties of capitalism: Protagonists, consenters, and antagonists. *World Politics*, 58 (2): 167–206. doi: 10.1353/wp.2006.0026

Larsen, T. P., Navrbjerg and Johansen, M. M. (2010). *Tillidsrepræsentanten og arbejdspladsen – Rapport I*. København: LO.

Madsen, J. S. and Due, J. (2008). *Den store illusion: eller stor ståhej for ingenting, FAOS' Forskningsnotater, nr. 95*. Copenhagen: Museum Tusculanum.

Martin, C. and Swank, D. (2012). *The Political Construction of Business Interests: Co-ordination, Growth, and Equality*. Cambridge: Cambridge University Press.

Meyer, J. W. and Rowan, B. (1977). Institutionalized organizations: Formal structure as myth and ceremony. *American Journal of Sociology*, 83 (2): 340–363. Available at: http://www.jstor.org/stable/2778293

Morel, N., Palier, B. and Palme, J. (2011). Beyond the welfare state as we knew it?. In: N. Morel, B. Palier and J. Palme (eds.) *Towards a Social Investment Welfare State?: Ideas, Policies and Challenges*. Bristol: Bristol University Press, pp. 1–30. doi: 10.2307/j.ctt9qgqfg.8

Navrbjerg, S. E. and Ibsen, C. L. (2017). *Arbejdsgiver-organisationer i Danmark: Fra passiv tradition til aktiv tilpasning*. København: Københavns Universitet.

Scharpf, F. (1999). *Governing in Europe: Effective and Democratic?* Oxford: Oxford University Press.

Sisson, K. (1987). *The Management of Collective Bargaining*. Oxford: Blackwell.

Suchman, M. (1995). Managing legitimacy: Strategic and institutional approaches. *Academy of Management Review*, 20 (3): 571–610.

Traxler, F., Blaschke, S. and Kittel, B. (2001). *National Labor Relations In Internationalized Markets: A Comparative Study Of Institutions, Change, And performance*. Oxford: Oxford University Press. doi: 10.1093/acprof:oso/9780198295549.001.0001

8 Employers' Associations in Australia

Peter Sheldon and Louise Thornthwaite

Introduction

Employers' organizations (EOs) in Australia include many often long-established and well-entrenched employers' associations (EAs). These are voluntary, membership-based, not-for-profit organizations with a labour-market mission. Most are mixed EAs which also have a product market function. Historically, the legislative regulation of industrial relations (IR) frameworks and processes, as well as of EAs as formal parties to the IR system, has institutionally embedded EAs through formally assigning them particular institutionalized roles and tasks, as we explain below. Legislative requirements have also shaped their internal processes, mandating adherence to transparency in governance and to internal democratic accountability. Despite major legislative changes in recent decades, crucial aspects of the overall architecture remain, retaining for EAs their central, legitimated roles and purpose. In Australia, this retention marks EAs out as a specific, influential and emblematic form of EO.

In this chapter we use Mancur Olson's (1971) seminal work on the collective action problem as a frame to understand better the particularities of Australian EAs – as membership-based, voluntary and not-for-profit bodies. Olson identified the conditions under which individuals would act in the collective interest when, as he argued, rational self-interested individuals normally would not act in the group interest. In examining the collective organization of employers through EAs, we draw on Olson's concepts of *collective goods* and *selective goods*, which he identified as necessary incentives to engender collective organization. To these incentives, we add our concept of *elective goods* (Sheldon and Thornthwaite 2004). We explain these terms below. In Australia, as the roles of EAs have changed in recent decades, so have the associated emphasis on the goods (services) they offer and provide to members. They concentrated on collective goods for much of the 20th century and increased their offerings of selective goods over this time. However, since the substantial dismantling of the centralized IR framework in the early 1990s, they have increasingly also focused on offering elective goods.

DOI: 10.4324/9781003104575-10

Before proceeding, we need to add in the interests of comprehensiveness, that in addition to traditional Australian EAs, there are other organizations with very limited or no involvement in labour market and IR activities, such as local 'chambers of commerce'. As well, there has been a recent proliferation of subscription-based private consultancies. Both EAs and these other EOs play important roles in representing, resourcing and assisting employers' IR and human resource management (HRM) interests.

Nonetheless, their areas of focus are often distinctly different, they operate on different business models, and they have different relationships with their members or customers. At times, what they provide is complementary; at other times they compete for employer attention and revenues through their offerings. Mostly, EAs provide a broader suite of services – including campaigning capabilities – than other EOs which tend to tailor their offerings more narrowly to commercial demand. More fundamentally, these other EOs operate within an IR world largely shaped by traditional EAs. Furthermore, EAs continue to play crucial representative roles in institutional IR at both strategic policy and day-to-day operational levels, and are influential, pro-business interlocutors in policy debate and development regarding the larger political economy.

The most consistent research on EAs in Australia appears in the *Journal of Industrial Relations*' annual reviews of 'Employer and Employer Associations Matters in Australia'. In recent years, these have been the work of some of the field's main researchers, including Michael Barry (e.g. 1995)You 2016You 2016, Bruce Hearn Mackinnon (e.g. 2006), Trish Todd (e.g. 2012),Todd 2012 and this chapter's authors. They chart the main developments within the EA world, its internal dynamics, relationships with governments and sympathetic lobby groups/think tanks, unions and the tribunal and court systems as well as EAs' main activities. This chapter relies heavily on that body of work, including our own studies covering nearly 30 years.

Accordingly, the first section articulates our conceptual frame, and explains its application to the changing roles of EAs in Australia, within a context of changing membership patterns. The second section provides a historical analysis of the role of EAs within Australia's nearly century-old 'arbitral model' and their more recent campaigns to replace or greatly reduce that model. The third and fourth sections summarize the current EA landscape and activity. The final section introduces some major challenges EAs confront as representatives of a business world facing contested legitimacy challenges.

The Collective Action Problem and Australian EAs

Olson's (1971) research on the collective action problem argues that for individuals to act collectively, either coercive devices or selective incentives are required to overcome the challenges of potentially conflicting interests. Olson's insights help link association purpose, strategy, activity and financial sustainability. His concepts of *collective goods* and *selective goods* are especially pertinent for capturing the full scope of Australian association activities until the 1990s. As we explain below, it is their commitment to providing collective goods that most marks out EAs from other types of EOs. For reasons we also explain below, their changing operational contexts from the 1990s have also encouraged some EAs to offer what we have termed *elective goods* (Sheldon and Thornthwaite 2004). It is in the provision of elective goods, and to a lesser extent selective goods, that new forms of EO have most competed with traditional EAs. Table 8.1 presents the key elements of these three types of offerings: collective, selective and elective goods. It distinguishes the core goods (services) of EOs in terms of their design, the intended beneficiaries, pricing, and the actual beneficiaries.

EAs have typically formed when employers combine and then collectively organize to find responses to shared labour market challenges, most notably from unions and state intervention. They also form or act to confront labour shortages and associated phenomena of labour poaching, employee turnover and upward wage bidding that may face categories of employers: by locality; industry; or production process. These EAs then provide (all) these employers, whether members or not, with 'collective goods' (Olson 1971): standardized, non-exclusive solutions to employers' 'class' needs; and they provide these free of charge. In Australia as elsewhere, this has included EAs leading or supporting employers in multi-employer collective bargaining; representing them before IR tribunals/courts and on policy consultation bodies; lobbying governments; and mounting public policy campaigns.

EAs also participate in bodies providing professional or product standard accreditation. For some, this is a core activity related to maintaining or improving ethical standards within that industry. In Australia, association concern for ethical conduct has involved questions of product/service quality and promoting 'good employer' behaviours on matters like workplace health and safety and diversity management. It also once but seemingly no longer, prioritized 'taking wages out of competition' by actively discouraging destructive cost-minimization competition based on individual employers undercutting minimum wage standards (Thornthwaite and Sheldon 2021).

However, EAs face 'free-rider' problems where their members' subscriptions pay for collective goods that advantage non-members too. This dynamic can encourage individual employer decisions to not join or to leave an association, putting at risk the association itself. To overcome this 'collective action' challenge to recruiting and retaining members, EAs have also typically developed 'selective goods' (Olson 1971). These are free and mostly standardized services, *solely available to members*,

Table 8.1 Types of core goods (services) EOs provide

Type of goods	Design of goods	Intended beneficiaries or targets	Price	Actual beneficiaries or affected employers	Examples
Collective	Standardized	Members	Free	All employers in category (including 'free riders')	Collective bargaining coordination; institutional representation; lobbying; public relations
Selective	Standardized	Financial members only	Free	Financial members only	Economic, industry, legal and IR information; training; networking
Elective	Customized	Anyone who will pay for it (members and non-members)	Commercial pricing (with discounts to member)	Anyone who will pay for it (members gain via discounted price)	IR and HRM policy consultancy; firm-based training; firm-level IR and HR strategy development; customized legal advice and representation

that encourage and reward membership. Important selective goods include employer advisory call-centre services; information on macroeconomic, trade and labour market trends; published advice on regulatory compliance; bargaining guidelines; social and organizational opportunities for networking; and training courses in legal compliance and people management.

In recent decades, despite new EAs having formed in emerging industries, there has been a substantial decline in the number of Australian EAs, through collapses, closures, mergers and acquisitions. Conterminously, a small number of prominent EAs have grown across several dimensions, including expansion into emerging areas of employment (Sheldon and Thornthwaite 2003). Their survival and success flowed mostly from absorbing other EAs, widening recruitment boundaries, expanding well beyond traditional IR activities and reinventing service delivery.

General association decline has followed factors like the substantial declines in manufacturing activity and employment, and legislative interventions into the labour market, particularly to the detriment of unionism and protective labour regulation. These factors largely reflect the impact of the adoption, in the mid-1980s to early 2000s, of what were called 'economic rationalist' (now 'neo-liberal') mindsets by successive Liberal-National Coalition governments (and, sometimes, Labor governments). Association re-invention has largely come through strategic and innovative adaptation, although not all EAs who experimented have been successful.

The attraction of association membership has also been beset by ideological shifts within corporate ranks and structural and cultural changes within, particularly, larger firms. One outcome has been the greatly reduced prominence of the corporate IR function relative to others, most notably with the emergence of HRM (and its more unitarist, recent incarnations). Thus, while many larger firms may have once belonged to multiple EAs, they have greatly reduced their spread of memberships or opted out entirely. This was already apparent in the late 1990s but has since gone much further (Sheldon and Thornthwaite 1999: 5; Sheldon et al. 2016).

Where membership once reflected a longstanding and often personalized commitment to a collective, representative organization or even to an employer movement, it is now a more transactional matter; senior managers look for the 'value proposition' membership provides within competing unit budget priorities (Sheldon et al. 2016). Many EAs face increasing product-market competition from management consultants, legal and accounting practices. For example, in 1995, 74% of private sector employers with more than 20 employees were association members. This was down from 82% in the 1980s. Densities were highest among large and very large firms and in manufacturing. For instance, density in 1995 for firms with between 200 and 459 employees was 88%

(Sheldon and Thornthwaite 1999: 4–5). Nonetheless, while data on current Australian association membership density are not available, it does not seem to have fallen anywhere near the same extent as union density (in 2020, at about 14%).

Seeking to adapt, some EAs have added 'elective goods' (Sheldon and Thornthwaite 2004) to their offerings. As Table 8.1 indicates, while *selective* goods are standardized, free of charge and only offered to association members, *elective* goods are customized, commercially-priced, fee-based products and services offered to both members and non-members alike – although members mostly enjoy a price discount. By offering elective goods, EAs seek to compete more directly with commercial competitors, whether other EOs or consultancies and legal practices. It therefore provides those EAs with opportunities to gain both members and revenue.

Employers' Associations under the Arbitral Model

Australian EO history can be roughly divided into three periods, but we mainly focus on the second and third periods. The first covers the later decades of British colonization from 1788 to 1901, the year of the nation's birth as a federation and its first compulsory arbitration legislation, in the state of New South Wales (NSW). EAs organized along craft and product market lines had already developed in colonial Australia during the second half of the 19th century. Many also had trade or professional-related functions. In the second period, from 1901 to the early 1990s, the 'arbitral model' dominated IR until gradually succumbing to successive waves of explicit neo-liberal challenges. The third period has continued and entrenched those dynamics.

During the early decades after 1901, existing and new EAs came to operate within and to depend upon Australia's systems of arbitration courts and various tribunals that parliaments established across the federal (or national) jurisdiction and the six states and two territories. It was these tribunals, rather than governments, that were largely responsible for the development of legislated employment standards in Australia until 2005 (McCallum 2011).

Almost all employment standards were, and some still are, embedded in 'awards'. Currently titled 'modern awards', they are an impoverished version of their predecessors. Awards are legally enforceable determinations. Together, they have provided the regulatory frameworks for employment relationships and the standing, rights and responsibilities of employers, EAs and unions as formal parties to any particular award. Indeed, arbitration systems had the overarching purpose of producing binding awards, although most awards were not the result only of compulsory arbitration. Rather, they came through processes of collective bargaining, supported by tribunal-based conciliation conferences.

Compulsory arbitration conditioned these processes as BATNA (best alternative to a negotiated agreement) for both parties, the likely arbitrated and legally enforceable outcome if they failed to reach agreement. Simplifying greatly, the early process for establishing awards was for one party, mostly union(s), to lodge claims with an arbitration tribunal. Employers who sought inclusion in the process of determining those claims became 'respondents'. Over time, as EAs largely took on that respondent role, the process then covered all their registered members. Whereas in some European countries, employer membership of an association can be compulsory, membership of an EA (or any EO) in Australia has always been voluntary (Deery and Plowman 1991). Nonetheless, institutional support for association recruitment through multi-employer bargaining, such as via 'extension clauses', was available under state-based systems but not the federal system. There, unions, in looking to make or vary an award, formally had to add each company they were targeting ('roping them in') when making their claims (Deery and Plowman 1991: 384). We focus here on the federal system.

The federal industrial tribunal has worn various names over the years, the most recent incarnation being the Fair Work Commission. Henceforth, we refer to all such tribunals as 'the Commission'. Earlier federal incarnations, like the [federal] Commonwealth Court of Conciliation and Arbitration (1904–1956) and the Commonwealth [later Australian] Conciliation and Arbitration Commission (1956–1988) signalled that body's processual powers. Later titles, like the Australian Industrial Relations Commission (1988–2010), emphasized their subject matter. More recent incarnations, with an eye to populist branding, have been the Australian Fair Pay Commission (2006–2009), Fair Work Australia (2009–2013), and most recently, the Fair Work Commission. In 1990, some 47% of Australia's employees worked under state awards and about 32% under federal awards (Plowman and Rimmer 1992: 9). State-award coverage was particularly high in Queensland and Western Australia. From the early 1990s, there was a continuing drift towards the federal system. This intensified after passage of *The Workplace Relations Amendment (Work Choices) Act 2005* which delivered almost all jurisdictional authority to the federal tribunal (Riley and Sarina 2006).

Working with Arbitration Tribunals

As explained earlier, industrial tribunals in Australia have depended, for their purpose and functioning, upon the existence and engagement of unions and EAs as claimants and respondents. In developing IR law, the Commission often prioritized problem-solving – in particular, dispute resolution – rather than more formalistic black letter reasoning. EAs (and unions) largely depended upon in-house technical experts to manage routine cases before tribunals. These IR practitioners, often called 'industrial officers' or 'advocates', developed within an association's internal labour market. Sometimes not qualified lawyers, their expertise lay in their deep working knowledge of the IR systems' rules and procedures – relevant awards, statute and case law – and tribunal personalities and cultures. They developed skills in reaching agreements that might satisfy both parties.

Registration, as respondents, embedded EAs' institutional legitimacy within those systems and access to their processes. This granted their provision of these collective goods immeasurable advantages for attracting and retaining members as well as enhancing their standing before governments. EAs therefore came to largely define their identities, policies, and practices through participation within those systems (Plowman and Rimmer 1992).

David Plowman, a highly influential scholar of Australian EAs, argues that when national EAs emerged in the early 20th century, they largely did so in response to the development of arbitration systems. Initially, they unsuccessfully attempted to destroy the federal arbitration court, after its establishment in 1904, by challenging its constitutionality. Subsequently, their litigation was more successful in restricting that court's operations. Soon however, EAs accommodated themselves to and embedded themselves in the new system. For Plowman, this engagement with statutory tribunal systems rather than with their member firms, came to define EAs' de facto purpose and orientation (Plowman 1988, 1989). Furthermore, Plowman argued, Australia's EAs – in contrast to those in other western countries – were strategically reactive, reliant for their agendas on what arbitration tribunals produced, often following from union initiatives. Here, Plowman's 'reactivity thesis' pointed to the apparent lack of association interest in re-shaping Australia's bargaining structure.

Barry (1995) refuted Plowman's origins story with evidence of EAs emerging in response to traditional labour market challenges well before arbitration legislation. Nonetheless, Plowman's reactivity thesis remained an influential, essentialist explanation of Australian EAs' character. Our own historically contingent work, covering the decade from the late-1980s (Sheldon and Thornthwaite 1993, 1999; Thornthwaite and Sheldon 1996), has countered that essentialism. During those years, an intense policy struggle between two leading EAs provided strong evidence that EAs had adopted high-level strategic initiatives to remake Australia's bargaining structure (see next section). Nonetheless, our arguments did not undermine the relevance of Plowman's thesis for earlier decades.

Breaking the Arbitral Model

From the late 1980s to the mid-1990s, the Business Council of Australia, a policy-focused EA composed of chief executives of most of Australia's largest companies, generated increasingly neo-liberal IR policy packages before skilfully and incessantly campaigning for them. Taken together, they aimed to increase management's unilateral prerogatives by weakening the reach and impact of both the Commission and unions, across the labour market and within individual workplaces. While initially spurned by most mainstream EAs, their proposals meshed with those from some small and medium enterprise (SME)-based EAs and an influential neo-liberal think tank, the HR Nicholls Society, whose propaganda served to make Business Council proposals seem less outlandishly anti-worker.

Founded in 1986 with strong corporate and Coalition politician support, the HR Nicholls Society's explicit aim was to destroy the arbitral model in favour of individual common law contracting and unconstrained managerial prerogatives. Crucial to their campaign was their public attacks on what they pejoratively called the 'IR Club': IR professionals implicated in accepting and servicing an arbitral model that supported and protected employee collectivism and regulatory protections of employees. 'Club' members included association officials, embedded in and supportive of that model, as well as union officials and tribunal personnel (Sheldon and Thornthwaite 1999).

Public campaigning by the Business Council was hugely successful in gaining media and parliamentary traction – including within the federal Labor government. The core objectives were to remove or reduce the role of arbitral tribunals in managing Australia's bargaining structure, compulsorily decentralize all collective bargaining to enterprise or workplace levels, increase possibilities for US-style union avoidance and for non-union bargaining, and create 'choice' for individual statutory employment agreements (Sheldon and Thornthwaite 1999). When, for their own purposes, important unions supported a stronger decentralization push, the Commission acquiesced in 1991, adopting an enterprise bargaining framework that removed itself from the system's central role. These decisions helped induce ever broader consensus for fundamental changes within the employer world, including among major EAs that had previously defended the Commission's role and centralized bargaining (Sheldon and Thornthwaite 1993, 1999; Thornthwaite and Sheldon 1996).

While the largest initial regulatory changes came under Labor in 1992 and 1993, from 1996 a now more virulently anti-union national government introduced laws that responded to much EA lobbying and propaganda. These enforced the decentralization of collective bargaining (almost exclusively) to the enterprise (Thornthwaite and Sheldon 2012); severe statutory limitations on the scope of bargaining and award content; the effective banning of union-engendered pattern bargaining and secondary (solidarity) boycotts; reductions in Commission oversight; the severe withering of the right to strike and union rights and activism. They also legalized lockouts and other employer power tactics. For a time (2005–2008), legislation also elevated individual 'agreement-making' above collective instruments (Hearn Mackinnon 2006; Riley and Sarina 2006).

These changes to Australia's IR framework reduced the need for EAs to lead or coordinate multi-employer bargaining and removed some of their work in the Commission, such as those longstanding, core IR collective goods that distinguished EAs from most other EOs. In turn, those trends diminished the felt need to associate among larger employers who traditionally contributed the bulk of EAs' dues. When legislation shifted most state-jurisdiction activity into the federal arena, it also greatly reduced the IR collective goods' vocations of many state-based EAs, forcing some into mergers or closures. Almost all these legislative changes weakening the sustainability of EAs' membership-bases reflected unceasing lobbying and propaganda campaigns by EAs themselves – albeit, not necessarily those most damaged by these effects.

There were also other changes associated with the transformed IR framework and additional regulatory interventions that have impacted EAs both specifically and generally, including: first, an expansion in individual employment rights; second, increased IR legalism; third, reduced union density and influence; and fourth, diminished employment security. Individual employment rights legislation, for instance, flowered alongside the breaking of the arbitral model. EAs fought hard to reduce the force of some of these – for example, unfair dismissal protections – but others, like those related to anti-discrimination, parental leave and domestic violence leave are too publicly popular for them to attack.

These provisions have substantially increased the volume of members' calls on EA selective goods expertise while providing market opportunities for other types of EOs. Given that larger firms can afford in-house expertise or access it through top-tier legal practices, this growing demand for selective goods has largely come from (low-fee) SME members. As most EAs have a preponderance of SME members, this too has challenged their financial sustainability as they struggle to compete with other EAs and for-profit firms. Rising average costs of providing selective goods increasingly coexists with falling average revenues from membership dues.

Second, the decentralization of bargaining, often mis-characterized as 'de-regulation', generated a substantial increase in the system's legalism, exemplified by much longer statutes and accompanying regulations. While the *Industrial Relations Act, 1988*, a high point of the arbitral model, had 360 pages, the radically 'deregulatory' *Work Choices Act, 2005* had more than 750. This neo-liberal statutory prescription and proscription sought to substantially reduce the Commission's autonomy and powers to manage the IR system and wider labour market, as well as to eradicate union activism. Further, the *Work Choices* legislation cost the Coalition the 2007 election (and the Prime Minister, his parliamentary seat). Labor governments (2007–2013) reversed important parts of the *Work Choices* agenda but, under intense EA pressure, also left much intact. When Labor left office, leading EAs immediately urged the Coalition to re-embrace that agenda (Sheldon and Thornthwaite 2013; Todd 2012).

Third, EAs' overall victory in re-shaping the nation's bargaining structure contributed to heavy declines in union density and greatly reduced union capacities to monitor and report workplace breaches. EAs had earlier rationalized their agenda as fostering enterprise bargaining. However, that agenda, by substantially shifting power to employers, contributed to enterprise bargaining's substantial decline. With unions broadly weakened, many employers eschew the direct costs and union engagement that comes with collective bargaining, preferring to leave their workforces covered by the less generous – to employees – underlying awards (Gahan et al. 2018). These developments have helped stunt wages growth, leading to a steep decline in labour's share of national income (Stanford 2018).

Fourth, EAs have achieved reductions in employment security, facilitating the emergence of Australia's high levels of atypical and insecure employment. Increasingly too, EAs have defended the growing use of work that firms (often bogusly) classify as independent contracting. These firms thereby avoid a range of regulatory and financial responsibilities of employment (Hearn Mackinnon 2006; Knox 2018; Stewart and Stanford 2017). Fractured forms of work in on-line platform and gig jobs join other faces of labour market exploitation within franchised businesses and business groups, supply chains and labour hire or temporary work agency arrangements. EAs that support legal arrangements putting labour costs into extreme downward competition ultimately support those companies at the expense of member organizations that properly employ their workers.

These regulatory changes have radically shifted Australia away from being a country where a strong union movement and powerful tribunal systems contributed to relatively egalitarian wages structures and widespread, and largely enforced, employee protections. In fact, the ILO has repeatedly found that Australia's IR legislation breaches the country's commitments under ILO core conventions regarding freedom of association, right to strike and collective bargaining (McCallum 2011). Nonetheless, at the start of 2021, a federal tribunal system – albeit its autonomy greatly constrained – still sets minimum wages annually, adjudicates some other wage questions and oversees the remnants of the award system. In many ways, it remains at the core of labour market regulation.

The Main Areas of Contemporary EA Activity

Facing severe product market pressures, many Australian EAs (and other EOs) now need to invest much more heavily in recruiting and retaining members, particularly through selective and elective goods. Indeed, 'business development' is now a central function of many (not-for-profit) EAs.

Collective Goods

The most traditional area of representative activity concerns the functioning and outcomes of the formal, institutional IR system. Currently, this involves activity in five main areas. First, given the almost complete withering of multi-employer collective bargaining, the representative activities of EAs now focus much more on engagement within the Commission and other tribunals that regulate labour markets or produce public policy regarding them. This involves them in the development of submissions to annual minimum wage cases, periodic reviews of modern awards, and one-off inquiries into such issues as parental leave, sex discrimination, modern slavery or workplace health and safety.

Leading EAs, like Australian Industry Group (Ai Group) and Australian Chamber of Commerce and Industry (ACCI) (Australian Industry Group (Ai Group) 2019, 2021; ACCI 2021), also invest heavily in individual rights' cases, particularly those with test-case potential, such as over legal definitions of 'casual' employment. These forms of engagement, whether over collective or individual IR matters, demand substantial resources in staff time and expertise: internal consultation; commissioning or undertaking research; developing legal arguments; lobbying governments and engaging with media.

The second main area reflects leading EAs' apparently insatiable desires to re-shape the IR system to produce ever greater managerial prerogative. Calls for more fundamental change have emanated particularly from ACCI, Ai Group, Australian Mines and Metals Association (AMMA) and the Business Council. Mostly these are highly distributive demands, even if couched in integrative rhetoric; they threaten to weaken what remains of union and individual labour rights. In pursuing these campaigns, EAs use various combinations of submissions to official inquiries, lobbying government, propaganda to the media, social mobilization campaigns and electioneering. Overall, they seek change by pushing governments – not employers – to do things differently – via legislation or other interventions.

These EAs publicly blame IR failings for nearly everything that seems to be wrong with industry and the economy and, despite winning substantial concessions over three decades, they always demand more. With many of their claims – for example regarding productivity improvement – the issues might be settled in other countries by collective bargaining, better public policy, improvements to education and skills formation structures, or more effective organizational management by employers themselves. For Australian EAs instead, the strategy dwells almost exclusively on demands for further regulatory change aimed at increasing the freedom of employers to contract – at the expense of employees – or reducing their labour costs in other ways. However, apart from the period 2005–2007, they have repeatedly faced difficulties in persuading a Senate majority to vote for their most extreme legislative proposals (Hearn Mackinnon 2006; Sheldon and Thornthwaite 2003, 2020; Thornthwaite and Sheldon 2021).

Leading EAs have also expanded their public relations and lobbying well beyond IR (Sheldon et al. 2019). EAs' arguments that what is good for business is *necessarily* good for the Australian economy, and hence all Australians, are increasingly difficult for them to sustain (see below). Nonetheless, EAs have strongly advocated 'trickle-down economics' via reducing tax rates for large corporations and upper-income individuals at a time of wages stagnation and/or chronic income insecurity for most (Sheldon and Thornthwaite 2020). Another challenge, particularly for the Business Council, has been the resurgence of EA complaints of contractual maltreatment of SMEs by big corporations (Sheldon and Thornthwaite 2020). Ironically, the Coalition government has felt compelled to relax competition law to give SMEs 'collective bargaining' rights vis-à-vis large oligopsonies.

A third and growing representational focus has emerged following exposure of widening and deepening employer IR malfeasance. This has particularly involved systematic wage underpayments (or theft) by many employers, large and small, and sham contracting arrangements. EAs have largely defended the reputations of these companies from rising media, public and parliamentary criticism, rebutting calls to introduce criminal sanctions against company owners and senior managers. EAs have also fought hard to minimize state regulation of 'sham' independent contracting, most recently among gig-economy workers who deliver food (Hearn Mackinnon 2006; Sheldon and Thornthwaite 2020; Thornthwaite and Sheldon 2021).

Fourth, EAs have been able to bring more creative and integrative perspectives to issues like vocational education and training, mental health in the workplace, matters related to disability and care, youth unemployment and government infrastructure investment. This broader canvass requires them to consult with members, (sometimes) unions, external experts, educational institutions and NGOs. It requires policy analysis and development, submissions, and often time-consuming lobbying and representation before government, parliamentary committees and commissions of inquiry.

Finally, Business NSW has brought some of these themes into its pro-business campaigning ahead of elections. These campaigns are often large-scale social mobilizations that bring together head office officials and affiliated local chambers of commerce. An innovative, new form of collective good, this campaigning focuses on raising awareness, joining local priorities with state-wide association priorities. It has hugely expanded Business NSW's network of affiliated local chambers (Sheldon et al. 2019).

Selective and/or Elective Goods

For Australia's EAs, bargaining decentralization has brought greater product market competition for their selective and elective goods. Within larger companies, competitors include HRM departments that take IR activities in-house or outsource them to specialized legal practices and consultancies. Greater employer unitarism and the IR system's increased legalism also encourage preferences for litigation over bargaining. All these choices suggest that many larger employers see themselves as customers not members of an employer movement or any particular EA.

These challenges to the financial sustainability of many EAs have encouraged adaptive experimentation. Some EAs have provided more and better selective goods. This is a pattern especially apparent in EAs defined by sector or occupation rather than territory because they tend to continue to face more of the traditional IR challenges that EAs developed to meet. It appears to be the case in traditional blue-collar areas and in private services like retailing and childcare (e.g. CCSA 2021; Master Builders NSW 2020; National Retail Association 2021).

Member companies appear to most value access to a member advisory call centre as a selective good. Other selective goods, increasingly provided electronically, include: dissemination of information updates and advice on legal, labour market and other economic matters; and support for employers concerning their day-to-day HR policies and practices. Some EAs also provide templates to member employers engaged in enterprise bargaining, and guidelines on developing workplace policies, including most recently on Covid-19 safe working (Sheldon et al. 2016; Thornthwaite and Sheldon 2021).

Increasingly too, EAs offer members free advertising opportunities or packages and/or use of the EA's logo to brand and promote their firms. Business SA also offers 'opportunities to engage with senior political and business leaders' and 'opportunities to engage with federal politicians and executive level business leaders' among its selective goods packages (Business SA 2020).

Many EAs, and particularly territorial ones, have substantial *elective* goods offerings. For employers involved in enterprise bargaining, this can include tailored guidance and direct support. EAs also provide HRM consultancy services – as elective goods – including on organizational culture, performance management, coaching, diversity management and HR audits. Some also offer elective goods on business/trade advice, environmental sustainability, technical monitoring and compliance, and grant-writing assistance (Business NSW 2020; Master Builders NSW 2020; Master Builders Australia 2021; Sheldon et al. 2016; VCCI 2020). As well, many EAs have developed alliance programmes with external business service providers that members can access with a discount – for example, in accounting, IT, travel, insurance, utilities, technical specifications and testing, and quality assurance.

Another innovation is for larger EAs to establish an in-house specialist legal practice. This allows them to compete directly with external legal practices while taking advantage of the EA's reputation for expertise and membership commitment. By offering discounted fees for members, these legal practices aid membership recruitment and retention. Some EAs have also converted law-related selective goods provided by their IR practitioners, and particularly the costly services, into elective goods delivered by their legal practices. These arrangements, which can reduce EA costs and raise revenue, are particularly attractive to larger firms who may otherwise be hard to recruit as members.

A few EAs have experimented with reinventing their business models more fundamentally. These rely less on membership dues and more on revenues from elective goods or accessing government funding. This creates tensions between associational and commercial priorities and identities. In taking this road, some EAs no longer speak only of 'members' that they represent and service but of 'members and clients' (Sheldon et al. 2016).

Some of the larger ACCI territorial affiliates, like Business NSW, the Victorian and Queensland Chambers, and Business SA, have fragmented the notion of membership into what amounts to a range of (member-customer) packages. Instead of a traditional membership dues structure that broadly reflects size of member firm (by workforce size), these new fee structures offer different price packages, each with a different level of selective goods entitlement.

For example, Business NSW has changed its membership offerings several times over the last decade, sometimes responding to disquiet from its SME membership annoyed at losing valued selective goods (Sheldon et al. 2016). Currently it offers two membership packages. The cheaper 'Business Networker' provides 'webcasts, webinars, advice, tools & documents' plus access to 'at least three events' as the main offerings. The more expensive 'Business Workplace' package provides these, plus access to 12 workplace advice line calls – a very low level of access when sectoral EAs typically offer unlimited access to theirs. Both packages provide voting rights plus 5% discount on in-house legal services (Business NSW 2020). Most other formerly selective goods – like training and briefings – are now elective goods, as would be the case for much IR advice, now available via the in-house legal practice.

The Victorian Chamber of Commerce and Industry offers four distinctly different membership packages, each providing tiered access to selective and (discounted) elective goods. The cheapest membership package ('Networker') costs A$350 per year, the most expensive ('Connect'), A$8,200. The former seems to offer more for less than at Business NSW. The latter is vastly more expensive than its comparator at

Business NSW and offers much more, including unlimited access to the advice line. Both packages strongly feature member discounts for elective goods – like training and briefings – that used to be selective goods (VCCI 2020).

After trying price-based tiered membership packages, the Queensland Chamber has done something entirely different. It has now differentiated its membership packaging first by theme and then by price. Each of the 11 packages includes theme-specific services – such as for HRM or international trade – as well as more universal selective goods plus member-discounted elective goods. Universal selective goods include the 'Employer Assistance Hotline', but these are rationed by dues level (CCIQ 2021; Sheldon et al. 2016).

These examples stand in stark contrast to the more traditional EA business models still operating in sectoral EAs. These latter tend to embrace more strongly a member-association model and levy dues accordingly. A telling example is the National Retail Association (2021) which charges A$500 per year to all members and provides a very full list of collective and selective goods.

EAs and Social Licence Challenges

Exposure of widespread corporate misbehaviour has weakened the sense of legitimacy accorded to (especially big) business in Australia, raising deeper issues of 'social licence to operate'. Furthermore, it has provoked unpredictable and unexpected dynamics across individual firms, institutional shareholders, civil society actors, governments and EAs. The concept of 'social licence' has similarities with ideas of corporate social responsibility (CSR), environmental, social and governance (ESG) concerns and the 'triple bottom line'. However, in Australia today, it carries a more collective notion pertaining to entire industries or big business rather than the corporate strategies of single firms. Inherent is the assumption of trust in relation to civil society expectations regarding how any business will operate. One implication of these changing social dynamics has been that, increasingly, large corporations are making their decisions on EO membership based on non-IR issues.

Leading EAs are aware that, as in other countries, corporate social licence has become more tenuous, as public discontent about deepening inequality has flared into forms of angry populism (see the chapter by Morgan). In adopting positions on related issues, some EAs appear to recognize that they are making choices between obvious short-term and possible long-term business and organizational advantage, between narrowly pro-business (pro-self) and pro-social orientations. However, strongly influencing is the felt need to recruit and retain members as 'individual customers' they service, rather than as part of a collective movement they might lead as a collective good.

Thus, on wage theft, for instance, while EAs do not always publicly defend miscreant employers from criticism, they often produce rationalizations suggesting innocent errors. They have also largely absented themselves from public condemnations and from publicly making the case for imposing stronger ethical standards on the business world, even if this means stronger regulation. Accordingly, it seems that EAs have largely absented themselves from adopting the role of business' social conscience, again as a collective good, walking away from their historic vocation of standing for 'the good employer' (Thornthwaite and Sheldon 2021).

Nonetheless, constituency seems to matter. For example, the (big) Business Council has repeatedly called for a substantial increase in welfare benefits for the unemployed. ACCI, close to the anti-welfare Coalition government and representing predominantly labour-intensive MNEs, rebuts such suggestions. For its part, during 2018, within the non-partisan and politically centrist Ai Group, active members held major, even passionate discussions on the policy implications of anti-business sentiment. At quarterly meetings of their National Executive Advisory Council, they pushed Ai Group to do more regarding business mis/behaviour, to increase its messaging regarding CSR (Sheldon and Thornthwaite 2020; Thornthwaite and Sheldon 2019, 2021).

Major employers and some EAs have also become increasingly divided over climate change policy. Global-scale mining and oil/gas corporations like BHP, Rio Tinto and Woodside and major local corporations now explicitly accept climate science and its implications for their operations, in Australia and abroad, and have been re-shaping their policies accordingly. Corporate realpolitik reflects how quickly the consensus on climate science and decarbonization policy is developing internationally, especially among 'customer' nations. Moreover, these enormous corporations also face social movement campaigning directed at major shareholders, including superannuation (pension) funds, universities, religious bodies and third-sector organizations. Some of these campaigns directly target EAs for their role in Australia's public policy paralysis over climate change.

More influential however have been campaigns targeting leading companies to pressure their EAs and even threaten disaffiliation, to shift them from climate change denial or passivity. Targeted companies have included BHP, Rio Tinto and Origin; targeted EAs included the Business Council, AMMA and Minerals Council of Australia. In recent years, leading corporations like BHP, Telstra, Qantas and Westpac have publicly pushed their EOs to change direction; BHP even disaffiliated from at least one EA on this issue. The Business Council, reflecting diverse currents within its membership, has faced repeated criticism for publicly accepting the science but failing to adopt policy that would address it. Conversely, Ai Group, which hosts an Energy and Climate Leaders' Group that includes renewable energy companies, continues its longstanding, pragmatic, science-led stance, repeatedly urging the federal government to initiate coherent policy action in that direction (Sheldon and Thornthwaite 2020; Thornthwaite and Sheldon 2019, 2021).

Conclusion

In prioritizing, as IR collective goods, publicity campaigns and lobbying for ever more incursions against legal protections for employees and unions, EAs have also, unwittingly, created challenges to their own organizational survival. Many smaller EAs have collapsed or been absorbed into a few, larger and more successful organizations, or have outsourced activities to them. Leading EAs and some smaller industry/occupational/regional ones that have survived have largely reinvented themselves to retain and attract members, reducing and reframing the IR collective goods they offer, while focusing ever more on selective and elective goods that members purchase, respectively, through price-tiered membership levies or via commercial fees. In general, collective IR goods seem ever less important for attracting and retaining members.

A key theme that has carried through the history of EAs in Australia, and which has been particularly prominent in the constant calls for legislative change to employment rights and the industrial law framework, has been the tradition of employer representation focusing on getting governments – not employers – to do things differently. One emerging irony of this approach has been that once EAs deliver institutional changes they believe employers demand, employers tend to lose interest with their gains, as they have with enterprise bargaining, and seek to further increase their unilateral freedom to contract in other ways, such as sham contracting. Perhaps a further emerging irony is that on social licence issues, it is employers that are calling for EAs to do things differently.

References

Australian Chamber of Commerce and Industry (ACCI) (2021). *Current Members*. Available at: https://www.australianchamber.com.au/membership/current-members/ [accessed 25 January 2021].
Australian Industry Group (Ai Group) (2019). *AI Group Membership: Good News for Business*. Available at: https://cdn.aigroup.com.au/Membership/2019/Ai_Group_Membership_Brochure_Feb_2019.pdf [accessed 20 January 2021].
Australian Industry Group (Ai Group) (2021). *About AI Group*. Available at: https://www.aigroup.com.au/about/ [accessed 20 January 2021].
Barry, M. (1995). Employer associations: Assessing Plowman's reactivity thesis. *Journal of Industrial Relations*, 37 (4): 543–561. 10.1177%2F002218569503700403
Barry, M. and You, K. (2017). Employer and employer association matters in Australia in 2016. *Journal of Industrial Relations*, 59 (3): 288–304. 10.1177%2F0022185617693873

Business NSW (2020). *Why Join?* Available at: https://www.businessnsw.com/Members/why-join[accessed 12 February 2021].

Business SA (2020). *Become a Member.* Available at: https://www.business-sa.com/LiveMenu/Membership/Membership-2020 [accessed 14 February 2021].

CCIQ (2021). *Become a CCIQ Member when You Purchase One of These Products.* Available at: https://www.cciq.com.au/membership/ [accessed 15 February 2021].

CCSA (2021). *Do You Need Expert Support Today?* Available at: https://www.ccsa.org.au/member-support/ [accessed 15 February 2021].

Deery, S. and Plowman, D. H. (1991). *Australian Industrial Relations.* Sydney: McGraw-Hill.

Gahan P., Pekarek, A. and Nicholson, D. (2018). Unions and collective bargaining in Australian in 2017. *Journal of Industrial Relations,* 60 (3): 337–367. 10.1177%2F0022185618759135

Hearn Mackinnon, B. (2006) Employer matters in 2005. *Journal of Industrial Relations,* 48 (3): 85–401. 10.1111/j.1472-9296.2005.00166.x

Knox, A. (2018). Regulatory avoidance in the temporary work agency industry: Evidence from Australia. *Economic and Labour Relations Review,* 29 (2): 190–206. 10.1177%2F1035304618765526

Master Builders Association of NSW (2020). *Become a Member.* Available at: https://www.mbansw.asn.au/become-member [accessed 10 February 2021].

Master Builders Australia (2021). *About Master Builders.* Available at: https://www.mbansw.asn.au/about-master-builders [accessed 20 January 2021].

McCallum, R. (2011). Legislated standards: The Australian approach. In: M. Baird, K. Hancock and J. Isaac (eds.) *Work and Employment Relations: An Era of Change.* Sydney, Australia: The Federation Press, pp. 6–16.

National Retail Association (2021). *Services.* Available at: https://www.nra.net.au/services/ [accessed 14 February 2021].

Olson, M. (1971). *The Logic of Collective Action: Public Goods and the Theory of Groups.* Cambridge, MA: Harvard University Press.

Plowman, D. H. (1988). Employer associations and bargaining structures: An Australian perspective. *British Journal of Industrial Relations,* 26 (3): 371–396.

Plowman, D. H. (1989). *Holding the Line: Compulsory Arbitration and National Employer Co-ordination in Australia.* Cambridge: Cambridge University Press.

Plowman, D. H. and Rimmer, M. (1992). *Bargaining Structure, Award Respondency and Employer Associations.* UNSW Studies in Industrial Relations no. 33, Kensington, NSW: Industrial Relations Research Centre, University of New South Wales.

Riley, J. and Sarina, T. (2006). Industrial legislation in 2005. *Journal of Industrial Relations,* 48 (3): 341–356. 10.1177%2F0022185606064789

Sheldon, P. and Thornthwaite, L. (1993). Ex Parte Accord: The Business Council of Australia and Industrial Relations Change. *International Journal of Business Studies,* 1 (1): 37–55.

Sheldon, P. and Thornthwaite, L. (eds.) (1999). *Employer associations and Industrial Relations Change: Catalysts or Captives?* Sydney: Allen & Unwin, chapters 1, 2, 3, 4 and 9.

Sheldon, P. and Thornthwaite, L. (2003). Employer matters in Australia in 2002. *Journal of Industrial Relations,* 45 (2): 224–253. 10.1111/1472-9296.00082

Sheldon P. and Thornthwaite L. (2004). Business or Association? The strategic response of employer associations to the decentralisation of bargaining in Australia. *Economic and Labour Relations Review*, 15 (1): 128–158. 10.11 77%2F103530460401500106

Sheldon, P. and Thornthwaite, L. (2013). Employer and employer association matters in Australia in 2012. *Journal of Industrial Relations*, 55 (3): 386–402. 10.1177%2F0022185613480747

Sheldon, P. and Thornthwaite, L. (2020). Employer and employer association matters in Australia in 2019. *Journal of Industrial Relations*, 62 (3): 403–424. 10.1177%2F0022185620908908

Sheldon, P., Paoletti, F., Nacamulli, R. and Morgan, D. (2016). Employer association responses to the effects of bargaining decentralization in Australia and Italy: Seeking explanations from organizational theory. *British Journal of Industrial Relation*, 54 (1): 160–191. 10.1111/bjir.12061

Sheldon P., della Torre, E. and Nacamulli (2019). When territory matters: Employer associations and changing collective goods strategies. *Human Resource Management Journal*, 29 (1): 17–35. 10.1111/1748-8583.12201

Stanford, J. (2018). The declining labour share in Australia: Definition, measurement and international comparisons. *Journal of Australian Political Economy*, 81: 11–32.

Stewart, A. and Stanford, J. (2017). Regulating work in the gig economy: What are the options? *Economic and Labour Relations Review*, 28 (3): 420–437. 10.1177%2F1035304617722461

Thornthwaite, L. and Sheldon, P. (1996). The Metal Trades Industry Association, Bargaining Structures and the Accord. *Journal of Industrial Relations*, 38 (2): 171–195. 10.1177%2F002218569603800201

Thornthwaite, L. and Sheldon, P. (2012). Employer and employer association experiences of enterprise bargaining: Being careful what you wish for? *Labour & Industry*, 22 (3): 255–274. 10.1080/10301763.2012.10669439

Thornthwaite, L. and Sheldon, P. (2019). Employer and employer association matters in Australia in 2018. *Journal of Industrial Relations*, 61 (3): 382–401. 10.1177%2F0022185619834323

Thornthwaite, L. and Sheldon, P. (2021). Employer and employer association matters in Australia in 2020. *Journal of Industrial Relations*, 63 (3): 357–376. 10.1177/00221856211000406

Todd, T. (2012). Employer and employer association matters in Australia in 2011. *Journal of Industrial Relations*, 54 (3): 344–360. 10.1177%2F0022185 612442285

Victorian Chamber of Commerce and Industry (VCCI) (2020). *Join the Chamber*. Available at: https://www.victorianchamber.com.au/membership/ join [accessed 14 February 2021]

You, K. and Barry, M. (2016). Intra-industry competition among employer associations: A case study of the retail sector. *Labour & Industry*, 26 (2): 1–18. 10.1080/10301763.2016.1162937

9 German Employers' Associations and their Strategy of Deliberate Neglect

Martin Behrens

Introduction

The initial formation of German Employers' Associations (EAs) dates to the second half of the 19th century when the collective voice of employers was formed in response to the rise of the trade union movement (Paster 2012). As Bunn has put it: '[p]ooling resources for strike defence, coordinating lockouts, and securing agreements among employers not to take competitive advantage of other employers during work stoppages, were the primary purposes which brought German employers together into organizations that developed into modern employers' associations' (Bunn 1984: 169). Following the rebuilding of the German economy after World War II the so-called collective bargaining autonomy (*Tarifautonomie*) was established as one of the core principles of German labour relations. Through the constitutional guarantee of collective bargaining autonomy, unions and EAs are empowered to determine wages, hours and working conditions free of state interference.

While the collective bargaining law allows for two different forms of collective bargaining; plant-level bargaining as well as industry-wide (multi-employer) collective bargaining, the latter dominates. By law, collectively agreed standards apply to the constituency of both parties to a multi-employer collective agreement; that is all member companies of an EA which is party to the agreement as well as all members of the signatory union which are employed by those companies. As those employers covered by an agreement do not want to create incentives for employees to join a union, they do not discriminate between union members and non-members and consequently apply the collectively agreed standards to their entire workforce. Due to this system of industry-wide collective bargaining, the capacity of employers to organize has been crucial in bringing collectively-agreed standards to a majority of German employees. Despite a union density of less than 17%, it is still the case that more than 50% of all workers are covered by a collective agreement (both forms: single employer and industry-wide agreement; see Visser 2019). As other mechanisms for stabilizing

DOI: 10.4324/9781003104575-11

collective bargaining coverage, for example the extension of collective agreements, play only a marginal role in Germany labour relations (see Behrens and Traxler 2003), maintaining viable EAs is in the prime interest of labour unions.

In the following we will first introduce the most important functions and structures of German EAs before moving to collective bargaining as the key function of EAs. As our analysis of changes in collective bargaining structures and policies will show, competing interests within associations, in some cases expressed with reference to the small-large firm divide, can be considered as one of the driving forces for the weakening of multi-employer bargaining. In the following we will argue that beyond these varying geometries of interests, which accompany the changing integration of large and small firms within (international) production networks, strategic choice at the level of the association matters as well. As the title of this chapter suggests and as will be shown, the decline of EAs collective bargaining function can – to a significant degree – be associated with employers' fading capacity and willingness to maintain representative structures. As Streeck and Thelen have described in their analysis of different types of gradual transformation within developed political economies, keeping institutions alive requires active maintenance by way of adapting those institutions to changing circumstances (Streeck and Thelen 2005: 30). As our account on the introduction of bargaining-free membership within German EAs will show, a revision of long-established rules for membership sets in motion a process whereby an institution assimilates new practices resulting in institutional displacement. As Mahoney and Thelen have argued (2010: 23), change agents act consciously, by way of institutional displacement, as they are visibly challenging old procedures as they reject the status quo.

Forms and Structures of Employers' Representation

The interests of business are covered by two different systems of representation. First, there are product-market related interests of business represented by industry associations, with the Confederation of German Industry (BDI) being the national-level peak organization of those interests. Among other points, the BDI and its affiliates are in charge of issues such as tax policies, technical standards, energy supplies and industrial policy. Second, there is a system of representation for labour-market related interests which focuses on issues such as collective bargaining, labour and employment law but also vocational education. Labour-market related interests are represented by a national peak confederation, the BDA (Confederation of German Employers' Associations). The BDA organizes about 700 EAs which are directly or indirectly affiliated with the peak federation. In addition, in a smaller number of industries we find associations which represent both the labour and product-market interests of companies within one structure. However, in most areas the separation into two separate systems of representation – at least up to now – remains in place (Schroeder and Weßels 2017).

Below the level of the BDA peak confederation, the organizational structures of the employers are fairly heterogeneous, with variation occurring between, in some cases even within, certain industries or sectors. While the interests of private banks, for example, are represented at the federal level because the major EA, *AGV Banken*, represents banks from the entire country, membership in the metal and engineering industry is at the state level (in some cases even below) with one of Gesamtmetall's state level or regional affiliates. Because the BDA maintains two parallel structures, one regional structure with a state-level unit in almost every state (in total 14 units as in two cases two states are represented by one association) as well as an industry structure with 48 peak-level associations in total, this structure allows for multiple layers of representation, also partly overlapping.

In addition, within the structure of the BDA we find small associations side by side with some heavyweights such as Gesamtmetall and its state-level affiliates, which represent employers in the automobile, metal, machine-tool and electronics industries, or the BAVC (*Bundesarbeitgeberverband Chemie*) representing employers in the chemical engineering industry. While the larger associations are usually equipped with sufficient resources and thus are able to provide their members with a broad spectrum of membership services, many of the smaller associations find it difficult to mobilize the funds necessary to hire staff to provide membership services beyond collective bargaining. Larger and more resourceful associations can support their members in a variety of ways. They not only negotiate collective agreements, they also provide the expertise to apply those agreements. Other services include advice in the area of labour and employment law (even representing companies' interests in the courts), assistance in public relations and the training of employees.

Affiliates enjoy a large degree of autonomy in their relationship vis-à-vis the BDA as their peak confederation. Despite some responsibilities in the case of the extension of collective agreements, the prerogative in the field of collective bargaining is mostly with BDA's affiliates. The BDA, in turn, pursues a coordinating function in the field of political lobbying. Much as their counterparts, the unions, BDA representatives are a powerful voice at public hearings in the parliaments, at both federal and state level, and thus have some influence on the process of law making.

Maintaining a unified voice in the case of political lobbying as well as at the bargaining table is a daunting task as EAs represent firms within a certain market segment or associational domain which compete for both customers and skilled labour, and must represent these somewhat contradictory interests of competitors within a single organization (Behrens 2018: 770). German EAs address this problem by introducing a dense network of formal rules and procedures which actively shape members' interests (Behrens 2011). Such rules concern the process of admitting members to the association, assigning voting rights to categories of members, the mobilization of resources, and provisions on dispute resolution. Of particular importance are rules on the insulation of different spheres of interest. While secrecy clauses in the byelaws of many associations seek to protect members' confidential business information from their competitors, EAs have also introduced a special brokerage function which accompanies the position of a managing director. Directors are mostly recruited from the ranks of university-trained attorneys (in some cases engineers) while the presidents of EAs are selected from the associations' membership (Schroeder and Silvia 2014: 350). While presidents represent their association in the public and vis-à-vis the unions, managing directors are entrusted with the day-to-day operations of the association. Because they do not have any commercial interests on their own, they serve as neutral interest brokers for the competing interests among the associations' membership.

About 27% of EAs, for which byelaws could be retrieved, also provide internal arbitration panels, which are intended to resolve conflict between individual members and the association or among members. Procedures for the operation of such panels are often modelled on rules applied in public courts and in some cases even allow a panel decision to be appealed in front of a higher-level arbitration panel. Sanctions which are ordered by such panels vary substantially and can include fines, censure and the suspension of voting rights or exclusion from elected positions within the EAs (Behrens 2011: 118–122).

As EAs do not have access to state subsidies, they have to raise funds through membership subscriptions and from savings. As Streeck and Visser (2006: 250) have pointed out, some associations built up considerable savings during the post-war years which allow them 'to finance their operation more or less entirely out of the current proceeds from their invested capital'. Most associations, however, depend on membership subscriptions as a major source of income. As shown in Table 9.1, the most common base for calculating members' subscriptions is the total wage bill. About 45 percent of the 163 associations, for which data was available, apply this scheme. Standard provisions vary between 0.1% and 0.2% of the total wage bill. About 10% of associations calculate membership subscriptions based on companies' gross income while 11% use the number of a company's employees as the benchmark for members' payments. A flat rate payment, with a fixed standard payment per member company, is the absolute exception, with less than 3% of associations applying this scheme.

As these data show, while resource mobilization on the part of employers is mostly a function of a company's ability to pay, the members' voice in terms of voting rights follows more egalitarian principles. More

Table 9.1 Basis for the calculation of membership subscriptions in employers' associations (n = 163)

Calculation mode	Percent
Flat rate payment per member	2.5
Net or gross wage bill	45.4
Company turnover	10.4
Number of employees	11.0
Other	30.7

Source: Based on WSI database on employers' and industry associations (2006).

than 64% of those EAs which admit companies to membership (instead of other associations), guarantee one vote per member. Weighted voting rights (according to company revenue, number of employees or establishments within a company) apply to only 18% of EAs and another 6% assign votes based on membership fees (other categories: 12%). This close association between means-based (membership fees) and egalitarian (voting rights) principles mostly benefits small and medium-sized companies. In most EAs small and medium-sized member companies benefit from services provided with the help of resources mobilized by the big member companies. As we will see in the following section, balancing the interests of different categories of members is an enduring challenge within EAs.

Collective Bargaining: Decentralization and Flexibilization

Collective bargaining is pivotal for the majority of German EAs. As Figure 9.1 shows, however, the share of the total workforce which is covered by an industry-wide agreement is in constant decline in both parts of the country, east and west Germany. While in 1995, 72% of west German employees were still covered by collectively agreed standards for wages hours and working conditions, this share declined to 46% by 2019 (decline in east Germany was from 56% in 1996 to 34% in 2019).[1]

It should be noted, however, that the data presented in Figure 9.1 represents both, public and private sector employees. While collective bargaining on the side of private employers is mostly conducted by EAs, collective bargaining in the public sector is conducted for the three different levels of state administration, with the municipal and federal governments joining forces in a collective bargaining alliance and the federal states (*Länder*) negotiating separate agreements for their constituency (Keller 2013). In addition, there is also a separate bargaining structure for employees of the Church, which is known as the 'third way'. Church employees

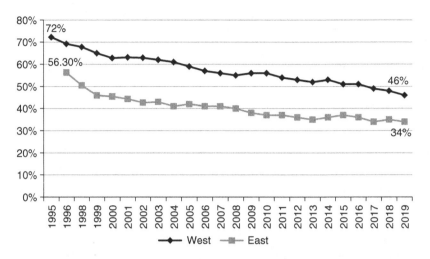

Figure 9.1 Share of employees covered by a multi-employer collective agreement.
Source: Based on IAB Establishment Panel, Ellguth and Kohaut 2020: 279.

are not allowed to strike and their working conditions, in contrast to the public and private sector, are determined by special commissions.

The decline of bargaining coverage in the private (non-Church) sector is mostly the result of the fading ability of German EAs to organize most companies within their jurisdiction, either because of membership decline or because of members choosing a new bargaining-free membership status, the so-called 'OT' membership. 'OT' is the short form for 'without collective bargaining coverage' (*ohne Tarifbindung*) and means that those associations offer an opt-out clause to their membership. Individual companies can maintain membership of the association but are exempt from applying the terms and conditions of the industry-wide collective agreement to their workforce. As members, companies can still benefit from all other services provided by that association but are free to either determine standards for wages, hours and working conditions with workers individually or to negotiate a separate company-level collective agreement. Despite these general trends or developments, it should be noted, however, that in terms of absolute coverage there is substantial variation in respect to company size and industry. While coverage in large companies is significantly higher than in small firms, we also find differences between certain industries and sectors: Coverage is highest in public administration, in banking/insurances, and construction and lowest in private services such as information/communication, retail and transportation. Part of this between-industry variation is driven by differences of average company-size but also by the varying willingness and capacity of EAs to organize companies. As the examples of nursing homes/hospitals, slaughterhouses and car-repair shops show, bargaining coverage in some areas is low because there are no or only weak EAs available to bargain with unions. This problem is most apparent in nursing, which employs more than one million employees. Attempts to improve wages within this occupation and to attract more people to work in nursing (a daunting problem during the COVID-19 pandemic) has had limited success because of the decentralized bargaining structure in this sector and deficient representational structures on the employers' side.

Membership Decline

Membership decline, a first root cause for declining bargaining coverage, began to be a major concern for the future of the German bargaining systems in the early 1990s (Schroeder and Ruppert 1996). Variables which are associated with the likelihood of companies leaving an EA cover a broad range of issues. One set of explanations focuses on specific firm-level characteristics such as size, location (east or west Germany) or industry (Addison et al. 2013; Ellguth and Kohaut 2010, Lehmann 2002; Kohaut and Schnabel 2003). The idea behind these accounts is that changes within the German political economy, such as competitive pressures arising from the integration into the global economy, new supplier-OEM (Original Equipment Manufacturer) relationships or changing forms of corporate governance, affect companies' preferences for membership in an EA.

A second set of explanations focuses on the associational level (see Helfen's contribution in this volume). As 'ideational brokers' (Campbell 2004: 105) the leadership of EAs and their normative orientations towards social partnership are critical for understanding institutional stability (Behrens and Helfen 2016: 337). The value of such an organizational perspective became most obvious in times of rapid change. Deliberation on the direction of collective bargaining has occurred on several occasions in German post-war history. One of those moments of intense debate occurred in the decade following German unification, a decade shaped by a difficult macroeconomic environment for Germany's export-oriented industry, which coincides with the time when EAs' membership decline became an issue.

In the early 1990s German EAs, led by Gesamtmetall, voiced criticism of the results of collective bargaining, arguing that collectively-agreed standards were too rigid and allowed too little flexibility. Gesamtmetall called for the introduction of opening clauses in multi-employer agreements, allowing firm-level actors to adjust collectively-agreed standards to the specific needs of individual companies. While unions did not entirely resist these demands for controlled decentralization, they voiced fierce opposition to forms of disorganized (or 'wildcat' or 'unauthorized') decentralization. In the case of organized decentralization, unions would be in the position of a gate keeper as they have the final word on plant-level deviation from collectively-agreed standards (Bispinck and Schulten 1999; Traxler 1995). Parts of the employer camp, however, sought to bypass union control and threatened to strike unauthorized side-deals with their works councils (Hassel 1999). The position of EAs on this issue turned out to be ambivalent: On the one hand, employers somewhat welcomed wildcat decentralization as a powerful tool to support their case on the need for bargaining reform, on the other hand this form of unauthorized transfer of bargaining responsibilities not only violates bargaining law but also interferes with the institutional role of EAs as the primary bargaining agent from the business side.

These tensions surfaced in the early 1990s, when the conflict on the future of collective bargaining escalated. Dieter Kirchner, Gesamtmetall's managing director, emphasized that the year 1994 was decisive for the fate of the entire bargaining system (*Handelsblatt* 29.12.1993) and argued that in a move of massive wildcat decentralization more and more companies would undermine collective agreements by way of negotiating side deals with their local works councils (*Handelsblatt* 29.9.1993). The situation worsened after IG Metall won a new collective agreement for the metal-engineering industry in the Bavarian district. Criticism within the employers' camp escalated when some industry federations such as that of the mechanical engineering industry (VDMA), the federation of the electronics (ZVEI) and auto industries (VDA) threatened to take bargaining responsibilities from Gesamtmetall and to bargain on their own (*Frankfurter Rundschau* 09.06.1995). This is remarkable because within the dual structure of business-interest representation, collective bargaining is the prerogative of EAs rather than industry associations. This development came just weeks before Gesamtmetall's managing director, Kirchner, even threatened to dissolve his organization altogether if the union did not collaborate in an effort to reform the collective agreement (*Frankfurter Rundschau* 25.07.1995), with some observers, however, assuming, this to be a 'cry for help' rather than 'a statement of intent' (Thelen 2000: 158).

Even when the collapse of EAs in Germany's leading industry failed to materialize, these events and developments from the early 1990s indicated the extent of tensions within the employers' camp. As some observers have emphasized (Silvia 2013: 201–211; Streeck 2009; Thelen 2000; Traxler et al. 2007) associations found it increasingly difficult to reconcile the competing interests of large and small/medium-sized companies within one association. In a traditional view on German EAs, the co-existence of large and small companies within one association served to maintain an equilibrium of interests. Because of their limited ability to pay membership subscriptions, small companies contribute only a small share of an EAs revenue but benefit substantially from their services. As small companies rarely have their own HR departments or specialized lawyers, they frequently take advantage of EA support in the field of labour and employment law, and advice on the application of a collective agreement. Large companies, in turn, contribute a large part to an association's budget without being dependent on EAs' services (Traxler 1995: 32). Larger companies still benefit, however, as they can hide behind the limited ability of the smaller EA members to accept substantial wage hikes and thus receive favourable collective bargaining settlements.

According to some observers, this mutual gains logic has been challenged in recent times. Streeck, for example, pointed out that tension increased when large firms, which dominated EAs, forced small and medium-sized supplier firms to cut their prices: 'Roughly at this point, a formerly self-reinforcing institutional configuration became self-undermining, and perhaps ultimately self-destructive' (Streeck 2009: 52). As the data presented in Figure 9.1 indicates, however, collective bargaining decline occurred across the board and not just in the metal engineering industry with its strong emphasis on supplier-OEM relationships. Another finding also indicates that the small vs. large firms-rationale does not suffice to explain declining support for multi-employer bargaining. As an analysis of employers' support for social partnership with unions reveals, it is mostly EAs dominated by large companies which distance themselves most intensively from traditional collective bargaining institutions (Behrens and Helfen 2016: 349–350).

Introduction of Bargaining-free Membership

Pressures on the system of collective bargaining increased when in the 1990s several EAs started to offer an 'OT' membership status, which turned out to be another root cause for the ongoing decline of collective bargaining coverage. Bargaining free membership is a remarkable departure from long-established employment relations institutions as collective bargaining is considered the key function of an EA. The introduction of this new OT membership status cleared the way for the liberalization of the German bargaining system by way of gradually transforming the very nature of an EA.

Reasons for this new strategy of allowing members to distance themselves from bargaining coverage vary. Three different explanations can be identified in the literature. A first explanation sees OT as a response to ongoing membership decline. By way of allowing members to opt out, it would keep those members from leaving the association who were dissatisfied with the results of collective bargaining (Haipeter 2017: 307; Haipeter and Schilling 2006; Kinderman 2005: 454). Increasing bargaining power, a second reason, focuses on the bargaining process. EAs might use the threat of large numbers of members changing their membership status and 'fleeing' collective bargaining coverage to gain concessions from unions during negotiations (Schroeder and Silvia

2014). Finally, in a more radical sense OT might be used as a device for ending multi-employer collective bargaining altogether. Once a critical mass of member companies has switched to OT-status, 'the EA would change its character from a collective bargaining organization into a mere service agency or lobby organization' (Behrens and Helfen 2019: 54). These three motivations are not exclusionary as, for example, reversing membership decline can be accompanied by a strategy for increasing an EA's bargaining power.

OT membership status originated on the periphery, rather than at the centre of organized employers' interest representation. When in 1990 the EA for the Wood and Plastics Industry, Rhineland-Palatinate (*Verband der Holz- und KunststoffindustrieRheinland-Pfalz*), introduced bargaining-free membership for the first time (Völkl 2002) this was still a controversial practice, carrying a stigma of 'deviance' even within the employers' camp (Schroeder 1995: 56). It took until 1995 for the state-level labour court in the Rhineland Palatinate to confirm that the new membership status did not violate the law, before other EAs followed by changing their byelaws to allow the introduction of OT. For German employers this issue was crucial because if the courts had denied their approval of OT, a full reinstatement of the collective agreements for all members would have been the result (Deinert and Walser 2015: 28). Apart from jeopardizing the competitive positions of companies, introducing a faulty new membership status would have exposed associations to the risk of damage to reputation and further alienation between associations and firms.

Based on survey data (Wirtschaftsverbände in Deutschland 2012), it is estimated that about half of all German EAs offer their members an opt-out opportunity (Behrens and Helfen 2019), somewhat contradicting the narrative that it is mostly small firms that oppose traditional collective bargaining institutions. Multivariate statistical analysis reveals that associations dominated by small firms resist the introduction of OT-membership, while the highest share of associations with this new membership form is to be found within the ranks of associations dominated by medium-sized companies with between 101 and 250 employees (Behrens and Helfen 2019: 63). It should be noted, however, that just introducing an opt-out clause into an associations' byelaws does not necessarily attract members into this new membership status. While the introduction of this clause is a choice to be taken at the associational level, taking advantage of OT is a decision to be taken by each company individually: either an existing member converting its status from bargaining coverage to non-coverage or a new entry preferring OT-membership over regular membership status.

As the following Table 9.2 shows, at least in the case of Gesamtmetall, one of the BDA's largest and most powerful affiliates, the use of bargaining-free (OT) membership status is becoming increasingly

Table 9.2 Membership development of Gesamtmetall, 2000–2016

	Total membership (firms)	Share OT/total membership (firms)	Total number of employees	Share OT/total membership (employees)
2000	6,252	0%	2,122,472	0%
2001	6,093	0%	2,103,799	0%
2002	5,704	0%	2,061,622	0%
2003	5,109	0%	1,922,167	0%
2004	4,774	0%	1,859,026	0%
2005	5,861	24.4%	1,986,792	8.3%
2006	6,113	31.1%	2,003,115	11.2%
2007	6,321	36.4%	2,065,812	14.0%
2008	6,366	38.8%	2,101,471	15.7%
2009	6,334	40.2%	2,016,986	15.8%
2010	6,437	42.3%	2,025,127	16.5%
2011	6,565	44.4%	2,117,464	17.6%
2012	6,774	46.8%	2,180,014	18.6%
2013	6,813	47.5%	2,209,605	19.3%
2014	6,903	48.5%	2,254,665	19.8%
2015	7,009	49.7%	2,259,058	20.2%
2016	7,110	50.4%	2,284,120	20.7%
2017	7,144	52.1%	2,359,642	22.0%
2018	7,223	53.5%	2,451,248	23.1%
2019	7,317	55.3%	2,515,859	24.3%

Source: Gesamtmetall, own calculation.

popular among member companies. After its introduction in the mid-2000s, OT membership status expanded within Gesamtmetall and, in fact, accounts for the association's entire membership growth in the second half of the decade. In 2019, the last year for which data is available, more than 50% of all member companies chose the 'bargaining-free' status. When looking at the right side of Table 9.2 it is also apparent that OT-membership status is an issue for small and medium-sized firms rather than for large companies: in 2019, while representing 55.3% of all member companies, OT firms only accounted for 24.3% of all employees employed by Gesamtmetall's member firms.

As these findings suggest, in terms of its impact on the support of traditional collective bargaining institutions, company size turns out to be an ambivalent category. It is mostly associations dominated by large firms which challenge the cherished concept of social partnership while, in turn, associations dominated by small firms tend to resist the introduction of bargaining-free membership and thus keep the door closed for those companies who are looking for an easy escape from collective bargaining. Once the door is open, and OT-membership status in place, however, it is mostly small and medium-sized companies which take advantage of this option. To fully understand the specific influences in this two-level decision structure – offering OT in the first place and using this option once it is established – further research would be required.

Factors Stabilizing EAs

With collective bargaining coverage being in decline for more than 25 years, scholars have raised the question of how to stabilize employers' collective interest representation. One approach is based on government regulation. While in general, collective bargaining autonomy free of state interference is a cherished key principle of German labour relations, there are also demands for new laws to stabilize multi-employer bargaining. One approach is extending collective agreements; a second one is the introduction of procurement clauses.

In most European countries, the extension of collective agreements to those companies and their employees who are not directly covered is a common procedure (Hayter and Visser 2018). Despite an initiative by the German 'grand coalition' government (coalition between Chancellor Merkel's party CDU and the social democrats, SPD) to improve conditions for extension, however, the number of collective agreements subject to this procedure has remained very limited with less than 2% of all multi-employer agreements being subject to extension (Schulten 2019: 23–24). The use of public procurement laws as a second approach for strengthening bargaining coverage has so far failed to significantly improve bargaining coverage. Procurement laws, which would make government spending conditional to firms complying with collectively agreed standards, became less effective after the European Court of Justice restricted the use of such pay clauses without being able to completely abandon them (Sack et al. 2016)[2]. The rationale behind these two approaches is to restrict the cost-benefits available to those outsider companies, which are not covered by a multi-employer agreement (either because they are not a member of the EA or because they have chosen bargaining-free membership). As long as companies have to obey collectively-agreed standards, either because of extension or procurement laws, there is little to be gained from leaving an EA, or not joining in the first place, or choosing an OT-membership status respectively. It should be noted, however, that such a perspective is somewhat disputed within the ranks of EAs. As for example Rainer Dulger, president of Gesamtmetall has argued, it could not be a major goal of collective bargaining autonomy to aim at 100% collective bargaining coverage (Dulger 2019: 49). From this perspective there are concerns that high coverage would increase wage levels and thus production costs (Lesch et al. 2018: 870). As indicated above, this reasoning would be very much in line with two of the motivations for the introduction of OT-membership: increasing EA's bargaining power and reversing membership decline.

Besides these proposed changes in the regulative environment of collective bargaining, scholars have also found that changes in the economic environment have the potential to influence employers' perceptions of key principles of multi-employer bargaining. Based on the data of a follow-up survey of EAs (Wirtschaftsverbände in Deutschland 2005/2006 and 2012) Helfen has found that compared to the year 2005/2006, when this survey was conducted for the first time, in the year 2012 the support of EAs for some key concepts of collective bargaining improved. While in 2005/2006 only 24.1% of representatives of EAs agreed with the statement: 'German social partnership is an advantage in international competition', by 2012, after the world financial crisis, this share had increased to 66.7% (Helfen 2013). Apparently, the experience of joint efforts to stabilize the German economy during and after the crisis strengthened the appreciation held by employers for traditional institutions of wage determination. This is also suggested by the following survey results: While in 2005/2006 only 19.2% agreed that 'Unions are a reliable partner' this share had increased to 37.4% in 2012. Finally, the share of EAs, which agreed with the statement 'Negotiations of collective agreements are characterized by factual debates' increased from 14.4% (2005/2006) to 32.5% in 2012.

As these findings indicate, it is not just companies' cost-benefit analysis that informs their preferences vis-à-vis multi-employer bargaining (and thus regarding membership in an EA) but also their experiences with those institutions. Such experiences can be nurtured by situations of crisis, such as the world financial crisis, but also by certain experiences with collective bargaining. As research has shown, support shown by employers for key institutions of collective bargaining improves when they perceive their success in previous bargaining rounds to be positive (Behrens and Helfen 2016).

Conclusions

As this brief account on the structures and development of employers' interest representation in Germany has shown, the employers' stance vis-à-vis key institutions of industrial relations in general and collective bargaining in particular, has varied. In the early 1990s it appeared that a major strand within leading EAs sought to depart from the traditional model altogether while during the past decade, in the aftermath of the world financial crisis, the most radical voices within the employers' camp have remained silent. One possible explanation for these inconsistent policies of German employers can be found in the work of Martin and Swank (2012). As employers' interests are politically constructed, the varying capacities of countries to produce highly organized EAs reflect 'the interplay of party politics and the government structures that set the rules of the game' (Martin and Swank 2012: 3). As far as the German case is concerned, they argue, the fragmented structure of the state has resulted in 'failure to promote concertation among social partners' (Martin and Swank 2012: 208) and thus resulted in a decline of the coherence of EAs (ibid., 209).

This would explain why in Germany – more than in other countries – the interest representation of employers is subject to employers' strategic choice. As the introduction of bargaining-free membership suggests, EAs act consciously when changing the rules of membership and thus, in the terms of the concept introduced by Streeck and Thelen (2005), are the drivers of institutional displacement. Old procedures and rules such as combining membership with collective bargaining coverage are abandoned and set in motion a process of gradual change whereby more and more of EAs' member companies choose not to be covered by a multi-employer agreement. As a result, this process of incremental change is providing grounds for the liberalization of collective bargaining. As so often in the political economy, however, powerful societal actors such as EAs take decisions under conditions they cannot control. This provides access points for other actors such as unions, works councils and governments but also makes decisions possible due to learning gained from earlier experiences.

Notes

1 In addition to those employees covered by an industry-level agreement in 2019 another 7% of the workforce in west and 11% in east Germany were covered by a company (single employer) agreement (Ellguth and Kohaut 2020: 279).
2 The recent revision of the EU Posting of Workers Directive might reverse this trend and has much potential to support the introduction of procurement laws (see Seikel 2020).

References

Addison, J. T., Bryson, A., Teixeira, P., Pahnke, A. and Bellmann, L. (2013). The extent of collective bargaining and workplace representation: Transitions between states and their determinants. A comparative analysis of Germany and Great Britain. *Scottish Journal of Political Economy*, 60 (2): 182–209. 10.1111/sjpe.12007

Behrens, M. (2011). *Das Paradox der Arbeitgeberverbände. Von der Schwierigkeit, durchsetzungsstarke Unternehmensinteressen kollektiv zu vertreten*. Berlin: edition sigma.

Behrens, M. (2018). Structure and competing logics: The art of shaping interests within German employers' associations. *Socio-Economic Review*, 16 (4): 769–789. 10.1093/ser/mwx037

Behrens, M. and Traxler, F. (2003). Collective bargaining coverage and extension procedures. *EIR Observer*, February: i–viii.

Behrens, M. and Helfen, M. (2016). The foundations of social partnership. *British Journal of Industrial Relations*, 54 (2): 334–357. 10.1111/bjir.12151

Behrens, M. and Helfen, M. (2019). Small change, big impact? Organisational membership rules and the exit of employers' associations from multi-employer bargaining in Germany. *Human Resource Management Journal*, 29 (1): 51–66. 10.1111/1748-8583.12210

Bispinck, R. and Schulten, T. (1999). Flächentarifvertrag und betriebliche Interessenvertretung. In: Walther Müller-Jentsch (ed.) *Konfliktpartnerschaft. Akteure und Institutionen der Industriellen Beziehungen*. Munich and Mehring: Rainer HamppVerlag, pp. 185–212.

Bunn, R. F. (1984). Employers' associations in the Federal Republic of Germany. In: J. P. Windmuller and A. Gladstone (eds.) *Employers Associations and Industrial Relations. A Comparative Study*. Oxford: Clarendon Press, pp. 169–201.

Campbell, J. L. (2004). *Institutional Change and Globalization*. Princeton, NJ: Princeton University Press.

Deinert, O. and Walser, M. (2015). *Tarifvertragliche Bindung der Arbeitgeber. Bindungswille und –fähigkeit der Arbeitgeber und ihrer Verbände als juristisches und rechtliches Problem*. Baden-Baden: Nomos.

Dulger, R. (2019). Es braucht keine neue, sondern eine andere Partnerschaft. In: S. Kampeter (ed.) *Sozialpartnerschaft 4.0. Tarifpolitik für die Arbeitswelt von morgen*. Frankfurt/New York: Campus, pp. 47–51.

Ellguth, P., and Kohaut, S. (2010). Auf der Flucht? Tarifaustritte und die Rolle von Öffnungsklauseln. *Industrielle Beziehungen/The German Journal of Industrial Relations*, 1 (4): 345–371.

Ellguth, P. and Kohaut, S. (2020). Tarifbindung und betriebliche Interessenvertretung: Aktuelle Ergebnisse aus dem IAB-Betriebspanel 2019. *WSI-Mitteilungen*, 73 (4): 278–285.

Frankfurter Rundschau 09.06.1995. "Es brodelt bei Gesamtmetall".

Frankfurter Rundschau 25.07.1995. "IG Metall wittert 'Bankrott'".

Haipeter, T. (2017). OT-Mitgliedschaften und OT-Verbände. In: W. Schroeder and B. Weßels (eds.) *Handbuch Arbeitgeber- und Wirtschaftsverbände in Deutschland*. 2nd edition. Wiesbaden: Springer VS, pp. 305–336.

Haipeter, T. and Schilling, G. (2006). *Arbeitgeberverbände in der Metall- und Elektroindustrie. Tarifbindung, Organisationsentwicklung und Strategiebildung*. Hamburg: VSA.

Handelsblatt 29.09.1993. "Mitglieder drohen mit der Flucht aus den Verbänden, wenn die Wende nicht gelingt".

Handelsblatt 29.12.1993. "Flächentarifvertrag ist nur durch Flexibilität zu retten".

Hassel, A. (1999). The erosion of the German system of industrial relations. *British Journal of Industrial Relations*, 37 (3): 483–505. 10.1111/1467-8543.00138

Hayter, S. and Visser, J. (2018). *The Application and Extension of Collective Agreements: Enhancing the Inclusiveness of Labour Protection*. Geneva: International Labour Organisation.

Helfen, M. (2013). Sozialpartnerschaft bei Arbeitgeberverbänden: „Schnee von gestern" oder vor der Renaissance? *WSI-Mitteilungen*, 66 (7): 482–490. 10.5771/0342-300X-2013-7-482

Keller, B. (2013). Die Arbeitgeber des öffentlichen Sektors: Institutionelle Stabilität und sozio-ökonomischer Wandel. *WSI-Mitteilungen*, 66 (7): 500–509. 10.5771/0342-300X-2013-7-500

Kinderman, D. (2005). Pressure from without, subversion from within: The two-pronged German employer offensive. *Comparative European Politics*, 3 (4): 432–463. 10.1057/palgrave.cep.6110064

Kohaut, S. and Schnabel, C. (2003). Zur Erosion des Flächentarifvertrags: Ausmaß, Einflussfaktoren und Gegenmaßnahmen. *Industrielle Beziehungen*, 10 (2): 193–219.

Lehmann, K. (2002). *Stabilität und Veränderung der Flächentarifbindung von Arbeitgebern in Deutschland*. Münster: LIT.

Lesch, H., Schneider, H., and Vogel, S. (2018). Rückzug aus der Flächentarifbindung: Empirischer Forschungsstand und Implikationen für eine Stabilisierung des Tarifsystems. *SozialerFortschritt*, 67 (10): 867–886.

Mahoney, J. and Thelen, K. (2010). *Explaining Institutional Change. Ambiguity, Agency, and Power*. Cambridge: Cambridge University Press.

Martin, C. J. and Swank, D. (2012). *The Political Construction of Business Interests. Coordination, Growth and Equality*. Cambridge: Cambridge University Press.

Paster, T. (2012). *The Role of Business in the Development of the Welfare State and Labor Markets in Germany. Containing Social Reforms*. London/New York: Routledge.

Sack, D., Schulten, T., Sarter, E. K. and Böhlke, N. (2016). *Öffentliche-Auftragsvergabe in Deutschland. Sozial und nachhaltig?* Baden-Baden: Nomos.

Schroeder, W. (1995). Arbeitgeberverbände in der Klemme. Motivations- und Verpflichtungskrisen. In. R. Bispinck (ed.) *Tarifpolitik der Zukunft. Was wird aus dem Flächentarifvertrag?* Hamburg: VSA, pp. 44–63.

Schroeder, W. and Ruppert, B. (1996). *Austritte aus Arbeitgeberverbänden: Eine Gefahr für das deutsche Modell?* Marburg: Schüren.

Schroeder, W. and Silvia, S. J. (2014). Gewerkschaften und Arbeitgeberverbände. In: W. Schroeder (ed.) *Handbuch Gewerkschaften in Deutschland*. 2nd edition. Wiesbaden: Springer VS, pp. 337–365.

Schroeder, W. and Weßels, B. (2017). Die deutsche Unternehmerver-bändelandschaft: vom Zeitalter der Verbände zum Zeitalter der Mitglieder. In: W. Schroeder and B. Weßels (eds.) *Handbuch Arbeitgeber- und Wirtschaftsverbände in Deutschland*. 2nd edition. Wiesbaden: Springer VS, pp. 3–28.

Schulten, T. (2019). German collective bargaining – from erosion to revitalization? In: M. Behrens and H. Dribbusch (eds.) *Industrial Relations in Germany. Dynamics and Perspectives*. WSI-Mitteilungen, Special Issue 2019. Baden-Baden: Nomos, pp. 11–30.

Seikel, D. (2020). Die Revision der Entsenderichtlinie. Wie der lange Kampf um die Wiedereinbettung exterritorialisierten Arbeitsrechts gewonnen wurde. *WSI-Working Paper* 212 (August 2020), Düsseldorf.

Silvia, S. (2013). *Holding the Shop Together. German Industrial Relations in the Post-war Era*. Ithaca and London: ILR-Press/Cornell University Press.

Streeck, W. (2009). *Re-Forming Capitalism. Institutional Change in the German Political Economy*. Oxford: Oxford University Press.

Streeck, W. and Thelen, K. (2005). Introduction: Institutional change in advanced political economies. In: W. Streeck and K. Thelen (eds.) *Beyond Continuity. Institutional Change in Advanced Political Economies*. Oxford and New York: Oxford University Press, pp. 1–39.

Streeck, W. and Visser, J. (2006). Conclusions; Organized business facing internationalization. In: W. Streeck, J. R. Grote, V. Schneider and J. Visser (eds.) *Governing Interests: Business Associations facing Internationalization.* London/New York: Routledge, pp. 242–272.

Thelen, K. (2000). Why German employers cannot bring themselves to dismantle the German model. In: T. Iversen, J. Pontusson and D. Soskice (eds.) *Union, Employers, and Central Banks. Macroeconomic Coordination and Institutional Change in Social Market Economies.* Cambridge: Cambridge University Press, pp. 138–169.

Traxler, F. (1995). Farewell to labour market associations? Organized versus disorganized decentralization as a map for industrial relations. In: C. Crouch and F. Traxler (eds.) *Organized Industrial Relations in Europe. What Future?* Aldershot: Ashgate, pp. 3–19.

Traxler, F., Brandl, B. and Pernicka, S. (2007). Business Associability, activities and governance. In: F. Traxler and G. Huemer (eds.) *Handbook of Business Interest Associations, Firm Size and Governance: A Comparative Analytical Approach.* London/New York: Routledge, pp. 351–406.

Visser, J. (2019). *ICTWSS Database. Database on Industrial Characteristics of Trade Union, Wage Setting, State Intervention, and Social Pacts in 41 Countries between 1960 and 2019. Version 6.1.* Amsterdam. Available at: http://uva-aias.net/nl/ictwss

Völkl, Martin (2002). *Der Mittelstand und die Tarifautonomie. Arbeitgeberverbände zwischen Sozialpartnerschaft und Dienstleistung.* Munich and Mehring: Rainer Hampp Verlag.

Part III

Different Types of Employers' Organizations

10 Countervailing Power and the Role of State Threats: The Case of Pro-religious Employers' Organizations in Turkey

Lisa Ahsen Sezer

Introduction

The concept of countervailing power has been used to explain the origins and development of Employers' Organizations (EOs). It suggests that threats from organized labour and/or state legislation push employers into coordination to countervail trade union and the state's legislative powers to pre-empt labour market regulations (Barry and Wilkinson 2011). However, union power, multi-employer bargaining, and the threat of collective labour regulations have declined. Proponents of the structural power hypothesis (e.g. Baccaro and Howell 2017; Culpepper 2011) have also argued that neoliberal governments have expanded employer discretion and translated business and employer interests into policy, thereby making EOs as collective organizations redundant. Yet employers continue to organize and to shape the employment relationship in new ways beyond collective bargaining while EO density rates have remained relatively stable (e.g. Baccaro and Howell 2017; Brandl and Lehr 2016). There are even new types of mixed EOs with adjusted functions and structures, such as employer forums in the UK (Bowkett et al. 2017). It is important to understand why and how EOs continue to emerge despite a weakened need for countervailing power.

Recent studies show that even in a context of weak union power, the state can continue to exert pressure on employers through individual rights legislation (Gooberman et al. 2019). This chapter builds on such recent extensions to explore new pressures of countervailing power through a historical analysis of EOs in Turkey until 2012. Existing explanations cannot sufficiently resolve the origins and development of a new type of EO in Turkey (Sezer 2019), and of EOs across other transition and developing economies, where trade union and employment legislative threats are particularly low. In Turkey, pro-religious EOs emerged from the 1990s onwards, with structures based on collaborative alliances among pro-religious employers, civil society organizations, and politicians; and with functions focused on support in political power struggles.

DOI: 10.4324/9781003104575-13

I argue that a necessary condition for such a new type of EO in Turkey to emerge and develop were state[1] and political actors' threats towards employer collective action. These threats combined with the perceived exclusion from political and corporatist channels to incentivize vulnerable civic actors to organize EOs in collaboration. While the state's legislative powers are a recognized condition in the countervailing power argument, broader state threats are not usually included as an incentive for employer organization. However, state threats can go beyond job regulatory issues to include autonomous collective action in the industrial relations (IR), civil society and political systems. The focus on regulatory institutions in the IR literature also misses the crucial role that individual state and political actors can have, especially after episodes of crises, on EO emergence and development. This chapter therefore combines countervailing power insights with the agency-centric political entrepreneurship stream (e.g. Markus 2007; Schneider 2004, 2010; Sinha 2005). The latter focuses on the role of actors in wider power contests and their effect on employer organization.

This chapter proceeds by first discussing the countervailing power and political entrepreneurship literatures. Second, the context of Turkey and its EOs are briefly introduced. Third, the chapter analyzes the conditions under which pro-religious EOs emerged. The discussion and conclusion provide a synthesis of the results along with a discussion on the theoretical contributions to the IR literature.

Old and New Pressures of Countervailing Power

IR approaches historically analyze the interaction among employment relations actors, trade union structures and the changing pressures they exert on EOs as globalization advances. Researchers in the countervailing power tradition have discussed multiple reasons why they would expect EOs to decline. Trade union densities have declined, employers increasingly exit multi-employer bargaining, statutory collective bargaining extension and coordination mechanisms feature loopholes, and union access to industrial action has been restricted. The overall effect is to make EOs increasingly redundant as organizations to countervail state and union power. Yet EO density rates are neither uniform cross-nationally, nor across industries, reigniting a debate on the conditions under which EOs emerge and are sustained. The EO revitalization literature has shown how organizations have restructured their functions and organizational structures to make domain changes of associations. Traditionally, EOs used to focus on employment matters and were differentiated from trade organizations that represent employers' product market interests. However, such pure organizations have become very rare. Instead, most EOs are now mixed organizations, where collective functions such as collective bargaining, skill provision, and corporatist policy-making, are now layered or bolstered with additional commercial selective or elective goods (e.g. Ibsen and Navrbjerg 2019). Most EOs have adapted their functions to serve member interests through selective goods such as specialized HR and legal support, product market services and tailored lobbying. Structurally, mergers and thus a change in membership base and greater concentration of EOs have become common adaptation strategies; and EOs have also entered alliances with new IR actors. New types of EOs have thus emerged as organizations shift their functions and/or structures.

To understand the resilience of EOs under reduced union and legislative threat, the countervailing power concept was recently extended to include new pressures from the state and CSOs (civil society organizations) (Heery et al. 2012), through a regime of individualized employment legislation (Barry and Wilkinson 2011; Gooberman et al. 2019). European Social Dialogue, European Union and national legislative powers with a focus on individual, rather than collective rights regime have provided renewed in-centives for employers to coordinate their activities in EOs. In the UK, the 'active regulatory state presented EOs with fresh opportunities to act as a buffering mechanism, lobbying government to secure favourable changes in the law and mediating the impact of law on member firms' (Gooberman et al. 2019: 11). With a trend towards increased occupational licensing and 'soft' forms of international labour laws, EOs have also adjusted their functions to provide licensing or codes of conduct for particular industries and thereby privately regulate labour markets. CSOs have exerted re-inforcing pressures on EOs to create and implement the new individual rights-based employment regime, leading to the development of a new type of EO: issue-based employer forums (Bowkett et al. 2017), which represent employer interests in equality and diversity, disability and corporate social responsibility. Union and regulatory threats, reinforced by new identity-based movements in some cases, are new sources of countervailing em-ployer power.

Economic and financial liberalization, combined with pressure from tight fiscal policies, have forced governments in developed and transition economies to rely increasingly on the third sector and capital to support macroeconomic governance and public goods provision. In most late developing countries across Latin America, Africa and Asia, business is more dependent on the state to drive industrialization and policy-input, and access to political elites become key selective incentives among EOs (Schneider 2004). Neoliberal international institutions and national governments have mostly weakened fledging trade unions, with limited collective IR legislations and underdeveloped collective bargaining. Therefore, EOs have often long performed such mixed labour and pro-duct market functions.

This chapter builds upon recent extensions of countervailing power in an environment of low union power, and where 'new social movements' mobilizing around individual identities constitute important IR actors. Individual employment rights regimes and mobilization based on non-work identities such as gender, race, ethnicity, and religion, have increasingly complemented collective bargaining in the UK (Gooberman et al. 2019) and US (Piore and Safford 2006). Similar conditions can also be observed in the 'Global South'. However, state-driven third sector growth as in liberal market economies is not a sufficient condition to explain the origins and developments of new EOs across a wide range of late-developing settings. State-led development and weak business development often foster rent-seeking relations between state actors and business groups (e.g. Buğra 1994). Nevertheless, mixed EOs that focus on achieving political aims, and cooperate with civil society, have been observed in several Latin American countries, Indonesia, and Turkey (Sezer 2019).

Political and State Actors

In order to understand these cases, it is important to move beyond trade unions or regulatory institutions as sources of countervailing power. The political entrepreneurship stream gives primacy to micropolitical institutions, to state and political actors and how they shape the incentives offered by the political system to organize employers (Markus 2007; Martin 1994; Martin and Swank 2012; Polsky 2000; Schneider 2004, 2010; Sinha 2005). This literature suggests two major strategic interests behind political entrepreneurs' organization of employers. Firstly, EOs can promote efficient policymaking by providing adequate information. The aggregation of business interests and provision of market information through peak EOs to prevent rent-seeking was a key motivator of European corporatism of the 1970s (Schmitter 1974). Secondly, EOs can support political and state elites in various power contests (e.g. electoral competition, struggles between executive and legislature) (Markus 2007). For example, in the US, political candidates were found to shape and mobilize employer interests to support their campaigns (Polsky 2000). US presidents also mobilized employers to offset competition with parliament (Martin 1994).

Schneider (2004) found that state actors, by threatening employers' trade interests, played a key role in shaping the initial development of EOs in several Latin American countries. Strong, encompassing EOs then developed in Chile, Colombia and Mexico over time due to the policy-access granted by individual state actors, whereas no economy-wide associations developed in Argentina or Brazil. Schneider (2010) argues that employers distribute their political investments into various influence channels according to their returns; and these returns depend mostly on state actors as they shape opportunities offered by the political system. Where state actors prefer to deal with organized capital through encompassing EOs and neo-corporatist channels (rather than through personal networks or political parties), this incentivizes employers to invest into EOs that exercise political influence (Schneider 2004). This chapter argues that if employers are excluded from such policy-making channels, then they may invest in new, alternative forms of organization. It is especially under conditions of high vulnerability after crises, e.g. through high electoral volatility or after a military coup, that political elites look to business to acquire information for complex policymaking, and to facilitate effective policy implementation. While Schneider (2004) focuses on politicians' incentive to enhance government effectiveness, the present and other studies focus on the role of power contests. Sinha (2005) showed that employer collective action in India formed into encompassing, developmental organizations because of active support by key state actors and in response to political competition by other EOs. Markus (2007) also finds that in post-communist countries, intra-executive power struggles were key. In Russia, Putin gave EOs access to economic policy-making to allow the President to increase pressure on state agents.

The above literatures have shown that threats by individual state and political actors can trigger employers to organize either by threatening employment legislation (Barry and Wilkinson 2011; Gooberman et al. 2019), employers' trade interests (Schneider 2004, 2010), or by state agents involving employers in wider political power contests, polarizing EOs along political lines (e.g. Markus 2007; Sinha 2005). The Turkish case illustrates that state threats need to include further historical political-institutional factors to understand the origins of EOs. This chapter analyzes how three types of interlinked state threats unintentionally pushed religiously-motivated employers to organize in alternative channels. Firstly, state threats towards class-based organization in fledgling IR systems appeared through the exclusion of formal EOs in general, and religiously-motivated SMEs in central and southern Anatolia in particular. Secondly, state threats towards an independent civil society and political system, with military governance fostering a weak political party and civil society system. This made individual politicians alternate between incentivizing and/or threatening EOs based on their changing power interests and ultimately polarized EOs. Finally, state threats included an ideological dimension which fragmented employers along pro-secular and pro-religious lines and pushed pro-religious actors to organize in collaboration as elite networks, whereas existing EOs, corporatist channels and political parties remained closed to them.

Employers' Organizations in Turkey

EOs in Turkey are divided along politico-ideological lines, with separate organizations existing for secular and pro-religious employers (Sezer 2019).

The main organization in Turkey that deals with the collective IR is TISK (Turkish Employers' Confederation), an umbrella confederation of sectoral EOs. Employers can join both the TISK affiliates and the mixed, voluntary EOs. The focus of this chapter is on the latter.

In Turkey, the competition among EOs has been part of a power contest between broad pro-religious and pro-secular political alliances. A new, seemingly moderate, secular, and pro-Western pro-religious coalition began to collaborate from the late 1990s until 2013. This coalition consisted of the incumbent Justice and Development Party (AKP), which has formed successive majority governments since 2002; the Gülen community, one of the most influential international Islamic movements; and the economy-wide voluntary business associations linked to these groups, Müsiad (Independent Industrialists' and Businessmen's Association), founded in 1990; and Tuskon (Turkey Industrialists' Confederation), founded in 2005, and closed in 2016. In 2012, Tuskon, a federation, represented approximately 33,260 companies, making it the largest of the EOs. Over the past 40 years, this coalition has gradually displaced the traditional pro-secular coalition of military leaders, top bureaucrats and state-nurtured holding companies organized in the pro-secular Tüsiad. Tüsiad (Turkey Industrialists' and Businessmen's Association) was established as the first voluntary EO to represent the large and secular employers, which were nurtured by the Kemalist elites in the Istanbul-Marmara region before economic liberalization. Its membership comprises a small, albeit economically powerful section of employers; about 600 members representing 2,500 firms in 2011.

The Gülen movement, centred around the preacher Fethullah Gülen, embodied a socio-economic and seemingly moderate branch of Islam. An international, informal network of education and business networks in media, health and trade provided its financial resources. Tuskon was the movement's business arm, founded in 2005 by gathering existing local associations under one roof. There has been an 'extensive purge of all Gülen linked groups since 17 December 2013' (Özcan and Gündüz 2015: 23). The Gülen community was declared a terrorist organization in Turkey in October 2015, and individuals or organizations, suspected of being affiliated to the movement have been imprisoned, purged and closed since the attempted coup of 16 July 2016. With the Gezi Protests in 2013, the AKP's authoritarian turn began as it resorted to top-down control, and internal conflicts among the pro-religious coalition intensified. These tensions culminated in the attempted July 2016 coup, the consequences of which are beyond the focus of this study. In order to extend the conditions under which new types of EOs emerge and develop, this chapter analyzes the case study of pro-religious EOs in modern Turkey, tracing their development since the formation of the modern Turkish state until 2012.

State Threats, and the Ideological Polarization of Employers from 1923–2012

Early Threats Promoting the Emergence of Pro-religious EOs

Authoritarian military and bureaucratic governance across decades severely hampered the development of a strong, independent political party system and of civil society organizations. After the formation of the Turkish Republic in 1923, a one-party state emerged with the centralized bureaucracy and military serving as the state elite. The state set up major industrial state-owned enterprises to nurture a Turkish bourgeoisie based on Kemalist ideology. The basic principles of Kemalism were republicanism, secularism, nationalism, populism, statism and reformism. Class-conflict, highly feared by the Kemalists due to its threat to the newly-established nation state, was to be prevented by organizing society in 'harmoniously' functioning occupational groups (Parla and Davison 2004).

State threats in Turkey have long included a politico-ideological dimension. With the formation of the Turkish Republic, Islam was eliminated from the public realm. Instead, Islam was institutionalized in the form of a state-interpreted, official version as an integral part of the government structure. Brotherhoods, religious sects, educational and other religious institutions that had been an integral part of the Ottoman Empire for centuries were forbidden but continued to exist 'underground' as popular spiritual ethical movements (Yavuz 2003).

After World War II, Turkey formally developed into a multi-party democracy. The newly elected centre-right government limited the autonomy and power of the bureaucracy, thereby creating mistrust between the powerful military and bureaucracy on the one hand, and the political regime on the other (Zürcher 2004) – a trend to worsen in the next decades.

The shift to multiparty democracy in the 1950s gave incentives for the fragmentation into dual representational structures of employer representation (Bianchi 1984). The new political elites were in a vulnerable position against the bureaucratic and military elites, and therefore attempted to cultivate informal alliances with both the new corporatist channels as well as the emerging holding companies (later to organize in the EO Tüsiad), and trade unions. Corporatist channels, i.e. 'vertically structured, quasi-monopolistic peak associations' were established in key economic sectors (Bianchi 1984: 142). In 1952, the Chambers of Trade and Commerce (TOBB) were founded; the most influential semi-official business association with obligatory membership. Restricted unionization was also allowed in 1947; but political activities of associations and strikes were banned (Bianchi 1984).

Both the limited unions, as well as the business activities restricted to Chambers, remained under state tutelage, functioning as extended government arms. In addition to the legal constraints for associational activity and the continued financial dependence of the emerging business class, patronage politics between dominant actors persisted. All these factors inhibited the development of a class consciousness, which further weakened the actors. As the ruling Democratic Party (DP) government became politically weaker, it aimed to gain the support of the business community by empowering the Chambers by granting them important public functions, e.g. the allocation of import quotas. However, at the same time, informal controls and harassment increased. The rival party, the Kemalist RPP (Republican People's Party), mobilized outside of corporatist structures. This had the unintended consequence of introducing a new dimension of pluralism into the politics of business and labour in the following decade as neither private, nor corporatist channels could emerge as channels for interest representation and had little influence on policy-making. State threats towards collective action had unintentionally given incentives for the development of a dual representational system in IR. This is a heterogeneous and unstable system of interest representation, marked by a 'division of associational life into two distinct legal and structural categories' (Bianchi 1984: 365). It is not state corporatist because of the absence of a unified Kemalist elite controlling an authoritarian state.

The decline in the perceived social status and political power of the military personnel incentivized a group of officials to stage a military coup in 1960. The DP was closed and the Prime Minister as well as two ministers executed, sending a strong message to not violate the limits of political behaviour set by the military.

After the 1960 military coup, economic development was still to be steered through the compliant corporatist structures. The 1961 Constitution was liberal in the realm of associational activity and furthered democratization, leading to the establishment of the first voluntary EO, Tüsiad, in 1971 and further trade unions. However, state elites remained hostile to collective action and a totally pluralistic view of interest groups due to the unitarist Kemalist ideology. Bianchi (1984) argues that the governments deliberately aimed to promote many weak and fragmented voluntary associations to prevent effective collective action. Many large businesses profited from protectionist measures through unmediated direct networks. Support mechanisms included the provision of cheaper input material and credits, and infrastructure investments. As Turkish business increasingly consolidated its presence in the industrial sector and in society in the 1960s, it began to criticize economic policies and demanded participation in public policy.

In 1965, the successor to the banned DP, the pro-business Justice Party (JP) formed a majority government until the next military coup in 1971. Several short-lived coalition governments ruled the country during the 1970s (Zürcher 2004). The high political instability of the 1970s increased the power of the military and accelerated the fragmentation of labour and business, weakening the collective organizations' capacities for solidarity and mass action. Prime Minister Demirel reacted to the growing competition between the ruling JP and the Kemalist RPP by tightening control over the Chambers and the trade union Türk-İş, first strengthening, but then gradually withdrawing their public functions. The newly emerging voluntary associations were met with hostility. The competing RPP on the other hand, tried to mobilize the constituencies of the autonomous and left-wing Confederation of Progressive Trade Unions of Turkey (Bianchi 1984).

Favouritism of big business and state repression alienated large segments of the business and labour communities, incentivizing the organization of further, competing voluntary organizations. On the employer side, fragmentation occurred mainly between EOs organizing state-nurtured business groups that emerged before economic liberalization; and pro-religious EOs that organized the new Islamic capital that developed in central and south-eastern Anatolian industrial centres alongside the Islamic movement after economic liberalization. Big business distanced itself from groupings representing the whole business community, culminating in the establishment of Tüsiad in 1971. Tüsiad, which represents mainly big and pro-secular businesses from the Istanbul region, was formed as a class organization to consolidate the status of the business community (Buğra 1994). The leadership of TOBB and its role as predominant spokesman for business was further undermined with the formation of TISK, as well as the Union of Chambers of Industry, a loose and informal coalition within TOBB (Bianchi 1984). TISK became the single central organization of employers, engaging in wage bargaining vis-à-vis organized labour. Tüsiad became recognized as the third representative of the private sector and emerged as a key political actor beginning in the late 1970s. With the foundation of Tüsiad, state-business relations changed significantly, as the corporatist legacy ended and voluntary EOs began to become more influential. However, both the Chambers as well as the voluntary systems remained excluded from policy-making as particularistic relations gained further strength (Bianchi 1984).

As a counterpart of rigid state secularism, Islamism made its first formal political appearance in Turkey in the 1970s when Necmettin Erbakan formed successive political parties as part of the Islamist National Outlook Movement (NOM, Milli Görüş Movement). He became Chairman of TOBB in 1969 with the support of small merchants and middle-income Anatolian businessmen as he aimed to improve the voice of provincial SMEs in TOBB decision-making and policy. He was soon removed from this position due to his perceived backwardness and religiosity (Fabbe et al. 2020). Not able to join pro-business, conservative political parties (e.g. the JP), Erbakan formed alternative political parties in the 1970s. These Islamist parties continued to successfully mobilize both the poor and pious as well as the new upwardly mobile Anatolian industrialists (e.g. Demir et al. 2004) who felt alienated by the Chambers and were excluded from the 'elitist' Tüsiad leadership, both controlled by big business interests. This early grassroots mobilization of pious Anatolian SMEs marks the beginning of alternative, pro-religious employer collective action.

1980–2001: The Emergence of Pro-religious EOs

After the military coup in 1980, a harsh constitution was implemented to depoliticize, control and restrict interest group activity and extend the powers of the military further (Buğra 1994). This Constitution regulated Turkish IR until recent amendments. Interest group associations lost the right to pursue political and class-based aims; it was illegal to use religious symbols for political purposes, and parties' organizational links with civil society were further constrained (Hale and Özbudun 2009).

After both the 1971 and 1980 military coups, the respective Islamist parties of Erbakan's NOM were closed. After the 1980 coup, the military and international community encouraged instead moderately pro-religious movements such as the Gülen community. The aim was to strengthen moderate over other Islamist movements, and to supplant class organization by promoting the uniting force of Islam. This increasing ideological opening contributed to the later pro-religious electoral victories of the current Islamic movement. The incumbent President Erdoğan had become Mayor of Istanbul as representative of the NOM's Welfare Party Refah Partisi (RP) in 1994. The RP had even entered a coalition government in 1995, and Erbakan became prime minister for a short period before the RP collapsed as the Constitutional Court closed it down in 1997. Several Müsiad members were imprisoned in 1997. This postmodern coup in 1997 left deep marks and contributed to the moderation and reshuffling of the Islamic movement. A young and reformist wing within the Islamist NOM established the AKP in 2001. By supporting this then more moderate group, Anatolian business elites, who had an economic interest not to further confront the secular state, arguably contributed to the temporary moderation of Islamist politics in Turkey.

The hostility of political elites towards business to take part in public policy making grew even stronger than before, although or because of the introduction of full trade and financial economic liberalization. State elites barely allowed lobbying and threatened repressive state intervention. State autonomy increased due to the centralization of economic decision-making and the legal environment restricting associational activities.

For a while the Chambers functioned as before, i.e. as extended arms of the government (Bianchi 1984). Formal meetings with interest group association did not include consultation or shared decision-making. Prime Minister Özal increasingly ignored the Chambers, withdrew their public functions, and thereby eliminated their quasi-public role. Thus, Chambers were further weakened as interest associations and, in terms of particu-laristic relations, became overshadowed by voluntary associations. Tüsiad emerged as the key political player from the 1980s onwards.

With the shift towards an export-oriented regime, SMEs gained eco-nomic power in an environment characterized by diverse inter-firm lin-kages of suppliers, subcontractors and end users. Anatolian SMEs and industrialists relied on informal grassroots networks and a pattern of pooling private resources for growth, and profited from new export in-centives, preferential credits and privatization deals. SME development became a stronger focus of industrial policy in the 1990s. This led to the development of a new generation of industrial centres in central-and southeastern Anatolia rivalling traditional industrial growth centres in the Istanbul-Marmara regions. These new industrialists increasingly demanded representation and policy-input but felt excluded from ex-isting employer representational channels.

The strengthening of the business class, however, was not com-plemented by weakening clientelistic relations (Buğra 1994). In the context of a weak party system vis-à-vis the military, political elites continued to struggle for electoral support by strengthening clientelistic ties. The allo-cation of resources continued to be based on connections to political elites rather than on merit and clear criteria, which resulted in further un-certainty, rent-seeking activity and hostility between bureaucratic, poli-tical and business elites, and the continued fragmentation of the already weakened labour movement and of the business community. The cleavage in the business community is represented in the division between the pro-secular Tüsiad, and the pro-religious Müsiad. The pro-religious Müsiad was formed in 1990 by businessmen of mainly export-oriented SMEs in Anatolian towns with an explicit pro-religious orientation (Demir et al. 2004). Müsiad first had close ties to Erbakan's NOM, but later reshuffled their alliance to a more 'moderate' movement – the AKP and Gülen movement. Excluded from policy-input in the Chambers and from the 'elitist' Tüsiad, and threatened by military coups against conservative and Islamist parties, pro-religious SMEs formed the Müsiad. It was formed with the goal of displacing the pro-secular business and states elites in collaboration with Islamic movements (Sezer 2019). Müsiad increasingly challenged the established distributional channels between government agencies and big business but could not participate in policy-making in this decade. Nevertheless, Tüsiad and Müsiad became vocal organs of interest representation with an important public opinion forming role (Buğra 1994), alongside the Gülen-affiliated Tuskon (after 2005).

The Pro-religious Coalition in Power (2002–2013)

A young group within the Islamist NOM established the AKP in 2001. The AKP came to power in 2002 and has formed multiple majority governments since then. However, both the AKP and pro-religious employers had an inherent high vulnerability vis-à-vis the powerful and Kemalist bureaucracy, state elites and military at the time of the AKP's inception, after repeated military coups ousting Islamists in the NOM and the EO Müsiad. This increased their need for the support of social groups outside the state apparatus and forced them to publicly withdraw their political aims to turn themselves into a socio-economic and seemingly moderate movement (Yavuz 2003). The pro-religious EO Müsiad and various civil society organizations, especially the Gülen movement and its EO Tuskon from 2005, have formed a key support base for the AKP. The AKP like its NOM predecessors provided state and municipal provisions to both the urban poor and the aspiring Anatolian business elites via pro-religious EOs, CSOs, including brotherhood networks, and new, flexible public institutions. The latter have been supported through a new patronage regime in privatizations, public tenders, infrastructure and construction projects, and cheap credit through public banks. The AKP maintains close contacts with like-minded civil society organizations active in the sub-province, mainly to guide and inform voters of the various social welfare programmes conducted by government institutions (Hale and Özbudun 2009). Through such support mechanisms, pro-religious political actors opposed secular institutions and aimed to establish their own pro-religious finance to replace old secular business elites (Buğra and Savaşkan 2014).

At the turn of the millennium constitutional amendments driven by the European Union accession process reduced military interference in associational life and lifted the ideological boundaries of political parties, further facilitating the rise of this Islamic movement. A crucial turning point was the attempted 2008 coup: the military feared the introduction of an Islamist state by the AKP and brought the case of the party's closure to the constitutional courts. Such a renewed state threat after the 1997 coup further facilitated pro-religious politicians and employers' framing of themselves as oppressed victims, and successfully branding themselves as an anti-establishment movement. The court proceedings ultimately failed, resulting in only a fine, but gave the AKP further incentives to resort to resentment politics and to start court proceedings against suspected "Kemalist" elites. As AKP elites have increasingly captured elite state positions, ideological threats are now turned against supposed Kemalist elites.

The AKP forged periodic alliances with liberals, nationalists and Islamic organizations. They initially adopted moderately Islamic frames and won international allies, by not only supporting International Monetary Fund and neoliberal reforms, but also by pursuing European Union accession. However, the party turned authoritarian as Erdoğan increased his control of the party. The AKP also tightened party control over the judiciary, police, education, military, and the business community by controlling capital flows. There was a brief period of increased independence from military governance of political parties and of civil society at the beginning of the millennium. However, the AKP since strengthening during the 2007 elections and after the 2008 post-modern coup, perpetuated this cycle through its authoritarian turn. State threats against civil and political society based on political ideology thus have continued.

The Chambers became overpowered by individual businessmen organized in Tüsiad, Müsiad, and Tuskon after the AKP's rise. SME development became an even stronger focus of the AKP government. Especially during the AKP's vulnerable phase from 2001 until 2007, the three voluntary EOs temporarily had more policy-input, e.g. becoming important interlocutors for the policy-makers in the Europeanization process, also influencing foreign policy. However, the government's relations with the biggest politically connected business groups continued to exist independent of these EOs (Buğra and Savaşkan 2014). Despite the shift towards export-orientation and the business class growing stronger, relations did not weaken. Especially as the AKP centralized power after 2007, it became less reliant on aggregated policy support from EOs. EOs increasingly transformed into clientelist exchange network organizations once again and capital became ever more politicized and polarized.

Nevertheless, pro-religious EOs have fulfilled important political, trade, and employment functions: better government relations and high-level political connections allowed pro-religious EOs to provide selective goods, such as preferential access to financial institutions, information, or export promotion incentives. Pro-religious EOs also provided HR training and services, while fulfilling public services in private-public partnerships (Sezer 2019). In exchange, pro-religious employers and EOs created local electoral support for the AKP, both indirectly by creating jobs and investing in local development projects (e.g. public schools) and directly by directing their employees to vote for the AKP or providing campaign financing. The rise of Islamic capital has laid bare internal conflicts among the pro-religious coalition, between the Gülen community and the AKP after 2013, which is beyond the scope of this analysis.

In sum, state threats by Kemalist state elites and exclusion from centrist political parties as well as EO and corporatist channels contributed to Erbakan's and later Erdoğan's populist Islamic mobilization of Anatolian SMEs. This polarized the business community into pro-secular and pro-religious employers and incentivized the latter to organize outside of formal channels alongside other vulnerable political and civic actors. Repeated military coups, and authoritarian governance severely hampered autonomous collective action and weakened and fragmented politicians, who attempted to garner worker, employer or civil society support against the strong state elite. Unitarist Kemalist ideology and restrictions on associational activity had not only weakened political and civil society, but also the IR actors. Both the corporatist and pluralist

representational channels were left to oscillate between state en-
couragement and repression. Shifting elites asymmetrically favoured
pro-secular big business, excluding labour and SMEs, and aggravated
employers' ideological polarization. State and political threats; exclusion
of pro-religious employers; and the promotion by state elites of 'moderate Islamic movements' all inadvertently gave rise to a new collaborative pro-religious movement, including pro-religious EOs, the Gülen
movement, and the AKP.

Conclusion

This chapter contributes to calls to explore new pressures on EOs as the
state's IR legislative threats and union power have declined as sources
prompting countervailing power reactions. Such extensions allow the
continued resilience of EOs to be explained, along with the emergence of
new types with new functions and alternative structures. Besides the
individual rights regime (Gooberman et al. 2019), this chapter makes
two main contributions to the countervailing power literature: Firstly,
the analysis widens the nature from regulatory threats to include state
threats towards independent collective action in the IR as well as political and civil society systems; and secondly, it shows the role of political
and state actors. Such state threats can overlap with ideological or other
broad social cleavages, bringing ideology to the fore in political and
employer mobilization.

The Turkish case illustrates that employers can form their own EOs in
collaboration with other vulnerable political and civic actors to countervail the state's political-ideological threats. Pro-religious EOs originated from employers' exclusion from representational channels and
threats towards independent collective action that unintentionally pushed employers to organize. By doing so pro-religious EOs formed an
alternative, and legitimate, channel for policy-input, access, and support
in political power contests.

Schneider (2004, 2010) showed that state actors' threats towards
employers' trade interests can spur EO development, depending on
whether state actors prefer to interact with employers via political parties, individual elite networks, corporatist channels or encompassing
voluntary EOs. The political entrepreneurship literature (e.g. Markus
2007; Sinha 2005) has also shown that EOs can fulfil important functions in wider political power contests. Based on this insight, this chapter
argues that if traditional political and IR structures (i.e. political parties,
existing EOs, neo-corporatist structures, elite networks), either exclude
certain employer interests, or are organizationally too weak to sufficiently represent them, employers may form new types of EOs. For example, by entering into informal, coalitions with civil society and
political actors or parties as observed in Turkey. State threats which were

directed at the exclusion of pro-religious, vulnerable actors were important motivators for employers in Turkey to organize. While in developing country contexts such exclusion is often the result of direct state repression, exclusion may also be the result of weakened capacities of traditional EOs and corporatist channels, such as in the US and UK. Where capital's aims cannot sufficiently be achieved through 'traditional' political or IR structures, such new types of EOs may emerge. Such conditions can provide the impetus for a range of actors to form a new type of EO by adjusting their structures – in the Turkish case to an informal coalition with CSOs and politicians – and their functions to include support in political power contests.

Such an inclusion of micro-political institutions and of wider state threats into the employment relationship can better explain EO origins in the 'Global South' and expand the countervailing power concept to such contexts. The boundary conditions of competitive markets (Barry and Wilkinson 2011; Gooberman et al. 2019) and some level of federalism or decentralization (Doner and Schneider 2000; Sinha 2005), as identified in previous literature, also applied to the Turkish context. Economic opportunities provided by gradual economic liberalization as well as gradual democratization provided openings and opportunities for collective organizing. Incentives for employer organization from individual state actors are also relevant in industrialized contexts, and are underplayed in the EO revitalization literature. Especially as mixed EOs have shifted their logic of influence to the state and focus on lobbying, it is crucial to analyze EOs as political actors that are part of wider political power contests, emerging because of state threats.

Note

1 By state I refer to the extensive and interconnected administrative, bureaucratic, legal and coercive system that has the authority to make rules, which govern a society, including actors from the government, and the armed forces. Political society is the arena in which contestations take place, including political parties as key actors.

References

Baccaro, L. and Howell, C. (2017). *European Industrial Relations since the 1970s: Trajectories of Neoliberal Transformation*. Cambridge: Cambridge University Press.

Barry, M. and Wilkinson, A. (2011). Reconceptualising employer associations under evolving employment relations: Countervailing power revisited. *Work, Employment and Society*, 25 (1): 149–162. 10.1177%2F0950017010389229

Bianchi, R. (1984). *Interest Groups and Political Development in Turkey*. Princeton, NJ: Princeton University Press.

Bowkett, C., Hauptmeier, M. and Heery, E. (2017). Exploring the role of employer forums – The case of Business in the Community Wales. *Employee Relations*, 39 (7): 986–1000. 10.1108/ER-11-2016-0229

Brandl, B. and Lehr, A. (2016). The strange non-death of employer and business associations: An analysis of their representativeness and activities in Western European countries. *Economic and Industrial Democracy*, 40 (4): 1–22. 10.11 77%2F0143831X16669842

Buğra, A. (1994). *State and Business in Modern Turkey: A Comparative Study*. Albany, NY: SUNY Press.

Buğra, A. and Savaşkan, O. (2014). *New Capitalism in Turkey: The Relationship between Politics, Religion and Business*. Northampton, MA: Edward Elgar Publishing.

Culpepper, P. D. (2011). *Quiet Politics and Business Power: Corporate Control in Europe and Japan*. Cambridge: Cambridge University Press.

Demir, Ö., Acar, M. and Toprak, M. (2004). Anatolian Tigers or Islamic capital: Prospects and challenges. *Middle Eastern Studies*, 40 (6): 166–188. 10.1080/ 0026320042000282937

Doner, R. F. and Schneider, B. R. (2000). Business associations and economic development: Why some associations contribute more than others. *Business and Politics*, 2 (3): 261–288. 10.2202/1469-3569.1011

Fabbe, K., Özlale, Ü. and Balıkçıoğlu, E. M. (2020). Islamic capitalism and the rise of religious-conservative big business. In: A. M. Colpan and G. Jones (eds.) *Business, Ethics and Institutions*. New York: Routledge, pp. 97–122.

Gooberman, L., Hauptmeier, M. and Heery, E. (2019). The evolution of employers' organisations in the United Kingdom: Extending countervailing power. *Human Resource Management Journal*, 29 (1): 67–81. 10.1111/1748-8583.12193

Hale, W. and Özbudun, E. (2009). *Islamism, Democracy and Liberalism in Turkey*. London: Routledge.

Heery, E., Abbott, B. and Williams, S. (2012). The involvement of civil society organizations in British industrial relations: Extent, origins and significance. *British Journal of Industrial Relations*, 50 (1): 47–72. 10.1111/j.1467-8543. 2010.00803.x

Ibsen, C. L. and Navrbjerg, S. E. (2019). Adapting to survive: The case of Danish employers' organisations. *Human Resource Management Journal*, 29 (1): 36–50. 10.1111/1748-8583.12182

Markus, S. (2007). Capitalists of all Russia, unite! Business mobilization under debilitated Dirigisme. *Polity*, 39 (3): 277–304. 10.1057/palgrave.polity.2300083

Martin, C. J. (1994). Business and the new economic activism: The growth of corporate lobbies in the sixties. *Polity*, 27 (1): 49–76.

Martin, C. J. and Swank, D. (2012). *The Political Construction of Business Interests: Coordination, Growth, and Equality*. Cambridge: Cambridge University Press.

Özcan, G. B. and Gündüz, U. (2015). Political connectedness and business performance: Evidence from Turkish industry rankings. *Business and Politics*, 17 (1): 41–73. 10.1515/bap-2013-0037

Parla, T. and Davison, A. (2004). *Corporatist Ideology in Kemalist Turkey: Progress or order?* Syracuse, NY: Syracuse University Press.

Piore, M. J. and Safford, S. (2006). Changing regimes of workplace governance, shifting axes of social mobilization, and the challenge to industrial relations theory. *Industrial Relations: A Journal of Economy and Society*, 45 (3): 299–325. 10.1111/j.1468-232X.2006.00439.x

Polsky, A. (2000). When business speaks: Political entrepreneurship, discourse and mobilization in American partisan regimes. *Journal of Theoretical Politics*, 12 (4): 455–476. 10.1177%2F0951692800012004006

Schmitter, P. C. (1974). Still the century of corporatism? *The Review of Politics*, 36 (01): 85–131.

Schneider, B. R. (2004). *Business Politics and the State in Twentieth-Century Latin America*. Cambridge: Cambridge University Press.

Schneider, B. R. (2010). Business politics in Latin America: Patterns of fragmentation and centralization. In: D. Coen, W. Grant and G. Wilson (eds.) *The Oxford Handbook of Business and Government*. Oxford: Oxford University Press, pp. 307–329.

Sezer, L. A. (2019) Employers' organisations as social movements: Political power and identity work, *Human Resource Management Journal*, 29 (1): 67–81. 10.1111/1748-8583.12209

Sinha, A. (2005). Understanding the rise and transformation of business collective action in India. *Business and Politics*, 7 (2): 1–35. 10.2202/1469-3569.1112

Yavuz, M. H. (2003). *Islamic Political Identity in Turkey*. Oxford; New York: Oxford University Press.

Zürcher, E. J. (2004). *Turkey: A Modern History* (3rd Revised edition). London; New York: I.B. Tauris.

11 Representing the Interests of Quebec Employers: The Contribution of Regional Employers' Organizations

Mélanie Laroche

Introduction

As established in the new regionalism literature, industrial relations scholars have identified the sub-national regional space "as an important level of institutional adaptation" (Almond et al. 2017). These authors recognize that a variety of actors – firms and Employers' Organizations (EOs), unions, government actors and civil society representatives – interact at different levels of governance, including the regional level, in order to adapt labour markets and business systems to their respective visions of economic development (see also MacKinnon 2012; Phelps and Fuller 2001). While there has been some weakening of social dialogue in its more traditional form at the national level, there has been in some countries instead a strengthening and diversification of the issues addressed within institutions at lower levels (Medina and Molins 2018), including in Canada (Almond et al. 2014). This increased importance of the regional level and this gradual transformation of political and economic structures has necessarily led to a revision of the roles and functions of the actors who interact with and within public institutions.

In this chapter, we address one of the actors involved in these regulatory arenas, regional EOs, which have received little attention in previous works. Although employer interests have been the subject of many European studies, the reality is different in North America, in particular because of the decentralized nature of the industrial relations system and, consequently, the less historically prominent role of EOs. Yet in Canada, particularly in Quebec, employers and their organizations have been able to organize themselves in such a way as to influence political and economic developments, in addition to driving many changes within the industrial relations system. Quebec's specific institutional context favours a more varied and organized collective action by employers at different levels of the industrial relations system. In this territory where the unionization rate is higher than in other Canadian provinces, where collective bargaining is bipartite and decentralized, where labour regulation is more developed and where there are sectoral

DOI: 10.4324/9781003104575-14

or provincial consultative institutions, we observe that EOs are more active and seek to acquire greater influence over the rules related to employment. By revealing the various forms, levels of representation and different roles of these organizations, we contribute to some of the work that has demonstrated a certain revitalization of EOs to counter new sources of regional political power (Gooberman et al. 2019, 2020b).

Employers' Collective Action

The literature generally presents EOs as a means used by employers to represent and promote their interests (Grimshaw and Hayter 2020), whether in respect to employees and their representatives in collective bargaining or with the state through consultation, negotiation or lobbying (Brandl and Lehr 2019). We recognize a *variety of organizational forms* amongst EOs, related to their values and ideology, their form and structure, the characteristics of their representatives and economic importance, which we consider as the *logic of representation* of these organizations (Schmitter and Streeck 1981).

EOs' strategic choices in terms of representation will necessarily influence their *logic of action*, which refers not only to their influence on public policy and collective negotiation (Schmitter and Streeck 1981), but also to consultative institutions. While trade associations focus on representing product market interests, EOs focus on labour market interests (Grimshaw and Hayter 2020; Traxler 2008). Different motivations, such as union power and legislative frameworks or economic uncertainties associated with globalization, lead employers to increasingly turn to EOs to extend their influence beyond the workplace, to have a say in all the regulations developed with respect to employment (Behrens 2004).

How can we determine/explain whether these organizations will be able to play a more or less active role in the territories they cover? One of the approaches put forward in the literature on the varieties of capitalism suggests that collective action among employers will differ between liberal market economies and coordinated market economies (Grimshaw and Hayter 2020; Hall and Soskice 2001). EOs are, indeed, very involved in economic governance in coordinated economies, whereas they have less space for action in liberal economies. Some scholars have, nevertheless, observed a certain stability of EOs, even in more liberal economies, while several factors contribute to putting them under pressure (Behrens 2018; Laroche 2016).

These pressures stem, on the one hand, from the strong desire of employers to decentralize industrial relations and to reintegrate them into the realities of their own enterprises, making EOs vulnerable and diminishing their capacity to act collectively (Grimshaw and Hayter 2020; Traxler 2006). They are also weakened by the growth of transnational enterprises, which are less dependent on these forms of groups to represent their interests, given their resources, size and impact (Schneider and Grote 2006). Other authors have also observed that small and medium businesses are also less likely to join EOs even when it could prove advantageous to do so (Brandl and Lehr 2019; Laroche 2012; Laroche and Murray 2012; Zhu et al. 2017).

On the other hand, transformations, such as changes in production networks (Dicken 2003), the expansion and diversification of global value chains (Gereffi et al. 2005) and the vertical disintegration of companies (Doellgast and Greer 2007), have also created strong pressure on firms to collaborate, in addition to contributing to modifying the forms and functions of EOs. Collective employer action, thus, assumes various configurations and leads to the establishment of diverse interest groups participating in the public debate via both formal and informal forums (Saurugger and Grossman 2006). For example, participation in various labour market institutions, networks of business representatives, political party financing, lobbying and financing of think tanks or the press are all efforts to influence public opinion.

In some cases, EOs are also having to change their organizational structures and member services to better serve the needs of firms. In the past, EOs took on certain traditional functions such as collective bargaining as a way of benefiting from a better balance of power and avoiding union whipsawing (Barry and Wilkinson 2011). This function, with the decline of unionization and the decentralization of industrial relations in many countries, has become less important due to a diminished interest in collective action for a number of large firms, since they are able to autonomously manage employment related activities (Gooberman et al. 2019; Sheldon and Thornthwaite 2005). EOs may also play the role of political and social actors, either by participating in different collaborative bodies and public consultations (Gooberman et al. 2019; Laroche 2016), or by acting as lobbyists to ensure that employers' interests are taken into account in state policies.

In addition to these traditional roles, Gooberman et al. (2019) add two other functions of EOs: providing services to businesses and working to develop common standards among businesses. Over the past decades, significant upheavals, such as the decentralization of industrial relations, have indeed led employers' associations to modify their associational models. These forms of adaptation have been observed in many countries, notably in Europe (Grimshaw and Hayter 2020), but also in Asia (Zhu et al. 2017) and in North America (Laroche 2012). Faced with the increasingly diverse needs of small businesses, EOs have had to increase services from those offered traditionally, as the main incentive to attract new members or retain current members and, therefore, ensure the survival of employers' associations (Brandl and Lehr 2019).

Certain associations offer consulting services with regard to human resource management while others may provide legal, workplace health and safety, or fiscal advice. As a result, a significant problem arises for these associations: they must absorb the higher costs of offering new services at the same time as experiencing significant revenue losses caused by the departure of large firms (Markey and Hodgkinson 2008). To adapt to these changes, EOs have adopted an associative model which falls between that of traditional representation and of offering individualized services, often on a commercial basis (Laroche 2012; Sheldon and Thornthwaite 2005). Finally, they have also adapted their actions with an emphasis on common standards amongst employers (Gooberman et al. 2020a), for example, the development of recognized labour standards or the promotion of better practices which may, notably, enhance their corporate image.

Another important transformation observed concerns the levels of representation of employer interests. Collective action among employers is indeed unfolding within a multilevel representation structure where large national sectoral EOs coexist with smaller regional associations. As a matter of fact, EOs may act at various levels, starting at the industrial subsector or sectoral level (Kohler-Koch et al. 2017). In addition, territorial or geographical associations cover local, regional and national or even international levels (Behrens 2018; Sheldon et al. 2016). Furthermore, Behrens (2018) notes that associations acting at lower levels of the industrial relations system often become affiliated with associations at higher levels, thus resulting in a complex network of associations ensuring the representation of employer interests at multiple levels.

At the heart of this complex structure of representation, some organizations, especially those at higher levels, have been marginalized as a result of the decline in industrial relations (Brandl and Lehr 2019) while others, such as regional organizations, have experienced a revival in their activities. For example, Gooberman et al. (2019, 2020b) argued that sub-UK EOs experienced some rejuvenation at the dawn of the 2000s as the creation of regional parliamentary bodies allowed them to mobilize new power resources.

In Spain, Medina and Molins (2018) have shown that territorial EOs act on many issues, such as environmental policies, urban planning and regeneration, industrial restructuring, technological transfer and training, policies on employment and labour markets or local welfare policies. These authors have also clearly demonstrated that territorial social dialogue and, therefore, the action of regional EOs, will be all the more intense when the region differs from the national state in terms of its identity and its public policies. They also add that tensions between national and sub-national governments are important sources of mobilization for regional elites: the latter could, for example, mobilize to defend the language of their territory and make it an important identity base for their nation.

Quebec: A Favourable Territory for Regional Employers' Organizations

These observations reinforce the choice of Quebec as a field of study. It is true that in North America generally and in Canada specifically, EOs have historically played a less prominent role in the industrial relations systems than unions. Decentralized labour relations systems (Crouch 1993) and a poor tripartite tradition (Katz et al. 2004) explain this weaker development of employer collective action. Although there was some movement towards centralized bargaining in Canada following the Second World War, this trend was quickly reversed at the turn of the 1980s. The severe recession of 1981–1982, deregulation in many industries and increased competition from non-unionized and foreign firms killed many of the expanded negotiations in Canada (Hébert 1992). On the other hand, we observe a very different trend in Quebec and a strong dynamism of EOs at the sectoral level. Several factors may help explain this distinct trajectory of employer collective action in Quebec.

Almond et al. (2014) describe Canada as a liberal market economy, although they acknowledge that, with a larger welfare state and a more employee-friendly employment system, it is distinctive in a North American context. These authors also recognize that Canadian provinces enjoy an extremely high level of autonomy over most domestic affairs and issues related to the governance of employment and skills. This may have contributed to the distinct evolution of the Quebec industrial relations system. On the one hand, this system was inspired by the American Wagner Act of 1935 and adopted many of its principles, such as grassroots union recognition, monopoly representation and decentralized collective bargaining at the establishment level (Laroche and Jalette 2016). On the other hand, Laroche and Jalette (2016) consider the Quebec system to be an exception on the North American continent because of the union density, its labour laws which are among the most progressive, and their tripartite consultation mechanisms deployed at supra-enterprise levels.

First, the distinctive character of Quebec's institutional framework is justified by the strength of the labour movement (ISQ 2020): union density (39.3% in 2019) in this province is the highest in Canada (29.1% nationwide). Second, Quebec's labour relations legislation is different (Coutu et al. 2019) and is traditionally considered more favourable to unions and to collective bargaining. Finally, despite a system of labour relations that favours local bargaining, a tradition of supra-enterprise consultation was established in the Quebec institutional landscape very early on. In the 1930s, the Act respecting the extension of collective agreements (the Decrees Act) encouraged the establishment of joint committees in several economic sectors in Quebec, where the partners had to discuss issues related to industrial development. In the wake of the

"Quiet Revolution," this trend became more pronounced, and several institutional innovations were put in place to allow the social partners to discuss issues such as training, industrial strategies and regional and local development (Laroche 2013). Since then, Quebec has remained unique in North America in terms of social dialogue. Over the years, several forums for exchange between social partners have been created to act at various levels, whether provincial, sectoral, regional or local.

In terms of economic development, Quebec has also pursued a rather social-democratic interpretation of neo-liberalism (Almond et al. 2014), manifested in the establishment of regional economic intervention funds in which multiple actors, including EOs, are involved. Quebec's social actors are concerned with fostering a constructive dialogue to plan economic development while promoting social innovation, in other words, to develop strategies that promote the competitiveness of businesses and the well-being of workers (Laroche 2016). In the early 2000s, for example, regional projects called Action concertée de coopération régionale de développement (ACCORD) were created throughout Quebec. Essentially, this was a strategic approach to regional economic development that aimed more specifically to build a regional productive system that is competitive on the North American and global levels in each of the regions of Quebec, through the identification and development of niches of excellence that could become their brand image. According to Laroche (2016), this ACCORD project is a form of economic development based on industrial clusters that highlight the complementary expertise of players in the regions and sectors targeted. Once again, this Quebec economic development strategy has strongly encouraged employers to coalesce to become key players in these concertation institutions.

On the political front, there is another key element to consider. Almond et al. (2014) point out that electoral politics in Quebec has for many years been strongly oriented towards the choice between Quebec independence or federalism. As these authors have recognized, this political dynamic has led the provincial government not only to attempt to develop a strong Quebec identity, but also to direct economic coordination in a distinct manner, one of the objectives being the development of a francophone business class. These elements, as Medina and Molins (2018) have observed elsewhere, are powerful motivations for Quebec employers to cooperate.

Therefore, we hypothesize that Quebec's specific institutional characteristics call for more varied forms of collective employer action than elsewhere in the country. Since organized collective action seeks to diminish environmental uncertainties, we might believe that in a context where union power is greater, where labour regulation is more developed, even restrictive for the employer (Behrens 2004), and where there are sectoral or provincial consultative institutions, EOs should be more active and seek to acquire greater influence over the rules related to employment.

Methodology

The results presented in this chapter stem from a combination of data collection strategies. First, in order to track EOs in Quebec, we adapted the methodology proposed by Gooberman et al. (2020a). Therefore, we identified EOs through an Internet search. In Quebec, we first counted employers' associations involved in the development and management of existing ordinances in certain economic sectors. As well as identifying employer representatives acting at the level of major provincial and sectoral consultative bodies, we also analyzed employers' associations listed in the Quebec Registry of Lobbyists. In addition, we did research on the Web, using key words to complement our initial efforts on the websites of organizations.

We used the same selection criteria to identify associations: (1) the members are primarily employers who pay a fee to the association; (2) the organizations must play a role in the field of industrial relations, human resource management or labour; and (3) the associations act solely on the provincial level (in Quebec), thus excluding Canadian and international associations.

Empirical Findings

Fragmented and Interconnected Employer Collective Action

Quebec employers are generally associated with four major EOs which act at the provincial level, but also include affiliated enterprises, and employers' associations acting at lower levels. The foremost EO is the Conseil du Patronat du Quebec (CPQ) which represents the interests of more than 70,000 employers of various sizes, from all sectors (private and public) and regions of Quebec, who are affiliated, directly or through an intermediary, with 70 sectoral associations. The CPQ is certainly the most influential EO in Quebec. Furthermore, it is unique in North America in that it constitutes a veritable employers' confederation along the same lines as Quebec's major central union bodies. Therefore, the rationale for joining this organization is of a general nature, since it represents private enterprises in Quebec vis-à-vis the government, unions and public opinion. The CPQ does not intervene in its members' collective negotiations, but it is active on a number of key issues in industrial relations, such as those of the workforce, regulation, public finances, workplace health and safety, etc. (Van Schendel and Gabriel-Tremblay 2020). For its part, the Fédération des Chambres de Commerce du Quebec (FCCQ) [Federation of Quebec Chambers of Commerce] brings together 130 regional chambers from the entire territory of Quebec and represents more than 50,000 enterprises from all economic sectors. This association aims at the development of firms and an entrepreneurial culture spurring innovation and competition between enterprises. This EO may also take positions on major issues related to labour, employment or professional training.

Two other EOs are active at the provincial level and have favoured different membership approaches: one according to the size of member firms; and the other according to business orientation. The Quebec branch of the Fédération canadienne de l'entreprise indépendante [the Canadian Federation of Independent Business] (FCEI) has a mandate to defend and represent the interests of small and medium-sized businesses (SMEs) in Quebec (20% of its 110,000 Canadian members come from Quebec). Since firms of this size are not fully present in other associations, they came together to exercise greater influence in the process of developing economic policies and labour force regulation. Finally, the Manufacturiers exportateurs du Québec [the Quebec Export Manufacturers] (MEQ) represents, as its name indicates, manufacturing and export companies. It supports its members in their issues regarding labour, innovation and exports, as well as representing them vis-à-vis the government. It wants to equip its members and enable them to be competitive at both the local and the international level.

In addition to participating in various parliamentary commissions and representing the interests of their members to the government, these four large EOs are actively involved in the principal Quebec collaborative institutions. Nevertheless, employer collective action in Quebec is not limited to these associations. When we analyze Quebec employers more closely, we lift the veil on a much more complex organizational structure, which functions at a number of levels and covers a wide range of activities.

As seen in Figure 11.1, 201 EOs are active in the territory of Quebec, representing varied interests and acting at different levels. While the vast majority of associations (194 out of 201) recruit employers directly, few large sectoral or provincial associations (7 out of 201) also recruit associative members. In addition, we were able to observe that the networking strategy of associations involves enterprises not only joining a sectoral EO but, in addition, attempting to ensure that their interests are represented by the major provincial EO, which speaks out on labour issues, as well as by their Canadian association, so that their interests are also represented vis-a-vis the federal government.

Some of the EOs identified (8 out of 201) have adopted a more universal approach to membership; therefore, they welcome all enterprises, regardless of the sector in which they are operating, their size or even their intended markets. Very few EOs have also chosen to represent the interests of small and medium-sized enterprises (SMEs). As indicated, these companies can join the Quebec branch of the FCEI, which may explain the relatively limited number of EOs involved in this niche.

Quebec EOs also act at different levels of the industrial relations system, especially due to the various local, regional, sectoral or provincial social dialogue spaces that have been created in this territory. Our analysis shows

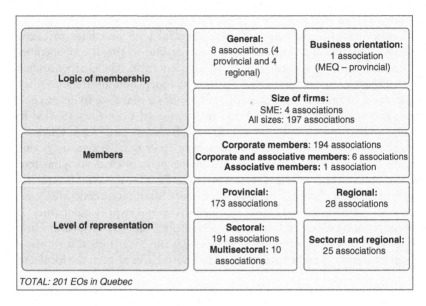

Figure 11.1 The logic of representation of Quebec EOs.

that 86% of associations (173 associations) act at the provincial level and 14% at the regional level (28 associations). A very large proportion of employers' associations (95%) act within the same industrial sector (Table 11.1) and some of them are also constituted on a regional basis (25 sectoral and regional associations).

While, in certain sectors (mining extraction, quarrying and petroleum and gas extraction; real estate, rental and leasing services, accommodation and food services, finances and insurance, other services; and public administration), few associations are active, in others collective employer action seems clearly more fragmented. This is the case, for example, in the agricultural sector, forestry, fishing and hunting (31 EOs) and construction (28 EOs) and, to a lesser extent, in the manufacturing sector (20 EOs). Therefore, EOs are organized, not only according to sector, but also as a function of regions or even a number of subsectors, so as to maximize the community of interests among the members. These smaller associations are usually members of the provincial association which covers the sector.

In light of these findings, it is possible to speak of a significant fragmentation of employer collective action in Quebec, signifying that the fields of representation covered by each of them are more limited and that they should be more representative of their members' interests (Traxler 2004). Overall, this degree of fragmentation of collective employer action is greater in the tertiary sector in which we find 56% of the sectoral employers' associations identified, compared to the primary and secondary

Table 11.1 Quebec sectoral EOs

Sector	Number of associations	Sector	Number of associations
Agriculture, forestry, fishing and hunting	31	Professional, scientific and technical services	11
Mining extraction, quarrying and petroleum and gas extraction	4	Administrative services, support services, waste management services and sanitation services	7
Construction	28	Accommodation and food services	2
Manufacturing	20	Other services (except public administration)	3
Transportation and storage	11	Finance and insurance	1
Wholesale trade	2	Tourism and recreation	11
Retail commerce	19	Education, health and social assistance	16
The information industry and the culture industry	15	Public administration	4
Real estate services and rental and leasing services	1		
		TOTAL	191

sectors which, respectively, account for 18% and 26%. Despite this strong degree of fragmentation, Quebec employers, nonetheless, ensure that they maintain their capacity for influence by establishing a web of interconnected associations which act at different levels and can represent their varied interests. In practice, certain employers will prefer to join together in an association with other employers with very similar interests, for example at the subregional or local level, and be affiliated to a sectoral association which will take over on more transversal issues in the industry or will ensure the representation of employers' interests on questions related to work and the labour force.

Logic of Action: A Representation Adapted to the Diversified Needs of the Members

These strategic choices of employers' associations in terms of representation necessarily influence their logic of action and their capacity to influence public policies, labour relations and labour market institutions.[1]

A limited number of associations may be considered pure employers' associations (2%), the form which is most involved in grouping together employers with respect to their field of labour relations (Traxler 2008). These groups often belong to the same branch of activities and act as representatives in collective bargaining, signing collective agreements in the name of their members. In fact, these associations are, above all, active in the sectors subject to specific arrangements of labour relations which favour the centralization of collective negotiations, such as sectors subject to the Collective Agreement Decree Act and the construction industry and public sector.

More than 9 out of 10 EOs identified are mixed associations and speak out on economic development questions as much as on industrial relations. Therefore, these EOs offer their members different services relative to labour, notably with reference to collective bargaining (42 associations). Pure employers' associations and mixed associations also offer a range of specialized services regarding industrial relations. For example, a high proportion of EOs (135 out of 201) offer consulting services on human resource management and on labour relations or labour law (Figure 11.2).

It should also not be suprising to observe that many of these associations (168 associations) are involved in professional training and workplace health and safety. Indeed, this result is not surprising in the Quebec context where the legislative framework imposes certain constraints on employers with respect to professional training, and where the social dialogue on the adaptation of the skills of the labour force to meet the needs of enterprises is highly developed (Laroche 2013). The rules governing workplace health and safety are also restrictive for employers who may feel the need to benefit from expert advice on how to better develop their strategies for prevention or how to minimize costs.

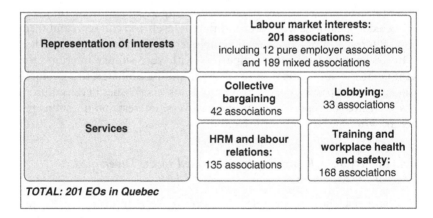

Figure 11.2 The logic of action of Quebec employers' organizations.

Finally, 33 associations are actively involved in the representation of employers' interests, either with political decisionmakers, or in consultative labour market institutions. First, the large provincial EOs ensure political representation at various levels of government. Then, because of the social dialogue tradition developed in Quebec, EOs are active in many intermediary institutions to influence training practices, industrial strategies and regional and local development (Laroche 2013). Specifically, the large provincial employers' associations (CPQ, FCCQ, FCEI, and MEQ) are members of permanent consultative bodies, for example: (1) the Conseil Consultatif sur le travail et la main d'œuvre [the Advisory Council on Labour and Employment] (CCTM), an organization dedicated to the development and maintenance of collaboration between employer and union organizations, in order to guide and support governmental action in the areas of labour and the workforce; (2) the Commission des partenaires du Marché du Travail [the Labour Market Partners Board] (CPMT), a body for collaboration between employers' representatives, the labour force, the educational milieu, community organizations and governmental organizations, which aims to improve the functioning of the labour market and the development of the qualifications of the labour force (CPMT, Internet site); and (3) the Commission des normes, de l'équité, de la santé et de la sécurité du travail [the Commission for Standards, Equity, and Workplace Health and Safety] (CNESST). They also sit on numerous administrative boards of public organizations such as the Caisse de dépôt et de placement [the Quebec Deposit and Investment Fund], the Commission des droits de la personne [the Human Rights Commission], the Office de la langue française [the Office for the French Language], the Régie des rentes du Quebec [the Quebec Pension Board] (RRQ) and other socio-economic organizations. They have also been called upon on many occasions to participate in informal consultative activities, notably during various economic summits.

For their part, the large sectoral associations which bring together smaller associations that have targeted more limited areas of representation, or which are active at the local and regional level, also have a significant influence on a number of levels. It is worth noting that they exercise activities of political representation on issues which have an impact on their own economic sector. They are also present on permanent consultative bodies. They are represented in the Comités sectoriels de main-d'œuvre [Sector Based Workforce Committees] (CSMO) which aim to define the development needs of the labour force specific to their economic sector of activity by proposing measures to stabilize employment and to reduce unemployment, and develop vocational training. The sectoral associations are also members of Comités régionaux des partenaires du marché du travail [the Regional Committees for Partners in Labour Market Development] (CRPMT), the mandate of which is to define the key issue of the labour market in a given region and to develop various solutions to remedy the problem. They may also be called upon to participate in the project "Action concertée de coopération régionale de développement" [Concerted Action for Regional Development Cooperation] (ACCORD) which consists of a strategic regional and sectoral economic development process.

Conclusion

Employers in Quebec have been able to organize themselves over the years to better defend their interests on multiple levels, within many collaborative bodies, and to speak out on numerous economic issues related to the labour market. Overall, we find that the decentralized nature of the Quebec system of industrial relations has certainly contributed to developing a cartography of EOs which is distinct from that of European countries and is notably characterized by a strong degree of fragmentation of collective action among employers. This fragmentation calls for an enhanced understanding of the foundations of the complementarity of the actions of these associations at various levels of the system of industrial relations. Indeed, it is thanks to this complex grid, developed among different forms of EOs acting at various levels, that employers succeed in seizing opportunities and driving changes within the systems of industrial relations and economic development throughout Quebec.

The configuration of Quebec collective employer action supports various findings in the literature. First, we have noted that the employer representation in this territory consists of a multilevel structure in which certain associations represent the interests of employers in various economic subsectors and act in different local forums. These EOs are affiliated with larger provincial sectoral associations which assume responsibility for representing their interests at the provincial level. In turn, these associations will establish links with Canadian and international associations, to invest in various locations where they can exercise their influence (Behrens 2018; Gooberman et al. 2019; Kohler-Koch et al. 2017; Sheldon et al. 2016).

The case of Quebec effectively illustrates to what degree regional EOs can play a determining role in the economic development of a territory and on issues related to labour and employment. As with the findings of Gooberman et al. (2019), Quebec EOs have known how to use different sources of power at their disposition within an institutional environment which strongly encourages the involvement of social partners. First, the more progressive labour laws (Coutu et al. 2019) and the stronger union density can justify further collective action by employers wanting to ensure that their interests are taken into consideration on questions related to labour and employment (Behrens 2004).

What particularly distinguishes Quebec, and which favours the establishment of this multilevel network of EOs remains the long tradition of consultation which allows social partners to become involved in a number of issues. This singular Quebec trajectory can be explained by various factors as we have seen, notably the political context which encouraged Quebec actors to foster a strong identity in this territory (Almond et al. 2014), and even to develop a francophone business class. These findings support the ideas of Medina and Molins (2018) and illustrate to what extent regional EOs can be leading actors when the institutional context encourages participation, indeed experimentation, by social actors on a number of issues related to economic development, to employment or labour. The Quebec model of industrial relations is, therefore, not only unique in North America due to these laws, these consultative mechanisms or the vitality of union organizations, but this is also true due to the dynamism of its EOs, which underscores the value of studying the regional level to better understand the historical trajectories of business systems and labour markets.

Note

1 In addition to the EOs, we identified 304 associations with interests related to the product market. This result reflects the capacity of employers to organize themselves to invest effectively in places where they may exercise an influence on the question of economic development. Indeed, the government has historically established different collaborative organizations in which employers may assert their interests in this sphere. Up until 2015, employers had the possibility of influencing economic development at the local level, through local development centres (LDCs) aiming to encourage economic development and the creation of employment in a given territory, by mobilizing local actors (Loubier 2008). Since that time, this mission has been entrusted to Quebec municipalities, requiring employers and their associations to exercise influence on municipal elected officials. In 2020, the government of Quebec announced the creation of Accès entreprise Quebec, an initiative to reinforce support and investment services offered to enterprises in all Quebec regions, with a view to accelerating regional economic development (Crête, Le Devoir, November 11, 2020). This new governmental strategy, which aims to reinforce the role of regional municipal counties in economic development, confirms the necessity for employers to rely on an influential network at the local and regional level. As mentioned, Quebec employers also have the opportunity to represent their interests within collaborative bodies, both regional and sectoral, with the projects of Action concertée de coopération régionale de development (ACCORD). Thus, this Quebec initiative encourages the bringing together and networking of business people and enterprises within the same region who share a common vision and who work together to develop a strategy of economic development in their sector (Laroche 2016).

References

Almond, P., Gonzalez, M. C., Gunnigle, P., Lavelle, J., Balbona, D. L., Monaghan, S. and Murray, G. (2014). Multinationals and regional economies: Embedding the regime shoppers? *Transfer*, 20 (2): 237–253. 10.1177%2F1 024258914526101

Almond, P., Gonzalez, M. C., Lavelle, J. and Murray, G. (2017). The local in the global: Regions, employment systems and multinationals. *Industrial Relations Journal*, 48 (2): 115–132. 10.1111/irj.12150

Barry, M. and Wilkinson, A. (2011). Reconceptualising employers' associations under evolving employment relations: Countervailing power revisited. *Work, Employment and Society*, 25 (1): 149–162. 10.1177%2F0950017010389229

Behrens, M. (2004). New forms of employers' collective interest representation? *Industrielle Beziehungen*, 11 (1–2): 77–91.

Behrens, M. (2018). Structure and competing logics: The art of shaping interests within German employers' associations. *Socio-Economic Review*, 16 (4): 769–789. 10.1093/ser/mwx037

Brandl, B. and Lehr, A. (2019). The strange non-death of employer and business associations: an analysis of their representativeness and activities in Western European countries. *Economic and Industrial Democracy*, 40 (4): 932–953. 10.1177%2F0143831X16669842

Commission des Partenaires du Marché du travail (2021). Available at: https://www.cpmt.gouv.qc.ca/ [accessed on 11 February, 2021].

Coutu, M., Fontaine, L. L., Marceau, G., Coiquaud, U. and Bourgault, J. (2019). *Droit des rapports collectifs du travail au Québec*. Montreal: Les Éditions Yvon Blais.

Crête, M. (2020). Québec Crée des CLD 2.0. *Le Devoir*, 11 November 2020. Available at: https://www.ledevoir.com/politique/quebec/589464/quebec-cree-des-cld-2-0 [accessed on 11 February, 2021].

Crouch, C. (1993). *Industrial Relations and European State Traditions*. New York: Oxford University Press.

Dicken, P. (2003). *Global Shift: Reshaping the Global Economic Map of the 21st Century*, 4th ed. London: Sage.

Doellgast, V. and Greer, I. (2007). Vertical disintegration and the disorganization of German industrial relations. *British Journal of Industrial Relations*, 45 (1): 55–76. 10.1111/j.1467-8543.2007.00602.x

Gereffi, G., Humphrey, J. and Sturgeon, T. (2005). The governance of global value chains. *Review of International Political Economy*, 12 (1): 78–104. 10.1080/09692290500049805

Gooberman, L., Hauptmeier, M. and Heery, E. (2019). The decline of employers' associations in the UK, 1976–2014. *Journal of Industrial Relations*, 61 (1): 11–32. 10.1177%2F0022185617750418

Gooberman, L., Hauptmeier, M. and Heery, E. (2020a). A typology of employers' organisations in the United Kingdom. *Economic and Industrial Democracy*, 41 (1): 229–248. 10.1177%2F0143831X17704499

Gooberman, L., Hauptmeier, M. and Heery, E. (2020b). The decay and revival of sub-UK employer organisation: A response to Dr Ritson. *Labor History*, 61 (5–6): 417–422. 10.1080/0023656X.2020.1830958

Grimshaw, D. and Hayter, S. (2020). Employment relations and economic performance. In: J. Kelly and C. Frege (eds.) *Comparative Employment Relations in the Global Economy*, 2nd ed. London: Routledge, pp. 139–169.

Hall, P. A. and Soskice, D. (2001). *Varieties of Capitalism: The Institutional Foundations of Comparative Advantage*. Oxford: Oxford University Press.

Hébert, G. (1992). *Traité de Négociation Collective*. Boucherville: Gaëtan Morin editor.

Institut de la statistique du Québec (2020). *La présence syndicale au Québec.* Available at: https://statistique.quebec.ca/fr/document/la-presence-syndicale-au-quebec [accessed on 11 February, 2021].

Katz, H. C., Wonduck, L. and Johee, L. (2004). *The New Structure of Labor Relations: Tripartism and Decentralization.* Ithaca, NY: Cornell University Press.

Kohler-Koch, B., Kotzian, P. and Quittkat, C. (2017). The multilevel interest representation of national business associations. *West European Politics,* 40 (5): 1046–1065. 10.1080/01402382.2017.1303244

Laroche, M. (2012). Action collective patronale sur fond de crise: vers une reconfiguration du modèle associative. *Canadian Review of Sociology/ Revue Canadienne de Sociologie,* 49: 271–291. 10.1111/j.1755-618X.2012. 01295.x

Laroche, M. (2013). Le dialogue social au Québec: quels impacts au niveau local? *Regards sur le travail,* 9 (2): 1–14.

Laroche, M. (2016). Le dialogue social économique dans le secteur de la transformation de l'aluminium: dynamisme et concertation des entreprises pour favoriser la compétitivité de la filière industrielle. In: D. Fraboulet, M. Margairaz and P. Vernus (eds.) *Réguler l'économie. L'apport des Organisations Patronales. Europe, XIXe-XXe siècles.* Rennes: Les Presses Universitaires de Rennes, pp. 309–323.

Laroche, M. and Jalette, P. (2016). Transformation des relations du travail au Québec: tendances récentes en matière de syndicalisation, de négociation et de convention collective. In: D. Andolphatto and S. Contrepoids (eds.) *Syndicats et dialogue social: les modèles occidentaux à l'épreuve,* Brussels: éditions Peter Lang (Brussels), Collection "Travail et société.", pp. 209–225.

Laroche, M. and Murray, G. (2012). Coordinated employer collective bargaining and globalization: a study of the men's clothing industry in Quebec, 1974–2012. *Industrial Relations Journal,* 43 (6): 472–493. 10.1111/irj.12003

Loubier, S. (2008). *Les CLD: Des intervenants de première ligne,* Quebec City: Communiqué de L'Association des Centres Locaux de Développement du Québec.

MacKinnon, D. (2012). Beyond strategic coupling: Reassessing the firm-region nexus in global production networks. *Journal of Economic Geography,* 12 (1): 227–245. 10.1093/jeg/lbr009

Markey, R. and Hodgkinson, A. (2008). The impact of the workplace relations act on regional patterns of industrial relations: The Illawarra region of Australia, 1996-2004. *Journal of Industrial Relations,* 50 (5): 752–778. 10.1177% 2F0022185608094116

Medina, I. and Molins, J. M. (2018). Business association and multilevel dynamics in Spain and the UK. In: G. Lachapelle and P. Onate (eds.) *Borders and Margins: Federalism, Devolution and Multi-Level Governance.* Opladen, Berlin and Toronto: Barbara Budrich Publishers, pp. 167–183.

Phelps, N. and Fuller, C. (2001). Taking care of business: Aftercare and the state—multinational enterprise nexus in Wales. *Environment and Planning C: Government and Policy,* 19 (6): 817–832. 10.1068%2Fc0055

Saurugger, S. and Grossman, E. (2006). Les groupes d'intérêt au secours de la démocratie? *Revue française de science politiques,* 56 (2): 299–321.

Schmitter, P. C. and Streeck, W. (1981). *The Organization of Business Interests: A Research Design to Study the Associative Action of Business in the Advanced Industrial Societies of Western Europe*. Berlin: Wissenschafts-Zentrum Berlin.

Schneider, V. and Grote, J. (2006). Introduction: Business associations, associative order and internationalization. In: W. Streeck, J. Grote, V. Schneider and J. Visser (eds.) *Governing Interests Business Associations Facing Internationalism*. London and New York: Routledge, pp 1–18.

Sheldon, P., Nacamulli, R., Paoletti, F. and Morgan, D. E. (2016). Employer association responses to the effects of bargaining decentralization in Australia and Italy: Seeking explanations from organizational theory. *British Journal of Industrial Relations*, 54 (1): 160–191. 10.1111/bjir.12061

Sheldon, P. and Thornthwaite, L. (2005). Members or clients? employers' associations, the decentralization of bargaining, and the reorientation of service provision: Evidence from Europe and Australia. *Business and Economic History On-Line*, 3: 1–21.

Traxler, F. (2004). Employers' associations, institutions and economic change: A cross-national comparison. *Industrielle Beziehungen*, 11 (1–2): 42–60.

Traxler, F. (2006). Economic internationalization and the organizational dilemma of employers' associations: A comparison of 20 OECD countries. In: W. Streeck, J. R. Grote, V. Schneider and J. Visser (eds.) *Governing Interests: Business Associations Facing Internationalization*. London: Routledge, pp. 93–114.

Traxler, F. (2008). Employer organizations. In: P. Blyton et al. (eds.) *The SAGE Handbook of Industrial Relations*. London: Sage, pp. 225–240.

Van Schendel, V. and Gabriel-Tremblay, D. (2020). L'action collective des employeurs. In: P.-L. Bilodeau and D. Gabriel- Tremblay (eds.) *Les Fondements des Relations Industrielles*. Montreal: Chenelière Education, pp. 60–83.

Zhu, Y., Benson, J. and Gospel, H. (2017). A comparative perspective on employer collective action and employers' associations in Asia. In: J. Benson, Y. Zhu and H. Gospel (eds.) *Employers' Associations in Asia: Employer Collective Action*. London: Routledge, pp. 229–241.

12 Employers' Organizations and the Territorial Divergence of Employment Relations in Wales, Scotland, and Northern Ireland

Leon Gooberman and Marco Hauptmeier

Introduction

The importance of sub-national variations within Employment Relations (ER) is an emerging research theme (Locke 1992). While such research tends to focus on federal systems (Belanger and Trudeau 2009; Cobble and Merrill 2009), researchers have argued that sub-national divergence can exist elsewhere within more fluid multi-level governance systems (Almond et al. 2017; Beynon et al. 2012; Katz and Darbishire 2000).

Our recent research identified 447 Employers' Organizations (EOs) in the UK (Gooberman et al. 2018). Some served employer interests in one of the nations of Wales and Scotland, or the region of Northern Ireland. These three territories are part of the UK, but elected parliaments or assemblies have existed in each since the introduction of political devolution in 1999. Although employment law in Wales and Scotland remains the responsibility of the central UK Government, autonomous governments in each territory, and Northern Ireland, are responsible for state functions such as health and education services, transport, and local government.

However, while the ER literature has explored regional variations, the role of EOs within such variation has yet to be fully discovered, only emerging recently and tentatively as a research topic (Larouche in this volume; Gooberman et al. 2020). This chapter addresses this research gap by exploring territorial EOs in Wales, Scotland, and Northern Ireland, to ask: How do EOs contribute to distinctive ER in the devolved territories?

We argue that developments in Scotland, Wales, and Northern Ireland constituted a new pattern of employer organization that responded to the creation of politically devolved institutions, and the development of emergent but substantive territorial variations (Beynon et al. 2012; Heery et al. 2020). The responsibilities discharged by devolved governments helped EOs develop two new roles. The first is representing employers' interests within topics linked to work and ER that are within the jurisdiction of devolved governments. These include pay and conditions

DOI: 10.4324/9781003104575-15

within public health and education services, general labour market skills, and the emerging linkage between supplying or receiving financial support from devolved institutions and adhering to labour standards set by such bodies. The second is joining with territorial governments and unions within new structures, most notably public sector social partnerships, to make choices as to the extent to which some industry-specific elements of ER diverge.

But this new pattern does not imply the creation of fully divergent ER systems in the three territories. While devolved governments in Scotland and Wales often want to diverge from UK-wide ER, the retention of employment law in these territories by the UK Government has prevented the creation of new ER systems. Meanwhile, although the Northern Ireland Assembly has jurisdiction over employment law, political deadlock has restrained wholesale divergence. Most notably, the UK-wide trend over recent decades of declining numbers of EOs bargaining collectively (Gooberman et al. 2019b) is also apparent in all three territories, and has prompted a similar organizational refocusing towards service provision and lobbying as throughout the UK (Gooberman et al. 2018).

The remainder of this chapter is structured as follows. The next section discusses the literature on regional ER systems and identifies the lack of research on regional EOs, followed by an outline of our data sources and methodology. The following part provides a quantitative overview of our statistical data. Subsequent parts use qualitative data to explore how territorial EOs represent collective member interests through political representation and joint labour market regulation; and representing individual member interests through services such as training and advisory services. The chapter then concludes.

Representing Territorial Employer Interests

Locke (1992) studied regional variety within Italy to critique how ER theory was premised on different 'national models' to argue for a greater focus on sub-national variation. But much of the ER literature continued to assume that national settings were paramount given the role of states as 'midwives of institutional change' (Baccaro and Howell 2011: 551). Nevertheless, Crouch et al. (2009) argued that sub-national diversity can exist within national typologies such as Varieties of Capitalism (Hall and Soskice 2001), as such typologies focus on delineating the dominant model, not factors driving deviation. Katz and Darbishire (2000) identified how sub-national divergences were prompted by diverging employment practices clustered at firm level across different sectors, while Almond et al. (2017) analyzed relationships between multinational corporations and regional governments to argue that the latter can join with EOs and unions to make choices about the extent to which elements of their business system follow 'co-ordinated' or 'liberal' patterns.

But although sub-national research tends to focus on federal systems given their legislative capacity for enabling sub-national divergence (Belanger and Trudeau 2009; Cobble and Merrill 2009; Patmore 2017), the emergence of devolved institutions in the UK prompted some analysis. Beynon et al. (2012) argued that Wales features 'a patterned variation from the norm of UK industrial relations' embodied by public sector social partnerships (Bacon and Samuel 2016). Hyman (2008) argues that governments assume many roles to intervene in ER in addition to their role as legislator. The variety of levers used by devolved governments to impact ER in the absence of legislative powers was observed recently by a study of the Real Living Wage standard (Heery et al. 2020) which encourages employers to pay an hourly wage greater than the UK Government's statutory national living wage. The research argued that devolved governments used their status as employers, purchasers, funders, subsidizers, soft regulators, institution-builders, and patriotic ideologues to promote the Real Living Wage, while the UK Government was less enthusiastic. As a result, a higher proportion of employers in Scotland and Wales applied the Real Living Wage than in England. Nevertheless, sub-national divergence is limited by the asymmetric nature of devolution, where governance responsibilities are divided between UK and devolved institutions.

While recent literature has highlighted the importance of EOs as actors within ER (e.g.: Gooberman et al. 2018; Ibsen and Navrbjerg 2019), the recent trajectory of regional EOs has been neglected although Larouche in this volume examines their characteristics within Quebec, while Gooberman et al. (2020) provided an overview of one such organization in the UK. However, political scientists have studied how devolution impacted employer interest representation across commercial and trading issues. For example, Medina and Molins (2014: 286) analyzed the regional functions of country-level employer groups in Italy, Spain, and the UK to argue that 'devolution is the source of business mobilization at the regional level'.

Nevertheless, territorial and regional EOs were once an important part of ER in the UK, given their 19th century emergence to counter unions. Union organization reflected product market scope and when these expanded across the UK, unions and EOs grew in parallel. Subsequently, a multi-level organizational structure during the post-war heyday of collective bargaining enabled EOs to represent members' interests within such bargaining structures (Gooberman et al. 2019a). But the decline of institutional industrial relations (Brown et al. 2009) impacted on all EOs, as their primary function was to bargain collectively although dynamics differed across public and private industries. By 2011, only 16% of private sector employees in Britain were covered by bargaining (Van Wanrooy et al. 2013) and many EOs in Wales, Scotland and Northern Ireland closed, merged, or ceased to bargain.

However, pockets of territorial bargaining continued, most notably in Scotland where territorial institutions were more common than elsewhere. Meanwhile, national agreements collapsed from the 1980s. One example was the Engineering Employers Federation (EEF), renamed as Make UK in 2019. The EEF's substantive bargaining agreement collapsed in 1989. Meanwhile the EEF was a federation of regional and territorial EOs but those in England and Wales merged by 2008 within a centralized structure (McKinlay 2013) while those in Scotland and Northern Ireland became independent. But the ending of the national agreement prompted all to refocus on member services such as advising on human resource management, employment law, and health and safety; activities that were combined with a continuation of political lobbying (Gooberman et al. 2020). Nevertheless, 44% of employees in the public sector were still covered by bargaining in 2011 (Van Wanrooy et al. 2013). Some territorial EOs such as those within local government were involved in negotiating and implementing collective agreements covering pay and conditions. But many agreements changed in scope. They increasingly became frameworks granting autonomy to individual employers over implementation terms, weakening the role of EOs within collective ER. Overall, and despite some regional ER divergence within the UK, researchers have yet to explore fully the role of EOs within this process.

Data and Methodology

We drew our primary data from two sources examined between 2014 and 2017 for an ESRC funded project on UK EOs (Bowkett et al. 2017; Demougin et al. 2019a, 2019b, 2021; Gooberman et al. 2018, 2019a, 2019b, 2020; Heery et al. 2017). The first source was our database of 447 EOs. Our definition reflected changing ER. We did not restrict our analysis to bodies involved in collective bargaining; we also included those providing member services across work and employment.

We identified EOs active within Wales, Scotland, and Northern Ireland in our EO database (Gooberman et al. 2018). These were standalone EOs, such as the Welsh Local Government Association, or federated EOs such as the Scottish Fisherman's Federation. We have also considered UK-wide general EOs whose territorial functions were organizationally autonomous, and whose governance structures featured territorial representation. Three of these, the Federation of Small Businesses, the Confederation of British Industry, and Business in the Community had autonomous functions in all three territories. A fourth, the UK Chambers of Commerce, included umbrella bodies representing local chambers throughout Scotland and Northern Ireland, but not Wales. In total, we identified 52 territorial EOs. An additional source of data were 28 semi-structured interviews carried out with representatives of EOs, unions and experts in devolved territories; 8 in Wales, 9 in Scotland, and 11 in Northern Ireland.

Our methodology in this chapter uses a framework drawn from our research on UK EOs (Gooberman et al. 2018) that identified how EOs represented their members' interests within work and employment topics on a collective and individual basis. Collective member interests were represented through political representation and joint labour market regulation; and individual member interests through services such as training and advisory services.

Employer Organization Across the Devolved Territories

Of the 52 territorial EOs in our sample, 41 were standalone and federated EOs that represented employers in particular industries. Meanwhile, all 11 UK-wide EOs with autonomous regional functions were general EOs drawing their memberships from different industries. Of the 52 EOs, most (28 EOs, 52%) were based in Scotland, compared to 15 (29%) in Northern Ireland and 9 (17%) in Wales. Dates of foundation were not generally available, but most territorial EOs pre-dated the creation of politically devolved institutions in 1999.

Table 12.1 sets out the proportion of territorial and UK-wide EOs (Gooberman et al. 2018) carrying out selected activities.

The most frequent activity was lobbying, carried out by 73% of UK-wide EOs and 85% in devolved territories, with the similar occurrence driven by common pluralist political systems operating across the UK. There was also little difference in the incidence of training, provided by 69% of UK-wide EOs and 67% in devolved territories. Vocational training throughout the UK remains fragmented and market driven. EOs do not generally have a role although fragments remain of the more co-ordinated system in place before the 1980s. The key trend within UK-wide EOs over recent decades has been an increasing focus on providing services to individual members, a pattern shared with territorial EOs. For example, 47% of UK-wide EOs, and 46% of territorial EOs provided employment law advice designed to minimize legal risks to the employer. However, the proportion of territorial EOs (29%) carrying out activities linked to collective bargaining was far greater than those at a UK level

Table 12.1 Selected EO activities within devolved territories and the UK

Type of EO activity	UK	Devolved territories
Lobbying	73%	85%
Training	69%	67%
Employment law advice	47%	46%
Bargaining	13%	29%

(13%). But difference did not reflect different systems or approaches within devolved territories, reflecting instead the greater historic presence of autonomous governing institutions in Scotland.

While the continuation of a UK-wide ER system means that territorial and UK-wide EOs carry out similar types of activities, territorial EOs are operating in a political system different to that of UK-wide EOs. While such EOs operate primarily within terrain shaped by the central UK Government when representing the collective and individual interests of their members, territorial EOs instead focus primarily on political aspects shaped by devolved governments and the qualitative focus of their activities reflects this difference, as we now set out.

Collective Interest Representation

Political Representation

Most EOs in devolved territories (85%) engaged in political representation with devolved political institutions, either through formal structures or informal means. Our interviewees commonly stressed the importance of such representation. For example, one stated that

> the purpose of this office [based in a capital city of a devolved territory] is to try and analyze all the proposals that come forward [to] try and guide the process, influence how the regulation eventually comes out the far end [of the devolved political process].
> (Interview with representative of EO, private sector)

Territorial EOs were not generally seeking to offset organized labour but instead to persuade devolved governments to adopt policies more favourable towards the collective interests of their members. These cover issues apart from employment, but the role of devolved governments within education and economic development, as well as their status as employers, means that employment topics often appeared.

There were two methods of participating in formal political structures. One was making written submissions to, or appearing as witnesses before, parliamentary or assembly committees. Their purpose is to scrutinize the activities of devolved governments and their accountable bodies. Topic specific committees operate by issuing a call for evidence, before inviting witnesses to represent their organization before the committee and answer its questions. Parliamentary or assembly clerks then work with committee members to produce a report with recommendations, to which devolved governments usually issue a written response. As examples, the Northern Ireland EEF commented on the 2016 Employment Bill (Northern Ireland Assembly 2016) while the Farmers Union of Wales and National Farmers' Union Cymru appeared before Assembly committees to discuss regulating agricultural wages and conditions (National Assembly for Wales 2013a, 2013b). Committee clerks depend on a stream of witnesses to populate hearings. As an example of the volume of activity, 19 committees operated within the Scottish Parliament by 2020 (Scottish Parliament 2020). In 2017–2018 the Economy, Jobs and Fair Work Committee heard from 159 witnesses representing 115 organizations (Scottish Parliament 2018). One EO representative observed that 'I'm giving evidence tomorrow to a committee and in the last six months, I have given evidence five times' (Interview with representative of Scottish EO 7). Similar EO representation exists in Wales and Northern Ireland.

The other method of participating in formal structures is taking part in parliamentary or assembly groups. These are topic focused discussion bodies enabling EOs to access politicians who have chosen to join the group. For example, Colleges Scotland provided secretariat services to the Scottish Parliament's Cross-Party Group on Colleges, while the Federation of Small Businesses Wales provided similar services to the National Assembly's Small Business Group. Overall, cross-party groups dealt with a vast range of topics and their meetings tended to be informal. Opinions varied as to their effectiveness. One EO in Scotland argued that they 'tended to be quite abstract at times' (Interview with representative of Scottish EO 1) and questioned their effectiveness as lobbying fora, but a second EO welcomed the opportunity to 'discuss our issues' around skills and argued that cross-party groups enabled them to promote members' interests directly to politicians (Interview with representative of Scottish EO 4).

However, lobbying also depended on communication outside formal channels. One of our interviewees remarked that 'I've probably been to 20 dinners over the past 8 years [with] a series of different Ministers' (Interview with representative of Welsh EO 3) while a second stated that:

> Each government minister has a Special Political Advisor known as a SPAD, and these individuals are very, very influential. So I work very hard at developing relationships with those individuals […] and if there are any significant decisions to be made, it's unlikely that the Minister will make those without first consulting their SPAD. So I would work quite closely with those individuals on an informal basis.
> (Interview with representative of Northern Irish EO 6)

A common theme within our interviews was how the small size of devolved civil societies made access to politicians and officials far easier than within the national UK system. One EO representative observed that:

> Having a devolved administration […] has been very helpful. It's much more accessible, and it's made our job easier. In the past, a lot

of our activity had to be focused on Westminster, and Westminster's impenetrable, [the] Scottish Government is much more open.
(Interview with representative of Scottish EO 6)

When discussing how and why EOs lobby, many interviewees described a three-stage process of building credibility. The first was to be accepted as a body that represented their members' collective opinion. The second was to be accepted as a source of credible data. Both processes combined to enable the EO to be invited to access aspects of the policy development process, whether through formal mechanisms such as assembly and parliamentary committees or through informal mechanisms. One representative observed that:

We have to invest in these long-term strategies of [...] building these relationships. And it pays off by organizing [cross-party group] events, by meeting Ministers, by going to conference events [...] we tell the officials in Government departments that we're doing all these things. And therefore, they see us as an influential organization, and when we want to speak to the Minister, or there's a new Minister, they will say, "yes you need to speak to them".
(Interview with representative of Scottish EO 7)

The third and final stage was translating access into influence, although most EOs admitted that this cannot be quantified. Nevertheless, close-knit policy communities can ease the process of influencing policies from their inception to execution. One common tactic was to engage with political parties when drafting their manifestos. One EO representative observed that 'We'll often meet with them to talk about their manifestos before they start the drafting process and to say, "Look. Here's our ideas. What do you think?"' (Interview with representative of Scottish EO 1).

A second tactic was to participate in some of the many fora and working groups that characterize devolved governance. But while most EOs saw their work as what one representative defined as 'nudging the super-tanker. Just keep on pushing this sort of colossus in the right direction and nudging at the right time', others noted that if a government was unpopular with their industry, then a more combative approach might not change policy but could generate publicity that aided member recruitment and retention (Interview with EO representatives).

Joint Labour Market Regulation

Thirteen EOs (29%) were active within collective bargaining structures, seven in the public sector, and six in the private sector. While data on employee numbers covered by bargaining in devolved territories were not available, it was likely that those covered by private sector agreements were far fewer than those in the public sector with, for example, some 240,000 employees covered by the four collective agreements within Scottish local government (Interview with representative of Scottish EO 8). Private sector EOs active within collective bargaining were concentrated in Scotland. But concentration was driven by historical factors rather than more recent developments linked to devolution. Autonomous governing institutions of any description have long been more likely to exist in Scotland. This was prompted by its retention of a separate legal system, while a territorial government department tasked with overseeing a range of state functions and public services existed since the late 19th century, albeit controlled before devolution by the UK Government. As an example of historical continuity, one EO in Scotland, Scotland's Electrical Trade Association (SELECT), has since 1969 negotiated terms and conditions with Unite, the union for electrical contractors, in Scotland through the Scottish Joint Industry Board. Nevertheless, Scotland was also subjected to the UK-wide changes to institutional ER over recent decades. As an example of such trends, the Scottish Building Federation was a signatory to the UK-wide Construction Industry Joint Council agreements that set out employment terms and conditions to be followed by all members, but in recent years its members could instead work with the federation to develop bespoke terms and conditions.

By contrast, Wales lacked autonomous governing structures before political devolution, and territorial level bargaining structures were few even during the heyday of collective bargaining. Our data demonstrated that no private sector EOs engaged in Wales only collective bargaining while remaining bargaining was subsumed into broader arrangements. For example, electrical contracting employers' interests in Wales (and Northern Ireland) were represented within a Joint Industry Board solely by the London-headquartered Electrical Contractors Association. Meanwhile, territorial EO involvement in private sector collective ER within Northern Ireland was very limited, although the Construction Employers Federation worked with the Joint Council for the Building & Civil Engineering Industry to set out basic terms and conditions for employment in the industry.

While bargaining in the private sector by EOs in devolved territories was marginal, bargaining in the public sector was more common. But the extent to which divergence took place divided into three patterns. The first was where devolved arrangements diverged significantly from the approach adopted in England. This was apparent within colleges where bargaining in England evolved into a framework approach, but political pressure helped retain a more centralized approach elsewhere. For example, colleges in Wales used standard contracts to ensure consistency, while the approach in England featured model contracts that could be voluntarily used by colleges. Meanwhile, in Northern Ireland a more collective approach also existed as to the negotiation and implementation of working conditions, such as pay, hours of work, and holiday entitlement, although other areas were subject to greater management discretion.

The second pattern was where UK level bargaining structures remained in force, but divergence existed, again driven by political pressures. Terms and conditions applying to the more than one million employees of the National Health Service (NHS) throughout the UK, for example, are recommended by a Pay Review body formed from independent representatives. But some collective bargaining took place at devolved levels, with one NHS EO working with the unions to adopt elements of the agreement in England but also negotiated local adaptations, with the revised agreement subject to a ballot of union members. The final pattern saw institutional arrangements differing across devolved territories. One example was local government, where pay and conditions in Scotland were negotiated within separate institutional structures, but those in Wales, Northern Ireland, and England were agreed within one structure.

The second type of joint labour market regulation was that carried out by government bodies. Although ER in Scotland and Wales is retained by the UK Parliament at Westminster, the creation of new regulatory institutions was difficult but not impossible. The determination of devolved governments to diverge was reflected in the exceptional creation in 2016 of the Agricultural Wages Panel for Wales, a bipartite body that specifies statutory minimum wage floors and other conditions for all agricultural workers in Wales (Gooberman and Hauptmeier 2021). Such terms were set in England and Wales by the Agricultural Wages Board, until its abolition by the UK Government. But while ER was reserved to the UK parliament, agriculture was devolved. The Welsh Government wanted to create a new regulatory body and challenged the UK Government in the Supreme Court, which ruled that the National Assembly for Wales had responsibility over agricultural wage setting. The Welsh Government subsequently created the Agricultural Wages Panel for Wales, the first and only devolved wage setting body established since 1999. Thus, agricultural ER in Wales was regulated using bi-partite approaches commonly found in 'co-ordinated' business systems, as were activities in Scotland and Northern Ireland where longstanding agricultural wages boards remained. Nevertheless, the constitutional loophole that enabled this divergence was closed by subsequent legislation.

While the re-regulation of agricultural ER in Wales was exceptional, the use of partnership approaches to modulate public sector ER in devolved territories was more common. The clearest example was social partnership arrangements in devolved health services (Bacon and Samuel 2016). Health services in the UK are taxpayer funded through the NHS, free at the point of use, and controlled in Scotland and Wales by the Scottish and Welsh Governments, respectively. The creation of partnership fora involving employers, unions and governments reflected how both governments were controlled by political parties supportive of labour interests, as well as frequent interaction within tight knit policy making communities.

Within the Scottish NHS, the Scottish Partnership Forum produced extensive co-operation between unions, employers, and governments to dismantle an internal health market created before devolution by the UK Government, improve services and enhance staff terms and conditions. Nevertheless, union participation in the Wales Partnership Forum was initially restricted to discussing workforce issues as asymmetric devolution prevented the Welsh Government from reforming NHS governance. But the National Assembly for Wales gained more competencies from 2007 and dismantled the internal market, deepening partnership working with EOs and unions. An EO involved in one of these territorial fora described how they would typically help to progress a workforce issue through the structure by acting as the secretariat for an issue based sub-group:

> We would ensure that the work was progressed, any expert opinion or legal opinion was drawn into those discussions, and we would [...] ensure that it was progressed, consultation was undertaken, stakeholders were involved, and once a final agreement was reached, that would then go back to the Partnership Forum, get ratified and we would then send it out to the service saying, 'This is the agreed document.'
>
> (Interview with EO representative)

Finally, the Scottish and Welsh Governments were committed to social partnership approaches that drove the emergence of substantive subnational divergences through creating regulation impacting on areas including ER. As examples, the Scottish Government issued Statutory Guidance to incorporate 'fair work' considerations into public sector procurement (Scottish Government 2018), while the Welsh Government plans to promote 'fair work' throughout all its activities, including linking the receipt of financial support by employers to better employment practices (Welsh Government 2019). Occasionally, EOs become involved in such initiatives, deepening their involvement with devolved governments. One example was Employers for Carers collaborating with the Scottish and Welsh Governments to support businesses to become better environments for employees with caring responsibilities by promoting best practice policies, leading to the joint creation of a form of private voluntary regulation.

Individual Interest Representation

Territorial EOs addressed individual members interests through member services and organizational functions, often tailored to the specific territorial requirements of their members. Virtually all EOs provided networking events and business development seminars. Beyond these, the provision of training was common, with 35 organizations (67%) reporting such activity. Programmes were generally small in scale such as a Scottish EO providing bespoke training for companies undertaking culture change initiatives or seeking guidance as to how new legislation might affect Human Resource Management (HRM) functions (Interview with representative of Scottish EO 2). Others were larger, primarily where EOs retained a role within the few surviving traditional, industry-level, apprenticeship structures such as the Construction Industry Training Board. But territorial EO involvement within the governance of such apprenticeship structurers reduced over recent decades because of UK Government policy, with one EO representative arguing that 'we used to do a lot more than we do now, it's very diluted' (Interview with representative of Scottish EO 9).

Some EOs provided their own territorial level apprenticeship programmes, but scale again varied widely reflecting the UK-wide decay of many such schemes. One EO representative observed that:

> We used to have classroom-based apprenticeships and they would get time off work to attend the College, but demand shrunk [...] So we ended up, as an organization, taking the apprenticeships modules, getting a training assessor, and providing those courses ourselves.
>
> (Interview with representative of Scottish EO 4)

Another common method of representing individual interests was advising on employment law, a service offered by 24 EOs (47%). Many offered a helpline staffed by a commercial provider, with subscription income being used to fund 'free' access to the service. As an example, the Federation of Small Businesses in all three territories offered a legal helpline while its legal protection insurance also enabled members to representation in employment tribunals and personal injury cases. Meanwhile, the National Farmers' Union Cymru offered access to an employment law helpline although additional subscription charges applied.

Other EOs employed lawyers to provide representation, enabling them to offer a form of legal insurance service as part of their service offering. Scottish Engineering employed lawyers to represent members directly during employment tribunals that can include unfair dismissal, redundancy payments and protective awards, sex, race and disability discrimination, maternity rights, time off for public or union duties. In Northern Ireland, a primary focus of EEF Northern Ireland (once a federated part of the UK-wide EEF but later independent) was the comprehensive legal representation of members facing employment law claims within tribunals, with an EEF Northern Ireland representative arguing that the service covered the period 'from the start [of the claim] to the finish, to the appeal court, the whole lot, if it goes to appeal' (Interview with EEF Northern Ireland representative). Some claims were those relating to religious discrimination, where linkages between religion and conflict in Northern Ireland prompted the UK Parliament to pass the Fair Employment Act in 1976. This Act and its successors outlawed discrimination on religious grounds, and claims were adjudicated by a system of tribunals separate to those adjudicating on cases linked to other aspects of employment law.

But, overall, the services offered by territorial EOs aimed at individual members demonstrated a narrow conception of HRM and employment relations. EOs generally did not promote sophisticated HRM practices with the aim of improving employee performance and engagement. Instead, the evidence indicated that EOs and their members were largely concerned with procedural HRM and reducing risks stemming from employee application of employment law. Finally, some territorial EOs were active within recruitment, generally through the provision of a vacancy advertising service.

Conclusion

The ER literature has recognized the potential for regional divergence (Almond et al. 2017; Cobble and Merrill 2009; Locke 1992; Patmore 2017), including within devolved territories in the UK (Bacon and Samuel 2016; Beynon et al. 2012). Nevertheless, EOs at a sub-national level in the UK and elsewhere have been neglected, emerging only recently as a research topic within ER (Gooberman et al. 2020)Gooberman 2020 and Larouche in this volume (Chapter 11).

This chapter adds to this emerging literature by arguing that as the salience of bargaining fell throughout the UK, developments in Scotland, Wales, and Northern Ireland reflected a new focus of employer organization within devolved contexts. Territorial EOs responded to the emergence of devolved government that were often more sympathetic to labour interests than were UK Governments and pursued policies that impacted on ER to create emerging but substantive divergences within territorial ER. Divergent policies combined with the scale of devolved governments as employers, funders, and procurers to prompt EOs to develop two new roles in addition to their provision of individual member services and residual bargaining activity; one was a lobbyist of devolved institutions on topics including those linked to ER, and the other was taking part in new structures to regulate industry specific elements of ER.

Nevertheless, two qualifications should be made. One is that the new organizational pattern is very different from that which characterized the origins of regional EOs, where employers sought to countervail and manage pressure from employees by forming local and regional level EOs, which amalgamated into UK-wide associations and federations that focused on representing employers' interests within collective bargaining. The other is that the newer organizational pattern does not signify the creation of new territorial ER systems. The devolved governments of Scotland and Wales often want to diverge from the UK-wide ER system, but UK Governments have used their retention of employment law jurisdiction to limit such divergence. The Northern Ireland Assembly can diverge given its authority over ER, but it has been constrained by political deadlock.

In conclusion, the British state is often viewed as a centralized entity that has pursued neoliberal policies in recent decades. But devolution has enabled the creation of territorial governments far less favourable to such policies, prompting the gradual emergence of substantive territorial divergence within ER. Ongoing constitutional pressures, especially in Scotland, are likely to converge with devolved governments' desire to intervene more forcefully in the post-Covid economy and labour market to drive further divergence, such as those embodied in the 'social partnership' agenda. Such dynamics mean that devolved governments are increasingly important actors within territorial ER and have been creating new challenges to employers, prompting the pattern of collective employer organization to adapt in response.

References

Almond, P., Maria C., Gonzalez, M., Lavelle, J. and Murray, G. (2017). The local in the global: Regions, employment systems and multinationals. *Industrial Relations Journal*, 48 (2): 115–132. 10.1111/irj.12150

Baccaro, Lucio, & Howell, Chris (2011). A Common Neoliberal Trajectory. Politics & Society, 39(4): 521–563 10.1177/0032329211420082

Bacon, N. and Samuel, P. (2016). Social partnership and political devolution in the National Health Service: Emergence, operation and outcomes. *Work, Employment and Society*, 31 (1): 123–141. 10.1177%2F0950017015616910

Belanger, J. and Trudeau, G. (2009). The institutional specificity of Quebec in the context of globalization. *Canadian Labour Employment Law Journal*, 15 (1): 49–76.

Beynon, H., Davies, R. and Davies, S. (2012). Sources of variation in trade union membership across the UK: The case of Wales. *Industrial Relations Journal*, 43 (3): 200–221. 10.1111/j.1468-2338.2012.00676.x

Bowkett, C., Hauptmeier, M. and Heery, E. (2017). Exploring the role of employer forums - the case of Business in the Community Wales. *Employee Relations*, 39 (7): 986–1000. 10.1108/ER-11-2016-0229

Brown, W., Bryson, A. and Forth, J. (2009). Competition and the retreat from collective bargaining. In: W. Brown, A Bryson, J Forth et al. (eds.) *The Evolution of the Modern Workplace*. Cambridge: Cambridge University Press, pp. 22–47.

Cobble, D. S. and Merrill, M. (2009). The promise of service work unionism. In: M. Korczynski and C. L. MacDonald (eds.) *Service Work: Critical Perspectives*. New York and Oxford: Routledge, pp. 153–174.

Crouch, C. (2005). *Capitalist Diversity and Change*. Oxford: OUP.

Crouch, Colin, Schröder, Martin, & Voelzkow, Helmut (2009). Regional and sectoral varieties of capitalism. Economy and Society, 38(4): 654–678. 10. 1080/03085140903190383

Demougin, P., Gooberman, L., Hauptmeier, M. and Heery, E. (2019b). Employer organisations transformed. *Human Resource Management Journal*, 29 (1): 1–16. 10.1111/1748-8583.12222

Demougin, P., Gooberman, L. and Hauptmeier, M. (2019a). The unexpected survival of employer collective action in the UK. *Relations Industrielles / Industrial Relations*, 74 (2): 353–376.

Demougin, P., Gooberman, L., Hauptmeier, M. and Heery, E. (2021). Revisiting voluntarism: Private voluntary regulation by employer forums in the United Kingdom. *Journal of Industrial Relations*. Published online first. 10.1177%2 F00221856211038308

Gooberman, L. and Hauptmeier, M. (2021). *Union Coalitions and Strategic Framing: The Case of the Agricultural Advisory Panel for Wales*. Manuscript. Cardiff: Cardiff University.

Gooberman, L., Hauptmeier, M. and Heery, E. (2018). Contemporary employer interest representation in the United Kingdom. *Work, Employment and Society*, 32 (1): 114–132. 10.1177/0950017017701074

Gooberman, L., Hauptmeier, M. and Heery, E. (2019a). The evolution of employers' organisations in the United Kingdom: Extending countervailing power. *Human Resource Management Journal*, 29 (1): 82–96. 10.1111/1748-8583.12193

Gooberman, L., Hauptmeier, M. and Heery, E. (2019b). The decline of employers' associations in the UK, 1976 to 2014. *Journal of Industrial Relations*, 61 (1): 11–32. 10.1177/0022185617750418

Gooberman, L., Hauptmeier, M. and Heery, E. (2020). The decay and revival of sub-UK employer organization: A response to Dr Ritson. *Labor History*, 61 (5–6): 417–422. 10.1080/0023656X.2020.1830958

Hall, P. and Soskice, D. (eds.) (2001). *Varieties of Capitalism*. Oxford: OUP.

Heery, E., Gooberman, L. and Hauptmeier, M. (2017). The petroleum driver passport scheme: A case study in reregulation. *Industrial Relations Journal*, 48 (3): 274–291. 10.1111/irj.12179

Heery, E., Hann, D. and Nash, D. (2020). Political devolution and employment relations in Great Britain: The case of the Living Wage. *Industrial Relations Journal*, 51 (5): 391–409. 10.1111/irj.12306

Hyman, R. (2008). The state in industrial relations. In: P. Blyton, N. Bacon, J. Fiorito and E. Heery (eds.) *The Sage Handbook of Industrial Relations*, Los Angeles, CA: Sage, pp. 258–283.

Ibsen, Christian Lyhne, and Navrbjerg, Steen E. (2019). Adapting to survive: The case of Danish employers' organizations. *Human Resource Management Journal*, 58 (5): 1–15. 10.1111/1748-8583.12182

Katz, H. and Darbishire, O. (2000). *Converging Divergences, Worldwide Changes an Employment Systems*, Ithaca: ILR Press.

Locke, R. (1992). The demise of the national union in Italy: Lessons for comparative industrial relations theory. *Industrial and Labor Relations Review*, 45 (2): 229–249. 10.1177%2F001979399204500202

McKinlay, A. (2013). From Organised to Disorganised Capital? British Employer Associations, 1897–2010. In: G. Gall and T. Dundon (eds.) *Global Antiunionism: Nature, Dynamics, Trajectories and Outcomes*, London: Palgrave Macmillan, pp. 39–62.

Medina, I. and Molins, J. (2014). Regionalism and employer groups in Spain, Italy, and the UK. *Territory, Politics, Governance*, 2 (3): 270–286. 10.1080/21 622671.2014.954602

National Assembly for Wales (2013a). Environment and Sustainability Committee, E&S(4)-04-13, Paper 2, Inquiry into the proposed abolition of the Agricultural Wages Board – Evidence from the Farmers' Union of Wales. http://www.senedd. assembly.wales/documents/s13639/Paper%202.pdf [accessed on 24 June 2020].

National Assembly for Wales (2013b). Environment and Sustainability Committee, E&S(4)-04-13, Paper 3, Inquiry into the proposed abolition of the Agricultural Wages Board – Evidence from NFU Cymru. http://www.senedd.assembly.wales/ documents/s13640/Paper%203.pdf [accessed on 24 June 2020].

Northern Ireland Assembly (2016). *Report on the Employment Bill*. Belfast: Northern Ireland Assembly.

Patmore, G. (2009). The origins of federal industrial relations systems: Australia, Canada and the USA, *Journal of Industrial Relations*, 51 (2): 151–172. 10.11 77%2F0022185608101705

Scottish Government (2018). *Best Practice Guidance on Addressing Fair Work Practices, Including the Living Wage, in Procurement*. Edinburgh: Scottish Government.

Scottish Parliament (2018). *Economy, Jobs and Fair Work Committee: Annual Report 2017–18* [online] https://sp-bpr-en-prod-cdnep.azureedge.net/published/ EJFW/2018/6/1/Economy--Jobs-and-Fair-Work-Committee--Annual-Report-2017-18/EJFWS052018R04.pdf [accessed on 24 June 2020].

Scottish Parliament, Current Committees [online] https://www.parliament.scot/ parliamentarybusiness/committees.aspx [accessed on 24 June 2020].

Sheldon, P., Nacamulli, R., Paoletti, F. and Morgan, D. E. (2016). Employer association responses to the effects of bargaining decentralization in Australia and Italy: Seeking explanations from organizational theory. *British Journal of Industrial Relations*, 54 (1): 160–191. 10.1111/bjir.12061

Van Wanrooy, B., Bewley, H., Bryson, A., Forth, J., Freeth, S., Stokes, L. and Wood, S. (2013). *The 2011 Workplace Employment Relations Study: First Findings*. London: Department for Business, Innovation and Skills.

Welsh Government (2019). *A More Equal Wales: Strengthening Social Partnership*, Cardiff: Welsh Government.

Welsh Government (2020). *Fair Work Wales, Report of Fair Work Commission*, Cardiff: Welsh Government.

Part IV

International and Comparative Employer Interest Representation

13 Comparing Higher Education Employer Organization

Geoffrey White and Laurence Hopkins

Introduction

Employer organization varies between countries according to a range of contextual factors. These can include the legal context and the degree to which employer organization is required within institutional frameworks, but wider employment relations contexts also explain differences in approach between countries. Little research has focused on international comparisons of employer bodies in the past although there have been some notable exemptions (for example: Sisson 1987; Traxler 2004; Windmuller and Gladstone 1984). In this chapter we compare Employers' Organizations (EOs) in three countries but within the same sector – higher education (HE). The three EOs are the Australian Higher Education Industrial Association (AHEIA), Faculty Bargaining Services (FBS) in Canada and the Universities and Colleges Employers Association (UCEA) in the UK. Our three case study countries have common features in terms of their HE systems – possibly because of their common language and history (both Canada and Australia modelled their universities on the UK) but, as we shall argue in this chapter, there are important differences which emanate from contextual factors. These include the way in which HE is organized and funded, the degree of central regulation by the state, the relative strength of labour unions and, most importantly, the different employee relations systems in place in each country.

The information and data for this comparison were gathered by the authors between October 2014 and June 2019 with some additional updating in 2020 where required. The primary source of information informing the nature and activities of the three EOs is largely documentary research using literature – mainly the documentation and notes from four employer international symposia, held respectively in 2012 (London), 2014 (Vancouver) 2017 (Sydney) and 2019 (London), and member-only content available from the three organizations' websites. The four international symposia also provided the opportunity to conduct ten interviews with key staff members of all three organizations. The information was collated according to a data framework covering

DOI: 10.4324/9781003104575-17

the legal framework for industrial relations, union organization and structures, bargaining role of the employer organization, employer organization objectives, member services and relationship with government. Secondary sources of data were used to supplement and fill any gaps in understanding.

In making our comparison, we consider the impact of the three explanatory variables for employer organization identified by Schmitter and Streeck (1999): (1) to reduce competition between employers in the same sector, (2) to respond to the countervailing power of employee organization and, lastly, (3) to influence and respond to interventions by the state in the labour market (for example through legislation). We argue that 'countervailing power' is the most important explanation for employer organization in the three countries, with all three employer bodies facing well organized trade unions which necessitates coordination and information sharing between employers. In two of our countries, Australia and Canada, collective bargaining is decentralized to individual higher education institutions (HEIs) and there are therefore no multi-employer agreements to take wages out of competition. However, this does not mean that coordination between HEIs does not aid containment of pay growth and help curtail 'pattern bargaining', the union strategy of targeting particular employers to set benchmarks for the rest of the sector. The ability to respond to interventions by the state is also an important factor in all three countries. While not subject to direct state intervention in bargaining as found in the public sector, funding constraints and political expectations place similar pressures on employers in terms of containing pay growth. We also argue that, while domestic and global competition for students and research funding has increased substantially, this factor is less important in explaining the rationale for employer organization in each country.

We begin the chapter by reviewing the literature on the rationale for employer organization and particularly the importance of countervailing power and the role of collective bargaining. This is followed by a brief discussion of the funding context for HEIs in the three countries. We then describe the key features of the three EOs. We then consider the role of the state, the countervailing power of labour unions, and the role of collective bargaining. We then discuss the role and services of the three organizations in providing 'private goods' (Olson 1971) that are only available to members. Finally, we conclude by discussing to what extent the Schmitter and Streek explanatory variables and Olson's theory help to explain the rationales for our three EOs.

Why Do Employers Organize?

Schmitter and Streeck (1999) argue that there are three main reasons why employers seek to form class or sectoral organizations. The first is to avoid the systematic contradictions and crises that affect capitalism by reducing the effects of free competition. This is often described as 'taking wages out of competition'. By enabling the EO to negotiate on their behalf, pay levels can be kept at an affordable level for the weakest employers while stopping stronger employers from using pay as a competitive lever within the labour market. The second reason is to coordinate a response to the power of organized labour or 'countervailing power' (Barry and Wilkinson 2011). This was a particularly important factor in the establishment of EOs in the 19th and 20th centuries (Tolliday and Zeitlin 1991). By coordinating a response to labour power within a sector, employers can avoid being isolated and picked off by targeted industrial action or pattern bargaining. The third reason is to deal with interventions in markets by the state and the outcomes of political democracy, including labour legislation. By coordinating the response to state regulation of the labour market, employers can present a unified voice in influencing both the form and structure of labour relations practice. This can often take the form of access to selective 'private' goods in the form of intelligence, advice, and training (Olson 1971), which are not available to non-members.

Traxler (2004) defined two main types of EO, those that primarily exist to represent labour market interests and those that are more concerned with trade matters. There are separate 'trade' bodies' in HE in all three countries (Universities UK, Universities Canada, and Universities Australia) that deal with non-employment issues, so our three organizations are clearly all of the first type.

The literature on EOs indicates a strong correlation between the presence of collective bargaining and the existence of EOs (Traxler 2000, 2004). As Gooberman et al. (2020: 4) state: 'collective bargaining is often regarded as the quintessential activity of EOs'. Indeed, employer organization as a response to employee demands was central to the existence of such formations in the past and was previously viewed as the defining characteristic of an employers' association (Windmuller and Gladstone 1984). This relationship proved valid as the diminishing importance of collective bargaining in developed economies was accompanied by a considerable decline in the number of EOs (Gooberman et al. 2020; Katz and Darbishire 2000; Purcell 1995; Sisson 1987). This decline in collective bargaining and trade union density has been sharpest in the private sector with trade union density and collective agreement coverage relatively stronger in the public sector across OECD countries (OECD 2017).

Traxler (2000) reinforces the importance of institutional factors and especially the extension of collective agreements and union density that underpinned the relevance of EOs. Multi-employer bargaining was central to the membership strength of EOs because such extension could only be achieved through multi-employer settlements. Sisson (1987: 5) makes the important point that 'market control can be achieved only by multi-employer bargaining; single employer bargaining cannot contribute to market control because it affects only one employer'. The argument follows that, if union power declines, so too does the requirement for multi-employer bargaining and hence the need for EOs. From this observation, Traxler (2004: 56) concluded that: '... the fate of employer associations is closely linked to the fate of multi-employer bargaining'.

An explanation for the choice of bargaining behaviour by employers, and hence the need for employer coordination, may relate to their 'ideology', i.e. their attitudes towards and opinions of the benefits of union recognition and collective bargaining (Sisson 1987). Other writers have noted the differences in the attitudes of employers between countries while the Varieties of Capitalism framework (Hall and Soskice 2001) indicates that collective organization among employers is less of a priority in Liberal Market Economies (LMEs) than in Coordinated Market Economies (CMEs). Colvin and Darbishire (2013) argue, however, that even within LMEs – or the 'Anglo-American model' – there are marked variations in employment relations and hence the role of employer organization. They argue that until recently three distinct separate models existed within LMEs – the 'Wagner Act' model of the USA and Canada, the 'voluntarist' model of the UK and Ireland and the 'award systems' of Australia and New Zealand. As we will argue, this distinction is particularly useful when comparing the three case studies in this chapter.

Even where bargaining is decentralized there may still be coordination by both employers and unions (Soskice 1990) and it has been noted that bargaining patterns and employer coordination may be observed at sectoral level (Arrowsmith and Sisson 1999; Sisson and Marginson 2002). A common tactic of unions under decentralized systems, relevant to this study, has been pattern bargaining whereby certain bargaining units at industry or company level set the pace for the other units (Capelli 1990; Traxler et al. 2008).

The Higher Education Context

HEIs in each of our three countries enjoy institutional autonomy which is an important factor regarding the nature of industrial relations and employer organization. Despite this autonomy, there is still a high level of regulation and a high reliance on national or state/provincial government support, either directly or in the form of income-contingent loans to students. With the burden of higher education funding shifting from the taxpayer to the individual student in all three countries, tuition fees are critical to higher education finance. This shift has also enabled a move to demand-led systems with money following the student, while growth in international student numbers has created a significant income stream independent of the state in all three countries. This has had important consequences for bargaining as a significant proportion of income is now subject to greater variability from year-to-year. In Canada for example, the share of government funding for post-secondary education fell from 84% in the 1980s to 57% in 2012 (Canadian Federation of Students 2013). In 2018–2019 the proportion was just 46% with 35% from provincial and territorial governments (Stats Canada 2020). Tuition fees provide the main source of non-government income (29% of the total in 2018–2019). In Australia, government funding (both federal and state) for higher education, excluding tuition fee loans, represented 51% of revenue in 2019 with tuition fees accounting for a further 33.5% (Ferguson 2021). As a result of tuition fee reform in England, direct government investment in higher education comprised just 24% of total income while tuition fees, including international tuition, comprised 49% of all income in 2018–2019 (HESA 2020). Due to devolution of higher education funding in the UK, there are different systems in Scotland, Wales, and Northern Ireland with Wales and Northern Ireland closely resembling the English model, while Scotland still provides free undergraduate tuition to Scottish domiciled students.

Retrenchment in public funding following the 2008–2009 recession has also had an impact on financial sustainability with HEIs in the UK seeing a cash freeze in research funding until 2015–2016 and a significant reduction in capital expenditure (Universities UK 2015). In Canada, reductions in funding for higher education across the provinces has resulted in above inflation fee increases. Australia did not suffer the same economic consequences of the 2008–2009 financial crisis and it continued to increase investment in higher education during the post-crisis period. Following this strong investment growth, an A$2.8 billion cut over two years was announced in 2017 alongside an increase in tuition fees that increased the proportion of funding from tuition fees from 42% to 46% (Australian Government 2017).

The pressure on public finances and funding for higher education has affected bargaining outcomes in Canada and the UK. In the UK, public sector pay policy (2010 onwards) instituted pay freezes for all but the lowest paid, followed by a 1% restriction on annual pay increases. While the pay policy did not cover higher education directly, it constrained the autonomy of the sector in terms of pay outcomes with the government urging the sector to exercise pay restraint (White and Hopkins 2015). In Canada, more direct pressure was placed on universities in Alberta, British Columbia, Manitoba, Ontario, and Quebec, resulting in pay freezes at 19 out of 53 HEIs in those provinces in 2010–2011 (FBS 2016). Meanwhile, the University of Manitoba was again under pressure to freeze wages in 2017 (CBC News 2017).

Our Three Case Study Organizations

Our three case study bodies vary in their origins, roles and services to members (see Table 13.1). The oldest is the UK's Universities and

Table 13.1 Our three case studies

	Universities and Colleges Employers Association (UCEA)	Australian Higher Education Industrial Association (AHEIA)	Faculty Bargaining Services (FBS)
Date of formation	1994*	1990*	2005
Staff	16	10	8 (including field officers)
Bargaining groups covered	All HE staff (except professoriate and senior managers)	All HE staff	Academic staff only
Membership (HE institutions)	162	32	71
Governance	Board comprised of 16 Vice-Chancellors, Principals and University Council Chairs or members nominated by Universities UK, Guild HE and the Committee of University Chairs.	Executive committee of six drawn from membership.	Two governing entities - FBS Management Committee of seven and the CAUBO Board of Directors. The Committee has representation from six regional groups, the CAUBO Board of Directors, and the CAUBO HR Committee.
Objectives	1) To provide information. 2) To be a source of expertise. 3) To lead on sector approaches to pensions challenges. 4) To provide a framework supporting negotiations at multi-employer and institutional levels.	To provide advice, guidance, assistance with local bargaining, training, research and lobbying activities for members.	To support institutions in both bargaining and academic contract administration. Offers access to several databases, newsletters and newsfeeds, and provides training to members.

Sources: Based on AHEIA, FBS and UCEA. * Both AHEIA and UCEA were created through mergers of earlier employers' bodies in different sub-sectors of tertiary education. FBS was created by the Canadian Association of University Business Officers, a professional body.

College Employers Association (UCEA), formed in 1994 from a merger of two previous bodies – one representing the pre-1992 or 'old' universities and one representing the polytechnics and colleges that became universities after 1992. The UK's 162 HEIs are defined as 'independent not-for-profit charities' and UCEA has them all in membership. Employer organization in HE in the UK developed alongside the creation of collective bargaining machinery and has a relatively long history compared to the other two countries, beginning after World War 2 (White 2014). In 1988 the Education Reform Act removed further education colleges and polytechnics from local government control and created two new funding councils – the Polytechnics and Colleges Funding Council and the Universities Funding Council. In 1992 the Conservative Government granted university status to some 30 polytechnics under the Further and Higher Education Act 1992, resulting in single funding bodies for HE being established in each of the four countries of the UK. This new funding regime further complicated the collective bargaining arrangements for the sector, which in turn led to the creation of a single negotiating forum, JNCHES (the Joint Negotiating Council for Higher Education Staff), and a single EO, UCEA, in 1994. UCEA covers all four jurisdictions of the UK.

In similar fashion to the UK, the Australian Higher Education Industrial Association (AHEIA) was established in 1990 as an amalgam of two older organizations: the Australian Universities Industrial Association and the Australian Advanced Education Industrial Association, both of which were formed during the mid-to-late 1980s. Decision-making, regulation, and governance for higher education are shared among the Australian Government, the State and Territory Governments and the institutions themselves. Some aspects of higher education are the responsibility of States and Territories – in particular, most universities are established or recognized under State and Territory legislation. Universities are self-accrediting institutions, and each university has its own establishment legislation (generally State and Territory legislation) and receive most of their public funding from the federal Australian Government, through the Higher Education Support Act 2003. There are 37 public universities funded by the national government and 2 private Universities. AHEIA has 32 of these HEIs in membership.

Faculty Bargaining Services (FBS) is the youngest of the organizations, having been established by the Canadian Association of University Business Officers (CAUBO) in 2005. Interestingly, FBS was created as a direct response to union control of bargaining information. In Canada, collective bargaining takes place at institutional level and is further complicated by the fact that HE funding is organized at provincial level, rather than federal. In some cases, provincial governments place restrictions on bargaining outcomes and pay awards will often reflect more the state of the provincial economies (e.g. ability to pay) than national priorities. The

Canadian Association of University Teachers (CAUT), an umbrella body for local faculty associations, has run an effective campaign of pattern bargaining for some years and has coordinated the collection and dissemination of pay award data across all institutions for its members. This led to the creation of a de facto employers' body to assist institutions with local bargaining. The aim of FBS is to support participating institutions in both bargaining and academic contract administration. As part of these services, the website offers access to several Canadian databases, newsletters, and newsfeeds. It also provides training to members.

The Role of the State

Our three case study organizations fall conveniently into the three variants of LMEs identified by Colvin and Darbishire (2013). In Canada, labour law is a responsibility of the individual provinces (except for federally regulated industries and the federal civil service) and is modelled on the US Wagner Act 1935 that provides for long-term collective agreements which preclude industrial action during the life of the contract (Thompson and Taras 2011). Unlike the USA, however, in Canada there is no limit to the scope of bargaining. An important legal and structural change took place in HE in the late 1960s when academic staff opted for collective bargaining under provincial private sector employment law, which was less restrictive than that governing the public sector (Jones and Weinrib 2012). Collective bargaining in Canada is typically uncoordinated with single employer, single union bargaining (OECD 1994). There are few EOs and very few instances of multi-employer bargaining (Traxler 2004). The key component of the 'Wagner' model is the majority principle, which enables recognition of a union as the bargaining agent if it can win a majority among designated workers and exclusivity of that union. In Canada, FBS therefore operates primarily as a data collection and advisory service, rather than being directly involved in bargaining at institutional level.

In contrast to Canada, in Australia labour law is the responsibility of both the federal and state governments and is based on a system of legally enforceable industry specific national 'awards' (in effect minimum wage levels) with compulsory conciliation procedures to deal with disputes (Lansbury and Wailes 2011). Australia is relatively new to enterprise level pay bargaining – for over 100 years pay was determined by Federal Tribunals and applied across the board. Enterprise bargaining was introduced across the Australian economy in 1992/1993, with cross-party support. Under the Australian legislation, EOs have a legal status under the award system and hence AHEIA is the designated employer body for tertiary education under the Federal Fair Work (Registered Organisations) Act 2009. In Australia, the 2009 Fair Work Act (Registered Organisations) (FWA) regulates the formation, registration, and conduct of trade unions and enables the creation and registration of 'enterprise associations' with at least 20 members within the same enterprise. However, the trade union movement in Australia is characterized by large, sector-oriented unions (Forsyth 2012) and collective agreements made under the FWA apply to all relevant employees within the enterprise, not just trade union members. Australia is the only example in this study of attempted direct state intervention in HE employment relations. The Howard government passed the Higher Education Workplace Requirements (HEWRs) legislation in 2005. These requirements linked university funding directly to the acceptability to Government of workplace enterprise agreements in HEIs (Rosewarne 2005).

The UK represents the third variation of the LME model, with its tradition of 'voluntarism' and a dislike for legal intervention. While there has been increasing intervention by the state in employment regulation since the 1980s, collective agreements remain voluntary and have no legal status in terms of enforcement. There are also no restrictions on the use of industrial action during the term of an agreement. UCEA is the only association among our three examples that continues to negotiate nationally across the four jurisdictions of the UK on behalf of the great majority of HEIs.

Countervailing Trade Union Organization

Trade unions representing academic staff exist in all three countries and exhibit healthy membership densities. Unlike in countries, where academic staff may be prohibited from joining unions all three countries in our study guarantee legal rights for HE employees to organize and collectively negotiate on pay and conditions. In Canada, where recognition has been obtained, the majority rule principle puts all academic staff in membership.

Although the legislation and institutions that regulate trade unions are different, there are similarities in the strength of the trade union movements in each of the countries relative to the general decline in union membership across the wider economy. Membership data, available for the UK and Australia, reveals that the sector has a membership density resembling that of the public sector with disaggregated data in the UK indicating that it is much stronger among the academic population (UCEA 2013). In Australia the National Tertiary Education Union (NTEU) was formed in 1993 as a result of a merger of five tertiary education unions. Although NTEU membership has declined marginally, from 26,879 in 2004 to 25,405 in 2016, density has fallen more markedly due to a 37.2% increase in full-time equivalent staff. The NTEU has operated a strong centralized and strategic approach to bargaining supported by industrial action threats and actions and most

Australian HEIs deal with the NTEU for all staff, including non-academic (Sydney Symposium 2017).

In Canada, HE is the most highly unionized sector in the economy with unionized faculty in all but two HEIs (Hughes and Bell 2015). In contrast to Australia, and atypically for Canada, each Canadian HEI negotiates with its own faculty staff association, most of which are affiliated to the CAUT. CAUT is not a trade union as legally defined but plays an important role in coordinating the activities and bargaining strategies of the faculty associations (Sydney Symposium 2017). The union provides academic staff salary data, a bargaining manual, a benefits survey, and a collective agreement database to its members.

In UK, there are two occupational trade unions representing academic staff in higher education – the Universities and Colleges Union (UCU) and the Educational Institute of Scotland (EIS). Support staff are represented by Unison, Unite and the GMB. The trade union movement in HE is strong relative to the wider UK economy where density in 2013 was 26.3% (UCEA 2013). This compares to public sector density of 52.7% in 2016 and 53.3% in the wider education sector. The density is around one-third for academic staff and one-fifth for support staff (UCEA 2016) and membership increased significantly in 2018–2019. In terms of the national negotiations, the academic trade unions have resorted to industrial action regularly since 2006, most effectively in 2006 when a lengthy campaign, including a marking boycott, led to a pay award worth 15% over three years.

Industrial action, including action short of a strike, remains common in HE although it is occasionally limited in its operational or bargaining impact. In Canada and Australia, in line with legal requirements, such action is legally confined to the period around the negotiation of a new contract. In all three countries trade unions also run active and visible campaigns on employment issues with casualization of academic staff a recent focus in all three countries. While the national negotiations in the UK require a centralized response from the unions, labour unions in Australia and Canada are also clearly coordinated, albeit with differences in the way this is achieved. In Canada, CAUT plays a coordinating role in terms of information, intelligence and strategy, while in Australia there is a dominant national union (NTEU) that adopts a pattern bargaining strategy.

A key outcome from the difference in employment relations history and legislative frameworks is the type of collective bargaining arrangements in place in each country. In both Canada and Australia, collective agreements are legally binding, negotiated at institutional level and long term, usually three to four year, contracts. In Canada there must be legally binding union recognition agreements in place for collective bargaining to take place (only two Canadian HEIs do not recognize unions). There are also differences in the coverage of collective agreements between the three countries. The collective agreements at institutional level in Australia cover terms and conditions for all HE staff, both academic and support, reflecting the national award for the sector. This wide coverage of HE employees also reflects the fact that the main trade union (the National Tertiary Education Union - NTEU) covers all staff. In Canada there are separate arrangements for 'full-time faculty' (permanent contract staff), contingent academic staff, and other academic-related staff. Support staff may be covered by separate agreements with other unions. The UK is the only one of the three countries which conducts negotiations at national level for most but not all HE staff, albeit limited primarily to the annual uplift to a national pay spine. While negotiations over the pay uplift figure normally take place annually in the UK, comprehensive reviews of local institutional agreements are less frequent. Around 10–15 UK HEIs negotiate pay at institutional level although most remain members of the EO and tend to follow, at a minimum, the level of general increases awarded at national level. A key outcome of these differences in collective bargaining arrangements is that AHEIA's bargaining services cover all HE employees while UCEA only covers staff below professor and senior manager (whose salaries are determined individually by each institution) for national bargaining purposes. In Canada FBS's services only cover academic and related staff.

More importantly, the collective agreements at institutional level in both Canada and Australia are much more detailed in their scope and cover a range of employment issues. In contrast, the annual national agreements in the UK tend to be only one or two pages long, detailing the pay uplift to be applied and terms of any joint working to be carried out between the parties. In terms of their status, Australian agreements are enforceable through Fair Work tribunals and in Canada through the courts at provincial level. In contrast, the agreements made at the UK Joint Negotiating Committee for HE Staffs (JNCHES) only acquire legal status through references made within individual contracts.

Participants in the collective bargaining process also differ. In Australia, negotiations normally take place between a single employer and primarily one trade union whereas in Canada each employer negotiates with a local faculty association, most of which are affiliated to the national umbrella organization, the CAUT. In both these countries the EO is not involved directly in institutional negotiations. In the UK, in contrast, at national level it is the EO that negotiates with the officers and lay representatives from the five trade unions recognized at national level. Negotiations over institutional terms and conditions in the UK are conducted locally, although these are typically less comprehensive in scope and less frequently changed than bargaining on similar terms in Australia and Canada.

In terms of pay structures, there is a strong similarity in academic grading structures across the three countries. The national academic grades A–E in Australia are set out in the National Award but with salary boundaries agreed locally. In Canada there is a three-stage grade structure for academic staff used nationally with salary boundaries determined locally. In the UK, while a national pay spine sets the incremental pay points, actual grade structures are determined through job evaluation at institutional level although most follow a similar academic hierarchy. However, at professor level, where HEIs determine their own approach to pay in the UK, there is largely a market and merit pay system in operation with academic discipline and individual accomplishments determining salary. This market pay system is underpinned by market data provided by UCEA and other commercial providers.

Role and Services

Although the context for each EO is different, there is similarity in the functions and services provided, except for the organizations' roles in collective bargaining. UCEA is the only body that plays a direct role in negotiating at national level with trade unions. The other two organizations are primarily co-ordinators of information to ensure symmetry of information at bargaining tables while also providing local assistance to individual institutions in their bargaining. In Australia AHEIA retains a statutory role as an employers' association for the sector and therefore can represent members before the FWA concerning approval of agreements (especially where contested) and applications for the cessation of industrial action. This status involves the organization advising members on the award and general industrial matters and representing them, on either an individual or collective basis, before industrial tribunals and internal disciplinary and appeal committees. FBS has no such role and is not formally constituted as an employers' body. It is primarily an information service providing guidance and information for collective bargaining purposes, interpretation of agreement terms and training of negotiators. In terms of membership density, all three organizations have high levels of membership among their potential constituencies. UCEA has nearly 100% membership while AHEIA has 86% and FBS 75%.

It is evident from all three cases that collection of data on pay agreements and pay levels is a critical part of the service to members, although the type of information differs in each case. In the case of AHEIA and FBS, the provision of data covers contract conditions, salary levels, and salary increases. In both cases the agreements are eventually available in the public domain, but it is the collation and structuring of the information that is important. The more detailed content required for the Australian and Canadian collective agreements leads to a much greater interest in data which compares institutional agreements and, because these are legally binding documents, a strong concern among employers about ensuring that the language used in the contracts is correct. In the case of UCEA, occupational salary surveys providing detailed information on levels of actual salaries and total earnings are a fundamental part of the association's service, but in Australia and Canada salary surveys are left to the market with either recruitment or professional services firms fulfilling this role where required.

Beyond the collective bargaining support and contract information, the organizations are broadly similar in offering training and networking events as well as information related to employment issues affecting the sector. FBS is more limited to the extent that it does not cater to the specific employment law contexts in each province/territory. However, FBS operates a field officer model where each officer has responsibility for certain provinces or territories and can therefore both develop stronger local relationships with universities and concentrate on specific contexts. UCEA's broader employment support is centralized with a helpline for members and has no permanent regional presence, although it operates a Scottish committee and maintains close relationships with Universities Scotland and Universities Wales.

One difference between the three organizations, however, is the degree of lobbying and public relations activity conducted. Given that both UCEA and AHEIA operate as traditional EOs it is not surprising that they are involved in lobbying activities with government on behalf of their members, but this is not the case in Canada where the Federal government does not play a direct role. A recent example of lobbying activity by UCEA was over the Government's new post-Brexit im-migration salary thresholds, where the proposed changes would have excluded some early career academic roles. Only UCEA has a dedicated communications and PR team.

Another difference is the role of the EO in pensions negotiations. In the UK pension schemes are largely national in scope. There are two schemes covering academic staff (one for pre-92 and one for post-92 institutions) while support staff belong to either local government schemes or local schemes. In Australia there is also a national super-annuation scheme for academic staff (Grieve 2020) but in Canada pensions are a matter for individual institutions. UCEA is the only organization to provide a dedicated pensions advice service.

Discussion

The rationale for employer organization in the three countries has strong similarities although the way employers have responded varies between them. We find that only two of the factors identified by Schmitter and Streek apply to our three case study countries – a response to the countervailing power of labour unions and the role of the state. Reducing competition between employers is not a stated objective of any of the three organizations and we find little evidence of this in their practice. A third factor, however, may relate to Olson's (1971) concept of 'private goods' – the provision of member-only services, which is clearly a major role for all three organizations.

To Respond to the Countervailing Power of Employee Organization

Multi-employer bargaining to counter the power of labour organizations is clearly not a pre-requisite for employers' organization in the three countries. While this could feasibly be offered as an explanation for the origins and strength of UCEA, AHEIA has maintained its role as an employer association without currently having a direct negotiating role in bargaining. While AHEIA's existence can perhaps be explained by the institutional framework for industrial relations in Australia, its active role in co-ordinating employers engaged in bargaining indicates that it is not merely a product of legislation. Indeed, there was more overt and visible co-ordination of four Western Australian universities in 2016 and 2017 supported by AHEIA (NTEU 2016).

The case of FBS is more interesting still as there is no statutory re-quirement for employer representation and, like the USA, little history of employer organization in Canada. With FBS, the countervailing power thesis offers the most logical rationale for a body which has as its pri-mary objective the collection and sharing of collective agreements and related intelligence. This explanation is also logical in the other two countries. Trade union density in HE is high in comparison to the wider economy in all three countries and there is evidence that trade unions continue to use the threat of industrial action and indeed act when thought necessary. It is also clear that there is strong central coordination on the union side in Australia and Canada where enterprise-level bar-gaining is taking place, either through a single national union (NTEU) or an association of faculty associations (CAUT).

Nonetheless the countervailing power thesis is not entirely satisfac-tory, given that several industries in these countries have similar levels of trade union membership but no formal co-ordination among em-ployers on collective bargaining. The ability of academic trade unions to adversely affect university operations also appears to be limited, particularly when compared to those sectors where the product is more perishable or time sensitive. Reputational damage, however, is perhaps a more important factor for HEIs in responding to such action and is an important consideration in all three countries. The key to decen-tralized arrangements in Australia and Canada is perhaps the level of trade union co-ordination relative to the employers, which when weighted towards the side of labour can enable effective pattern bargaining strategies to emerge.

To Influence and Respond to Interventions by the State

The legislative frameworks for industrial relations in the three countries are certainly important in determining the structure of the collective bargaining arrangements but do not appear to be a determining factor in the nature or strength of employers' organization. While FBS is not a certified 'employers' association', its main services are like the other two organizations, except for AHEIA's statutory role regarding the FWA and UCEA's direct role in national bargaining. Multi-employer negotiations are no longer the norm in the UK, but this has not deterred HE employers from remaining UCEA members and signing up to the national agreement.

The three cases also highlight the potential differences between the organization of employers in the private sector and in a 'not-for-profit' sector where opportunistic temptations and management of diverse interests are reduced. Higher education is also less exposed to the forces of globalization that have been identified in some studies as a driver for trade union decline and decentralization in collective bargaining (Calmfors et al. 2001; Gaston 2002; Thelen and van Wijnbergen 2003). Although international tuition is less regulated and has been an important independent source of income for HEIs in recent years, HEIs are primarily competing on reputation and not price in the international market so salary levels are not a determining factor.

Regarding the quasi-public sector status of HEIs, the role of government funding and regulation of the HE sector appears important with examples of the government directly and indirectly involving itself in sector industrial relations in a manner it would not in the private sector. Coordination of employer responses in bargaining may therefore be important in justifying the outcomes in terms of taxpayer or student 'value for money'. Uncoordinated approaches might expose outliers to public criticism and act as a strong incentive for HEIs to keep contract agreements within the norms indicated from survey data. In all three countries there is evidence of increasing government and public interest in the cost of HE and pay levels, especially for senior staff (see Hutton 2011 for example), and with the rise in student fees increasing interest by students in what they are paying for (Jones 2010; Rolfe 2002). The more active role of government in public sector and quasi-public sector collective bargaining is as important as is the ongoing strength of trade unions within the public sector in the three case study countries.

Finally, the provision of 'private goods' (Olson 1971) available only to members is found to be a key factor in explaining the rationale for the three EOs. The provision of key bargaining intelligence, legal advice, and training of HR staff was found to be a valuable resource for member institutions in all three countries.

Conclusions

Through the three case studies we set out to explore the factors that influence and explain the rationale for employer organization in the HE sectors in Australia, Canada, and the UK. Our argument was developed from Schmitter and Streeck's (1999) three explanations for employer organization. We have argued that, while there are similarities between the HE systems between the three countries in terms of their independence from direct state regulation of pay (unlike most public services) and their competition for overseas students, in other respects the role of the state in HE funding and regulation of academic affairs exerts stronger constraints on institutions which encourage collective responses. Taking wages out of competition (at least in terms of pay growth if not pay levels) through centralized collective agreements is only found in the UK but this does not mean decentralized bargaining negates a need for coordination on the part of employers in the other two countries. The presence of countervailing power in the form of well organized national employee organizations in all three cases necessitates a coordinated response. The examples of Australia and Canada show that coordination is required at least to reduce information asymmetry in the bargaining process that can occur when there is strong co-ordination among trade unions. The provision of bargaining data, advice, and training is therefore a key attraction for members. It appears that data collection and dissemination is even more important when pay determination and employment contracts are decentralized. In these cases, the employers' organization rationale is less 'strength in numbers' than 'access to numbers'.

References

Arrowsmith, J. and Sisson, K. (1999). Pay and working time: Towards organisation-based systems? *British Journal of Industrial Relations*, 37 (1): 51–75. 10.1111/1467-8543.00118

Australian Government (2017). *The Higher Education Reform Package.* Canberra: Australian Government.

Barry, M. and Wilkinson, A. (2011). Reconceptualising employer associations under evolving employment relations: Countervailing power revisited. *Work, Employment and Society*, 25 (1): 149–162. 10.1177%2F0950017010389229

Calmfors, L., Booth, A., Burda, M., Checchi, A., Naylor, A. and Visser, J. (2001). Part I. The future of collective bargaining in Europe. In: T. Boeri, A. Brugiaviani and L. Calmfors (eds.) *The Role of Unions in the Twenty-First Century*. Oxford: Oxford University Press, pp. 1–156.

Canadian Federation of Students (2013). *Funding Fact Sheet*. Ottowa: Canadian Federation of Students.

Capelli, P (1990). Is pattern bargaining dead? A discussion. *Industrial and Labor Relations Review*, 44 (1): 152–155.

CBC News (2017). U of M was threatened with funding cuts unless it froze wages, Manitoba Labour Board hears. *CBC News*, 3 May 2017. Available at: http://www.cbc.ca/news/canada/manitoba/u-of-m-wage-freeze-faculty-labour-board-1.4098429 [accessed 8 July 2021].

Colvin, A. and Darbishire, O. (2013). Convergence in industrial relations institutions: The emerging Anglo-American model? *Industrial relations and Labor Relations Review*, 66 (5): 1047–1077. 10.1177%2F001979391306600502

FBS (2016). *Across-the-Board Salary Increases for Full-Time Faculty in Canada: 2008 to 2019*. Ottawa: Faculty Bargaining Services. Member only document.

Ferguson, H. (2021). A guide to Australian Government funding for higher education learning and teaching. *Parliament of Australia Research Paper Series 2020-21*. https://parlinfo.aph.gov.au/parlInfo/download/library/prspub/7921419/upload_binary/7921419.pdf [accessed 8 July 2021].

Forsyth, A. (2012). The evolving pluralistic approach to employee representation at the enterprise in Australia. In: H. Nakakubo and T. Araki (eds.) *A System of Employee Representation at the Enterprise: A Comparative Study*. Alphen aan den Rijn: Kluwer Law International, pp. 175–193.

Gaston, N. (2002). The effects of globalisation on unions and nature of collective bargaining, *Journal of Economic Integration*, 17 (2): 377–396.

Grieve, C. (2020). How the university revenue crisis will test its generous super system. *The Sydney Morning Herald*, 25 May 2020.

Gooberman, L., Hauptmeier, M. and Heery, E. (2020). A typology of employers' organisations in the United Kingdom. *Economic and Industrial Democracy*, 41 (1): 229–248. 10.1177%2F0143831X17704499

Hall, P. A. and Soskice, D. W. (2001). *Varieties of Capitalism: The Institutional Foundations of Comparative Advantage*. Oxford and New York: Oxford University Press.

HESA (2020). *HE Finance Plus 2018-19*. Cheltenham: Higher Education Statistics Agency.

Hughes, J. and Bell, D. (2015). Bargaining for contract academic staff at English Canadian Universities. *Journal of Collective Bargaining in the Academy*, 0 (35): 1–37.

Hutton, W. (2011), *The Hutton Review of Fair Pay in the Public Sector*. London: HM Treasury.

Jones, G. (2010). Managing student expectations – The impact of top-up tuition fees', *Perspectives: Policy and Practice in Higher Education*, 14 (2): 44–48. 10.1080/13603101003776135

Jones, G. A. and Weinrib, J. (2012). The Organisation of Academic Work and Faculty Remuneration at Canadian Universities. In: P. G. Altbach et al. (eds.) *Paying the Professoriate: A Global Comparison of Compensation and Contracts*. New York and London: Routledge, pp. 83–93.

Katz, H.C. and Darbishire, O. (2000). *Converging Divergences: Worldwide changes in Employment Systems*. Ithaca and London: ILR Press.

Lansbury, R.D. and Wailes, N. (2011). Employment relations in Australia. In: G. J. Bamber and N. Wailes (eds.) *International & Comparative Employment Relations: Globalisation and Change*. 5th Ed. London: Sage, pp. 117–193.

NTEU (2016). *Joint Statement – Embracing Future Opportunities*, 26 April 2016. Available at: http://www.nteu.org.au/library/view/id/6901 [accessed 8 July 2021].

OECD (1994). Collective bargaining: Levels and coverage. In: *OECD Employment Outlook, 1994.* Paris: OECD Publishing.

OECD (2017). Collective bargaining in a changing world of work. In: *OECD Employment Outlook 2017.* Paris: OECD Publishing.

Olson, M. (1971). *The Logic of Collective Action: Public Goods and the Theory of Groups.* Cambridge, MA: Harvard University Press.

Purcell J. (1995). Ideology and the end of institutional industrial relations: Evidence from the UK. In: C. Crouch and F. Traxler (eds.) *Organized Industrial Relations in Europe: What future?* Aldershot: Avebury, pp. 101–119.

Rolfe, H. (2002). Students' demands and expectations in an age of reduced financial support: The perspectives of lecturers in four English universities, *Journal of Higher Education Policy and Management,* 24 (2): 171–182. 10.1080/1360080022000013491

Rosewarne, S. (2005). Workplace reform and the restructuring of higher education. *Journal of Australian Political Economy,* 56: 186–206.

Schmitter, P.C. and Streeck, W. (1999). The organization of business interests: Studying the associative action of business in advanced societies. *MPIfG Discussion Paper 99/1.* March. Cologne: Max-Planck-Institute fur Gesellschaftsforshung.

Sisson, K. (1987). *The Management of Collective Bargaining: An International Comparison.* Oxford: Blackwell.

Sisson, K. and Marginson, P. (2002). Coordinated bargaining: A process for our times? *British Journal of Industrial Relations,* 40 (2): 197–220. 10.1111/1467-8543.00229

Soskice, D. (1990). Wage determination: The changing role of institutions in advanced industrialized countries. *Oxford Review of Economic Policy,* 6 (4): 36–61.

Stats Canada (2020). Financial information of universities for the 2018/2019 school year and projected impact of COVID–19 for 2020/2021.

Sydney Symposium (2017). Record of employers' association symposium held at Intercontinental Hotel, Sydney on 1 May 2017.

Thelen, K. and van Wijnbergen, C. (2003). The paradox of globalisation: Labor relations in Germany and beyond, *Comparative Political Studies,* 36 (8): 859–880. 10.1177%2F0010414003256111

Thompson, M. and Taras, D.G. (2011). Employment relations in Canada. In: G. J. Bamber and N. Wailes (eds.) *International & Comparative Employment Relations: Globalisation and Change.* 5th Ed. London: Sage, pp. 89–116.

Tolliday, S. and Zeitlin, J. (1991). *The Power to Manage? Employers and Industrial Relations in Comparative Historical Perspective.* London: Routledge.

Traxler, F. (2000). Employers and employer organisations in Europe: Membership strength, density and representativeness. *Industrial Relations Journal,* 31 (4): 308–316. 10.1111/1468-2338.00167

Traxler, F. (2004). Employer associations, institutions and economic change: A cross-national comparison. *Industrielle Beziehungen,* 11. Jg., Heft 1+2: 42–46.

Traxler, F., Brandl, B. and Glassner, V. (2008). Pattern bargaining: An investigation into its agency, context and evidence. *British Journal of Industrial Relations,* 46 (1): 33–58. 10.1111/j.1467-8543.2007.00664.x

UCEA (2013). *Survey of Trade Union Membership in HE 2013.* London: UCEA. Member only access.

UCEA (2016). *UCU Membership 2016*. London: UCEA. Member only access.
Universities UK (2015). *Efficiency, Effectiveness and Value for Money*. London: Universities UK.
White, G. (2014). *20th Anniversary History of UCEA*. London: UCEA.
White, G. and Hopkins, L. (2015). *Autonomy and Austerity – The Impact of Government Policy on Higher Education Reward Management since the 2008–09 Recession*. Paper presented to the 5th European Reward Management Conference, Brussels, 10–11 December 2015.
Windmuller, J. P. and Gladstone, A. (1984). *Employers' Associations and Industrial Relations: A Comparative Study*. Oxford: Clarendon Press.

14 International Employers' Organizations and Public Policy beyond National Boundaries

Kevin Farnsworth and Cangheng Liu

Introduction

Global and world-regional governmental organizations have grown in power and importance since the mid-20th century and, alongside them, the power, influence and engagement of non-governmental organizations, including employers' organizations, has increased. This chapter examines the views of employers operating at the international level by looking at the views expressed through international organizations. An examination of International Employers' Organizations (IEOs) is useful in revealing 'purer' forms of employer perspective than often emerges at the national level, free from the political struggles that exist within nation states. International employer perspectives are also important in pushing 'bottom line' issues up the international agenda.

Before proceeding with this chapter, it is useful to note that although we attempt here to distil the particular views of employers, the line between 'employer' and 'business' interest is inevitably blurry. Indeed, the distinction between 'businesses' and 'employers' as political actors or concerns, is seldom made. This is somewhat understandable because, at least at the international level, businesses and employers are often assumed to be synonymous. Indeed, the broad descriptor of such groups is business interest associations. Yet there are important distinctions between the two. The largest businesses are not necessarily the largest employers. For instance, large supermarkets employ more people than banks. Some businesses extract the majority of their 'surplus' or profit from employees, others less so. The apparel industry, for instance, profits from sweated labour (which it may or may not directly employ); international finance from speculation, lending and insurance; farming from livestock and the exploitation of the environment; tobacco from addiction. In terms of the wide range of social and public policies that might affect them, the interests and preferences of different employers and different businesses are inevitably diverse at least at the national level. At the international level, however, it is a little less clear-cut for two reasons. First, international regulations, controls and constraints are narrower and tend to be restricted to issues of trade, capital

DOI: 10.4324/9781003104575-18

controls and taxation. As research on national business perspectives has revealed, on these broad issues business opinion tends to be more united (Farnsworth 2008) compared to, for example, social policies. Second, international organizations themselves tend to focus on 'business' interests rather than 'employer' interests. Of the major organizations that organize across borders, the International Association of Employers uniquely states that it represents 'employers'. Again, this is both understandable and, in many ways, may be more accurate. All private businesses operating at the international level are likely to be employers, but not all employers are private businesses (as already noted). But what if, as this book does, we want to distil the views of employers and, specifically, views that are shaped by employment relations? The problem with broad appeal, representing all private sector businesses of different sizes in different sectors, tends to force organizations to gravitate towards common denominator issues.

The above has implications for research on international employer perspectives. In this chapter, we are interested in looking at international business opinion on a broad range of issues, but we are also interested in those that relate more specially to employment and employers. We take as our unit of analysis the Business and Industry Advisory Committee (BIAC) of the Organization for Economic Co-operation and Development (OECD), and the International Organisation of Employers (IOE). Before we look at these organizations, however, we discuss the power and influence of organized business at the international level.

Business Influence beyond the Nation State

Global social and public policy analysis has been critical of the tendency to privilege the economic above the social. The reason for such privileging is explained, by Wade (2002) as neoliberal hegemony where one set of arguments or ideas become so dominant that they inform thinking and effectively shut down alternative arguments. With regards to the implementation of the 1948 Universal Declaration of Human Rights, for instance, articles and covenants that underpin democracy and legal rights have, historically, been promoted above those that advocate social justice and economic redistribution (Evans 2005). What has tended to be missing from analysis is the contribution of business and employers at the international level to shaping dominant ideas. This is perhaps because the assumption is that neoliberal, pro-economy ideas naturally advantage business interests. Given that global politics also tends to be played out by national governments and international governmental organizations, it is easy to overlook the actual or virtual 'presence' of business and employers. Even if business and employer actors are invisible in high-level intergovernmental meetings that thrash out the most important and most binding agreements, their voice is echoed through that of government actors.

The ability of business and employers to influence through such mechanisms can be understood as 'structural power' (Hacker and Pierson
2002, Lindblom 1977). Although structural power is often discussed at the
national level, it is less discussed at the international level. One reason for
this is that one of the most basic dimensions of structural power is the
ability of businesses to exercise control over investment decisions
(Farnsworth 2004). If governments enact policies that businesses and
employers do not favour, they will halt, reduce or shift investment to more
favourable policy environments. Such 'investment strikes' are thought not
to have any relevance at the international level. However, it is not simply
the threat of divestment that may influence government policies.
Governments, and the political parties that run most of them, are often
connected to businesses through intricate financial and non-financial
ways. Governments are dependent for their own revenue on existing or
new business investments and taxes levied on profits and employee pay.
Their electability often closely mirrors the relative health of the economy.
The electorate also depend on businesses, as employers, for their jobs and
wages. Given their high level of dependence on continued business investment and profits, governments and employees have little choice but to
create and sustain the conditions which do not damage these (Offe and
Ronge 1984). And the more profitable the company and larger their
workforce, the more strategically important and powerful the company is
likely to be. Once politicians and citizens accept this, business is said to
assume a hegemonic position meaning that business interests are legit-
imized as the 'common interest' nationally (Lindblom 1977) which then
plays out at the international level.

International governmental bodies, for their part, are influenced by
similar concerns about competitiveness, economic and financial stability.
Some of the most important were constituted on the basis that they
would stabilize the global economy and facilitate trade, investment and
growth. The World Bank, International Monetary Fund (IMF) and the
General Agreement on Tariffs and Trade (GATT), which later morphed
into the World Trade Organization (WTO), were all established during,
or shortly after, the political and economic tumult of the Second World
War to help coordinate economic cooperation, growth and stability.
Inevitably, therefore, the broad, common business and employer interests, alongside broad national economic interests, establish the baseline
at the international level. Building on this, internationally organized
business and employer interests focus on the specifics and policy detail.
And as political and economic integration has continued apace with
globalization, so business and employer interests have sought to exploit
new openings that have arisen. Global business has been able to present
a relatively united front and form linkages with globalizing political
and bureaucratic élites and other members of the transnational capitalist
class (Sklair 2001). International business organizations have been

offered increasing opportunities and incentives to engage with International Governmental Organizations (IGOs) over the past 40 years or so. Whereas IGOs have gone out of their way to incorporate business voices within various committees and other decision-making bodies, labour and citizen groups have not been afforded the same advantages (Korten 1997, O'Brien 2002, Stiglitz 1998, Stiglitz 2002, Tesner 2000, Utting 2006). The creation of new channels and formalized linkages between IGOs and business organizations since the 1990s has further amplified the voices of global business organizations.

Beyond structure, business and employer representatives are deeply embedded within international governmental institutions. Business and employer interests have been very successful in organizing and exploiting new openings arising from the creation of supra-national governing or ideational institutions. Moreover, as a former 'insider' in the World Bank, Joseph Stiglitz (2002), notes, that this revolving door between business, the World Bank and IMF places senior business people at the heart of both of these international financial institutions so that they 'naturally see the world through the eyes of the financial community'. The following sections focus on the perspectives that international employers bring to the table.

International Employers' Organizations

The linkages between IGOs and business organizations have been further cemented since the 1990s. This has been the case especially within the European Union (EU) where more national sovereignty has been ceded and the scope and reach of international policy has been developed further than anywhere else. According to Transparency International (2015), the majority of meetings with lobbyists (75%) within the EU are with 'companies and industry representatives'. Of the top ten most influential international industry associations (under which all business and employer associations are included), the majority of meetings in Europe are accounted for by BusinessEurope. The remaining top ten are made up of sectoral associations and EuroChambers.

Table 14.1 identifies the largest IEOs, representing millions of companies across different sectors. The table outlines the organizations' mission statements and key concerns and focus. All organizations lay out their aims to represent the interests of their members, although only one, the IOE, states that it represents employers specifically. The IOE is also the only organization that mentions broad public or social policies as a key focus.

BusinessEurope, for instance, states that its main priority is to advocate for 'growth and competitiveness at the European level'.[1] EuroChambers campaigns for 'an integrated', globally competitive Europe where businesses can prosper and drive socio-economic progress (EuroChambers 2021). Interestingly, only one organization, the IOE, explicitly highlights

Table 14.1 Outline of the largest international employers' organizations

Name	Based	IGO links	Membership	Aims
IOE	Geneva, Switzerland	ILO	50 million businesses through 150 employers' organizations	1. To be a business voice shaping and driving the global agenda on employment and social policies; 2. To create a sustainable economic environment around the world that promotes free enterprise and is fair and beneficial to business and society; 3. To advocate for the interests of employers and business in international policy debates.
BIAC	Paris, France	OECD	7 million companies	1. Competence: A positive influence on OECD policy initiatives through sound knowledge; 2. Advocacy: Address business and industry needs at all OECD policy levels; 3. Coordination: to be the hub for all OECD developments that impact business.; 4. Thought leadership: Through an expert network.
ICC	Paris, France	WTO, UN, G20	45 million companies of all sizes and sectors	1. Promote international trade and investment as vehicles for inclusive growth and prosperity; 2. Support multilateralism as the best way to address global challenges and reach global goals; 3. Promoting inclusive and sustainable growth to the benefit of all; 4. Promoting international trade, responsible business conduct and a global approach to regulation; 5. To help members help adapt to the challenges of global trading.

Business Europe	Brussels, Belgium	EU Commission, Parliament and the Council, and Members States	20 million businesses, drawn from 40 business associations in 35 countries	1. To advocate for business growth and competitiveness at European level and representative for all-sized enterprises in 35 European countries whose national business federations are its direct members; 2. To work on behalf of member federations to promote business interests within European policymaking.
Eurochambers	Brussels, Belgium	EU	20 million businesses in Europe through 45 members	To focus on promoting business interests within topics including global Europe, single market, skills and entrepreneurship, Small and Medium Enterprises and economic policy and Sustainable Europe

the interests of 'employers' but all mention businesses. The IOE is also alone in discussing 'social policies', and only it and the ICC mention 'sustainable' growth. Perhaps this suggests that an organization focusing explicitly on the employment relationship is also more likely to focus on different methods of extracting value out of workers through more active social policies? The IOE is linked to the International Labour Organization (ILO) and claims to have more members than any other employers' organization. The ICC has more links with the UN, WTO and the G20.

The ICC is interesting here because it was the first international organization to have consultative status with the UN and, since 2016, was the first business organization to be granted observer status by the General Assembly of the UN. The majority listed here have links with at least one international governmental organization. And some (BIAC, IOE) have formal or constitutionally guaranteed positions as regular advisor organizations as part of tripartite decision-making structures. This influences the focus of the organization. BIAC naturally confines itself to matters that are central to the OECD and, in contrast to the other organizations covered in the table, outlines a list of relatively vague aims.

In order to capture the views of international employers, in the remaining sections we examine the IOE together with BIAC.

Examining the Views of International Employers' Organizations

For IEOs, and IGOs for that matter, public and social policies are directly tied to economic performance. Social policies are defended when they operate to boost the economy, especially during periods of economic crisis (Blyth 2013, Farnsworth and Irving 2012). For global business and employer interests, the analysis tends to be the other way around: social policy is viewed as being affordable only if economies are populated by productive and profitable companies and underpinned by strong economic growth. The general position was laid out by the Head of the IOE in a memo setting out the business position to G7 Labour Ministers:

> *Without a vibrant private sector there are no jobs, no decent work and no economic growth. Sustainable economic growth, based on productivity and an enabling environment for business, together with decent work are the pillars that underpin social justice.*
>
> (IOE 2019)

Social policies that might directly contribute to economic stability and growth and, more importantly, business-need satisfaction, may be promoted, but greater effort has tended to go into arguing for tax cuts (especially on corporations) and public expenditure cuts.

IEOs have lobbied hard to ensure that IGOs prioritize the needs and concerns of employers in formulating social policy, especially in the human capital sphere relating to skills, flexibility, and adaptability within the labour force. Towards this end, calls have been made to bring business voices into public services. The IOE, for instance, stated that:

> *The education sector will need to work much more closely with business to ensure that programmes are developed and continuously updated to meet future skills requirements. Critical to avoiding structural unemployment will be public support for enabling job transitions and mobility.*
>
> (IOE 2017)

Since they play such an important, or potentially important, role in meeting business-needs, education and training provision has been prioritized and more heavily defended than other public/social policy areas by IOEs. Social protection benefits, for instance, have tended to be viewed with more circumspection. They have been defended in instances where they might function to smooth out employment markets, but they are considered viable only in certain circumstances (BIAC 1998). Social policies that might be used to reduce disincentives to work, halt the propensity towards early retirement and increase the productivity of workers have all been promoted. A mix of policies were advocated by BIAC and IOE in a joint statement (along with Deloitte) that would support young people with a carrot and stick approach: 'make work pay' schemes underpinned by conditionality and benefit sanctions (Deloitte et al. 2015). These policies are the opposite of those advocated by BIAC's sparring partner in the OECD, the Trade Union Advisory Committee (TUAC).

High social security costs and accompanying administrative burdens, BIAC has argued, undermine profitability and ultimately increase unemployment (BIAC 1998); hence strict qualifying conditions, time limitations, the retention of work incentives and conditionality based on the acceptance of employment tend to be promoted. This is especially pressing, as argued by a joint report on youth unemployment by Deloitte, IOE and BIAC: *'some carrots and sticks [are] needed to encourage youth to take action to find a job'* (Deloitte et al. 2015).

Similarly, sufficiently wide gaps between benefits and the lowest pay rates in order to maintain work incentives are considered to be crucial (BIAC 1981). Such basic principles are important, according to BIAC, if social protection systems are to remain viable (BIAC 1998). In the case of pensions, business has advocated greater private provision and argued for more flexibility in the age of retirement (BIAC 1998). Whether in pensions or other forms of social protection, the key for business is that employers should be able to shed surplus labour with relative ease but retain workers as economic conditions dictate.

The approach of the IOE to social policy tends to be a little more supportive, recognizing their importance in supporting different groups, including the self-employed. The key reason for this is that the IOE is a key advisory body to the ILO.

Social security systems, for the IOE, need to evolve to changing patterns of employment including the increase in self-employment across many states whilst considering the need to control additional costs on business:

> [...] *social protection schemes, both private and public, will need to adapt to a greater number of self-employed needing coverage, and employees will need to have the possibility to collect social protection benefits from different employers and countries. Current social protection schemes and benefits may need to develop further to respond to this new reality without creating strains on sustainability or incurring unnecessary costs for business.*
>
> (IOE 2017)

Not surprisingly, crisis points tend to interrupt the thinking of business actors. IEOs have responded to recent crisis events, such as the 2007/2008 financial crisis, sovereign debt crisis from 2009, austerity and the Covid-19 pandemic from 2020 as requiring significant interventions. Previous strategies to promote 'less' government tend to be replaced with calls to increase support, especially where employers might benefit. This statement from the IOE released in the aftermath of the health pandemic illustrates this well:

> [R]elief needs to be easily accessible to ensure sustainability of healthy businesses and workers. Businesses need support to offset cost induced by government measures such as paid sick and family care leave, adjusting workplaces, worker quarantine, and/or remote working. This includes the opportunities to [temporarily] replace sick workers.
>
> (IOE 2021)

The strength of support for more active government illustrated here goes against much of the business discourse over the past four decades (Farnsworth and Irving 2012). Whilst business is not as opposed to social policy as is often assumed, the prevailing view is best described as pragmatic. And in crisis and change lies opportunities:

> *The private sector has the ability and potential to contribute to moving those in the informal sector to the formal one through the*

> *gig economy; generate production and employment through riding the technological progress; create global networks and platforms; collaborate with universities and other educational institutions to promote innovation; and help develop training methods and curriculum to meet future labour needs and demands.*
>
> (IOE 2019)

What is interesting here is that what the IOE identifies as a solution to unemployment – the 'gig economy' – is widely viewed to be part of the problem in that 'new work' is often 'temporary, poor quality and exploitative' work (IOE 2017).

The state tends to be viewed as an important guarantor of certain minimum social conditions, and, in some instances, funding, but, with the exception of schooling, greater private involvement in state services, as a substitute for the public sector, has also been actively encouraged (BIAC 1996). Thus, whilst the major international business organizations tend to regard state-funded and state regulated, but not necessarily state provided, schooling as essential (Farnsworth 2005), such support varies by level of qualification. A far greater role for the state is envisaged for lower-level schooling than for the further and higher education sectors, within which an expanded role for the private sector is encouraged.

More generally, on the question of provision, IEOs tends to favour targeted provision funded and delivered by a combination of efforts, both public and private. In those areas dominated by the state and with strong public support, for instance health care, an expansion of private insurance is advocated.

Business associations face an interesting dilemma when it comes to state provision. On the one hand, many of their members want to see reductions in certain types of 'unproductive' welfare measures and the taxes required to fund them. On the other hand, if openings can be created for them, public services provide huge market opportunities for private businesses to win lucrative contracts with the state. And, as already noted, heavy state intervention is required to stabilize and/or rescue the economy during financial crises in particular. The perceived tensions are captured by the IOE:

> *Companies looking to invest in health face different types of obstacles. [...] negative perceptions of private involvement in health care provision may translate [to] barriers such as [...] price controls and disadvantageous contract terms and conditions, discrimination in favour of non-profit investors [or] overly prescriptive requirements on the contracting parties.*
>
> (IOE 2020)

What the IOE fails to mention here is the weight of evidence that has emerged in recent years that draws attention to the inflated costs and inefficiency of a large proportion of public–private partnerships in the past or concerns connected with over-inflated pharmaceutical charges (BIAC 2020).

In pensions, an area that has been under attack from a number of quarters in recent years, IEOs have defended state provision, provided it is supported with robust occupational and private provision (BIAC 2015). In both instances, a mixed-economy approach is favoured, in which the state, the market, the voluntary sector and families together share the burden of funding and delivering welfare provision (Powell 2019). And on the question of the method and impact of funding, IEOs generally favour provision that is funded by employees or consumers and pays little attention to equity issues. Redistribution, where it occurs, should be horizontal, across lifetimes, rather than vertical, from rich to poor.

What emerges from this analysis of IEOs and their approach to social policy is a remarkably clear and coherent position on social policy, even over time, which places economic needs, and the needs of businesses and employers, above social welfare concerns. This does not necessarily translate into 'less' state activity, but it does translate into targeted state interventions that are justified only if theydo not undermine private investment and profits. What is also clear, however, is that profits can be protected or boosted by (certain forms of) social and public provision.

Conclusions

This chapter has examined the role of IEOs in steering global public and social policy. The differences between business and employers' interests have been teased out, although most organizations do not distinguish between business in general and employers (although the IOE is an exception). The key focus of this chapter has been on those issues that arise for businesses as private sector employers. But it also identifies some differences in approach between two of the leading representatives of employers and businesses at the global level: BIAC, a self-identified representative of 'business' focuses less than the IOE, as an international representative of employers, does on social policies, citizen's wellbeing and social welfare issues. One explanation for this divergence is because employers invariably need to be more deeply embedded within national systems of education, social protection and pensions. And they are likely to have to concern themselves with employee-welfare questions. This is not inevitably the case for private businesses generally. Profitable businesses with smaller, skilled workforces are, as we argued above, likely to have slightly different concerns than many other companies. And these differences in emphasis are important points of reference that need exploring in more detail going forward.

Note

1 The mission statement for BusinessEurope is displayed on its website, see www.businesseurope.eu/mission-and-priorities.

References

BIAC (1981). *A view from the entrepreneurs*, presented to the Conference on Social Policies in the 1980s. *The Welfare State in Crisis*. Paris: OECD.

BIAC (1996). *Productivity to the Rescue of Social Protection*. Paris: BIAC.

BIAC (1998). *Meeting of the Employment, Labour and Social Affairs Committee at Ministerial Level on Social Policy*. Paris: BIAC.

BIAC (2015). *BIAC Consensus Statement on: Draft Recommendation of the Council on the Core Principles of Private Pensions Regulation*. Paris: BIAC.

BIAC (2020). *Leveraging Investment for More Resilient Health Care Systems*. Paris: BIAC.

Blyth, M. (2013). *Austerity: The History of a Dangerous Idea*. Oxford: Oxford University Press.

Deloitte, IOE and BIAC (2015). *The youth employment opportunity understanding labour market policies across the G20 and beyond*.

EuroChambers (2021). *What we do and how we do it?* [*online*]. Available at: https://www.eurochambres.eu/about/who-we-are/what-we-do-and-how-we-do-it/#:~:text=EUROCHAMBRES'%20vision%20is%20an%20integrated, the%20pursuit%20of%20this%20vision. [Accessed March 2021].

Evans, T. (2005). *The Politics of Human Rights: A Global Perspective*. London: Pluto Press.

Farnsworth, K. (2004). *Corporate Power and Social Policy in Global Context: British Welfare under the Influence?* Bristol: Policy Press.

Farnsworth, K. (2005). International class conflict and social policy. *Social Policy and Society* 4 (2): 217–226. 10.1017/S1474746404002301

Farnsworth, K. (2008). Business and global social policy. In N. Yeates (ed.) *Understanding Global Social Policy*. Bristol: Policy Press, pp. 77–105.

Farnsworth, K. and Irving, Z. (2012). Varieties of crisis, varieties of austerity: Social policy in challenging times. *Journal of Poverty and Social Justice*, 20 (2): 133–147. 10.1332/175982712X652041

Hacker, J. and Pierson, P. (2002). Business power and social policy: Employers and the formation of the American welfare state. *Politics & Society*, 30 (2): 277–325. 10.1177%2F0032329202030002004

IOE (2017). *Understanding the Future of Work*. Geneva: IOE.

IOE (2019). *IOE Guidance Note on the ILO Global Commission on the Future of Work's Report*. Geneva: IOE.

IOE (2020). *IOE Position Paper on Economic Advocacy: Fiscal and Monetary Policies-What Matters Most in the Sustainability of Companies*. Geneva: IOE.

IOE (2021). *Policy Priorities for the Road to a Sustainable Job Recovery: World Employment Confederation and International Organisation of Employers Joint Position Paper.* Geneva: IOE.

Korten, D. C. (1997). *The United Nations and the corporate agenda.* [*online*]. Available at: https://americandiplomacy.web.unc.edu/1997/12/the-united-nations-and-the-corporate-agenda/ [Accessed 18 March 2021].

Lindblom, C. E. (1977). *Politics and Markets.* New York: Basic Books.

O'Brien, R. (2002). Organizational politics, multilateral economic organizations and social policy. *Global Social Policy,* 2 (2): 141–161. 10.1177%2F146801 8102002002739

Offe, C. and Ronge, V. (1984). Theses on the theory of the state. In: C. Offe (ed.) *Contradictions of the Welfare State.* London: Hutchinson, pp. 119–129.

Powell, M. (2019). *Understanding the Mixed Economy of Welfare.* 2nd ed. Bristol: Policy Press.

Sklair, L. (2001). *The Transnational Capitalist Class.* Oxford: Blackwell.

Stiglitz, J. (1998). More instruments and broader goals: Moving towards the post-Washington consensus. *Wider Annual Lecture.* New York: UN World Institute for Development Economics Research.

Stiglitz, J. (2002). *Globalization and Its Discontents.* London: Norton House.

Tesner, S. (2000). *The United Nations and Business: A Partnership Recovered.* London: Macmillan.

Utting, P. (2006). *Reclaiming dEvelopment Agendas: Knowledge, Power and International Policy Making.* Basingstoke: Palgrave.

Wade, R. H. (2002). US hegemony and the World Bank: The fight over people and ideas. *Review of International Political Economy,* 9 (2): 215–243. 10.1 080/09692290110126092

15 Beyond Social Dialogue: The Varied Activities of European Employers' Organizations

Mona Aranea, Leon Gooberman, and Marco Hauptmeier

Introduction

Literature on European Employers' Organizations (Eeos) tends to equate them with those employer bodies that are recognized as social partner organizations by the European Commission (2020) and engage with unions in cross-sectoral and sectoral social dialogue (Degryse 2015; Smismans 2008; Welz 2008). Over the last couple of decades, a rich literature has examined the roles of EEOs in cross-sectoral and sectoral dialogue, providing insights into the varied initiatives, processes, and outcomes of social dialogue in the EU (Arcq et al. 2003; Keller and Weber 2011; Marginson and Sisson 2004; Prosser 2016).

Social dialogue is an important area of EEO activity. However, the tendency of the literature to equate EEOs with those employer bodies that engage in social dialogue has crowded out other relevant EEO activities which this chapter highlights. For this purpose, our research broadened the definition of EEOs to consider all collective bodies representing employers in Employment Relations (ER), work and labour at the European level, capturing the full range and extent of EU-level employer interest representation.

Our approach reflects changes to definitions of national employers' organizations (EOs). Literature has equated EOs (or employers' associations) with those employer bodies that conduct collective bargaining (Windmuller and Gladstone 1984). However, as EOs adapted to new circumstances their roles and functions changed. Collective bargaining declined and some EOs ceased to bargain collectively, but still represented employer interests in other ways. Thus, more recent literature has defined EOs more broadly as including those bodies active across topics within ER, work and labour (Gooberman et al. 2018). The goal of broadening the research perspective has been to capture all employer interest representation, and thus national EO research has moved beyond a narrow focus on collective bargaining and in the same vein, this chapter on EEOs moves beyond a narrow focus on social dialogue.

DOI: 10.4324/9781003104575-19

This chapter argues that EEOs represent employer interests in the EU through the following activities: political representation, interaction with labour unions (including social dialogue), service provision and standard setting. First, EEOs lobby EU institutions, aiming to either influence, stall or prevent EU programmatic initiatives and legislation. Second, EEOs engage with labour unions in the context of EU institutions, namely cross-sectoral social dialogue; sectoral social dialogue committees; sector skills councils and the European alliance for apprenticeships; and, EU-funded projects. Third, EEOs provide services to their members, including informing them as to EU legislative initiatives, organizing events and networking opportunities for members, offering training, and providing services related to sectoral labour markets. Finally, EEOs contribute to standard setting in the EU, promoting sectoral work rules and defining jobs. EEOs pursue this voluntary agenda through accredited training, European professional training frameworks and codes of conduct.

Our research is based on quantitative and qualitative data. First, we created an EEO database, consisting of 136 EEOs, using organizational websites, EU archival records and the EU transparency register to collate information on each EEO. Data on each EEO are published in a 'Handbook of European Employers' Organisation' (Aranea et al. 2021a). Second, we complemented the database findings with information from more than 100 interviews. We primarily conducted interviews with EEO representatives and policy officers, but we also talked with actors who have knowledge of and interact with EEOs.[1]

Political Representation

EEOs' primary activity was political representation. Given the key employer focus on influencing EU institutions, the majority of EEOs had their main office or headquarters in Brussels (105 EEOs, 77.2%) and even more had at least one office in Brussels (118 EEOs, 86.8%). All 136 EEOs were registered with the European Transparency Register. This included the 70 EEOs recognized as social partner organizations in the EU, which possess consultation rights by being procedurally involved in the early stages of social and employment legislative initiatives, enabling the social partners to comment on the content and direction of European Commission proposals. This section focuses on the five formal channels for EEO political representation of their members' interests within work and employment; responding to European Commission consultations; meeting European Commission staff; participating in topic-specific expert advisory groups established by the European Commission; lobbying the European Parliament and representing employers on boards governing EU agencies.

EEOs' most frequent channel of political representation was responding to European Commission consultations (60 EEOs, 44.1%). EEOs issuing many position papers were the main cross-sectoral organizations such as BusinessEurope, European Centre of Employers and Enterprises providing Public Services (CEEP) and Small and Medium Enterprises United (SMEunited), alongside some sectoral EEOs who were directly affected by European Commission legislative initiatives. Topic areas of EEO consultation responses involved employment conditions, social protection, labour market regulation, and occupational health and safety, including the following indicative examples.

EEOs had an important focus on the European Pillar of Social Rights and subsequent proposals for legislation. For example, 20 EEOs responded to the European Commission's 2017 consultation on the Social Pillar. Their responses articulated a rejection of binding social policy. In their joint statement, several EEOs emphasized that "the subsidiarity principle, as enshrined in the Treaty, should be at the centre of policy orientation" (BusinessEurope et al. 2017). CEEP (2016) argued, "[r]especting the principle of subsidiarity will be key for the success and widespread acceptance of the European Pillar of Social Rights". The EEO demanded that "the European Pillar of Social Rights [...] should be a general strategic document which is not legally binding" (CEEP 2016). EuroCommerce, BusinessEurope and 11 other EEOs responded to the consultation with a joint call for "more competitiveness to sustain the social dimension of Europe", arguing that [...] "the persisting social problems in Europe are not due to a lack of social policy measures, but to a lack of global competitiveness" (BusinessEurope et al. 2017).

In response to the 2015 working time consultation, BusinessEurope and nine other EEOs, including InsuranceEurope, the International Road Transport Union and the European Banking Federation jointly wrote an open letter to the European Commission Vice-President for the Euro and Social Dialogue, Vladimir Dombrovskis, to express their views on the existing Working Time Directive. Employers lamented the Directive's "lack of flexibility", especially that "the non-regression clause in the directive limits the opportunity for flexibility in national transposing measures after the adoption of the directive". Employers argued against the introduction of additional legislation because "the world of work has changed considerably since the directive came into force. This creates the need for more flexibility in the organization of working time for both employers and workers" (BusinessEurope et al. 2015).

Seventeen EEOs responded to the European Commission consultation on fair minimum wages. Employers questioned the rationale, proportionality, and policy objectives of the EU initiative on fair minimum wages. The SMEunited position paper disputed the extent of low-wage work and commented on collective bargaining coverage: "Taking into account the low level of low paid workers without collective bargaining coverage, a dedicated European initiative on minimum wage would be dispropor-tionate". The Ceemet position paper, speaking on behalf of metal sector employers argued that the EU treaties excluded the issue of pay from EU competences and that higher wages would lead to further relocation of production away from Europe. BusinessEurope (2020: 2) argued that "wages exist to compensate the work performed, taking into account the way in which it is done and valued, including in the market and within the enterprise", while they regarded the policy goal to ensure a minimum income as the responsibility of national governments. Similarly, EuroCommerce argued that "issues such as income and poverty are better dealt with by national governments with the competence to redistribute wealth [...] than through blunt instruments such as minimum wages".

Overall, EEOs regularly used European Commission consultations to voice concerns about binding employment and social legislation. Most EEO policy officers argued that preventing additional employment reg-ulation was important to maintain competitiveness for their sector. In their view, the "European social policy agenda" was an attempt to regulate "things too much in detail", resulting in "a kind of overregulation" (in-terview with a sectoral EEO representative, 2018; interview with a cross-sectoral EEO representative, 2018). As one secretary general argued, "whenever the [EU] intervenes, this is well-meant but eventually has bad effects" (interview with a sectoral EEO representative, 2018).

The second channel used by EEOs was meetings with European Commission staff. Forty-two EEOs (30.9%) met with DG Employment staff between 2015 and 2019 to express their views on draft legislation and raise general or sectoral employer concerns. One sectoral EEO re-presentative explained that in some cases they met with DG Employment staff "so we can give input directly to the Commission" (Interview with a sectoral EEO representative, 2018). Meeting dates, participants and main topics addressed were available from European Commission websites and, since September 2019, also from the European Transparency Register.

The most frequent topic areas appearing in meeting records were em-ployment conditions, social protection and labour market regulation, in-cluding the following indicative examples. Fifteen EEOs met with DG Employment staff to address employment conditions and social protection, which included the European Pillar of Social Rights. Nine EEOs had meetings to discuss social dialogue. These EEOs represented mainly civil aviation sectors, SME employers and service industries. EEOs such as the Civil Air Navigation Services Organisation, Airports Council International – European Region or the Airport Services Association. Their discussions with DG Employment and DG Transport reflected the breakdown of social dialogue, and labour conflicts in the air traffic control sector. One EEO registered collective labour representation topic – strikes – as a topic of DG Employment meetings. Airlines for Europe met several times with DG Employment and DG GROW between 2015 and 2019 to discuss the economic impact of air-traffic-controller strikes on EU growth and jobs. Six EEOs met with DG Employment to discuss occupational health and safety. Finally, manufacturing and chemical sector employers used DG Employment meetings to raise employer concerns about expanding European regulation over hazardous substances at work.

The third channel for political representation used by EEOs was participating in topic-specific expert advisory groups established by the European Commission. Twenty-four EEOs (17.6%) participated in groups related to work and employment topics. The most active were the cross-sectoral organizations BusinessEurope, SMEunited and CEEP. Eleven EEOs participated in expert groups within general labour market regulation. Eight EEOs participated in expert groups in the topic area of occupational health and safety, including the European Cement Association and the Industrial Minerals Association – Europe. Seven EEOs participated in expert groups in the topic area of employment conditions and social protection with, for example, the European Agri-Cooperatives participating in groups on posting of workers and on un-declared work. Finally, six EEOs participated in groups covering training and professional development with, for example, the Pharmaceutical Group of the EU and the European Hospital and Healthcare Federation participating in the European workforce for health group.

The fourth channel for representing employer interest was lobbying the European Parliament. However, there was less evidence for such lobbying when compared to the European Commission. Eighteen EEOs (13.2%) participated in events or hearings at the European Parliament on topics related to work or employment. Only seven EEOs (5.1%) presented their views during hearings of the European Parliament's Employment and Social Affairs Committee between 2015 and 2018, including BusinessEurope, Ceemet and European Road Haulers Association.

EEO representatives also mentioned informal meetings with Members of the European Parliament. As one policy officer explained:

> We also meet bilaterally with members of the Employment Committee to give them our views on certain dossiers. I was in the European Parliament just earlier this afternoon [...]. I met with an MEP on a specific file to tell them what we think.
> (Interview with a cross-sectoral EEO representative, 2018)

Additional, more informal lobbying takes place through the industry forums of the European Parliament. For example, the European Forum for Manufacturing organized three dinner debates, one each on posting of workers, European social dialogue and the European Pillar of Social Rights. One EEO from the road transport sector organized a dinner debate in the European Parliament during the time of research. The EEO used the event to present employer perspectives on the EU mobility package, especially driver working conditions and working time, to over 100 participants, including Members of the European Parliament.

A fifth channel was EEO representation on the boards governing EU agencies active within employment relations and work topics, such as the European Agency for Safety and Health at Work, European Labour Authority and Eurofound. Such representation allowed EEO input to EU Agencies' work programme and monitor executive management, although influence was shared with other stakeholders.

Interaction with Labour Unions

Seventy-nine EEOs interacted with labour unions (58%). This included the 70 EEOs recognized as social partner organizations and nine additional EEOs that engaged with unions without official recognition. Advantages of being a recognized social partner EEO includes receiving funding for meetings and joint projects with unions and being able to negotiate binding collective agreement, which EU institutions can transpose into European law. In the following we discuss the four channels through which EEOs engage with unions; namely cross-sectoral social dialogue; sectoral social dialogue committees; sector skills councils and the European alliance for apprenticeships; and EU-funded projects.

The first channel was cross sectoral social dialogue. BusinessEurope, CEEP and SMEunited stood out as recognized cross-sectoral social partner organizations, along with their labour counterpart, the European Trade Union Confederation. Following the heyday of cross-sectoral dialogue in the 1990s when social partners negotiated three joint agreements that were transposed into EU law (Keller and Platzer 2003), EEOs focused instead on stalling new legislative initiatives. An exception was the revision of Parental Leave Directive in 2009, but EEOs and European union federations have not subsequently negotiated legally binding cross-sectoral agreements, instead focusing on non-binding joint declarations and programmatic statements (Clauwaert 2011). Meanwhile, six framework agreements, termed 'autonomous' agreements, were agreed between 2002 and 2020, covering telework (2002), work-related stress (2004), harassment and violence at work (2007), inclusive labour markets (2010), active aging (2017) and digitalization (2020).

The European Commission initiated a 'new push for social dialogue' in 2015, attempting to strengthen the role of the social partners but EEOs generally opposed this initiative as indicated by their position papers. These papers emphasized their desire for greater economic competitiveness and their linked rejection of new social and employment regulation. BusinessEurope called for European social dialogue to develop into a "reform partnership" and for unions to "acknowledge that European companies face severe global competition, and improved competitiveness alone will allow us to keep Europe's social model functioning". Employers criticized this drive for social dialogue as lacking a focus on reducing obstacles to job creation: "Nostalgia of the 1990s does not help. We need to address the current challenges" (BusinessEurope 2015).

The second channel was sectoral social dialogue committees. Over half of the EEOs engaged with unions in such committees, including nine that participated in a sectoral social dialogue without official recognition as European social partner organizations. EEOs used sectoral social dialogue committees to discuss employment and work matters in their sectors and to explore joint interests that existed in some areas such as health and safety and training and skill development, but mostly opposed negotiating joint regulation with unions or unilateral sectoral regulation by the European Commission. Most social partner EEOs (69, 44.8%) instead signed non-binding joint statements, declarations, or letters to the European Commission together with unions. Finally, EEOs attempted to contain the European Pillar of Social Rights initiative, seeking to exclude its topics from sectoral social dialogue committees.

Of the over 40 European sectoral social dialogue committees created since the early 2000s, only six have signed agreements that became EU Directives (Degryse 2015; Harvey and Turnbull 2015; Tricart 2019; Turnbull 2010). Five of these were highly internationalized sectors: maritime transport, civil aviation, railways, inland waterways, and fisheries. In these sectoral committees, employers and unions used agreements for a sectoral regulation of working time provisions, or to transpose global regulation stemming from the International Labour Organization into EU law, although the hospital and healthcare sector framework agreement on prevention from sharp injuries constituted an exceptional case of EU social partner regulation. In the early 2000s, the European Parliament debated European legislation that intended to prevent such injuries. As a response to this legislative threat, hospital sector employers formed the European Hospital and Healthcare Employers' Association and pursued a joint agreement with the sectoral union. Employers and unions intervened in the legislative process by negotiating a joint agreement and securing its transposition into an EU Directive in 2010. However, other sectoral social dialogues failed to jointly regulate their sector. The hairdressing sector organization Coiffure EU, for example, signed a sectoral workplace health and safety agreement with the service sector union UNI Europa in 2012, but the European Commission refused to transpose the agreement into EU law (Tricart 2019).

The third channel was sector skills councils and the European alliance for apprenticeships, where EEOs discussed skill development with unions. Twenty-eight EEOs (20.6%) participated with unions in European sector skills councils, funded by the European Commission to identify sector specific skills gaps and develop strategies to address such gaps. For example, social partners from the textile, clothing, leather, and footwear industry formed a European sector skills council to work alongside their sectoral social dialogue committee. Other sectors with European sector skills councils included automotive, commerce (retail and wholesale), audio-visual and live performance and marine technologies. EEOs also collaborated with unions in the European alliance for apprenticeships, which aimed to strengthen the provision and quality of apprenticeships. Large cross-sectoral EEOs such as BusinessEurope or the European Round Table for Industry took part, as did sectoral EEOs such as FoodDrinkEurope, UNIEP (the International Association of Painting Contractors), the fitness sector organization EuropeActive and the machine tool industry EEO (CECIMO).

The fourth and final channel was EU-funded projects, where 24 EEOs (17.6%) participated. Some projects grew out of sectoral social dialogue committees or from sector skills councils, but others existed separately. As examples, civil aviation EEOs pursued a joint social partner initiative promoting national level social dialogue within civil aviation, while construction sector organizations such as the European Builders Confederation engaged in joint EU-funded projects on health and safety together with labour. Eighteen EEOs (13.2%) participated alongside unions in the EU Healthy Workplaces Campaigns, run by the European Agency for Safety and Health at Work. Finally, a few EEOs used their campaign involvement to strengthen their credentials as employer representatives within occupational health and safety in the absence of social partner recognition. One example was the European Builders Confederation and the European Demolition Association, which participated in the campaign and enjoyed informal access to the construction sector social dialogue committee.

Service Provision

A third area of EEO activity was service provision to their members, across four main categories. The first was informing members as to new EU initiatives. Most EEOs (86.8%) provided information to their members on new legislative or programmatic EU initiatives. The most common topics within ER were health and safety, social dialogue, training, and employment and social protection. EEO members were particularly interested in plans for new EU legislation, as these might result in additional constraints or costs, prompting EEOs to provide an 'early warning system' about such plans. Such alerts can spur coordination between employers on the national as well as European level and result in EEO lobbying of political actors with the intention to prevent, water down or influence legislation. UNIEP, for example, used their newsletter to update members on legislative progress around carcinogens and mutagens at work, and on other pieces of health and safety regulation.

The second service provision category was membership networking. Most EEOs (88 EEOs, 64.7%) facilitated networking between members through events such as general assemblies (85 EEOs), conferences (72 EEOs) or workshops (42 EEOs). To incentivize participation, some EEOs scheduled them on the day before their social dialogue meetings with European union federations, for which the European Commission usually reimbursed EEO members' travel and accommodation costs.

The third service provision category was labour market services. Less than a third of EEOs (38 EEOs, 27.9%) compiled and provided information on their sectoral labour market, including comparison of national markets or skills. For example, UNIEP offered a comparison of different national qualification frameworks for painters, based on member input in the context of an EU-funded project. Sixteen EEOs developed and provided handbooks and policy implementation guides. For example, the European Industrial Gases Association provided guides on safety training for employees, and on employee involvement in environmental activities. One exceptional labour market service was the European Lotteries' online job portal, which none of the other EEOs offered. But unlike national EOs, EEOs did not provide specific legal advice on the management of labour or labour disputes in individual companies.

The fourth service provision category was training and staff development. Twenty-two EEOs (16.2%) offered non-certified training to their members (certified training is discussed in the next section on standard setting). For example, the European Association of Distance Teaching Universities provided training in virtual teaching skills, delivered in collaboration with members. The Euro Banking Association, representing the payment industry, regularly organized seminars on EU-level regulatory developments. The European Industrial Gases Association provided training on preventing accidents at work. The Federation of European Manufacturers and Suppliers of Ingredients to the Bakery Industry and the International Association for Soaps, Detergents and Maintenance Products jointly developed online training modules on the safe handling of enzymes in the workplace. Various chemical industry EEOs provided online training modules in conjunction with health and safety training materials for their national members.

Standard Setting

A fourth and less frequent area of EEO activity was standard setting, carried out across two categories. One was the provision of voluntary standards. Around one quarter of the EEO population (35 EEOs), all of them sectoral, provided some form of voluntary standards focused on employment, work, and jobs in European sectors. These standards were developed and promoted either unilaterally by EEOs or in conjunction with European unions. EEOs promoted such private voluntary regulation through accredited training and professional training frameworks, codes of conduct, benchmarking, and best practice sharing. Thirteen EEOs promoted work standards through accredited training, resulting in a professional qualification for employees. EEOs were either the sole provider of such training, or the courses were offered with member organizations or education providers. As examples, the European Association of Abnormal Road Transport and Mobile Cranes provided a European Crane Operator License, while the hairdressing sector organization Coiffure EU offered a European Hairdressing Certificate. Similarly, a few EEOs offered European professional qualification standards for jobs in their sector. For example, the European Confederation of Outdoor Employers promoted joint standards for outdoor animators, and the European Association of Sport Employers set standards for fitness workers.

Seventeen EEOs (12.5%) promoted standards through setting voluntary codes of conduct, often with the aim of preventing or pre-empting binding legislation. EEO codes were most likely to focus on standards in training and development, and health and safety. For example, the High Temperature Insulation Wool Industry Association operated a pan-European product stewardship programme that included occupational hygiene standards related to dust exposure in members' production sites. Other topics were, for example, gender equality or corporate social responsibility. Moreover, 23 EEOs (16.9%) established joint standards together with unions, often in the context of sectoral committees. These voluntary joint agreements included codes of conduct, frameworks, guidelines, or toolkits. For example, the European Telecommunications Network Operators' Association issued health and safety guidelines jointly with unions while the European Association of Sugar Manufacturers signed a joint corporate social responsibility code of conduct with the European agriculture sector union.

The other category within standard setting was informal benchmarking and the sharing of best practice, where some EEOs conducted informal benchmarking to help members improve their practices and standards. Examples included the European Asphalt Pavement Association publishing a good practice guide on asphalt workers' health protection, and the European Chemical Industry Council providing best practice guides as to employment conditions, including "Social Responsibility in the European Chemical industry" (2014). Twenty EEOs published best practice guides in collaboration with European union federations. For example, the Community of European Railway and Infrastructure Companies, the European Rail Infrastructure Managers and the European Transport Workers' Federation used an EU grant to develop a best practice guide on attracting and retaining female employees.

Conclusion

The main purpose of the chapter has been to broaden our understanding of EEOs. Previous research narrowly defined EEOs as social partner organizations registered with the European Commission. As this chapter demonstrates, a narrow focus excludes a range of other employer interest representation, and thus we considered all transnational employer bodies representing employer interests in the EU. Engaging with labour unions in cross-sectoral and sectoral social dialogue is a key EEO activity, but it is not the most important one. EEOs' central activity is political representation with a key focus being to avoid binding employment and social legislation which in their view increases costs for employers, limits flexibility and overall hinders their competitiveness vis-à-vis firms from other world regions.

EEOs represent such interests by responding to European Commission consultations; lobbying European Commission staff; participating European Commission expert advisory groups; lobbying the European Parliament and representing employers on boards governing EU Agencies. The chapter identified three additional areas in which EEOs represent member interests: interaction with unions, service provision and standard setting. Even in these additional areas, a key theme was avoiding binding employment and social regulation. In their interaction with unions, EEOs mostly stalled attempts by unions to negotiate binding agreements. Although EEOs still regularly engage with unions in social dialogue, agreeing to voluntary measures or joint declaration in social dialogue can be interpreted as a strategy to keep out the legislator and avoid binding EU legislation. Within service provision, EEOs have an important focus on informing members about EU legislative initiatives. In a way, this is an 'early warning system' about undesired developments in the EU, which can then spur employer lobbying at the EU level as well as the national level, where EEO members lobby their national governments that take part in EU political processes. Within standard setting, EEOs engage in private voluntary regulation through accredited training, European professional training frameworks and codes of conduct. These forms of voluntary regulation are flexible and can be freely amended if circumstances change, which is preferred over binding regulation, and thus, one key motive for self-regulation is again to pre-empt legislation by the European Commission.

EEO interest representation can be interpreted in the broader antagonistic context of economic (market making) and social (market constraining) EU integration (Meardi 2018; Prosser 2016). The EU has pursued economic integration through the liberalization of markets, removal of trade barriers between member states, creation of European single markets and introduction of a common currency and social integration through a variety of social and employment legislation, especially in the 1990s. In the 21st century this social dimension of European integration has made little progress, although the Juncker Commission introduced a new European Pillar of Social Rights. EEOs generally favour EU-wide economic integration but oppose social integration. An EEO representative reflected on this dualism: "As business representatives, we ask normally for the harmonization of [market] rules across the EU – but then for social issues, social protection, it should remain at national level" (Interview with a service sector EEO representative, 2019). Given that economic integration is much more advanced in the EU compared to social integration, the current course of EU integration is broadly in line with EEOs' articulated interests.

Note

1 For detailed information on the research methods see the appendix in Aranea et al. 2021a, 2021b. The described research methods, including the database methods, were developed initially in a broader project on EOs (Bowkett et al. 2017; Demougin et al. 2019a, 2019b, 2021; Gooberman and Hauptmeier 2021; Gooberman et al. 2018, 2019a, 2019b, 2020; Heery et al. 2017).

References

Aranea, M., Demougin, P., Gooberman, L. and Hauptmeier, M. (2021a). Handbook of European employers' organisations. *Hans Böckler Foundation Working Paper No. 225.* Düsseldorf. https://www.boeckler.de/fpdf/HBS-008096/p_fofoe_WP_225_2021.pdf [accessed 8 September 2021].

Aranea, M., Gooberman, L. and Hauptmeier, M. (2021b). What do European employers' organisations do? *Hans Böckler Foundation Working Paper No. 226.* Düsseldorf. https://www.boeckler.de/fpdf/HBS-008113/p_fofoe_WP_226_2021.pdf [accessed 24 September 2021].

Arcq, E., Dufresne, A. and Pochet, P. (2003). The employers: The hidden face of European industrial relations. *Transfer: European Review of Labour and Research,* 9 (2): 302–321. 10.1177%2F102425890300900210

Bowkett, C., Hauptmeier, M. and Heery, E. (2017). Exploring the role of employer forums – The case of Business in the Community Wales. *Employee Relations,* 39 (7): 986–1000. 10.1108/ER-11-2016-0229

BusinessEurope (2015). *Social Dialogue Should Develop in the Direction of a Reform Partnership,* press release.

BusinessEurope et. al. (2015). *Letter to Mr Valdis Dombrovskis, Vice-President for the Euro and Social Dialogue.*

BusinessEurope (2020). *Response to First Phase Social Partner Consultation on a Possible Action Addressing the Challenges Related to Fair Minimum Wages,* position paper.

BusinessEurope et al. (2017). *European Social Pillar,* position paper.

Clauwaert, S. (2011). 2011: 20 years of European interprofessional social dialogue: Achievements and prospects. *Transfer: European Review of Labour and Research,* 17 (2): 169–179. 10.1177%2F1024258911401403

Degryse, Christophe (2015). The European Sectoral Social Dialogue: An Uneven Record of Achievement? *SSRN Electronic Journal.* 10.2139/ssrn.2628064

Demougin, P., Gooberman, L. and Hauptmeier, M. (2019a). The unexpected survival of employer collective action in the UK. *Relations Industrielles/ Industrial Relations*, 74 (2): 353–376.

Demougin, P., Gooberman, L., Hauptmeier, M. and Heery, E. (2019b). Employer organisations transformed. *Human Resource Management Journal*, 29 (1): 1–16. 10.1111/1748-8583.12222

Demougin, P., Gooberman, L., Hauptmeier, M. and Heery, E. (2021). Revisiting voluntarism: Private voluntary regulation by employer forums in the United Kingdom. *Journal of Industrial Relations*, Published online first. 10.1177% 2F00221856211038308

European Centre of Employers and Enterprises Providing Public Services (CEEP) (2016). Opinion on the European Pillar of Social Rights. https://www.ceep.eu/ opinion-on-the-european-pillar-of-social-rights/ [accesed on 24 September 2021]

European Commission (2020). *List of EU Social Partner Organisations*. September 2019.

Gooberman, L. and Hauptmeier, M. (2021). *Union Coalitions and Strategic Framing: The Case of the Agricultural Advisory Panel for Wales*. Manuscript. Cardiff University.

Gooberman, L., Hauptmeier, M. and Heery, E. (2018). Contemporary employer interest representation in the United Kingdom. *Work, Employment and Society*, 32 (1): 114–132. 10.1177/0950017017701074

Gooberman, L., Hauptmeier, M. and Heery, E. (2019a). The evolution of employers' organisations in the United Kingdom: Extending countervailing power. *Human Resource Management Journal*, 29 (1): 82–96. 10.1111/1748-8583.12193

Gooberman, L., Hauptmeier, M. and Heery, E. (2019b). The decline of employers' associations in the UK, 1976 to 2014. *Journal of Industrial Relations*, 61 (1): 11–32. 10.1177/0022185617750418

Gooberman, L., Hauptmeier, M. and Heery, E. (2020). The decay and revival of sub-UK employer organization: A response to Dr Ritson. *Labor History*, 61 (5-6): 417–422. 10.1080/0023656X.2020.1830958

Harvey, G. and Turnbull, P. (2015). Can labor arrest the "sky pirates"? Transnational trade unionism in the European civil aviation industry. *Labor History*, 56 (3): 308–326. 10.1080/0023656X.2015.1042775

Heery, E., Gooberman, L. and Hauptmeier, M. (2017). The petroleum driver passport scheme: A case study in reregulation. *Industrial Relations Journal*, 48 (3): 274–291. 10.1111/irj.12179

Keller, B. and Platzer, H.-W. (2003). *Industrial Relations and European Integration: Trans- and Supranational Developments and Prospects*. Aldershot, England and Burlington, VT: Ashgate.

Keller, B. and Weber, S. (2011). Sectoral social dialogue at EU level: Problems and prospects of implementation. *European Journal of Industrial Relations*, 17 (3): 227–243. 10.1177%2F0959680111410960

Marginson, P. and Sisson, K. (2004). *European Integration and Industrial Relations: Multi-Level Governance in the Making*. New York: Palgrave Macmillan.

Meardi, G. (2018). Economic integration and state responses: Change in European industrial relations since Maastricht. *British Journal of Industrial Relations*, 56 (3): 631–655. 10.1111/bjir.12307

Prosser, T. (2016). Economic union without social union: The strange case of the European social dialogue. *Journal of European Social Policy*, 26 (5): 460–472.

Smismans, S. (2008). The European social dialogue in the shadow of hierarchy. *Journal of Public Policy*, 28 (1): 161–180. 10.1017/S0143814X08000822

Traxler, F. (2004). Employer associations, institutions and economic change: A cross-national comparison. *Industrielle Beziehungen*, 11(1/2): 42–60.

Tricart, J. P. (2019). *Legislative Implementation of European Social Partner Agreements: Challenges and Debates.* ETUI Research Paper-Working Paper.

Turnbull, P. (2010). From social conflict to social dialogue: Counter-mobilization on the European waterfront. *European Journal of Industrial Relations*, 16 (4): 333–349. 10.1177%2F0959680110384835

Welz, C. (2008). *The European Social Dialogue Under Articles 138 and 139 of the EC Treaty: Actors, Processes, Outcomes* (Vol. 36). Alphen aan den Rijn: Kluwer Law International BV.

Windmuller, J. P. and Gladstone, A. (1984). *Employers' Associations and Industrial Relations: A Comparative Study.* Oxford: Oxford University Press.

Index

Printed in the United States
by Baker & Taylor Publisher Services